CW00643384

ABBREVIATIONS.

T. _ Teacher P. _ Pupil A. _ Answer Q. _ Question R. _ Repeat Col. _ Columns Ar. _ Arrows M.M. Mälzel Metronome Ex. Example.

GALIN-PARIS - CHEVÉ METHOD,

as endorsed by

Rossini, Gounod, Felicien David

and OTHER MAESTROS.

AUTHORIZED BY THE MINISTRE D'EDUCATION IN FRANCE

ADOPTED IN BELGIUM AND SWITZERLAND.

AWARDED

GOLD MEDALS at the UNIVERSAL EXHIBITION

of LONDON 1862, PARIS 1867, 1878, 1889.

EASY POPULAR SIGHT-SINGING MANUAL

REVISED AND AUGMENTED

by

John Zobanaky.

THE RECOGNIZED EXPONENT IN AMERICA OF THE

GALIN-PARIS-CHEVÉ METHOD.

ELEMENTARY BOOK . Part I & II.

Copyright 1896 by John Zobanaky, Philadelphia, Pa.

A FEW APPROBATIONS
From well known Teachers and the Press.

"I take pleasure in expressing to you my entire approval of the GALIN-PARIS-CHEVÉ System of Sight Singing under your instruction . I have found this method of incalculable value to my pupils ." MRS. R. CAPERTON.

" . . . . . In fact, I am so convinced of its merits, that I recommend it to all ." EMIL GASTEL.

"I believe the system which you represent, is a great advance in Music." G. FETTER, Late Principal Normal School

' "You may use my name with my full consent, as I believe your system of teaching to be excellent ." H. A. CLARK, Mus. D.

"The merits of the GALIN-PARIS-CHEVÉ Method of Sight Reading have been most clearly shown by my pupils who have been in your classes . Wishing you the success you deserve, I am, etc" FREDERIC PEAKES .

"Such results, as far as I know, have never been equaled by any other system of Sight Singing; thereupon I gladly add my name to the many who have already given their approval to the GALIN-PARIS-CHEVÉ Method, as being one to solve the great actual desideratum, to learn how to read Music as we do our Mother Tongue." S. BEHRENS.

"I cannot adequately express my appreciation of the GALIN PARIS CHEVÉ Method for Sight Singing . I wish it could be adopted in every school of the country. ELEANOR EVEREST.

"I shall with pleasure send my pupils to you for this most necessary branch of instruction ." MRS. ABBOTT.

"I am glad to express my satisfaction and admiration for the ability displayed by you, in teaching the GALIN-PARIS-CHEVÉ Method in our NEW YORK CONSERVATORY . The results were fully up to my expectation, and I am sorry that you could not arrange matters in order to remain among our faculty." A. SAPIO, Late Director, Conservatory of Music of America .

"This system greatly facilitates the reading of music." PHILA PRESS.

"Judged by the results the Method is far superior to the old " PHILA TIMES.

"Music for the Millions ." PHILA. PUBLIC LEDGER.

"Mr. Zobanaky's method undoubtedly surpasses all others . It is the only method by which such remarkable results can be achieved ." RITER FITZGERALD.

"It may be truly said that by this method the art of teaching music has attained all the perfection of which it is susceptible ." DUPINEY DE VOREPIERRE ENCYCLOPEDIA. (Page 528.)

"It was only after it had caused a careful examination to be made that the *Ledger* drew attention to the GALIN-PARIS-CHEVÉ System, as one that might be made to solve the problem of popular musical education in the best sense, in connection with our common school system ." ED. PUBLIC LEDGER.

. . . . AND MANY OTHERS . . . .

FIRST LESSON.

Music is the art of producing and combining sounds.

Sound. Constitutive Element in Music. In listening to a singer or an instrumentalist, it can be noticed that musical noises are produced at a definite pitch. The pitches of these noises which can be ascertained have received the name of sounds and by their collection constitute **music.**

First qualification of sounds. Pitch. These sounds appear at unequal pitches, some low, some high. Therefore the first study must be the production of a sound at a required pitch. In vocal music this study is named: **Intonation.**

Second qualification of sounds. Duration. When listening with care, it will be noticed that these sounds can be of unequal duration; some very long, some very short. **Duration** is the second qualification of sounds and should be our next study.[1] Further more while watching a band passing the street it will be seen that those who follow keep step. This is caused by the occurence of a strong accented sound reappearing at equal distances and constitutes the time. We shall study separately first **Intonation**, or the study of sounds in regard to their pitch, second, **Time** or the study of sounds in regard to their duration.

Mode. By the disposition of sounds according to their relative pitch, two combinations are to be found, one which was intended to express gaity, happiness and joy is named **Major Mode** which we will study immediately, the other intended for melancholy and sorrow is named **Minor Mode** and will be studied later.

Scale. Each of these combinations is a sort of ladder which is named the **Scale** and composed of seven sounds.

The seven sounds of the Major Mode are named from the Italian syllables do, ré, mi, fa, sol, la, si, and pronounced doh, ra, me, fah, sohl, lah, se.

SIGNS FOR INTONATION.

We represent the seven words by the first seven numerals in this manner 1 2 3 4 5 6 7
DO RÉ MI FA SOL LA SI

In singing, the figures should not be named one, two, three, but do, re, mi, etc.

Three series of seven figures will be sufficient for the human voice,

---

[1] We shall not speak here of the strength nor the timbre which belongs to the higher studies.

1

three series of seven figures will be all that is needed, but in order to distinguish one series from another we shall place a dot underneath the figures for the low series thus: $\underset{\cdot}{1}$ $\underset{\cdot}{2}$ $\underset{\cdot}{3}$ $\underset{\cdot}{4}$ $\underset{\cdot}{5}$ $\underset{\cdot}{6}$ $\underset{\cdot}{7}$– none for the middle series thus: 1 2 3 4 5 6 7 – and a dot above for the high series thus: $\dot{1}$ $\dot{2}$ $\dot{3}$ $\dot{4}$ $\dot{5}$ $\dot{6}$ $\dot{7}$–

Example:_ the three series on one line

First Series	Second Series	Third Series
$\underset{\cdot}{1}$ $\underset{\cdot}{2}$ $\underset{\cdot}{3}$ $\underset{\cdot}{4}$ $\underset{\cdot}{5}$ $\underset{\cdot}{6}$ $\underset{\cdot}{7}$	1 2 3 4 5 6 7	$\dot{1}$ $\dot{2}$ $\dot{3}$ $\dot{4}$ $\dot{5}$ $\dot{6}$ $\dot{7}$
do ré mi fa sol la si	do ré mi fa sol la si	do ré mi fa sol la si
Grave or low Sounds.	Medium Sounds.	Acute or high Sounds.

STUDY OF MAJOR MODE.

Exercises for Intonation.

In the following Exercises – which will have to be studied by columns the sounds must be of equal duration, rather short in accordance with the distance which separates them; but, when they are set apart a little more for the eyes, the sounds must be likewise lengthened. In order to obtain a good tone, it will be well to have the pupils sing at a pitch that does not tire the voice, and, for **children**, head notes must be taken from A (LA) of the tuning fork. It is very important that every pupil should have the correct sound to start with, as given by the teacher.

If, in the class, the pupils do not know the intonation of the five sounds do, ré, mi, fa, sol, the teacher will sing them several times until **every one** of the pupils can sing them **correctly**; also, watch the right pronunciation. If it happens after several trials that some pupils cannot repeat any of these sounds, it would be advisable for them to listen to the first course, not to sing. The teacher can now begin to use the chart and pointer; if a chart is not at hand it can be traced on the blackboard in the following manner:

The figures must be large enough to be seen by all the pupils.

	$\dot{5}$	$\dot{5}$
$\dot{4}$		
	$\dot{3}$	
		$\dot{2}$
$\dot{1}$	$\dot{1}$	
		7
6		
	5	5
4		
	3	
		2
1	1	
		$\underset{\cdot}{7}$
$\underset{\cdot}{6}$		
	$\underset{\cdot}{5}$	$\underset{\cdot}{5}$

Begin by pointing to the first five notes; do, re, mi, fa, sol, in succession several times and let the pupils merely **name** each figure: 1, do, 2, re, 3, mi, etc. When the teacher is sure they know the names of the first five sounds, then they can sing from the chart exercise Nº 1 pointed by the teacher. When the little letter R is met under two notes it means to repeat the two sounds several times. When a larger space occurs between two notes each one should be held a little longer than the others. Each exercise is preceded by the words KEY OF..... which means to always name the sound indicated DO. For instance, the first exercise is Key of MI; we take the LA tuning fork and descending from it to MI, we stop there and giving the sound of MI the name of Do we are singing in the Key of MI: that is, we have started the new scale from the 3rd degree of the original scale of DO.

Nº 1.		Nº 2.		Nº 3.		Nº 4.	
1 2	1	5 4	5	1 2 3 4 5	1	5 4 3 2 1	5
1 2 3	1	5 4 3	5	1 2 3 4	1	5 4 3 2	5
1 2 3 4	1	5 4 3 2	5	1 2 3	1	5 4 3	5
1 2 3 4 5	1 5 R	5 4 3 2 1	5 1 R	1 2	1 5 R	5 4	5 1 R

The same work should be done for the intonation of the four notes $\dot{1}$ 7 6 5, to first *name* them by the syllables, do, si, la, sol, then the teacher will sing them and when all the pupils have sung them correctly then the study can begin with Nº 5. KEY OF RÉ.

Nº 5.	Nº 6.	Nº 7.	Nº 8.		Nº 9.		Nº 10.		Nº 11.	
$\dot{1}$765	567$\dot{1}$	$\dot{1}$765	56	5	$\dot{1}$7	$\dot{1}$	567$\dot{1}$	5	$\dot{1}$765	$\dot{1}$
$\dot{1}$765	567$\dot{1}$	$\dot{1}$765	567	5	$\dot{1}$76	$\dot{1}$	567	5	$\dot{1}$76	$\dot{1}$
$\dot{1}$765	567$\dot{1}$	$\dot{1}$765	567$\dot{1}$	5$\dot{1}$ R	$\dot{1}$765	$\dot{1}$5 R	56	5$\dot{1}$ R	$\dot{1}$7	$\dot{1}$

KEY OF RÉ.

Nº 12.		Nº 13.		Nº 14.		Nº 15.	
12345567$\dot{1}$		$\dot{1}$76554321		12345567$\dot{1}$		$\dot{1}$76554321	
1234567$\dot{1}$		$\dot{1}$7654321		1234567$\dot{1}$		$\dot{1}$7654321	
12	1	$\dot{1}$7	$\dot{1}$	1234567$\dot{1}$	1	$\dot{1}$7654321	$\dot{1}$
123	1	$\dot{1}$76	$\dot{1}$	1234567	1	$\dot{1}$765432	$\dot{1}$
1234	1	$\dot{1}$765	$\dot{1}$	123456	1	$\dot{1}$76543	$\dot{1}$
12345	1	$\dot{1}$7654	$\dot{1}$	12345	1	$\dot{1}$7654	$\dot{1}$
123456	1	$\dot{1}$76543	$\dot{1}$	1234	1	$\dot{1}$765	$\dot{1}$
1234567	1	$\dot{1}$765432	$\dot{1}$	123	1	$\dot{1}$76	$\dot{1}$
345671̇	1$\dot{1}$ R	$\dot{1}$7654321	$\dot{1}$1 R	12	1	$\dot{1}$7	$\dot{1}$

Dictation.

Dictation is very important in Music and produces quick results as experience has proved. For this first lesson the teacher will vocalize a few notes from preceding exercises on Ah, not more than five notes at one time; the pupils repeating together in the same manner.

Time.

The time is the result of a stronger accent, the return of which is periodical and regular and divides a musical phrase in parts of equal duration. *A measure* is the duration which occurs between two strong accents. *The bar* is a vertical line which is used to separate the measures. *The beat* is a unit of duration. It can be an articulation, a duration or a rest, it can also be the result of one or more sounds.

Signs in Time.

As we will not speak at present of division of beat, we shall say that each isolated sign, a figure, a dot or a cipher represents a beat; and, therefore a dot placed after a figure means to prolong that first sound one more beat. The cipher, representing the rest means to stop singing during one beat.

A measure is composed of all the signs included between two consecutive bars. We will for the present speak of two beat time.

Beating Time. The right hand should be used, taking care to only move the fore arm, keeping the elbow steady on the side of the body. When the forearm is raised as high as possible without moving the elbow, the point reached by the hand will be the limit for the upper beat; the down beat could be limited to striking the knee or the table, but generally the noise on the table is the cause of disturbance.

Two beat time. The teacher beats alone first asking the pupils to watch; then, stopping at the upper beat directs all pupils to imitate which they will do by raising their right hand then the teacher lowers the hand the class doing the same. Attention must be paid to have the motion done quickly to remain at each place the same duration of time; when the pupils are able to beat correctly, let them say: down, up, down, up. It is best to begin with a slow movement. The teacher must be well pleased if successful at the first lesson.

(1) All the keys given in this manual are intended for children; Adults can lower the pitch one or two degrees.

———•••———

A good practice is to always review the previous exercise of intonation faster. In the beginning of Musical Studies many children often find great difficulty in repeating the same sound; therefore, it is important that the teacher does not go too fast and state when coming to exercise N⁰ 17. that each note will be pointed twice except when returning to *Do*, the teacher's duty being to help the children by all possible means except prompting for the tone; only the sound to begin the exercise should be given and nothing else.

KEY OF MI.

N⁰ 16.	N⁰ 17.	N⁰ 18.	N⁰ 19.	N⁰ 20.
12345 1	1122334455 1	122334455 1	122345 1	123345 1
1234 1	11223344 1	1223344 1	12234 1	12334 1
123 1	112233 1	12233 1	1223 1	1233 1
12 1	1122 1	122 1	122 1	12 1
12345 1	1122334455 1	122334455 1	122345 1	123345 1
R	R	R	R	R

N⁰ 21.	N⁰ 22.	N⁰ 23.	N⁰ 24.	N⁰ 25.
543215	5544332211 5	5443322115	5443215	5433215
5432 5	55443322 5	5443322 5	54432 5	54332 5
543 5	554433 5	54433 5	5443 5	5433 5
54 5	5544 5	544 5	544 5	54 5
543215	5544332211 5	5443322115	5443215	5433215
R	R	R	R	R

KEY OF RÉ.

N⁰ 26.	N⁰ 27.	N⁰ 28.	N⁰ 29.
1̇765 1̇	1̇1̇776655 1̇	1̇776655 1̇	1̇7765 1̇
1̇76 1̇	1̇1̇7766 1̇	1̇7766 1̇	1̇776 1̇
1̇7 1̇	1̇1̇77 1̇	1̇77 1̇	1̇77 1̇
1̇765 1̇5 1̇	1̇1̇776655 1̇5 1̇	1̇776655 1̇5 1̇	1̇7765 1̇5 1̇
R	R	R	R

N⁰ 30.	N⁰ 31.	N⁰ 32.	N⁰ 33.
567 1̇	567 1̇	567 1̇	567 1̇
567 1̇ 5	556677 1̇1̇ 5	56677 1̇1̇ 5	5667 1̇ 5
567 5	556677 5	56677 5	5667 5
56 5	5566 5	566 5	566 5
567 1̇5 1̇	556677 1̇1̇55 1̇	56677 1̇1̇55 1̇	5667 1̇5 1̇
R	R	R	R

Dictation.

The teacher will vocalize on the vowel-Ah- singing the columns N⁰ˢ 1,2,3, 4,8,9,10,11, stopping at each line. Pupils answer on the same vowel.

Time.

The ***Strong Accent*** – When following a military band we soon keep step in good order. This regulating effect is due, as we have already said, to the stronger accentuation of a sound the regular and periodical return of which divides the musical phrase into parts of equal duration.

If we represent the sounds by vertical lines, taking care to trace the strong accents by longer lines, we will illustrate near enough for the sight the impression produced upon the ear by the alternating succession of the strong and weak sounds.–

Ex. 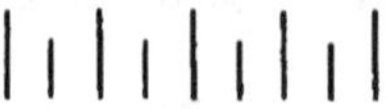

Classification of Measures. – In order that the ear may be able to ascertain the duration, it is neccessary for the strong sound to be heard every two, three or four units. Therefore there are measures of

Two Beats

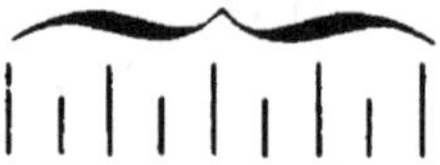

Three Beats

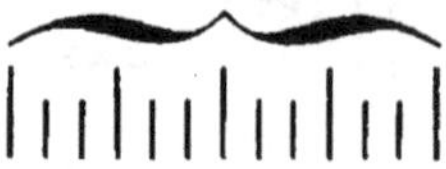

Four Beats

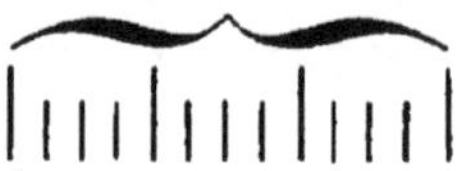

Remark. No particular kind of four beat measure ought to be made. In this measure really exists two strong beats; the first and the third. The result is, that for the ear it produces confusion with the two beat measure.

In reality in every two or three beats the ear only admits the accent - ed one.

Indications of strong beat. To mark the strong beat the measures are separated by vertical lines named bars. The strong accent is al - ways placed on the note following the bar.

Two beats in measure	1 2	3 4	5 4
Three beats in measure	1 2 3	4 5 4	3 2 3
Four beats in measure	1 2 3 4	5 4 3 2	

Ideas to Express. – The beat can be articulated sound, the prolon - gation of a sound, or a rest.

Signs in Measure. – The articulated beat is represented by figure, the prolongation by a dot, the rest by a cipher.

Each isolated sign, dot or cipher represents one beat and the number of signs between two bars is equal to the number of beats therein.

Ex. 1. Two beats measure	5 6	5 .	1̇ 7	6 0
Ex. 2. Three beats measure	5 4 3	3 . 2	3 0 4	5 . 0
Ex. 3. Four beats measure	5 5 1̇ 7	6 . 5 .	4 3 4 5	3 . 0 0

One dot after a figure means to prolong that sound one more beat. The cipher indicates that the P. stop singing during one beat.

P. after having learned to beat time will begin "Time Exercise No 1." But in order not to give two mental operations at once, it is advisable to have the pupils first beat the two-beat measure while watching them. When the regularity of motion is satisfactory the T. writes on the blackboard the following exercises; No 1, 2, 3, 4. They read, first following the small arrows the T. pointing to each sign successively, the P. saying *tä* for the figures and *ä* for the dots.

Time Exercises.

KEY OF FA.

No 1.				No 2.			
1 2	3 4	5 4	3 2	1 2	3 .	4 5	4 3
1 2	3 4	5 4	3 .	1 2	3 .	4 5	5 .
1 2	3 4	5 .	4 3	1 2	3 .	4 .	5 5
1 2	3 4	5 .	5 .	1 2	3 .	4 .	5 .
1 2	3 4	5 .	. .	1 2	3 .	2 .	. .

No 3.				No 4.			
1 .	2 3	4 5	4 3	1 .	2 .	3 4	5 5
1 .	2 3	4 5	5 .	1 .	2 .	3 4	5 .
1 .	2 3	4 .	5 5	1 .	2 .	3 .	4 5
1 .	2 3	4 .	5 .	1 .	2 .	3 .	2 .
1 .	2 3	2 .	. .	1 .	2 .	3 .	. .

THIRD LESSON.

For all the exercises of this book — Intonation or Time — the order of the lessons should be strictly followed. But if the pupils should have difficulty in a series they should review the one preceding similar to it. When a series of exercises has two kinds of arrows, long and short, it is understood that it is to be sung according to small arrows first but if trouble is experienced with the second column it would then be advisable to sing the two columns according to the indication of the large arrows

Intonation.

The small notes interpolated in many of these exercises must be *thought of* but *not sung*. Still, if in thinking the small notes the large one following could not be sung, it would be sufficient to lightly sing the small notes. The intonation of the next would therefore come itself.

KEY OF MI.

№ 34.

12	21	12	₂1
123	321	123	₃21
1234	4321	1234	₄321
12345	54321	12345	₅4321

№ 35.

54	45	54	₄5
543	345	543	₃45
5432	2345	5432	₂345
54321	12345	54321	₁2345

№ 36.

12345	54321	12345	₅4321
1234	4321	1234	₄321
123	321	123	₃21
12	21	12	₂1

№ 37.

54321	12345	54321	₁2345
5432	2345	5432	₂345
543	345	543	₃45
54	45	54	₄5

KEY CF RÉ.

№ 38.

1̇7	71̇	1̇7	₇1̇
1̇76	671̇	1̇76	₆71̇
1̇765	5671̇	1̇765	₅671̇

№ 39.

56	65	56	₆5
567	765	567	₇65
5671̇	1̇765	5671̇	₁765

№ 40.

1̇765	5671̇	1̇765	₅671̇
1̇76	671̇	1̇76	₆71̇
1̇7	71̇	1̇7	₇1̇

№ 41.

5671̇	1̇765	5671̇	₁765
567	765	567	₇65
56	65	56	₆5

Dictation.

The teacher sings the *second* columns of №ᔆ 34, 35, 36, 37, 38, 39, 40, 41, on Ah, stopping at every line, the pupils answering the same.

Time.

After having the class beat time a few seconds, the teacher goes back to the blackboard pointing as before the №ᔆ 1, 2, 3 and 4, pupils saying tä on the articulation and ä for the prolongation. Then the pupils are instructed to beat the time and *name* the notes, *not sing* them.

(Columns 1 & 3) When meeting a figure they will name it, if a dot they should only pronounce the vowel of the preceding notes.

Ex.	1	•	2	•	3	•	4	•	5	•
	do - o		ré - é		mi - i		fa - a		so - ol	

This explanation being well understood the pupils should beat two blank measures before starting, the teacher *only* saying down, up. At the third measure pupils begin to *name* the notes and beat to the end of the exercise.

FOURTH LESSON.
Intonation.

Review Nºˢ 34, 35, 36, 37, 38, 39, 40, 41, by large arrows. On account of the irregularity of the combinations of the following T.
will do well to write them on the blackboard announcing to the pupils to be on the lookout as sometimes some notes are repeated and some are not.

KEY OF MI.

Nº 42.

12345	54321
1122334455	554433221
122334455	544332211
122345	544321
123345	543321
123445	543221

Nº 43.

54321	12345
5544332211	1122334455
544332211	122334455
544321	122345
543321	123345
543221	123445

KEY OF RÉ.

Nº 44.

1̇765	567̇1̇
1̇1̇776655	5566771̇1̇
1̇77665	566771̇
1̇7765	5667̇1̇
1̇7665	56771̇

Nº 44½

567̇1̇	1̇765
5566771̇1̇	1̇1̇776655
566771̇	1̇77665
5667̇1̇	1̇7765
56771̇	1̇7665

Dictation.

Same as previous lesson.

Time.

After the pupils have beaten the time saying down, up, (without reading) the teacher gives them the same time exercises Nº⁵ 1 – 2 – 3 – 4. The pupils first saying tä ä, then *naming* notes as before. For the prolongation the teacher will remark to the pupils that as they have kept the same vowel in naming they will also keep *the same sound in singing*. Be careful to sustain the same sound whenever a prolongation occurs; giving a sort of accent on the dot. In case some should experience trouble, a sure way would be to make them sing, 1 1 2 2 3 3

do do ré ré mi mi

4 4 5 5 several times, then 1 . 2 . 3 . 4 . 5 .   Then

fa fa sol sol.   do-o ré-é mi-i fa-a so -ol.

5 5 4 4 3 3 2 2 1 1   5 . 4 . 3 . 2 . 1 .

sol sol fa fa mi mi ré ré do do ⁻   so -ol fa-a mi-i ré-é do-o

This exercise done the teacher gives the sound of FA and calls it DO, being sure all have the same DO before starting. The class then beats two blank measures, while the teacher says, down, up, down, up; then, following the large arrows they sing the syllables, beating time until they have read the four exercises.

FIFTH LESSON.
Intonation.

Take slowly and alone the *second* column of Nº⁵ 34, 35, 36, 37, 38, 39, 40, 41. If pupils have trouble take both columns of each number following large arrows. They will then no doubt get it correctly. The exercise should not be passed over until sung correctly as first stated. Then point to Nºs 42, 43, 44 & 44½ following large arrows.

Dictation.

Vocalize singly by column on ah, Nº⁵ 12, 13, 14 & 15 beginning at the third line – omit two first lines of each number – Pupils repeat also on ah; dictate one line at a time.

Time.

After a few beats with the hand – without reading – The same exercise is gone over; first, in speaking the sounds; secondly, in singing them. These exercises done divide the class in two; first division will sing the 1ˢᵗ line, second division the 2ⁿᵈ line, first division 3ʳᵈ line, second division 4ᵗʰ and so on alternately, asking them to continue beating time whether singing or not; otherwise, they would fail to attack the first note of their line in correct time. Then repeat the same exercise, the second division starting so as to exchange lines.

A Solfa is a succession of sounds arranged as a melody according to rules established in Music to be sung with the syllabic names of the notes. In the beginning of the study of music they should be very simple; in fact they should be the outcome of the exercises and be composed in accordance with the knowledge of Time and Intonation already mastered. Teacher writes on blackboard the following melody;   the class first beats the time and names the sounds; secondly, sings them – without beating.

KEY OF RÉ. (1-i)

№1. | 1 2 | 3 4 | 5 . | 5 . | 5 4 | 3 2 | 1 . | . . | 2 3 | 4 5 |
| 5 4 | 3 2 | 1 2 | 3 4 | 5 . | 5 . | 5 . | 6 7 | i . | 5 . | i 7 |
| 6 5 | i . | . . | i 7 | 6 5 | i 7 | 6 5 | 5 4 | 3 2 | 1 . | . . |

SIXTH LESSON.
Intonation.

For this lesson the following exercises should be studied according to *small arrows only.*

KEY OF RÉ.

Nº 45.

1 2 3 4 5 6 7 i	i 7 6 5 4 3 2 1	1 2 3 4 5 6 7 i	i 7 6 5 4 3 2 1
1 2	2 1	1 2	2 1
1 2 3	3 2 1	1 2 3	3 2 1
1 2 3 4	4 3 2 1	1 2 3 4	4 3 2 1
1 2 3 4 5	5 4 3 2 1	1 2 3 4 5	5 4 3 2 1
1 2 3 4 5 6	6 5 4 3 2 1	1 2 3 4 5 6	6 5 4 3 2 1
1 2 3 4 5 6 7	7 6 5 4 3 2 1	1 2 3 4 5 6 7	7 6 5 4 3 2 1
1 2 3 4 5 6 7 i	i 7 6 5 4 3 2 1	1 2 3 4 5 6 7 i	i 7 6 5 4 3 2 1

Nº 46.

i 7	7 i	i 7	7 i
i 7 6	6 7 i	i 7 6	6 7 i
i 7 6 5	5 6 7 i	i 7 6 5	5 6 7 i
i 7 6 5 4	4 5 6 7 i	i 7 6 5 4	4 5 6 7 i
i 7 6 5 4 3	3 4 5 6 7 i	i 7 6 5 4 3	3 4 5 6 7 i
i 7 6 5 4 3 2	2 3 4 5 6 7 i	i 7 6 5 4 3 2	2 3 4 5 6 7 i
i 7 6 5 4 3 2 1	1 2 3 4 5 6 7 i	i 7 6 5 4 3 2 1	1 2 3 4 5 6 7 i

№ 47.

1 2 3 4 5 6 7 i	i 7 6 5 4 3 2 1	1 2 3 4 5 6 7 i	i 7 6 5 4 3 2 1
1 2 3 4 5 6 7	7 6 5 4 3 2 1	1 2 3 4 5 6 7	7 6 5 4 3 2 1
1 2 3 4 5 6	6 5 4 3 2 1	1 2 3 4 5 6	6 5 4 3 2 1
1 2 3 4 5	5 4 3 2 1	1 2 3 4 5	5 4 3 2 1
1 2 3 4	4 3 2 1	1 2 3 4	4 3 2 1
1 2 3	3 2 1	1 2 3	3 2 1
1 2	2 1	1 2	2 1

№ 48.

i 7 6 5 4 3 2 1	1 2 3 4 5 6 7 i	i 7 6 5 4 3 2 1	1 2 3 4 5 6 7 i
i 7 6 5 4 3 2	2 3 4 5 6 7 i	i 7 6 5 4 3 2	2 3 4 5 6 7 i
i 7 6 5 4 3	3 4 5 6 7 i	i 7 6 5 4 3	3 4 5 6 7 i
i 7 6 5 4	4 5 6 7 i	i 7 6 5 4	4 5 6 7 i
i 7 6 5	5 6 7 i	i 7 6 5	5 6 7 i
i 7 6	6 7 i	i 7 6	6 7 i
i 7	7 i	i 7	7 i

Dictation.

Teacher sings by vocalizing on ah col. № 16, 21, 26, 30. Pupils re-peat the same on *ah*. (see page 5)

Time.

Take the same exercises as before—only sing them—and if all pupils have books they may sing from them; otherwise they can read from blackboard.

Solfa.

In reviewing Solfa № 1 increase speed in singing. Then point a few times: i 7 6 5 _ i 7 6 5 _ i 5 i 5 i _ i 7 6 5 4 3 2 1, before proceeding to № 2.

KEY OF RÉ. (1_i)

№ 2. | i 5 | i . | i 5 | i . | 7 6 | 5 4 | 3 2 | 1 . | 2 3 | 4 . |

| 3 4 | 5 . | i 7 | 6 5 | i 7 | 6 5 | i 5 | i . | i 5 | i . | 7 6 |

| 5 4 | 3 2 | 1 . | 2 3 | 4 . | 3 4 | 5 i | 5 4 | 3 2 | 1 1 | 1 . ‖

SEVENTH LESSON.

Intonation.

Take second col. of N.º.ˢ **45, 46, 47 & 48.** If pupils make mistakes take both col. following large arrows.

Dictation.

Take both col. of N.º.ˢ **34, 35, 36, 37, 38, 39, 40 & 41** separately, according to small arrows. Pupils repeat after teacher on *ah*.

Time.

Review the first four exercises following large arrows. Singing and beating should now be perfect.

Staff.

In order to express sounds use is made of five lines and four spaces called a staff.

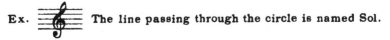

fifth line	
fourth line	fourth space
Ex: third line	third space
second line	second space
first line	first space

On these lines and spaces are set the notes. A sign is set at the beginning of the staff to name a line; that sign is called a Clef. There are three clefs but for the present we will only speak of the G or Sol Clef.

Ex.  The line passing through the circle is named Sol.

When knowing the name of a line we instantly know the others as per

Ex: 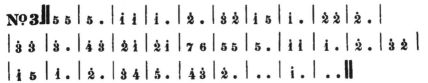 Illustrate.

Solfa.

Review N.º 2. Before taking up N.º 3 first name the sounds and beat the time. Then give the pitch of the new key and point on chart a few times:—
i̇ 7 6 5 i̇ 5 i̇ 5 i̇ 2̇ 3̇ 2̇ i̇ 5 i̇ 5 i̇ 5.

KEY OF SOL. (5_5)

N.º3 |5 5 |5 . |i̇ i̇ |i̇ . |2̇ . |3̇ 2̇ |i̇ 5 |i̇ . |2̇ 2̇ |2̇ . |

|3̇ 3̇ |3̇ . |4̇ 3̇ |2̇ i̇ |2̇ i̇ |7 6 |5 5 |5 . |i̇ i̇ |i̇ . |2̇ . |3̇ 2̇ |

|i̇ 5 |i̇ . |2̇ . |3̇ 4̇ |5̇ . |4̇ 3̇ |2̇ . |. . |i̇ . |. . ‖

EIGHTH LESSON.
Intonation.

KEY OF DO.

Repeat this line before beginning.

|1·2 3 4 5   5 6 7 i   i 2 3   3 2 i   i 7 6 5 ‖ 5 6 7 i 2 3   3 2 i 7 6 5|

№ 49.

5 6	5	3 2	3
5 6 7	5	3 2 i	3
5 6 7 i	5	3 2 i 7	3
5 6 7 i 2	5	3 2 i 7 6	3
5 6 7 i 2 3 5 3		3 2 i 7 6 5 3 5	
R		R	

№ 50.

5 6 7 i 2 3 5	3 2 i 7 6 5 3
5 6 7 i 2 5	3 2 i 7 6 3
5 6 7 i 5	3 2 i 7 3
5 6 7 5	3 2 i 3
5 6 5 3	3 2 3 5
R	R

№ 51.

5 6 7 i 2 3 3 2 i 7 6 5	5 6 7 i 2 3 3 2 i 7 6 5
5 6 7 i 2 2 i 7 6 5	5 6 7 i 2 i 7 6 5
5 6 7 i i 7 6 5	5 6 7 i i 7 6 5
5 6 7 7 6 5	5 6 7 7 6 5
5 6 6 5	5 6 6 5
5 6 7 i 2 3 3 2 i 7 6 5 3	5 6 7 i 2 3 3 2 i 7 6 5 3
R	R

As can be noticed № 51 has two vertical arrows on the left, which means that after having sung from top down as usual the same exercises should be repeated going back. Also № 52.

№ 52.

3 2 i 7 6 5 5 6 7 i 2 3	3 2 i 7 6 5 5 6 7 i 2 3
3 2 i 7 6 6 7 i 2 3	3 2 i 7 6 6 7 i 2 3
3 2 i 7 7 i 2 3	3 2 i 7 7 i 2 3
3 2 i i 2 3	3 2 i i 2 3
3 2 2 3	3 2 2 3
3 2 i 7 6 5 5 6 7 i 2 3 5	3 2 i 7 6 5 5 6 7 i 2 3 5
R	R

Dictation.

Vocalize the *first column* of № 45 dictating one line at a time. If satisfactory repeat on ah the *first column only* of № 46. see page 11.

Beginning with a new sign, the rest, represented by a cipher 0. We will give it a name – as the other signs – which will be To and say, To, every time we meet the cipher taking care to hold the syllable TO just as long as the notes *do, ré, mi* etc. Repeat the following several times *naming* them.

	1	0	2	0	3	0	4	0	5	0	
	do	to	ré	to	mi	to	fa	to	sol	to	

When satisfied with the preceding exercise have the class sing seve – ral times the following.

KEY OF FA.

	1	1	2	2	3	3	4	4	5	5	

then imitating the same sounds *sing* the syllable TO

as follows

x	1	1	2	2	3	3	4	4	5	5	
	to	to	to	to	to	to	to	to	to	to	

then have TO sung in the pitch of the preceding sound.

xx	1	0	2	0	3	0	4	0	5	0	
	do	to	ré	to	mi	to	fa	to	sol	to	

Staff.

Teacher will show that the staff of five lines is not always sufficient to write music and that use is made of short lines which are added ei- ther below or above; these small lines are named *Leger Lines*.

Ex.

Teacher may draw five lines and the Sol Clef on the blackboard with the figures 1 on the leger line, 3 on the first line, 5 on the second line and by means of a short pointer(the end of which can be split, insert a card cut in shape of an *oval dot* which can be made out of a cream col- ored bristol card, the size of which depends on the spacing of the lines : this oval card represents the note and is shifted by the teacher on to the lines or spaces.) Teacher may point slowly to a few lines and spaces of the first exercises in regular succession beginning with DO on the *leger line,* pupils naming them together promptly.

Solfa.

KEY OF MI. T_points on chart: 1765_1765_1515_1234567í
(5_1)

Nº4.	1 5	6 7	1 5	6 7	1 2	3 4	5 6	7 í	í 7	6 5	
	í 7	6 5	5 .	5 .	5 4	3 2	1 5	6 7	1 5	6 7	1 2
	3 4	5 í	5 .	6 .	7 .	í 7	6 5	5 4	3 2	1 .	. 0

NINTH LESSON.

Intonation.

Review exercises Nos 51 & 52 following *large* arrows but start from the last line going up after which read it again going down.

Dictation.

Nos 45 & 46 by *large arrows* making no stop except at the line. (page 11)

Time

The teacher writes on black-board exercises 5, 6, 7, 8, pupils saying "tä" for the articulation "to" for the rest. The second time, *name* the notes and the rests, 0, TO.

KEY OF FA.

No 5.				No 6.			
1 2	3 4	5 4	3 2	1 2	3 0	4 5	4 3
1 2	3 4	5 4	3 0	1 2	3 0	4 5	5 0
1 2	3 4	5 0	4 3	1 2	3 0	4 0	$\underset{\cdot}{3}$ 2
1 2	3 4	5 0	5 0	1 2	3 0	4 0	5 0
1 2	3 4	5 0	0 0	1 2	3 0	2 0	0 0

No 7.				No 8.			
1 0	2 3	4 5	4 3	1 0	2 0	3 4	5 5
1 0	2 3	4 3	2 0	1 0	2 0	3 4	5 0
1 0	2 3	4 0	5 5	1 0	2 0	3 0	4 5
1 0	2 3	4 0	5 0	1 0	2 0	3 0	2 0
1 0	2 3	2 0	0 0	1 0	2 0	3 0	0 0

Then go to lesson No 8 and sing Ex. × and ×× in time. (page 15.)

Staff.

Similar practice as at previous lesson.

Solfa.

KEY OF RÉ. (1-$\dot{2}$)

No 5. ‖ 5 6 | 7 $\dot{1}$ | 7 6 | 5 4 | 3 4 | 5 4 | 3 2 | 1 . | $\underset{\cdot}{7}$ 1 | 2 . |

| 3 4 | 5 . | 6 . | 7 $\dot{1}$ | 7 6 | 5 . | 5 6 | 7 $\dot{1}$ | 7 6 | 5 4 | 3 4 |

| 5 4 | 3 2 | 1 . | 2 3 | 4 5 | 6 7 | $\dot{1}$ $\dot{2}$ | $\dot{1}$. | 7 . | $\dot{1}$. | . 0 ‖

TENTH LESSON.
Intonation.

Review 2nd col. only of Nos 51 & 52.

KEY OF RÉ. |1 2 3 3 4 5 5 6 7 i i 7 6 5 5 4 3 ‖3 4 5 6 7 i i 7 6 5 4 3|

NO 53.

i 7 6 5 4 3 i	i 7 i
i 7 6 5 4 i	i 7 6 i
i 7 6 5 i	i 7 6 5 i
i 7 6 i	i 7 6 5 4 i
i 7 i	i 7 6 5 4 3 i 3

R

NO 54.

3 4 5 6 7 i 3	3 4 3
3 4 5 6 7 3	3 4 5 3
3 4 5 6 3	3 4 5 6 3
3 4 5 3	3 4 5 6 7 3
3 4 3 i	3 4 5 6 7 i 3 i

R   R

Sing the two following Nos. by descending arrow and afterward ascending.

NO 55.

i 7 7 i	i 7 7 i
i 7 6 6 7 i	i 7 6 6 7 i
i 7 6 5 5 6 7 i	i 7 6 5 5 6 7 i
i 7 6 5 4 4 5 6 7 i	i 7 6 5 4 4 5 6 7 i
i 7 6 5 4 3 3 4 5 6 7 i	i 7 6 5 4 3 3 4 5 6 7 i

NO 56.

3 4 4 3	3 4 4 3
3 4 5 5 4 3	3 4 5 5 4 3
3 4 5 6 6 5 4 3	3 4 5 6 6 5 4 3
3 4 5 6 7 7 6 5 4 3	3 4 5 6 7 7 6 5 4 3
3 4 5 6 7 i i 7 6 5 4 3	3 4 5 6 7 i i 7 6 5 4 3

Dictation.

Vocalize NO 47 making a stop at the vertical line. then NO 48. (page 12.)

Time.

Take Nos 5, 6, 7 & 8 by small arrows *naming* them once; singing at the second reading always beating time, watching that the syllable TO is sung on the same pitch as the preceding note.

Staff.

If pupils have books they can follow from them. Teacher giving a little tap with the stick to preserve the regularity and making a short stop at the double bars. Pupils will name them after which the teacher will point the following exercise on the Meloplast.[1] Pupils *naming* the following: do, ré, mi, etc. T. calling attention to the fact that do mi sol are on the lines, therefore ré, fa, are on the spaces

Nº 1.

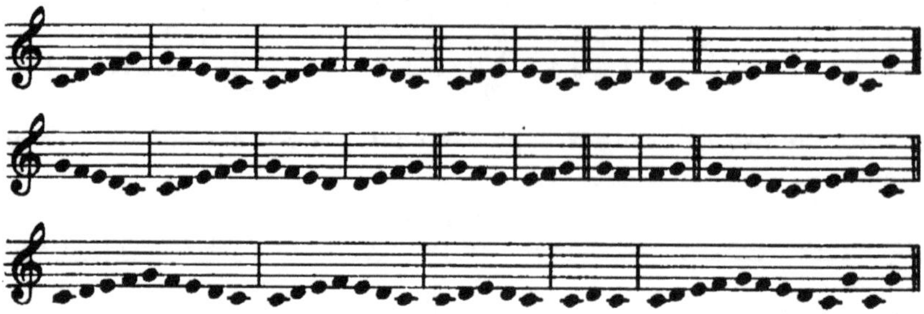

Solfa.

KEY OF MI. ($\underset{\cdot}{5}$ - $\dot{1}$)

Nº 6. ‖ 1 $\underset{\cdot}{5}$ | 1 $\underset{\cdot}{5}$ | 1 $\underset{\cdot}{5}$ | 1 2 | 3 4 | 5 6 | 5 . | 4 3 | 2 3 | 4 5 |
| 4 3 | 2 1 | $\underset{\cdot}{7}$ $\underset{\cdot}{6}$ | $\underset{\cdot}{7}$ 1 | 2 . | . . | 1 $\underset{\cdot}{5}$ | 1 $\underset{\cdot}{5}$ | 1 $\underset{\cdot}{5}$ | 1 2 | 3 4 | 5 6 |
| $\underset{\cdot}{7}$ $\dot{1}$ | 5 . | 6 . | 7 . | $\dot{1}$ 7 | 6 5 | 5 4 | 3 2 | 1 . | . 0 ‖

ELEVENTH LESSON.

Intonation.

Review the 2nd col. only of Nos 55 & 56 first ascending then descending. In the following exercises it is important for the teacher to carefully watch so that the FA is not sung too high. These exercises should be sung slowly.

---

(1) Blank staff on which exercises are pointed.

| 12345 54321 1765 | 5671 12345 | 54321765 | 56712345 |

№ 57.

54321765	5	54	5
5432176	5	543	5
543217	5	5432	5
54321	5	54321	5
5432	5	543217	5
543	5	5432176	5
54	5	54321765 R	5

№ 58.

56712345	5	56	5
5671234	5	567	5
567123	5	5671	5
56712	5	56712	5
5671	5	567123	5
567	5	5671234	5
56	55 R	56712345	55 R

№ 59.

54321765	56712345	54321765	5 6712345
5432176	6712345	5432176	6 712345
543217	712345	543217	7 12345
54321	12345	54321	1 2345
5432	2345	5432	2 345
543	345	543	3 45
54	45	54	4 5

№ 60.

56712345	54321765	56712345	54321765
5671234	4321765	5671234	4 321765
567123	321765	567123	3 21765
56712	21765	56712	2 1765
5671	1765	5671	1 765
567	765	567	7 65
56	65	56	6 5

Dictation.

1st vocalize by small arrows Nos. 49 & 50. P. repeating on *ah*. 2nd T. dictates on *ah* Nos 1,2,3,4. P. repeat now not only singing but at the same time *naming* the notes; that is, they must recognize every sound dictated, not wait for a whole series of sounds but try to recognize them quickly one by one and after the stop, repeat them from memory singing their names.(page 3.)

Time.

Review Nos. 5,6,7,8, singing by large arrows.Then divide the class into two parts and count the mistakes of each division.

Staff.

Name first from book, then T. will give the sound of MI for DO, then point slowly on the Meloplast the following : P. sing.

№ 2.

Solfa.

T. points on chart: 567_ 567_57_57_ 567i 5i5 i765_i75
KEY OF MI.(1-i)

№ 7. | 1 2 | 3 4 | 5 6 | 7 i | i . | 5 . | i . | . . | 7 6 | 5 4 |

| 3 2 | 1 2 | 3 . | 1 . | 5 . | 5 . | 5 6 | 7 5 | i . | 5 . | 5 6 |

| 7 5 | i . | . . | 7 5 | 6 7 | i 7 | 6 5 | 5 4 | 3 2 | 1 . | . 0 |

Duett.

Each part should be studied as a Solfa the first division singing the first line the second division the second line. Thereafter they can sing together each pupil taking care to listen to his or her own voice. If having spare time change parts, that is have the second division sing the first line and the first division sing the second line.

KEY OF SOL.(5-3) M.M. 120 | 1 1 | 2 2 | 3 3 | 2 .' | 1 1 | 2 3 | 2 2 | 1 . |
| 1 1 | 5 5 | 1 1 | 5 .' | 1 1 | 5 1 | 5 5 | 1 . |

TWELFTH LESSON.

Intonation.

Review by large arrowsNos. 59 & 60 but first ascending and then descending.

KEY OF RÉ.

```
    1 2 3 4 5   5 6 7 i        i 7 6 5   5 4 3 2 1   1 7 6 5
  5 6 7 1   1 2 3 4 5   5 6 7 i    i 7 6 5   5 4 3 2 1   1 7 6 5
    5 6 7 1 2 3 4 5 6 7 i          i 7 6 5 4 3 2 1 7 6 5
```

No 61.

```
5 6                      5
5 6 7                    5
5 6 7 1                  5
5 6 7 1 2                5
5 6 7 1 2 3              5
5 6 7 1 2 3 4            5
5 6 7 1 2 3 4 5          5
5 6 7 1 2 3 4 5 6        5
5 6 7 1 2 3 4 5 6 7      5
5 6 7 1 2 3 4 5 6 7 i  5 i
                         R
```

No 62.

```
i 7                                    i
i 7 6                                  i
i 7 6 5                                i
i 7 6 5 4                              i
i 7 6 5 4 3                            i
i 7 6 5 4 3 2                          i
i 7 6 5 4 3 2 1                        i
i 7 6 5 4 3 2 1 7                      i
i 7 6 5 4 3 2 1 7 6                  i
i 7 6 5 4 3 2 1 7 6 5 i 5
                           R
```

No 63.

```
5 6                            6 5
5 6 7                         7 6 5
5 6 7 1                      1 7 6 5
5 6 7 1 2                   2 1 7 6 5
5 6 7 1 2 3                3 2 1 7 6 5
5 6 7 1 2 3 4            4 3 2 1 7 6 5
5 6 7 1 2 3 4 5        5 4 3 2 1 7 6 5
5 6 7 1 2 3 4 5 6    6 5 4 3 2 1 7 6 5
5 6 7 1 2 3 4 5 6 7 7 6 5 4 3 2 1 7 6 5
5 6 7 1 2 3 4 5 6 7 i 7 6 5 4 3 2 1 7 6 5
```

No 64.

```
5 6                            6 5
5 6 7                         7 6 5
5 6 7 1                      1 7 6 5
5 6 7 1 2                   2 1 7 6 5
5 6 7 1 2 3                3 2 1 7 6 5
5 6 7 1 2 3 4            4 3 2 1 7 6 5
5 6 7 1 2 3 4 5        5 4 3 2 1 7 6 5
5 6 7 1 2 3 4 5 6    6 5 4 3 2 1 7 6 5
5 6 7 1 2 3 4 5 6 7 7 6 5 4 3 2 1 7 6 5
5 6 7 1 2 3 4 5 6 7 i 7 6 5 4 3 2 1 7 6 5
```

(page 14.)   ## Dictation.

1st vocalize by small arrows, first descending then ascending Nos. 51 & 52. 2nd T. vocalizes on *ah*, P. repeat singing & naming notes of Nos. 12 & 13. (Omit two first lines.) (page 3.)

Time.

Take the following by *small arrows*, calling attention to the fact that the duration and the rest will occur.

KEY OF FA.

Nº 9.

1 2	3 4	5 4	3 2
1 2	3 4	5 4	3 .
1 2	3 4	5 .	4 3
1 2	3 4	3 .	2 0
1 2	3 4	5 .	. 0

Nº 10.

1 2	3 .	4 5	4 3
1 2	3 .	4 3	2 0
1 2	3 .	4 0	3 2
1 2	3 .	4 0	5 0
1 2	3 .	2 .	0 0

Nº 11.

1 .	2 3	4 5	4 3
1 .	2 3	4 3	2 0
1 .	2 3	4 0	3 2
1 .	2 3	4 .	5 0
1 .	2 3	2 .	0 0

Nº 12.

1 .	2 .	3 4	3 2
1 .	2 .	3 4	5 0
1 .	2 .	3 0	4 5
1 .	2 .	3 0	2 0
1 .	2 .	3 .	. 0

Staff.

First name as before, then point on chart. Give the sound of Ré for DO and let the class sing it.

Nº 3.

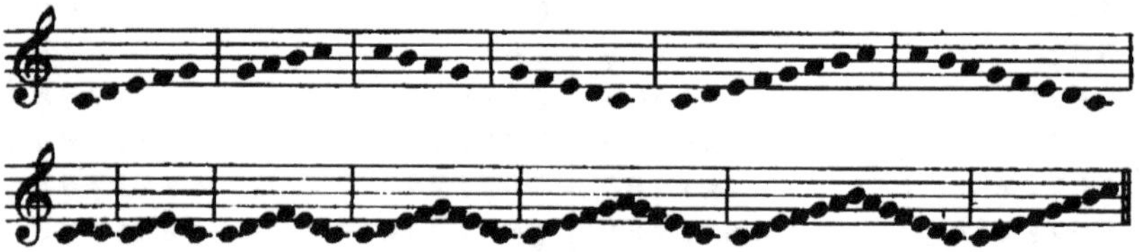

There are seven signs to represent the notes but we will only speak for the present of three: the whole note 𝅝, the half note 𝅗𝅥, the quarter note 𝅘𝅥 (Illustrate) T. points to each sign the whole class naming them together. The duration of the quarter note 𝅘𝅥 we will say counts one, the half note 𝅗𝅥 counts two and the whole note 𝅝 counts four. Question the class about the duration of these new signs after having illustrated on the blackboard thus:

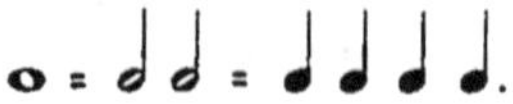

KEY OF RÉ. (4 _ i)

N° 8.‖ 1̣0 | 2̣3 | 1̣0 | 2̣3 | 45 | 45 | 43 | 2̣3 | 1̣0 | 2̣3 | 1̣0 |
| 2̣3 | 45 | 43 | 2. | 1̣0 | 5̣0 | 67 | 5̣0 | 67 | i̇7 | i̇7 | 65 |
| 6̣0 | 5̣0 | 67 | 5̣0 | 67 | i̇7 | 65 | 6. | 5. | 1̣0 | 2̣3 | 1̣0 |
| 2̣3 | 45 | 45 | 43 | 2̣3 | 1. | 2̣3 | 1. | 2̣3 | 45 | 67 | i̇. | .0 ‖

Duett.

KEY OF SOL. (5̣ - 3) M. M. 120

N° 2. ‖ 1 1 | 2. | 33 | 2.' | 1 1 | 2 2 | 3 2 | 1. ‖
         1 1 | 5̣. | 1 1 | 5̣.' | 1 1 | 5̣ 5̣ | 5̣ 5̣ | 1. ‖

THIRTEENTH LESSON.

Intonation.

Review N° 64 then the following Nos. 65, 66, 67 descending only.

KEY OF DO.

N° 65.

1 2 1	3̇ 2̇ 3̇
1 2 3 1	3̇ 2̇ i̇ 3̇
1 2 3 4 1	3̇ 2̇ i̇ 7 3̇
1 2 3 4 5 1	3̇ 2̇ i̇ 7 6 3̇
1 2 3 4 5 6 1	3̇ 2̇ i̇ 7 6 5 3̇
1 2 3 4 5 6 7 1	3̇ 2̇ i̇ 7 6 5 4 3̇
1 2 3 4 5 6 7 i̇ 1	3̇ 2̇ i̇ 7 6 5 4 3 3̇
1 2 3 4 5 6 7 i̇ 2̇ 1	3̇ 2̇ i̇ 7 6 5 4 3 2 3̇
1 2 3 4 5 6 7 i̇ 2̇ 3̇ 1 3̇	3̇ 2̇ i̇ 7 6 5 4 3 2 1 3̇ 1
R	R

N° 66.	N° 67.
1 2 2 1	1 2 2 1
1 2 3 3 2 1	1 2 3 3 2 1
1 2 3 4 4 3 2 1	1 2 3 4 4 3 2 1
1 2 3 4 5 5 4 3 2 1	1 2 3 4 5 5 4 3 2 1
1 2 3 4 5 6 6 5 4 3 2 1	1 2 3 4 5 6 6 5 4 3 2 1
1 2 3 4 5 6 7 7 6 5 4 3 2 1	1 2 3 4 5 6 7 7 6 5 4 3 2 1
1 2 3 4 5 6 7 i̇ i̇ 7 6 5 4 3 2 1	1 2 3 4 5 6 7 i̇ i̇ 7 6 5 4 3 2 1
1 2 3 4 5 6 7 i̇ 2̇ 2̇ i̇ 7 6 5 4 3 2 1	1 2 3 4 5 6 7 i̇ 2̇ 2̇ i̇ 7 6 5 4 3 2 1
1 2 3 4 5 6 7 i̇ 2̇ 3̇ 3̇ 2̇ i̇ 7 6 5 4 3 2 1	1 2 3 4 5 6 7 i̇ 2̇ 3̇ 3̇ 2̇ i̇ 7 6 5 4 3 2 1

Dictation.

1st T. vocalizes Nos. 53 and 55. P. repeat on *ah*. 2nd Nos. 14 and 15. P. repeat after T. singing and naming the notes. (Omit first two lines.) (page 3.)

Time.

Review by large arrows Nos. 9, 10, 11, 12, first by all the class, secondly each division taking a line one after another while all keep beating time.

Staff.

Name first, then give the sound of *Ré* for *Do* and let the class sing it.

N° 4.

Question about the new signs learned at the last lesson; also in regard to their duration. Show their transformation into figures thus: $\begin{array}{c} d \mid d \mid o \\ 1 \mid 1. \mid 1... \end{array}$

In the staff notation there are three ways to prolong a sound First the Dot (•) which adds one half to the duration of the preceding note. Ex: ♩. = ♩ ♩. Second the Tie (⌣) when wishing to prolong the last note over the next bar and also sometimes inside of a bar. Ex: ♩|♩.

Third, the sign for double duration (♩) or quadruple duration (o).

Ex: Four beats measure |♩♩♩♩|♩♩|o‖ Ex: of the three ways of prolongation. Staff Signs |♩ ♩|♩.♩|♩ ♩♩|♩♩♩♩‖ Remark: In the staff notation the dot is never used at the beginning of a measure.

Question about the duration of each of these last signs.

Solfa.

KEY OF RÉ. (1-i)

N° 9.‖ 1 2 | 3 2 | 1 2 | 3 2 | 1 2 | 3 4 | 5 i | 5 0 | 5 4 | 3 2 |

| 5 4 | 3 2 | 1 2 | 3 4 | 3 0 | 2 0 | 1 2 | 3 2 | 1 2 | 3 2 | 1 2 |

| 3 4 | 5 i | i . | 7 6 | 7 i | i 5 | 5 . | 6 5 | 5 4 | 3 2 | 1 . ‖

Duett.

KEY OF FA. (5-5) M. M. 120.

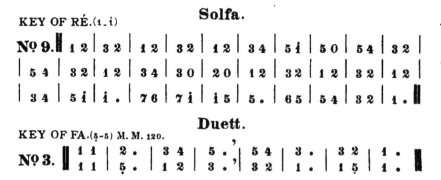

FOURTEENTH LESSON.

Intonation.

Review Nos. 66 and 67 following ascending arrow.

Study of the perfect Chord.

This study starting with the perfect chord requires great attention from T. and P.

It is very important that P. sing the following exercises slowly, listening to themselves.

The first line being sung in equal duration. In the second line the small notes should be sung softly, the large notes loudly; in the third line the small notes should be thought by the P., the T. giving time to think of them.

N⁰ 68.

1 2 3	3 4 5	5 4 3	3 2 1
1 2 3	3 4 5	5 4 3	3 2 1
1 2 3	3 4 5	5 4 3	3 2 1
1 3	3 5	5 3	3 1
1 3	5	5 3	1

N⁰ 69.

5 4 3	3 2 1	1 2 3	3 4 5
5 4 3	3 2 1	1 2 3	3 4 5
5 4 3	3 2 1	1 2 3	3 4 5
5 3	3 1	1 3	3 5
5 3	1	1 3	5

N⁰ 70.

1 3 5	5 3 1	1 3 5	5 3 1
1 3 5	3 1	1 3	3 1
1 3	3 1	1 3	1

N⁰ 71.

5 3 1	1 3 5	5 3 1	1 3 5
5 3 1	3 5	5 3	3 5
5 3	3 5	5 3	5

N⁰ 72.

1 3 1	1 3 5 1	5 3 5	5 3 1 5
1 3	1 3 5	5 3	5 3 1

N⁰ 73.

5 3 5	5 3 1 5	1 3 1	1 3 5 1
5 3	5 3 1	1 3	1 3 5

N⁰ 74.

1 3	3 1 3 5	5 3	3 5 3 1
1 3	3 1 3 5	5 3	3 5 3 1
1 3	1 3 5	5 3	5 3 1

N⁰ 75.

5 3	3 5 3 1	1 3	3 1 3 5
5 3	3 5 3 1	1 3	3 1 3 5
5 3	5 3 1	1 3	1 3 5

Dictation.

1st by small arrows descending Nos. 54 and 56 (page 17.)
2nd Col. 16, 17, 21, 22. P..sing and name. (page 5.)

Time.

1st Read by small arrows only, then read once more telling children when coming to the rest 0 (to) to try to say the *To* softly but be care - ful not to shorten the duration.

Nº 13.

1 2	3 4	5 4	3 2
1 2	3 4	5 4	3 0
1 2 ·	3 4	5 0	4 3
1 2	3 4	3 0	2 .
1 2	3 4	5 .	0 0

Nº 14.

1 2	3 0	4 5	4 3
1 2	3 0	4 3	2 .
1 2	3 0	4 .	3 2
1 2	3 0	4 .	5 0
1 2	3 0	2 .	0 0

Nº 15.

1 0	2 3	4 5	4 3
1 0	2 3	4 3	2 .
1 0	2 3	4 .	3 2
1 0	2 3	4 .	5 0
1 0	2 3	2 .	0 0

Nº 16.

1 0	2 .	3 4	3 2
1 0	2 .	3 4	5 0
1 0	2 .	3 0	4 5
1 0	2 .	3 0	2 .
1 0	2 .	3 .	. 0

Staff.

Give the sound of *RÉ* for *DO*. after P. have named.

Nº 5.

On the staff the rests are expressed by signs which correspond for the duration to the signs of articulation.

The quarter rest (Σ) corresponds to the quarter note ($\flat$); the half rest ▬ to the half note ($\flat$); the whole rest ▬ to the whole note (o). As the half and whole rests look very much alike the T. can remark that the half rest re - sembles a sailor hat, while the whole rest looks like the hat turned up-side down.

Articulated Sounds	Rests	Duration
♩	Σ	one
♩	▬	two
o	▬	four

Ex: Two beats measure. Ex: Three beats measure. Ex: Four beats measure.

Solfa.

KEY OF RÉ.(1.i)

Nº 10. | 5 6 | 5 i | 5 6 | 5 . | 5 4 | 3 2 | 3 i | 2 . | 5 6 | 5 i |
| 5 6 | 7 . | 6 . | 7 i | 7 6 | 5 . | 5 6 | 5 . | 5 i | 5 . | 6 5 |
| 6 5 | 6 5 | 4 3 | 5 6 | 5 . | 5 i | 7 6 | 5 4 | 3 2 | 1 . | . o |

Duett.

KEY OF FA (5 - 5) M. M. 120.

Nº 4. | 1 2 | 3 . | 3 4 | 5 . | 5 4 | 3 . | 2 3 | 1 . |
      | 1 7 | 1 . | 1 2 | 3 . | 3 2 | 1 . | 5 5 | 1 . |

FIFTEENTH LESSON.
Intonation.

Review Nos. 68, 69, 70, 71, 72, 73, 74, 75, first by *small* and after - wards by *large* arrows.

(page 19.)   ### Dictation.

1st vocalize in descending Nos. 57 and 58. 2nd Nos. 19, 20, 24 and 25 telling P. to watch carefully because, sometimes they will hear one sound repeated twice. (page 5.)

Time.

By large arrows Nos. 13, 14, 15, 16, each division singing every other line as before and beating time through entire exercise; T. counting the mistakes.

Staff.

P. first name then sing.

T. gives *RE* for *DO* as starting sound.

This sign [:‖:] means repeat. # NO 6.

Two - four $(\frac{2}{4})$ at the beginning of a piece indicates that each measure should contain the value of two quarter notes and that two beats should be counted between each bar. T. illustrates the transformation of the half note (♩)(1 •) and quarter note (♪)(1) into figures. When singing (♩) P. give an accentuation on the duration, thus *do - o*.

Solfa.

Name first, then let P. sing. # NO 6. A. T. gives sound of *DO* for *DO*.

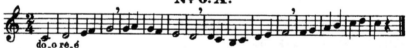

do - o re - 6

Though the gradation of difficulty is sensibly introduced in Solfa NO 11 it is preferable to work out the difficulty before singing the melody; for instance; care has been taken at bar NO 12. to prepare for the diffi - culty at bar NO 17 but some children from lack of attention may break at bar NO 17.

To overcome this, point on the chart Sol-La-Si-La-Sol, Sol-La-Si-Si-La-Sol after which have the first LA sung very softly then they will easily master Sol Si La Sol of course in the key in which they will sing the melody. Remark— It often happens that the second reading is worse than the first— the cause is that those who did well dislike to repeat for the sake of those who did poorly and at the second reading less attention is paid. On the contrary if the stated difficulty is first worked out the chances are they will all do well at first reading.

Nº 11. | 1 3 | 5 . | 5 1 | 5 . | 5 3 | 5 3 | 1 3 | 2 . | 1 3 | 5 . |

| 5 1 | 5 6 | 7 . | 6 5 | 6 7 | 5 . | 5 7 | 6 5 | 5 1 | 7 6 | 5 4 |

| 3 2 | 1 2 | 3 1 | 5 7 | 6 5 | 5 1 | 1 3 | 5 . | 5 . | 1 . | . 0 |

Duett.

KEY OF FA. (5-5) M.M. 120.

Nº 5. | 1 2 | 3 2 | 3 4 | 5 . | 5 4 | 3 4 | 3 2 | 1 . |
       | 1 7 | 1 5 | 1 2 | 3 . | 3 2 | 1 7 | 1 5 | 1 . |

SIXTEENTH LESSON.
Intonation.

KEY OF FA. Repeat each column two or three times.

Nº 76.

These exercises must be sung perfectly true and slowly. If some P. should experience trouble have the small notes sung lightly.

1 3 5 3 1	5 3 1 3 5	3 5 3 1 3
1 3 5 3	5 3 1 3	3 5 3 1
1 3 5 3 1	5 3 1 3 5	3 5 3 1 3
1 3 1 3 5	5 3 5 3 1	3 5 3 1 3 5
1 3 5 3 1	5 3 1 3 5	3 1 3 5
1 3 5 3 5	5 3 1 3 1	3 1 3 5 3
1 3 5 3 1 3	5 3 1 3 5 3	3 1 3 5 1

Dictation.

1st – Vocalize by large arrows, stopping at each vertical line, the 1st, 4th and 5th lines of Nos. 68 and 69. (page 25.)

2nd – Nos. 26, 27, 30, 31 P. repeating by singing the names of sounds. (page 5.)

Time.

In any kind of measure the relative importance of beats is different; for instance, in two beats the first one is much more important than the second. The first one is strong, the second is weak, thereby we have two kinds of prolongation emanating from one or the other beat.

As it is the first time this effect is presented to the P. the T. writes on black-board N°17 and has it executed first by saying *tä* for the arti - culated sound, *ä* for the prolongation; then in naming the notes taking care to carry the vowels of the preceding notes over the following du - ration thus _ ré-é, mi-i etc. doing the same when singing.

KEY OF SOL. Prolongation { simple _ prolongation of a strong beat.
{ syncopated _ prolongation of a weak beat.

N° 17.   N° 18.

1 2	. 3	3 4	3 2	1 2	0 3	3 4	3 2
1 2	. 3	3 1	2 .	1 2	0 3	3 1	2 0
1 2	. 3	3 .	2 3	1 2	0 3	3 0	2 3
1 2	. 3	3 .	2 .	1 2	0 3	3 0	2 0
1 2	. 3	3 .	. .	1 2	0 3	3 0	0 0
1 2	3 4	. 3 2	. 2	1 2	3 4	3 2	0 2
1 2	3 .	2 3	. 2	1 2	3 0	2 3	0 2
1 .	2 3	3 2	. 2	1 0	2 3	3 2	0 2
1 .	2 .	3 2	. 2	1 0	2 0	3 2	0 2
1 .	. .	2 3	. 2	1 0	0 0	2 3	0 2
1 2	. 3	3 2	. 2	1 2	0 3	3 2	0 2

Staff.

P. name first then sing slowly.
Give the sound of *MI* for *DO*.

N° 6.

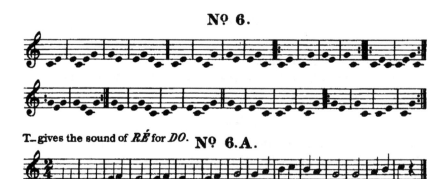

T. gives the sound of *RÉ* for *DO*. N° 6.A.

Question about signs on the staff already learned.

Great care should be taken, when a note is followed by a rest, not to carry the least sound of the previous articulation over the rest.

Solfa.

KEY OF RÉ. (1 _ $\dot{1}$)

Nº 12.

$\dot{1}$ 5	$\dot{1}$ 0	$\dot{1}$ 5	$\dot{1}$ 0	7 6	5 4	3 2	1 0	2 3	4 0
3 4	5 0	$\dot{1}$ 7	$\dot{1}$ 5	4 3	2 0	2 3	2 0	2 3	2 0
2 3	2 3	2 5	5 .	5 $\dot{1}$	$\dot{1}$.	7 6	7 $\dot{1}$	5 6	5 4
4 .	3 .	2 5	5 .	5 $\dot{1}$	$\dot{1}$.	7 6	5 4	3 2	1 .

Duett.

KEY OF MI. ($\underset{\cdot}{7}$ - 5) M.M. 120.

Nº 6.

1 2	3 4	5 4	3 2'	1 2	3 4	3 2	1 .
1 $\underset{\cdot}{5}$	1 2	3 2	1 $\underset{\cdot}{7}$'	1 $\underset{\cdot}{7}$	1 2	1 $\underset{\cdot}{5}$	1 .

SEVENTEENTH LESSON.

Intonation.

KEY OF FA.

Nº 77.

13531	53135	35313	5432	1
1353	5313	3531	2345	1
13531	53135	35313	4323	1
13135	53531	3531315	4325	1
13531	53135	3135	4345	1
13535	53131	31358	2123	1
135313	531353	31351	321$\underset{\cdot}{7}$	1

Dictation.

1st _ Take Nos. 70, 71, 72, 73, 74 & 75 on *ah* by small arrows. (page 25.)

2nd _ Nos. 34, 35, 38, 39 first columns only. (It will be understood hereafter that the second Dictation must always be sung on ah by T._ and repeated by P._who sings the *names* of the notes. (page 8.)

Time.

Review Nº 17 _ speaking the names of the notes first, then singing.

Staff.

Name first, then *sing* slowly giving the sound of *RÉ* for *DO*. Making a short stop at each bar.

Nº 7.

Nº 7. A.

Name notes first in time _ then class will sing _ Give *RÉ* for *DO* as starting sound.

Solfa.

KEY OF SOL. (5_5)

Nº 13.

1 5	1 3	1 5	1 0	1 5	1 3	1 5	1 0	2 0	3 1
2 0	3 1	5 4	3 2	1 7	6 5	1 5	1 3	1 5	1 .	1 5
1 3	1 3	5 .	5 4	3 2	5 4	3 2	5 4	3 2	1 .	. 0

In Music a Round is a melody so arranged that one part leads and after singing a certain number of measures is followed by each of the other parts successively in the same way thereby producing part - sing_ing.

When the first division starts from bar A and has reached B the second division should begin singing at bar A, both divisions continuing to the end at which, each division in turn immediately starts over again until the T_gives the signal to stop by striking rapidly a few times on the desk.

Nº 7. Round.

KEY OF FA.

(Advise P. to hum the rest so as to keep perfect time and to sing it first in unison once or twice before singing it in parts.)

A   B

‖1 1 |5 5 |6 6 |5 . |4 . |3 . |2 . |1 . |5 . |1 . |0 0 |0 0 |1 1 |

|5 5 |6 6 |5 . |4 . |3 . |2 . |1 . |5 . |1 . |0 0 |0 0 |5 5 |4 4 |

|3 3.|2 2 |5 . |5 . |0 0 |0 0 |5 5 |4 4 |3 3 |2 2 |5 . |5 . |0 0 |0 0 ‖

EIGHTEENTH LESSON.
Intonation.

Nº 78.

123	345	567i	i765	543	321
123	345	567i	i765	543	321
123	345	567i	i765	543	321
1	3	5 i	i 5	3	1

Nº 79.

i765	543	321	123	345	567i
i765	543	321	123	345	567i
i765	543	321	123	345	567i
i	5	3	1	1	3	5	i

Nº 80.

135i	i531	135i	i531
135	531	135	531
13	31	13	31

Nº 81.

i531	135i	i531	135i
i53	35i	i53	35i
i5	5i	i5	5i

Nº 82.

1 3 1	1 3 5 1	1 3 5 i 1
1 3 .	1 3 5	1 3 5 i

Nº 83.

i 5 i	i 5 3 i	i 5 3 1 i
i 5	i 5 3	i 5 3 1

Nº 84.

Nº 84 should be sung quickly making a pause on the last note of each group. repeat last line several times.

13	135	135i	i5	i53	i531
13	135	135i	i5	i53	i531
13	135	135i	i5	i53	i531
13	1 5 1	i	i5	i 3 i	1

Dictation.

1st _ Nos. 72, 73, 74, 75. (page 25.)

2nd _ Nos. 36, 37, 40, 41 first column only. (page 8.)

Time.

Review by arrow No. 17.

For the rests as for the prolongations, there are two cases: where the rest follows a strong beat or a weak beat, therefore; we have this division +

Rest { after a strong beat + rest properly said
{ after a weak beat + counter _ time.

The T_writes on black-board N⁰ 18, P_saying *tä* for every sign, except the rest (represented by the cipher) for which they will say *TO*. Then the class will name them as follows | 1 0 | 2 0 | etc._ then | DO TO | RE TO | at last sing them.

Staff.

P_*name first* then sing_ Give sound of *RÉ* for *DO*.

N⁰ 8.

Solfa.

KEY OF RÉ.(1_i)

N⁰14. | 5 3 | 1 . | 2 3 | 1 . | 5 3 | 1 i | 7 6 | 7 5 | 5 3 | 1 . |
| 2 3 | 1 3 | 5 . | 5 . | 1 . | . 0 57 | 6 . | 5 7 | 6 . | 5 7 |
| 6 7 | i 7 | 6 . | 5 7 | 6 . | 5 7 | 6 . | 5 7 | 6 7 | i 7 | 6 5 |

Duett.

Review last Round _ first with syllables, then singing la, la, la, on every note. P. thinking the syllables.

NINETEENTH LESSON.
Intonation.

Review Nos. 78, 79, 80, 81, 82, 83 (not 84) then begin Nos. 85 & 86. Have the class hold the notes that are repeated. It will do no harm to repeat each line two or three times, especially the last one.

P. will experience more trouble in descending from high *DO* to *MI* than in ascending from *MI* to high *DO*. The cause of this is that, the P. always find the key note better and quicker while the third degree is far less attractive — therefore, it will be well to have the P. think the missing *Sol* in the chord when descending.

KEY OF MI.

Nº 85.   Nº 86.

1 3	3 1 3 5	5 3 5 1̇	1̇ 5	5 1̇ 5 3	3 5 3 1	1̇ 5	5 1̇ 5 3	3 5 3 1	1 3	3 1 3 5	5 3 5 1̇
1 3	3 1 3 5	5 3 5 1̇	1̇ 5	5 1̇ 5 3	3 5 3 1	1̇ 5	5 1̇ 5 3	3 5 3 1	1 3	3 1 3 5	5 3 5 1̇
1 3	1 3 5	3 5 1̇	1̇ 5	1̇ 5 3	5 3 1	1̇ 5	1̇ 5 3	5 3 1	1 3	1 3 5	3 5 1̇
1 3	1 5	3 1̇	1̇ 5	1̇ 3	5 1	1̇ 5	1̇ 3	5 1	1 3	1 5	3 1̇

Dictation.

1st — Nos. 70, 71, 72, 73, 74, 75 by small arrows. (page 25.)

2nd — The second column of Nos. 34, 35, 38, 39. (page 8.)

Time.

Nºs 19 and 20 *naming notes* first and then singing by small arrows.

KEY OF FA.

Nº 19.   Nº 20.

1 •	• 2	3 5	3 2	1 0	0 2	3 5	3 2
1 •	• 2	3 5	5 •	1 0	0 2	3 5	5 0
1 •	• 2	3 •	2 5	1 0	0 2	3 0	2 5
1 •	• 2	3 •	5 •	1 0	0 2	3 0	5 0
1 2	• 3	5 •	• •	1 2	0 3	5 0	0 0
1 2	3 5	3 •	• 2	1 2	3 5	3 0	0 2
1 2	3 •	2 •	• 5	1 2	3 0	2 0	0 5
1 •	2 3	2 •	• 5	1 0	2 3	2 0	0 5
1 •	3 •	5 •	• 5	1 0	3 0	5 0	0 5
1 •	2 3	5 •	• 5	1 0	2 3	5 0	0 5
1 •	• •	5 •	• 5	1 0	0 0	5 0	0 5

Staff.

Name first then sing. Give the sound of *MI* for *DO*.

Solfa.

KEY OF RÉ.(1̣-i)

Nọ15.‖13│13│13│5i│53│13│25│5.│13│13│13│5i│
│53│13│2.│1.│25│5.│35│5.│43│25│43│21│
│25│5̣.│35│5.│i5│i5│31│5.│13│13│13│5i│
│53│13│25│5.│13│13│13│5i│76│54│32│1.‖

Duett.

KEY OF FA.(5̣-5) M. M. 120.

Nọ8.‖1.│2.│34│5.ꞌ│43│43│21│2.ꞌ│
      1.│5̣.│12│3.ꞌ│21│21│71│5̣.ꞌ│

│1.│2.│34│5.ꞌ│43│21│23│1.‖
│1.│5̣.│12│3.ꞌ│21│71│5̣5̣│1.‖

TWENTIETH LESSON.

Intonation.

KEY OF SOL.

	Nọ 87.				Nọ 88.		
567i	i2̇3̇	3̇2̇i	i765	3̇2̇i	i765	567i	i2̇3̇
567i	i2̇3̇	3̇2̇i	i765	3̇2̇i	i765	567i	i2̇3̇
567i	i2̇3̇	3̇2̇i	i765	3̇2̇i	i765	567i	i2̇3̇
5	i	i	3̇	3̇	i	i	5
5	i	3̇	3̇	3̇	i	5	5

Nº 89.

| 5 1̇ 5 | 5 1̇ 3̇ 5 | 3̇ 1̇ 3 | 3̇ 1̇ 5 3 |
| 5 1̇ | 5 1̇ 3 | 3̇ 1̇ | 3̇ 1̇ 5 |

Nº 90.

| 3̇ 1̇ 3 | 3̇ 1̇ 5 3 | 5 1̇ 5 | 5 1̇ 3̇ 5 |
| 3̇ 1̇ | 3̇ 1̇ 5 | 5 1̇ | 5 1̇ 3 |

Nº 91.

5 1̇ 3	3̇ 1̇ 5	5 1̇ 3	3̇ 1̇ 5
5 1̇	3̇ 1̇ 5	5 1̇	1̇ 5
5 1̇	1̇ 5	5 1̇	5

Nº 92.

3̇ 1̇ 5	5 1̇ 3̇	3̇ 1̇ 5	5 1̇ 3̇
3̇ 1̇ 5	5 1̇ 3̇	3̇ 1̇	1̇ 3̇
3̇ 1̇	1̇ 3̇	3̇ 1̇	3̇

Nº 93.

5 1̇	1̇ 5 1̇ 3̇	3̇ 1̇	1̇ 3̇ 1̇ 5
5 1̇	1̇ 5 1̇ 3̇	3̇ 1̇	1̇ 3̇ 1̇ 5
5 1̇	5 1̇ 3̇	3̇ 1̇	3̇ 1̇ 5

Nº 94.

3̇ 1̇	1̇ 3̇ 1̇ 5	5 1̇	1̇ 5 1̇ 3̇
3̇ 1̇	1̇ 3̇ 1̇ 5	5 1̇	1̇ 5 1̇ 3̇
3̇ 1̇	3̇ 1̇ 5	5 1̇	5 1̇ 3̇

Dictation.

1st – Nos. 78, 79, 80, 81, 82, 83, 84. When dictating Nº 84 call P.– attention to the lowest sound (*Do*) which is easily missed. (page 33.)

2nd – Second columns of Nos. 36, 37, 40, 41. (page 8.)

Time.

Review Nos. 19 & 20 across the whole line, following large arrows.

Staff.

Name first then sing. Give the sound of *Re* for *Do*.

Nº 10.

KEY OF RÉ. (1 – i)

Solfa.

Nº 16.
5 6	5 6	5 4	3 0	3 4	3 4	3 2	1 0	2 3	4 0
3 4	5 0	6 0	7 1̇	7 6	5 .	5 6	5 1̇	5 4	3 .	3 4
3 5	3 2	1 .	2 5	6 7	7 1̇	5 4	3 .	2 3	2 .	1 .

Duett.

KEY OF MI. (5 – 3) M.M. 90. Very slowly and softly.

Nº 9.
| 1 . | 1 2 | 3 . | 3 . | 2 1 | 2 2 | 3 . | 5 . | 5 6 | 5 . | 5 . | 4 3 | 2 2 | 1 . |
| 1 . | 1 7 | 1 . | 1 . | 5 6 | 5 5 | 1 . | 3 . | 3 4 | 3 . | 3 . | 2 1 | 7 7 | 1 . |

TWENTY-FIRST LESSON.

Intonation.

Review Nos. 87, 88, 89, 90, 91, 92, 93, 94 _ Then take N⁰ 95 first singing small and large notes alike, then small notes lightly.

N⁰ 95.

KEY OF DO.

1 3 1 5 1	5 1 3 1 5	3 1 5 1 3
1 3 1 5	5 1 3 1	3 1 5 1
1 3 1 5 1	5 1 3 1 5	3 1 5 1 3
1 3 1 5 1 3	5 1 5 1 3	3 1 3 1 5
1 5 1 3	5 1 3 1 5	3 1 5 1 3
1 5 1 3 1	5 1 3 1 3	3 1 5 1 5
1 5 1 3 1 5	5 1 3 1 5 1	3 1 5 1 3 1

Dictation.

1ˢᵗ _ Nos 85 and 86 stopping between the notes which are repeated thus:
T_ dictates *Do-Mi* on *ah*_ P_ repeat. Continue dictating *Mi-Do-Mi-Sol_
Sol-Mi-Sol-Do* etc. P_ repeating. (page 35.)

2ⁿᵈ _ Nos. 34, 35, 38, 39 by large arrows. stop at line. (page 8.)

Time.

Review Nos. 19 and 20 then Nos 21 and 22 by small arrows only _ Call
attention to the skipping of the octave 5-5. Repeat last line.

KEY OF FA.

N⁰ 21.

1 2	. 3	5 3	2 3
1 2	. 3	5 3	2 .
1 2	. 3	5 .	3 2
1 2	. 3	5 .	5 .
1 2	. 3	5 .	. .
1 2	3 5	3 2	. 3
1 2	3 .	2 5	. 5
1 .	2 3	2 5	. 5
1 .	2 .	3 2	. 5
1 .	. .	2 .	. .
1 2	. .	5 2	. .

N⁰ 22.

1 2	0 3	5 3	2 3
1 2	0 3	5 3	2 0
1 2	0 3	5 0	3 2
1 2	0 3	5 0	5 0
1 2	0 3	5 0	0 0
1 2	3 5	3 2	0 3
1 2	3 0	2 5	0 5
1 0	2 3	2 5	0 5
1 0	2 0	3 2	0 5
1 0	0 0	2 0	0 0
1 2	0 0	5 2	0 0

Staff.

Ask a few questions about the names and values of notes, rests etc.
Name first **then give sound of** ***RÉ*** **for** ***DO*.**

Nº 11.

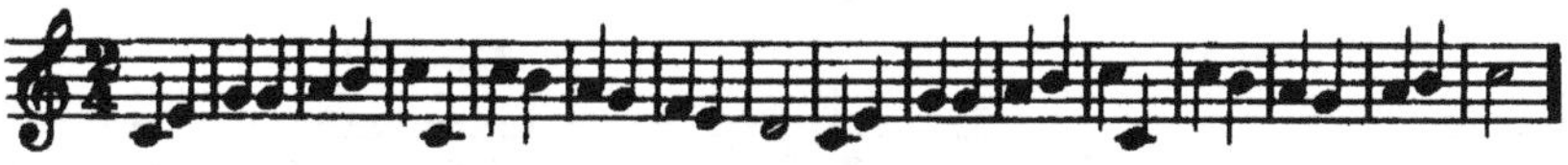

Solfa.

KEY OF MI. (5̣ - 1̇)

Nº 17. | 1 2 | 3 0 | 5 1̇ | 5 0 |[5] 5 4 | 3 2 | 1 7̣ | 6̣ 5̣ |[9] 1 3 | 3 5 | 5 1̇ | 5 0 |
|[13] 5̣ 6̣ | 7̣ 5̣ | 1 3 | 1 0 |[17] 2 3 | 2 0 | 2 1 | 7 0 |[21] 6̣ 7̣ | 1 7̣ | 6̣ 5̣ | 6̣ 0 |
|[25] 7̣ 1 | 2 0 | 3 5 | 5 0 |[29] 1̇ 7 | 6 1̇ | 7 6 | 5 . |[33] 1 2 | 3 . | 5 1̇ | 5 . |
|[37] 5 4 | 3 2 | 1 7̣ | 6̣ 5̣ |[41] 1 3 | 3 5 | 5 1̇ | 5 . |[45] 5̣ . | 6̣ 7̣ | 1 5̣ | 1 . ‖

Duett.

KEY OF FA. (5̣ - 6) M. M. 120.

Nº 10.

5 4	3 .'	4 3	2 .'	3 4	5 6	7 6	5 .'
3 2	1 .'	2 1	7̣ .'	1 2	3 4	5 4	3 .'
6 5	4 .'	5 4	3 .'	4 3	2 3	2 2	1 .
2 3	2 .'	1 2	1 .'	2 1	7̣ 1	5̣ 5̣	1 .

TWENTY-SECOND LESSON.

Intonation.

Review Nº 95 each column twice, then take Nos. 96, 97, 98, 99, 100, 101, 102, 103 by small arrows.

Nº 96.

3 4 5 5 6 7 1̇	1̇ 7 6 5 5 4 3
3 4 5 5 6 7 1̇	1̇ 7 6 5 5 4 3
3 4 5 5 6 7 1̇	1̇ 7 6 5 5 4 3
3 5 5 1̇	1̇ 5 5 3
3 5 1̇	1̇ 5 3

Nº 97.

1̇ 7 6 5 5 4 3	3 4 5 5 6 7 1̇
1̇ 7 6 5 5 4 3	3 4 5 5 6 7 1̇
1̇ 7 6 5 5 4 3	3 4 5 5 6 7 1̇
1̇ 5 5 3	3 5 5 1̇
1̇ 5 3	3 5 1̇

Nº 98.

3 5 3 3 5 1̇ 3	1̇ 5 1̇ 1̇ 5 3 1̇
3 5 3 5 1̇	1̇ 5 1̇ 5 3

Nº 99.

1̇ 5 1̇ 1̇ 5 3 1̇	3 5 3 3 5 1̇ 3
1̇ 5 1̇ 5 3	3 5 3 5 1̇

№ 100.   № 101.

3 5 ı̇	ı̇ 5 3	3 5 ı̇	ı̇ 5 3		ı̇ 5 3	3 5 ı̇	ı̇ 5 3	ɜ 5 ı̇
3 5	ı̇ 5 3	3 5	ʙ 3		ı̇ 5	5 ı̇	ı̇ 5	ʙ ı̇
3 5	5 3	3 5	3		ı̇ 5	5 ı̇	ı̇ 5	ı̇

№ 102.   № 103.

3 5	5 3 5 ı̇	ı̇ 5	5 ı̇ 5 3		ı̇ 5	5 ı̇ 5 3	3 5	5 3 5 ı̇
3 5	5 3 ʙ ı̇	ı̇ 5	5 ı̇ ʙ 3		ı̇ 5	5 ı̇ ʙ 3	3 5	5 3 ʙ ı̇
3 5	3 ʙ ı̇	ı̇ 5	ı̇ ʙ 3		ı̇ 5	ı̇ ʙ 3	3 5	3 ʙ ı̇

Dictation.

1st _ N⁰ˢ 89, 90, 91, 92, 93, 94 by large arrows stopping between the
notes which are repeated. (page 37.)

2nd _ N⁰ˢ 36, 37, 40, 41 by large arrows. (stop at line.)(page 8.)

Time.

Review Nos 21 and 22 first by small then by large arrows.

Staff. № 12.

Name first then give sound of *RÉ* for *DO.*

KEY OF DO. (1 _ ɜ̇)

Solfa.

№ 18. | ı̇ 3 | 5 ı̇ | 5 3 | ı̇ 0 | ı̇ 3 | 5 ı̇ | 3 5 | ı̇ 3 | 2̇ 0 | ı̇ 3̇ |
| 2̇ 0 | ı̇ 3̇ | 2̇ ı̇ | 7 6 | 5 4 | 3 2 | ı̇ 3 | 5 ı̇ | 5 3 | ı̇ 0 | ı̇ 3 |
| 5 ı̇ | 3 5 | ı̇ 3 | 2̇ . | ı̇ 3̇ | 2̇ . | ı̇ 2̇ | ı̇ . | 7 . | ı̇ . | . 0 ||

Duett.

After the class has mastered the following duett by notes have it sung very
softly.

Evening Bells. KEY OF MI. (5 _ 6) M. M. 96.

№ 11.	1 2	3 3	2 2	1 .'	3 4	5 5	4 4	3 .'
	To the	sound of	evening	bells	All that	lives to	rest re _	pairs,
	1 7	1 1	5̤ 5̤	1 .'	1 2	3 3	2 2	1 .'

	2 3	4 4	3 4	5 .	6 6	5 4	3 2	1 .	
	Birds un	_ to their	leaf _ y	dells	Beasts un	_ to their	fo _ rest	lairs.
	7̤ 1	2 2	1 2	3 .	4 4	3 2	1 7̤	1 .

TWENTY-THIRD LESSON.

Intonation.

Review Nos. 98, 99, 100, 101, 102, 103 by large arrows_then begin Nº 104, first with small notes. As the difficulty lies in descending from i to 3 it is advisable at the second reading of this exercise to prepare the class by having it sing i-5-3-3-3 i-5-3-3 i-3. KEY OF RÉ.

Nº 104.

→	→	→
5 i 5 3 5	3 5 i 5 3	i 5 3 5 i
5 i 5 3	3 5 i 5	i 5 3 5
5 i 5 3 5	3 5 i 3	i 5 3 5 i
5 i 5 3 5 i	3 5 3 i	i 5 i 5 3
5 3 5 i	3 5 i 5 3	i 5 3 5 i
5 3 5 i 5	3 5 i 5 i	i 5 3 5 3
5 3 5 i 5 3	3 5 i 5 3 5	i 5 3 5 i 5

Dictation.

1st_ Nos. 98, 99, 100, 101, 102, 103 making a stop between repeated notes.
2nd_ Nos. 45 and 46 first column only. (page 11.)

Time.

Review Nos. 21 and 22 by large arrows alternating each division with every other line.

Staff.

Name first then give sound of *RÉ* for *DO*.

Nº 13.

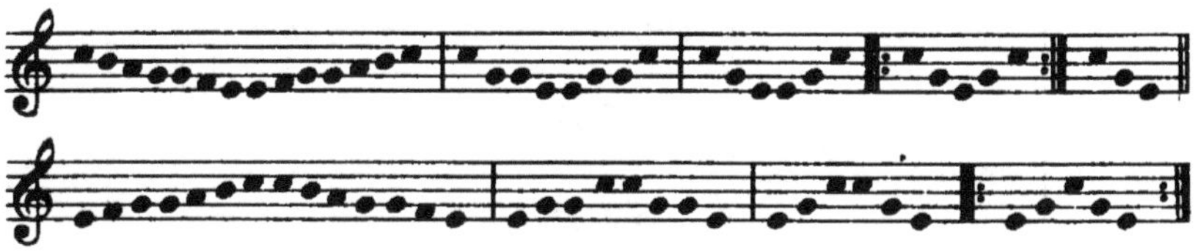

Solfa.

.KEY OF RÉ. (1-i)

Nº 19. | 1 3 | *f* 5 3 | 1 3 | 5 3 | 1 3 | 5 i | 5 . | 0 0 | *p* 4 5 | 4 5 | 3 5 | 3 5 |
4 3	2 1	2 .	0 0	*f* 1 3	5 3	1 3	5 3	1 3	5 i	7 .	0 0	*p* 6 7
i .	7 6	5 .	6 7	6 7	5 .	. 0	*f* 5 4	3 2	5 4	3 2	1 3	5 i
5 3	1 3	*p* 5 4	3 2	5 4	3 2	1 i	5 3	5 3	2 0	*mf* 1 3	1 3	3 5
3 5	5 i	5 i	i 7	6 .	*f* 7 6	5 4	3 i	5 3	1 .	2 .	1 .	. 0 ‖

Duett.

Review last duett with words.

TWENTY-FOURTH LESSON.

Intonation.

Review Nº 104. by single column then change the key for exercises 105, 106, 107, 108. Repeat last line of each exercise.

KEY OF SOL.

Nº 105.

5671	123	345	543	321	1765
5671	123	345	543	321	1765
5	1	3	5	5	3	1	5

Nº 106.

543	321	1765	5671	123	345
543	321	1765	5671	123	345
5	3	1	5	5	1	3	5

Nº 107.

51	513	5135	53	531	5315
51	513	5135	53	531	5315
51	513	5135	53	531	5315
51	5	3	5	5	53	5	1	5	5

Nº 108.

53	531	5315	51	513	5135
53	531	5315	51	513	5135
53	531	5315	51	513	5135
53	5	1	5	5	51	5	3	5	5

Dictation.

1st — Nº 95 by column with small notes. (page 38.)
2nd — Nos. 47 and 48 first column only. (page 12.)

Time.

Review Nos. 21 and 22 by large arrow, the whole class reading first line loudly, second softly, next loudly, next softly like an echo.

Staff.

Give the sound of *RÉ* for *DO*.

Nº 14.

Question about the signs used in the staff notation already learned.

Solfa.

A slur ⌣ placed under the numeral or notes means to sing in a smooth gliding manner when passing from one note to another.

The sign ◁ termed crescendo means to gradually increase the sound. Piano (meaning soft) is marked *p*. Mezzo-forte half loud *mf*.

KEY OF MI. (5-1)

p

NǪ 20. |5 1|1 0|5 1|1 0|2 3|1 3|2 3|1 5|5 1|1 0|5 1|1 0|

mf

|2 3|1 3|2 3|1 0|2 5|5 0|2 5|5 0|6 7|5 7|6 7|5 0|

sf

|2 5|5 0|2 5|5 0|6 7|5 7|6 7|5 . |5 1|1 . |5 1|1 . |

|2 3|1 3|2 3|1 5|5 1|1 . |5 1|1 . |2 3|4 5|6 7|1 . |

Duett.

Sing the notes only for this lesson.

NǪ 12.

Ariel's Song. KEY OF FA. (5-6) M.M. 132.

Fine.

1 1	5 5	6 6	5 0'	4 4	3 3	2 2	1 0
Where the	bee sucks	there lurk	I,	In a	cowslip's	bell I	lie;
On the	bat's back	I do	fly	Af-ter	summer	mer-ri-	ly.
1 1	3 3	4 4	3 0'	2 2	1 1	5 5	1 0

D.C.

5 5	4 4	3 3	2 0'	5 5	4 4	3 3	2 0
There I	crouch when	owls do	cry,	On the	bat's back	I do	fly.
3 3	2 2	1 1	5 0'	3 3	2 2	1 1	5 0

TWENTY-FIFTH LESSON.
Intonation.

Review Nos. 105 and 106.

KEY OF SOL.

NǪ 109. → → **NǪ 110.** →

5 1	1 5	5 1	1 5	5 3	3 5	5 3	3 5
5 1 3	3 1 5	5 1 3	3 1 5	5 3 1	1 3 5	5 3 1	1 3 5
5 1 3 5	5 3 1 5	5 1 3 5	5 3 1 5	5 3 1 5	5 1 3 5	5 3 1 5	5 1 3 5

NǪ 111. → **NǪ 112.** →

5 1	1 5 1 3	3 1 3 5	5 3	3 5 3 1	1 3 1 5	5 3	3 5 3 1	1 3 1 5	5 1	1 5 1 3	3 1 3 5
5 1	1 5 1 3	3 1 3 5	5 3	3 5 3 1	1 3 1 5	5 3	3 5 3 1	1 3 1 5	5 1	1 5 1 3	3 1 3 5
5 1	5 1 3	1 3 5	5 3	5 3 1	3 1 5	5 3	5 3 1	3 1 5	5 1	5 1 3	1 3 5

Repeat this last line several times.

Dictation.

1st _ NǪ 104 by columns with small notes. (page 41.)

2nd _ Second columns of Nos. 45 and 46 dictating an entire line at a time.

(page 11)

KEY OF SOL.

Time.

Nº 23.				Nº 24.			
1 2	. 0	3 5	3 2	1 2	. 0	3 5	3 2
1 2	. 0	3 1	5 0	1 2	. 0	3 1	5 .
1 2	. 0	3 0	2 5	1 2	. 0	3 .	2 5
1 2	0 0	3 .	5 0	1 2	. 0	3 0	5 .
1 2	. 0	5 .	0 0	1 2	0 0	5 .	. 0
1 2	3 5	3 2	. 0	1 2	3 5	3 2	. 0
1 2	3 0	2 5	. 0	1 2	3 .	2 5	. 0
1 .	2 3	2 5	. 0	1 0	2 3	2 5	. 0
1 .	2 0	3 2	. 0	1 0	2 .	3 2	0 0
1 .	. 0	2 5	0 0	1 .	0 0	2 5	. 0
1 2	. 3	5 2	. 0	1 2	0 3	5 2	. 0

Repeat last line.

Staff.

Name first then sing - give sound of *RÉ* for *DO*.

Nº 15.

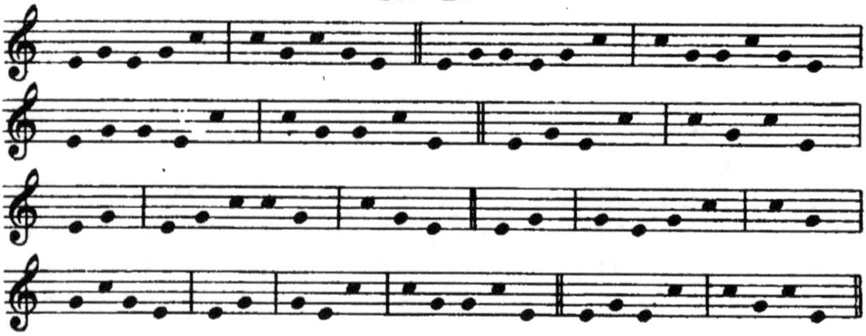

Solfa.

KEY OF RÉ.(1 - i)

Nº 21. *f* 1 5 | 0 0 | *p* 1 5 | 0 0 | *mf* 5 3 | 3 1 | 5 3 | 3 2 | *f* 1 5 | . 0 | *p* 1 5 | . 0 |
mf 5 3 | 3 1 | 5 5 | 1 0 | *f* i 7 | 6 0 | *p* i 7 | 6 0 | *mf* 7 i | 7 6 | 7 7 | 0 0 |
f i 7 | 6 0 | *p* 7 6 | 5 0 | *mf* 6 7 | 6 7 | 6 7 | 5 0 | *f* 1 5 | . . | *p* 1 5 | . . |
| 5 3 | 3 1 | 5 3 | 3 2 | 1 5 | . . | 5 6 | . . | 7 5 | i 1 | 5 5 | 1 . ||

Duett.

Review last duett with syllables then on *la* after which sing the words.

TWENTY-SIXTH LESSON.

Intonation.

KEY OF MI.

Nº 113.

5̣1	15̣	5̣1	15̣
5̣13	315̣	5̣13	315̣
5̣135	5315̣	5̣135	5315̣
5̣1351̇	1̇5315̣	5̣1351̇	1̇5315̣

Nº 114.

1̇5	51̇	1̇5	51̇
1̇53	351̇	1̇53	351̇
1̇531	1351̇	1̇531	1351̇
1̇5315̣	5̣1351̇	1̇5315̣	5̣1351̇

Nº 115.

5̣15̣	5̣135̣	5̣1355̣	5̣1351̇5̣	1̇51̇	1̇531̇	1̇5311̇	1̇5315̣1̇5̣
5̣1	5̣13	5̣135	5̣1351̇	1̇5	1̇53	1̇531	1̇5315̣
5̣1	5̣13	5̣135	5̣1351̇	1̇5	1̇53	1̇531	1̇5315̣
5̣1	5̣13	5̣135	5̣1351̇	1̇5	1̇53	1̇531	1̇5315̣
5̣1	5̣3	5̣5	5̣1̇	1̇5	1̇3	1̇1	1̇5̣

Dictation.

1st _ Nos. 109, 110, then 107. (page 43.)

2nd _ Second col. of Nos. 47, 48. Entire line at a time. (page 12.)

Time.

Review Nos. 23 and 24.

Staff.

Name first, then give the sound of *RÉ* for *DO* and let P_ sing.

Nº 16.

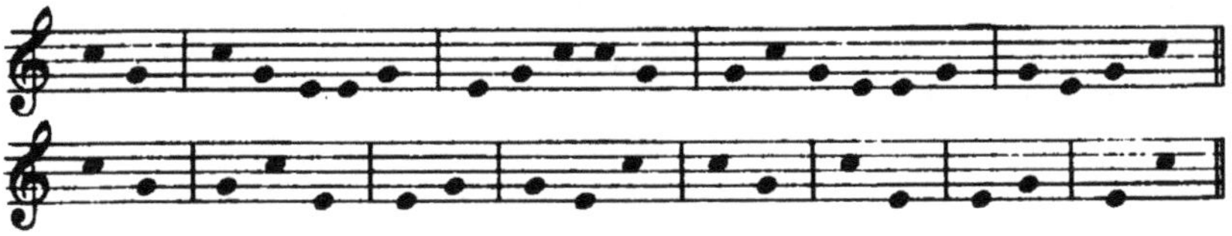

Solfa.

KEY OF RÉ. (1_1̇)

Nº 22. *f* 35 | 35 | 35 | 1̇0 *p* 54 | 35 | 31 | 20 *f* 35 | 35 | 35 | 1̇0 |

| *p* 76 | 57 | 1̇6 | 50 *f* 75 | 65 | 1̇5 | 65 | 75 | 67 | 65 | 3 . |

| *p* 25 | 67 | 76 | 71̇ | 5 . | 6 . | 5 . | . . *f* 75 | 65 | 1̇5 | 65 |

| 75 | 67 | 65 | 3 . *p* 11̇ | . . | 76 | 54 | 3 . | 2 . | 1 . | . 0 ‖

Duett.
Sing notes only at this lesson.

	1 3	5 0'	1 3	·5 0'	1 3	1 3	2 3	2 0'
Nọ 13.	Join our	throng	In a	song,	Come and	mer_ry	mer_ry	be;
	1 1	3 0'	1 1	3 0'	1 1	1 1	7 1	5 0'

3 3	4 3	2 2	3 2'	1 3	5 5	6 7	1 0
And with	gladness	Dispel	sadness,	Sing with	us in	heartfelt	glee.
1 1	2 1	5 5	1 7'	1 1	3 3	4 4	3 0

TWENTY-SEVENTH LESSON.
Intonation.
Review 113, 114, 115.

KEY OF MI.

Nọ 116.

5 1	1 5 1 3	3 1 3 5	5 3 5 1	1 5	5 1 5 3	3 5 3 1	1 3 1 5
5 1	1 5 1 3	3 1 3 5	5 3 5 1	1 5	5 1 5 3	3 5 3 1	1 3 1 5
5 1	1 5 1 3	3 1 3 5	5 3 5 1	1 5	5 1 5 3	3 5 3 1	1 3 1 5
5 1	1 5 3	3 1 5	5 3 1	1 5	5 1 3	3 5 1	1 3 5
5 1	5 1 3	1 3 5	3 5 1	1 5	1 5 3	5 3 1	3 1 5
5 1	5 1 3	1 3 5	3 5 1	1 5	1 5 3	5 3 1	3 1 5
5 1	5 3	1 5	3 1	1 5	1 3	5 1	3 5

Dictation.

1st – Nọ 109 down and up then Nọ 111 making a stop between the repeat - ed notes. (page 43 .)

2nd – Before beginning the exercises Nos. 12, 13, 14 and 15 which the class already have had the T. will announce that on account of the easy succession of notes P. have a tendency to guess the coming dictation; to prevent this the T. will skip one or more lines warning the P. to that effect. (see page 8 .)

Time.
KEY OF SOL. Following small arrows only.

Nọ 25.					Nọ 26.			
1	·	0 2	3 5	3 2	1 0	0 2	3 5	3 2
1	·	0 2	3 5	5 0	1 0	0 2	3 5	5 ·
1	·	0 2	3 0	2 5	1 0	0 2	3 ·	2 5
1	·	0 2	3 ·	5 0	1 0	0 2	3 0	5 ·
1	·	0 5	5 ·	0 0	1 0	0 5	5 ·	· 0
1	2	3 5	3 ·	0 2	1 2	3 5	3 0	0 2
1	2	3 ·	2 ·	0 5	1 2	3 0	2 ·	0 5
1	·	2 3	2 ·	0 5	1 0	2 3	2 ·	0 5
1	·	3 0	5 ·	0 5	1 0	3 ·	5 0	0 5
1	·	· 0	5 ·	0 5	1 0	0 0	5 ·	0 5
1	·	0 3	5 ·	0 5	1 0	0 3	5 ·	0 5

Name and observe time. Before singing give the sound of *RÉ* for *DO*.

Nọ 17.

Solfa.

KEY OF RÉ. (1 . i)

Nọ 23.
3 5	4 5	3 5	4 5	3 5	i 0	7 6	5 4	3 5	4 5	3 5	4 5
3 5	i 0	i 7	i 0	7 6	7 i	7 6	7 i	7 6	5 0	6 0	0 0
7 0	6 i	7 0	6 i	7 6	5 6	6 .	5 4	3 5	4 5	3 5	4 5
3 5	i .	7 6	5 4	3 5	5 i	i .	. 7	i 5	4 3	2 .	i 0 ‖

Duett.

Review last duett, first singing *every note* with the syllable *la* then applying the words.

TWENTY EIGHTH LESSON.

Intonation.

Do not forget the arrows on the side of Nọ 119 & 120.

KEY OF DO.

Nọ 117.

1 2 3	3 4 5	5 6 7 i̇	i̇ 2̇ 3̇		3̇ 2̇ i̇	i̇ 7 6 5	5 4 3	3 2 1
1 2 3	3 4 5	5 6 7 i̇	i̇ 2̇ 3̇		3̇ 2̇ i̇	i̇ 7 6 5	5 4 3	3 2 1
1 2 3	3 4 5	5 6 7 i̇	i̇ 2̇ 3̇		3̇ 2̇ i̇	i̇ 7 6 5	5 4 3	8 2 1
1	3	5 5	i̇ 3̇		3̇	i̇	5 5	3 1
1	3	5	i̇ 3̇		3̇	i̇	5	3 1

Nº 118.

$\dot{3}\ \dot{2}\ \dot{1}$	$\dot{1}$ 7 6 5	5 4 3	3 2 1	1 2 3	3 4 5	5 6 7 $\dot{1}$	$\dot{1}\ \dot{2}\ \dot{3}$
$\dot{3}\ \dot{2}\ \dot{1}$	$\dot{1}$ 7 6 5	5 4 3	3 2 1	1 2 3	3 4 5	5 6 7 $\dot{1}$	$\dot{1}\ \dot{2}\ \dot{3}$
$\dot{3}\ \dot{2}\ \dot{1}$	$\dot{1}$ 7 6 5	5 4 3	3 2 1	1 2 3	3 4 5	5 6 7 $\dot{1}$	$\dot{1}\ \dot{2}\ \dot{3}$
$\dot{3}$	$\dot{1}$ 5	5 3	1	1 3	5	5 $\dot{1}$	$\dot{3}$
$\dot{3}$	$\dot{1}$ 5	3	1	1 3	5	$\dot{1}$	$\dot{3}$

Nº 119.

1 3	3 1	1 3	3 1
1 3 5	5 3 1	1 3 5	5 3 1
1 3 5 $\dot{1}$	$\dot{1}$ 5 3 1	1 3 5 $\dot{1}$	$\dot{1}$ 5 3 1
1 3 5 $\dot{1}\ \dot{3}$	$\dot{3}\ \dot{1}$ 5 3 1	1 3 5 $\dot{1}\ \dot{3}$	$\dot{3}\ \dot{1}$ 5 3 1

Nº 120.

$\dot{3}\ \dot{1}$	$\dot{1}\ \dot{3}$	$\dot{3}\ \dot{1}$	$\dot{1}\ \dot{3}$
$\dot{3}\ \dot{1}$ 5	5 $\dot{1}\ \dot{3}$	$\dot{3}\ \dot{1}$ 5	5 $\dot{1}\ \dot{3}$
$\dot{3}\ \dot{1}$ 5 3	3 5 $\dot{1}\ \dot{3}$	$\dot{3}\ \dot{1}$ 5 3	3 5 $\dot{1}\ \dot{3}$
$\dot{3}\ \dot{1}$ 5 3 1	1 3 5 $\dot{1}\ \dot{3}$	$\dot{3}\ \dot{1}$ 5 3 1	1 3 5 $\dot{1}\ \dot{3}$

Dictation

Page 43.

1st _ Nº 110 down and up Nº 112 stopping between the repeated notes.
2nd _ Same as at previous lesson. Nºs 12, 13, 14 and 15 _(page 3.)

Time

Review Nº 25 and Nº 26 by small arrows first, then following large arrow.

Staff

Name first then give the sound of *RÉ* for *DO* before singing.

Nº 18.

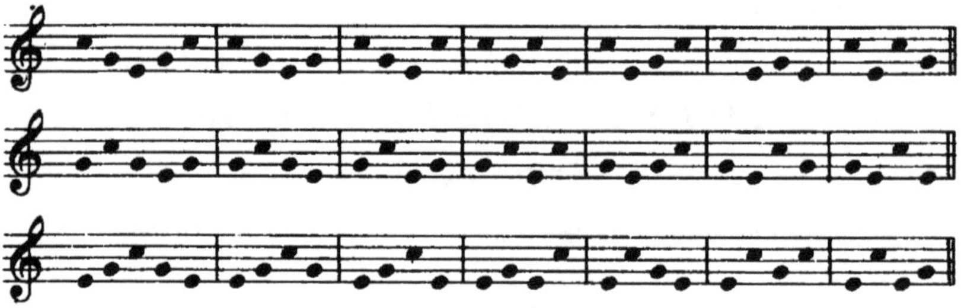

Solfa.

KEY OF SOL.(2 _ $\dot{5}$)

Do not forget to have P_ give an accentuation on the prolongation and it will be advisable to prepare for the first skip by using the missing note of the chord DO until no trouble is experienced in singing 5-$\dot{3}$.

No 24. ‖ % | 5 3 | . 1 | 5 3 | . 1 | 2 1 | 2 3 | 2 1 | 2 5 | 5 3 |

| . 1 | 5 3 | . 1 | 2 1 | 2 3 | 2 . | 1 . ‖ 2 3 | . 2 | 2 1 | 1 . | 7 1 |

| . 7 | 7 6 | 6 . | 5 6 | . 7 | 1 5 | . 3 | 2 1 | 7 6 | 5 4 | 3 2 | % ‖

Round.

Sing the notes *only* first in unison, then in three parts (see A, B, C,)— if trouble is experienced with the skip fa-ré, work it out by placing the missing note MI until it can easily be sung without it.

KEY OF RÉ.

A	5	6	7	1	7	6	5	. '
	Kind words	speak and	kind deeds	plan,			

B	3	4	2	3	5	4	3	. '
	Help each	oth _ er	when you	can,			

C	1	.	1	.	1	.	1	. '
	Kind		words		kind		deeds .	

TWENTY NINTH LESSON.
Intonation.

Review 119 and 120, then start 121, 122, 123, 124. Great care should be taken in Nos. 122 and 124 to have P. hold the last note of each group a little longer than the others, tell P. to not miss the DO.

KEY OF DO.

No 121.

1 3		1
1 3 5		1
1 3 5 1		1
1 3 5 1 3		1 3
	R	

No 122.

1 3	1 3 5	1 3 5 1	1 3 5 1 3
1 3 .	1 3 5	1 3 5 1	1 3 5 1 3
1 3	1 3 5	1 3 5 1	1 3 5 1 3
1 3	1 5	1	1	3

No 123.

3 1		3
3 1 5		3
3 1 5 3		3
3 1 5 3 . 1		3 1
	R	

No 124.

3 1	3, 1 5	3 1 5 3	3 1 5 3 1
3 1	3 1 5	3 1 5 3	3 1 5 3 1
3 1	3 1 5	3 1 5 3	3 1 5 3 1
3 1	3	5	3	3	3	1

Dictation.

1st _ Nº 113 both col. separately *no stop* in the middle of each line. Then only the first col. of Nº 115 stopping at the end of each group. p. 45

2nd _ Nº 45 both col. separately no stop in line and skipping line or lines making the same remark as at previous lesson. (page 11.)

Time.

KEY OF FA.

Nº 29.				Nº 30.			
1 2	. 3	2 5	. .	1 2	0 3	2 5	0 0
1 2	. 3	2 .	. 5̣	1 2	0 3	2 0	0 5̣
1 2	. .	5 2	. 3	1 2	0 0	5 2	0 3
1 2	. .	5 .	. 2	1 2	0 0	5 0	0 2
1 .	. 2	5 2	. .	1 0	0 2	5 2	0 0
1 .	. 2	5 5̣	. 2	1 0	0 2	5 5̣	0 2

Thereafter T. will start the class to beat the three beats measure, taking care that P. keep the elbow on the side of the body saying in moving the forearm Down, Right, Up _ making a sort of triangle.

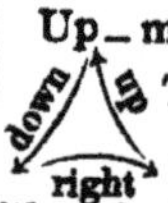
down
up
right

The T. will illustrate. Great care should be taken as generally children experience trouble with this kind of measure.(1)

Staff.

P. name first then sing. Give sound of *RÉ* for *DO*.

Nº 19.

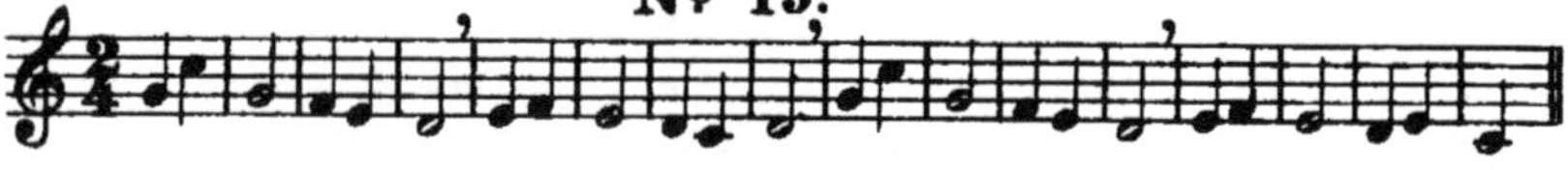

Solfa.

KEY OF RÉ. (1 _ 1̇)

Nº 25.

1̇ 5	1̇ 5	3 5	1 0	5 5	0 0	5 5	0 0	1̇ 5	1̇ 5	3 5	1 0	
2 5	5 0	6 7	5 0	2 .	0 2	3 5	5 0	2 .	0 2	3 5	5 0	1̇ 5	0 0
1̇ 7	6 5	4 3	4 5	4 .	3 0	1̇ 5	. 0	1̇ 7	6 5	4 3	2 5	1 .	. 0

Round.

Review last one then add words to it.

---

(1) In some countries the second beat is done on the left but beside being an awkward movement especially in a pause it does not give the room needed to show a crescendo in leading.

THIRTIETH LESSON.

Intonation.

Review 121 and 123 down and up.

KEY OF DO.

Nº 125.

1 3	3 1 3 5	5 3 5 1̇	1̇ 5 1̇ 3̇	3̇ 1̇	1̇ 3̇ 1̇ 5	5 1̇ 5 3	3 5 3 1
1 3	3 1 3 5	5 3 5 1̇	1̇ 5 1̇ 3̇	3̇ 1̇	1̇ 3̇ 1̇ 5	5 1̇ 5 3	3 5 3 1
1 3	1 3 5	3 5 1̇	5 1̇ 3̇	3̇ 1̇	3̇ 1̇ 5	1̇ 5 3	5 3 1
1 3	1 3 5	3 5 1̇	5 1̇ 3̇	3̇ 1̇	3̇ 1̇ 5	1̇ 5 3	5 3 1
1 3	1 5	3 1̇	5 3̇	3̇ 1̇	3̇ 5	1̇ 3	5 1

Repeat last line.

Dictation.

1st _ Nº 114 both col. separately no stop in lines then second col. of Nº 115 _ stopping at end of each group. (page 45)

2nd _ Nº 46 both col. separately no stop in lines skipping a line once in a while calling P_ attention to this fact. (page 11)

KEY OF FA.

Time.

Nº 31.				Nº 32.			
1 2	.3	2 5	0 0	1 2	0 3	2 5	.0
1 2	0 3	2 0	0 5̣	1 2	0 3	2 .	0 5̣
1 2	. .	5 2	0 3	1 2	0 0	5 2	.3
1 2	.0	5 0	0 2	1 2	.0	5 .	0 2
1 .	0 2	5 2	0 0	1 0	0 2	5 2	.0
1 .	0 2	5 5̣	0 2	1 .	0 2	5 5̣	.2

Same practice as at last lesson in regard to the three beats measure, see that the motion is done quickly and that the hand remains at each position an equal lenght of time.

Staff.

P _ *name first* then sing. Give sound of RÉ for DO.

Nº 20.

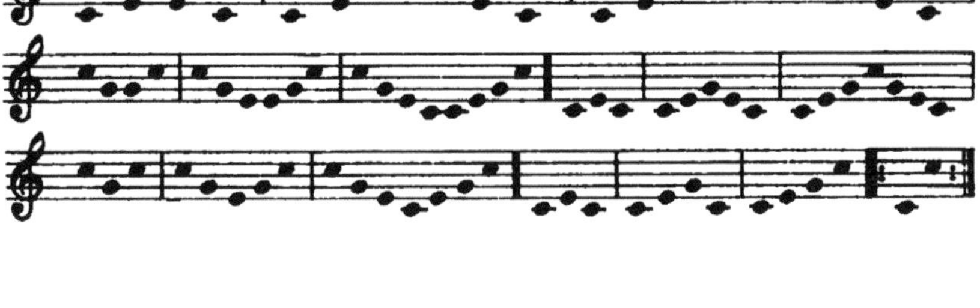

KEY OF MI.(1_i) **Solfa.**

This sign ⟩—⟨ stands for decrescendo and means to gradually sing softer.

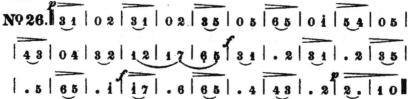

Nº 26. | 3 1 | 0 2 | 3 1 | 0 2 | 3 5 | 0 5 | 6 5 | 0 i | 5 4 | 0 5 |

| 4 3 | 0 4 | 3 2 | 1 2 | 1 7 | 6 5 | 3 1 | . 2 | 3 1 | . 2 | 3 5 |

| . 5 | 6 5 | . i | 1 7 | . 6 | 6 5 | . 4 | 4 3 | . 2 | 2 . | 1 0 ‖

Duett.

Give the sound of RÉ for DO.

Hurrah! for our native land For A _ me _ ri _ ca Hur _ rah!

THIRTY FIRST LESSON.
Intonation.

Great care should be taken with Nos. 126 and 127 especially with the interval $\hat{3}$ 3 with which P_ may experience trouble; small notes should not be neglected.

KEY OF DO. 1 2 3 3 3 4 5 5 4 3 3 3 4 5 5 4 3

Nº 126.

3455671̇1̇2̇3̇	3̇2̇1̇1̇765543
3455671̇1̇2̇3̇	3̇2̇1̇1̇765543
3455671̇1̇2̇3̇	3̇2̇1̇1̇765543
3 5 1̇ 3̇ 3̇	1̇ 5 3

Nº 127.

3̇2̇1̇1̇765543	3455671̇1̇2̇3̇
3̇2̇1̇1̇765543	3455671̇1̇2̇3̇
3̇2̇1̇1̇765543	3455671̇1̇2̇3̇
3̇ 1̇ 5	3 3 5 1̇ 3̇

Nº 128.

35	351̇	351̇3̇	3̇1̇	3̇15	3̇153
35	351̇	351̇3̇	3̇1̇	3̇15	3̇153
35	351̇	351̇3̇	3̇1̇	3̇15	3̇153
35	3 1̇	3 3̇	3̇1̇	3̇5	3 3

Nº 129.

3̇1̇	3̇15	3̇153	35	351̇	351̇3̇
3̇1̇	3̇15	3̇153	35	351̇	351̇3̇
3̇1̇	3̇15	3̇153	35	351̇	351̇3̇
3̇1̇	3̇5	3 3	35	3 1̇	3 3̇

Dictation.

1st_ Nº 116. Dictate by groups first and second col. Do not let P_ hold one note longer than another but if they find trouble in repeating certain sounds T_ can emphasize the said sounds until they can repeat them all alike. (page 46.)

2nd_ Nos. 49 and 50 first with the line of introduction. (page 14.)

Time.

Having practised the beating of three beats measure at the last two lessons, P_ ought to be able to do the following exercise, as this being the first of this new time, the intonation has purposely been made easy_ A little accent should still be made on the prolongation and the voice well sustained.

KEY OF FA.

Nº 33.				Nº 34.			
1 2 3	4 5 4	3 4 3	2 1 2	1 2 3	4 5 4	3 4 3	2 1 2
1 2 3	4 5 4	3 4 3	2 • 3	1 2 3	4 5 4	3 4 3	2 0 3
1 2 3	4 5 4	3 4 3	2 • •	1 2 3	4 5 4	3 4 3	2 0 0
1 2 3	4 5 4	3 • 4	3 2 3	1 2 3	4 5 4	3 0 4	3 2 3
1 2 3	4 5 4	3 • 4	3 • 2	1 2 3	4 5 4	3 0 4	3 0 2
1 2 3	4 5 4	3 • 4	5 • •	1 2 3	4 5 4	3 0 4	5 0 0
1 2 3	4 5 4	3 • •	2 1 2	1 2 3	4 5 4	3 0 0	2 1 2
1 2 3	4 5 4	3 • •	2 • 3	1 2 3	4 5 4	3 0 0	2 0 3
1 2 3	4 5 4	3 • •	2 • •	1 2 3	4 5 4	3 0 0	2 0 0

Staff.

P_ *name* first then sing. Give the sound of RÉ for DO.

This 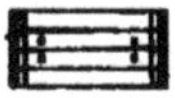 means to repeat.

Nº 21.

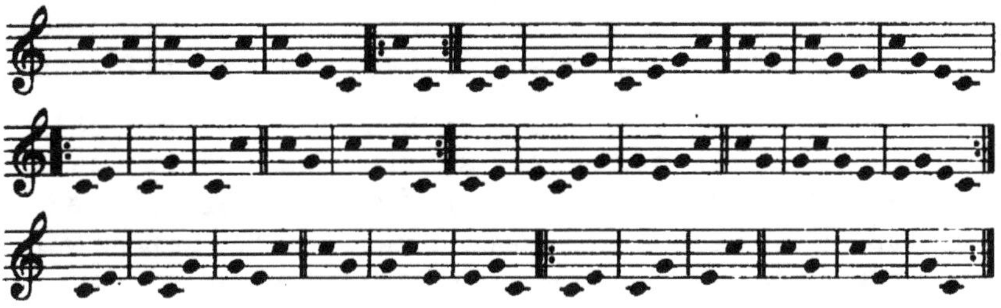

54 **Solfa.**

After having given Key note, first try measures 25 and 26 and if not correctly sung use should be made of the missing note SOL between FA and LA until all P_ skip with ease.

KEY OF DO. (1_ṡ)

№27 ⅗5 i | 5 i | 7 5 | 7 5 | i 5 | 4 3 | 3 . | 2 . | 23 | 45 | 43 | 5 i |
¹³ | 7 6 | 7 i | ż i | 7 5 | 5 i | 5 i | 7 5 | 7 5 | i 5 | 4 3 | 2 . | . . | 23 |
4 6	6 5	i .	¹ .	2 .	i .	. 0	25	67	65	3 .	i 7	6 i
7 6	7 i	⁴¹ ż i	. 7	7 6	. 7	67	67	6 .	. . .	0 5	67	65
3 .	i 7	67	i ż	2 .	⁵⁷ ż i	ż i	i 7	i 7	⁶¹ 7 6	76	5 .	. .	š

Round №16.

KEY OF DO. (1_ṡ)

A   B

| 1 2 | 3 1 | 3 4 | 5 . | i i | 7 7 | 6 6 | 5 . | 1 2 | 3 1 | 3 4 | 5 . | i ż | 3 i | 5 5 | i . |

THIRTY SECOND LESSON.
Intonation.

Review Nos 126 and 127 then 130, 131, 132, 133.
KEY OF DO.

№130.

3 5	5 3	3 5	5 3
3 5 i	i 5 3	3 5 i	i 5 3
3 5 i 3	3 i 5 3	3 5 i 3	i i 5 3

№131.

3 i	i 3	3 i	i 3
3 i 5	5 i 3	3 i 5	5 i 3
3 i 5 3	3 5 i 3	3 i 5 3	5 5 i 3

№132.

35	535i	i5i3	3i	i3i5	5i53
35	53ь1	i5i3	3i	i3i5	5iь3
35	53ьi	i5i3	3i	i3i5	5iь3
35	53i	i53	3i	i35	5i3
35	3ьi	5i3	3i	3i5	iь3
35	3ьi	5i3	3i	3i5	iь3
35	3i	53	3i	35	i3

№133.

3i	i3i5	5i53	35	535i	i5i3
3i	i3i5	5iь3	35	53ьi	i5i3
3i	i3i5	5iь3	35	535ьi	i5i3
3i	i35	5i3	35	531	i53
3i	3i5	iь3	35	3ьi	5i3
3i	3i5	iь3	35	3ьi	5i3
3i	35	i3	35	3i	53

Be careful that there is no confusion between the last lines of Nos. 132 & 133 and the last lines of exercises Nos. 128 & 129.

Dictation.

1st _ Nos. 119 & 120 by single columns. (page 48)

2nd _ Nº 51 1st col. down & up, after having started from $\dot{1}$765-5671̇-$\dot{1}$765-5671̇$\dot{2}\dot{3}$ as introduction. (page 14.)

KEY OF FA. **Nº 35.** **Time.** **Nº 36.**

1 2 3	4 . 3	2 3 4	3 2 3	1 2 3	4 0 3	2 3 4	3 2 3
1 2 3	4 . 3	2 3 4	3 . 2	1 2 3	4 0 3	2 3 4	3 0 2
1 2 3	4 . 3	2 3 4	5 . .	1 2 3	4 0 3	2 3 4	5 0 0
1 2 3	4 . 5	4 . 3	2 1 2	1 2 3	4 0 5	4 0 3	2 1 2
1 2 3	4 . 5	4 . 3	2 . 3	1 2 3	4 0 5	4 0 3	2 0 3
1 2 3	4 . 5	4 . 3	2 . .	1 2 3	4 0 5	4 0 3	2 0 0
1 2 3	4 . 3	2 . .	3 4 5	1 2 3	4 0 3	2 0 0	3 4 5
1 2 3	4 . 3	2 . .	3 . 2	1 2 3	4 0 3	2 0 0	3 0 2
1 2 3	4 . 3	2 . .	3 . .	1 2 3	4 0 3	2 0 0	3 0 0

Staff.

P_ name the notes first, then sing in the key of DO.

Nº 22.

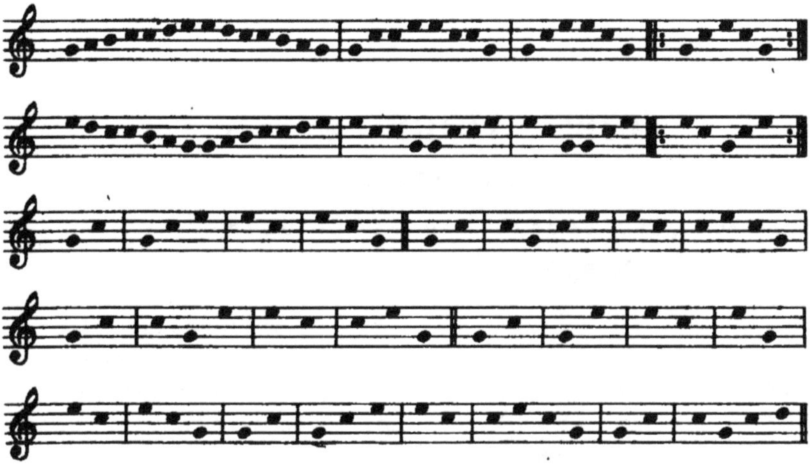

Solfa.

Before taking next Solfa, practice the interval 7-$\dot{2}$, placing between it the missing *DO* until all the class can skip without it.

KEY OF LA.(5.5)

N⁰ 28. |56|51|23|1.|2.|32|16|72|56|51|23|1.|31|

|75|6.|5.|52|2.|51|1.|57|65|51|23|52|2.|51|

|1.|71|71|71|32|56|51|23|1.|2.|32|16|72|56|

|51|67|6.|71|7.|12|1.|23|25|43|21|1.|6.|1.|0|

Duett. N⁰ 17.

P_ sing notes only.

Sing Birdie. KEY OF SOL.(3-6) M.M. 120.

1 7	1 2	3 .	2 .'	3 5	4 3	2 .	. 0 '
Sing a -	way my	bir -	die,	On your	perch so	high;	
1 5	3 5	1 .	7 .'	1 3	2 1	5 .	. 0 '

5 3	4 5	6 .	5 .'	3 5	3 2	1 .	. 0
Wintry	blasts are	o -	ver,	Summer	now is	nigh.	
1 1	2 3	4 .	3 .'	1 2	1 7	1 .	. 0

THIRTY THIRD LESSON.
Intonation.

KEY OF SOL. 123 34567123345 5432176543

N⁰ 134.

34	3	54	5	T_ will watch the *FA*
345	3	543	5	especially the high (up-
3456	3	5432	5	per) *FA* (4) P_generally
34567	3	54321	5	sing it too high
345671	3	543217	5	
3456712	3	5432176	5	
34567123	3	543217 65	5	
345671234	3	5432176 54	5	
34567123345	3 5	543217654	3 5	
	R		R	

Nọ 135.

3 4 5	5 6 7 i̇	i̇ 2̇ 3̇	3̇ 4̇ 5̇	5̇ 4̇ 3̇	3̇ 2̇ i̇	i̇ 7 6 5	5 4 3
3 4 5	5 6 7 i̇	i̇ 2̇ 3̇	3̇ 4̇ 5̇	5̇ 4̇ 3̇	3̇ 2̇ i̇	i̇ 7 6 5	5 4 3
3 4 5	5 6 7 i̇	i̇ 2̇ 3̇	3̇ 4̇ 5̇	5̇ 4̇ 3̇	3̇ 2̇ i̇	i̇ 7 6 5	5 4 3
3 5	i̇	i̇ 3̇	5̇	5̇ 3̇	i̇	i̇ 5	3
3 5	i̇	3̇	5̇	5̇ 3̇	i̇	5	3

Nọ 136.

3 5	3 5 i̇	3 5 i̇ 3̇	3 5 i̇ 3̇ 5̇	5̇ 3̇	5̇ 3̇ i̇	5̇ 3̇ i̇ 5	5̇ 3̇ i̇ 5 3
3 5	3 5 i̇	3 5 i̇ 3̇	3 5 i̇ 3̇ 5̇	5̇ 3̇	5̇ 3̇ i̇	5̇ 3̇ i̇ 5	5̇ 3̇ i̇ 5 3
3 5	3 5 i̇	3 5 i̇ 3̇	3 5 i̇ 3̇ 5̇	5̇ 3̇	5̇ 3̇ i̇	5̇ 3̇ i̇ 5	5̇ 3̇ i̇ 5 3
3 5	3 i̇	3 3̇	3̇ 3̇ 5̇	5̇ 3̇	5̇ i̇	5̇ 5	5̇ 3

Dictation.

1st_ Nos. 121, 122, 123, 124. (page 49.)

2nd_ Nọ 51 second col. down & up the entire line and T_ starts with i̇ 7 6 5 so P_ can recognize the first note with which to start. (page 14.)

Time.

KEY OF SOL.

Nọ 37.   ### Nọ 38.

1 2 3	4 . .	3 4 3	2 1 2	1 2 3	4 0 0	3 4 3	2 1 2
1 2 3	4 . .	3 4 3	2 . 3	1 2 3	4 0 0	3 4 3	2 0 3
1 2 3	4 . .	3 4 3	2 . .	1 2 3	4 0 0	3 4 3	2 0 0
1 2 3	4 . .	3 . 4	3 2 3	1 2 3	4 0 0	3 0 4	3 2 3
1 2 3	4 . .	3 . 4	3 . 2	1 2 3	4 0 0	3 0 4	3 0 2
1 2 3	4 . .	3 . 4	5 . .	1 2 3	4 0 0	3 0 4	5 0 0
1 2 3	4 . .	3 . .	2 1 2	1 2 3	4 0 0	3 0 0	2 1 2
1 2 3	4 . .	3 . .	2 . 3	1 2 3	4 0 0	3 0 0	2 0 3
1 2 3	4 . .	3 . .	2 . .	1 2 3	4 0 0	3 0 0	2 0 0

Staff. (Time.)

Time exercise should be ended with *DO.*

Give sound of RÉ for DO.

Nọ 23.

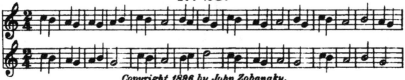

KEY OF SOL.(ₛ.ₛ̇) **Solfa.**

№ 29. ^{p} ₃₅ | ₁₅ | ₃₅ | ₁₅ | ₃₅ | ₁₃̇ | ₅̇.|.₃̇ | ₂̇₅̇ | ₃̇₁̇ |

| ₂̇₅̇ | ₃̇₁̇ | 77 | ₁₆ | ₅.|.4 |^p ₃₅ | ₁₅ | ₃₅ | ₁₅ | ₃₅ |

| ₁₃̇ | ₅̇.|.₃̇ | ₂̇₅̇ | ₃̇₁̇ | ₂̇₅̇ | ₃̇₁̇ |^p ₅̇.|.₂̇ |.₁.|.o ▌

Duett.

Review last duett by note first, then on *la*, then with words.

THIRTY FOURTH LESSON.
Intonation.

Review № 135. Look out for the *FA.*

KEY OF SOL.

№ 137.   № 138.

35	53	35	₅8	5̇3̇	3̇5̇	5̇3̇	₅5̇
35₁̇	₁̇53	35₁̇	₁53	5̇3̇1̇	1̇3̇5̇	5̇3̇1̇	₁3̇5̇
35₁̇3̇	3̇₁̇53	35₁̇3̇	₁3̇53	5̇3̇1̇5	51̇3̇5̇	5̇3̇1̇5	₅1̇3̇5̇
35₁̇3̇5̇	5̇3̇₁̇53	35₁̇3̇5̇	₁3̇1̇53	5̇3̇1̇53	351̇3̇5̇	5̇3̇1̇53	,51̇3̇5̇

№ 139.

3 5	5 3 5 1̇	1̇ 5 1̇ 3̇	3̇ 1̇ 3̇ 5̇	5̇ 3̇	3̇ 5̇ 3̇ 1̇	1̇ 3̇ 1̇ 5	5 1̇ 5 3
3 5	5 3 ₅ 1̇	1̇ 5 1̇ 3̇	3̇ 1̇ 3̇ 5̇	5̇ 3̇	3̇ 5̇ ₅ 1̇	1̇ 3̇ 1̇ 5	5 1̇ ₅ 3
3 5	5 3 ₅ 1̇	1̇ 5 1̇ 3̇	3̇ 1̇ 3̇ 5̇	5̇ 3̇	3̇ 5̇ ₅ 1̇	1̇ 3̇ 1̇ 5	5 1̇ ₅ 3
3 5	3	1̇	5	3̇	1̇	5	5̇ 3̇	5̇	1̇	3̇	5	1̇	3

Dictation.

1ˢᵗ_ № 125 by small groups. (page 51.)

2ⁿᵈ_ № 52. Second col. down and up.(page 14.)

KEY OF FA. № 39. **Time.** № 40.

1 . 2	3 4 5	5 4 3	2 1 2	1 0 2	3 4 5	5 4 3	2 1 2
1 . 2	3 4 5	5 4 3	2 . 3	1 0 2	3 4 5	5 4 3	2 0 3
1 . 2	3 4 5	5 4 3	2 . .	1 0 2	3 4 5	5 4 3	2 0 0
1 . 2	3 2 1	2 . 3	4 2 3	1 0 2	3 2 1	2 0 3	4 2 3
1 . 2	3 2 1	2 . 3	2 . 3	1 0 2	3 2 1	2 0 3	2 0 3
1 . 2	3 2 1	2 . 3	2 . .	1 0 2	3 2 1	2 0 3	2 0 0
1 . 2	3 2 1	2 . .	3 4 5	1 0 2	3 2 1	2 0 0	3 4 5
1 . 2	3 2 1	2 . .	3 . 2	1 0 2	3 2 1	2 0 0	3 0 2
1 . 2	3 2 1	2 . .	5 . .	1 0 2	3 2 1	2 0 0	5 0 0

Staff.

P.- name notes first, then sing. T.- gives the sound of LA for DO.

Nº 24.

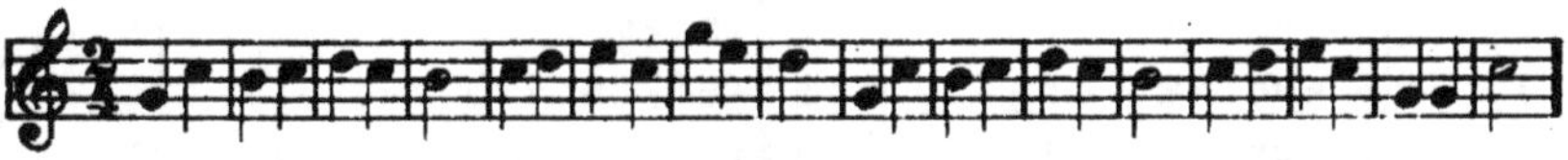

Solfa.

This sign 𝄐 in Music is termed ***a pause*** and means to hold the tone as long as the leader feels the neccessity of holding it and which at his signal or command is dropped.

KEY OF SOL. (5̣-5)

Nº 30. ‖ 0 5 | 5̣ . | 6̣ 7̣ | 1 . | 2 3 | 4 . | 5 6 | 5 . | 0 5 | 5̣ . |
Fine.
| 6̣ 7̣ | 1 . | 2 3 | 4 . | 5 5 | 1 . ‖ 2 1 | 7̣ 0 | 1 2 | 3 0 | 2 1 | *D.C.*
| 5̣ 0 | 1 3 | 5 . | 4 3 | 2 0 | 3 5 | 3 0 | 2 1 | 2 0 | 3 1 | 5 𝄐 ‖

Duett.

When a curved line extends under two or more figures it is intended when applying the words to sing all the notes so connected on one syllable.

Robin Redbreast. KEY OF SOL. (3̣-3) M.M. 144.

Nº 18.								
	3 . 1	3 . 1	2͜1 2	3 . 1'	3 . 1	3 . 1	2͜1 2	1 . 0
	Rob-in / What will	Red-breast / this poor	sings so / Rob-in	sweet-ly / do? For	In the / days of	fal-ling / scar-ci	of the / -ty are	year. / near.
	1 . 1	1 . 1	5̣ . 5̣	1 . 1'	1 . 1	1 . 1	5̣ . 5̣	3̣ . 0

THIRTY FIFTH LESSON.

Intonation.

Remark. When a dot follows a note in Intonation it means to hold the said preceding note twice as long.

KEY OF SOL.

Introductoryline for Nº 140. ‖ 1.5̣ 5̣12.5̣ 5̣123.5̣ | 32.15̣ 5̣12.15̣ 5̣1.7̣5̣ 5̣7̣.1 ‖

Repeat several times each half line then the whole line.

Introductoryline for Nº 141. ‖ 1.235 512.5 5123.5 | 53.215 52.15 521.5 517̣.1 ‖

60

№ 140.

1.512.523.532.521.517.571						
15 125 235 325 215 175 71
15 125 235 325 215 175 71
15 125 235 325 215 175 71

R| 15 25 35 25 15 75 1

№ 141.

1.512.523.532.521.517.571						
15 125 235 325 215 175 71
15 125 235 325 215 175 71
15 125 235 325 215 175 71

15 25 35 25 15 75 1

The notes DO, RE, MI, should be accented.

If reading from book P. must take notice of the skip from low *Sol* (5) to high SOL (5)

№ 142.

1 512 55 235 5 325 5 521 55 175 571
1 512 55 235 5 325 5 521 55 175 571
1 512 55 235 5 325 5 521 55 175 571

R| 15 255 355 255 155 755 1

№ 143.

155 1255 2355 3255 2155 1755 71
155 1255 2355 3255 2155 1755 71
155 1255 2355 3255 2155 1755 71

155 255 355 255 155 755 1

Dictation.

1st. No. 125 by small groups as at previous lesson. (page 51.)
2nd. Nos. 53 & 54 using introductory line first. (page 17.)

Time.

KEY OF SOL.

№ 41.

1 . 2	3 . 5	3 4 3	2 1 2
1 . 2	3 . 5	3 4 3	2 . 3
1 . 2	3 . 5	3 1 3	2 . .
1 . 2	3 . 5	5 . 3	2 1 2
1 . 2	3 . 5	5 . 4	3 . 2
1 . 2	3 . 5	5 . 5	5 . .
1 . 2	3 . 5	3 . .	2 1 2
1 . 2	3 . 5	3 . .	2 . 5
1 . 2	3 . 5	5 . .	5 . .

№ 42.

1 0 2	3 0 5	3 4 3	2 1 2
1 0 2	3 0 5	3 4 3	2 0 3
1 0 2	3 0 5	3 1 3	2 0 0
1 0 2	3 0 5	5 0 3	2 1 2
1 0 2	3 0 5	5 0 4	3 0 2
1 0 2	3 0 5	5 0 5	5 0 0
1 0 2	3 0 5	3 0 0	2 1 2
1 0 2	3 0 5	3 0 0	2 0 5
1 0 2	3 0 5	5 0 0	5 0 0

Staff.

P. name first, then sing. T. gives the sound of DO for DO.

No 25.

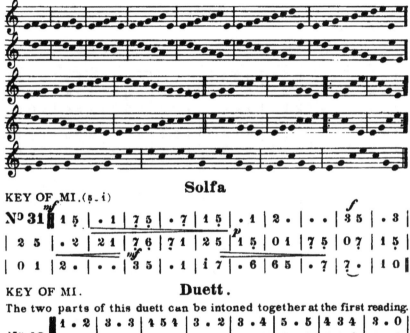

Solfa

KEY OF MI.(5.i)

No 31

mf								f	
1 5	. 1	7 5	. 7	1 5	. 1	2 .	. .	3 5	. 3
2 5	. 2	2 1	7 6	7 1	2 5	1 5	0 1	7 5	0 7	1 5
0 1	2 .	. .	3 5	. 1	1 7	. 6	6 5	. 7	7 .	1 0

KEY OF MI.   **Duett.**

The two parts of this duett can be intoned together at the first reading.

No 19.

1 . 2	3 . 3	4 5 4	3 . 2	3 . 4	5 . 5	4 3 4	3 . 0
1 . 7	1 . 1	2 3 2	1 . 7	1 . 2	3 . 3	2 1 2	1 . 0

2 . 3	4 . 5	6 6 6	6 . 5	5 . 6	5 . 5	5 6 7	i . 0
7 . 1	2 . 3	4 4 4	4 . 3	3 . 4	3 . 3	3 4 4	3 . 0

THIRTY SIXTH LESSON.

Review Nos. 140 & 141.   **Intonation.**

KEY OF DO.

No 144.				No 145.				No 146.		No 147.	No 148.
567	712	217	765	217	765	567	712	5	7275	72 757	27572
567	712	217	765	217	765	567	712	5	72 7	72 7 5	3757
567	712	217	765	217	765	567	712	5	7275	7275 7	27572
5 7	7 2	2 7	7 5	2 7	7 5	5 7	7 2	5	7572	727572	27275
5 7		2 2	7	5	2 7	5 5 7		2	5727 5	7 57 2	27572
5 7		2	7	5	2 7	5	7	2	5727 2	7572 7	27575
									572757	757275	27527

Dictation.

1st- Nos. 126 and 128. (page 52.)

2nd- No. 55 Second col. down & up; no stop in lines. (page 17.)

Time.

KEY OF SOL.

Nº 43.

1 . 2	3 . .	2 3 4	3 2 3
1 . 2	3 . .	2 3 4	3 . 2
1 . 2	3 . .	2 3 4	5 . .
1 . 2	3 . .	5 . 3	2 1 2
1 . 2	3 . .	5 . 3	2 . 3
1 . 2	3 . .	5 . 3	2 . .
1 . 2	3 . .	2 . .	3 4 5
1 . 2	3 . .	2 . .	5 . 5
1 . 2	3 . .	2 . .	5 . .

Nº 44.

1 0 2	3 0 0	2 3 4	3 2 3
1 0 2	3 0 0	2 3 4	3 0 2
1 0 2	3 0 0	2 3 4	5 0 0
1 0 2	3 0 0	5 0 3	2 1 2
1 0 2	3 0 0	5 0 3	2 0 3
1 0 2	3 0 0	5 0 3	2 0 0
1 0 2	3 0 0	2 0 0	3 4 5
1 0 2	3 0 0	2 0 0	5 0 5
1 0 2	3 0 0	2 0 0	5 0 0

Staff.

P- name first, then sing. T- gives the sound of DO for DO.

Nº 26.

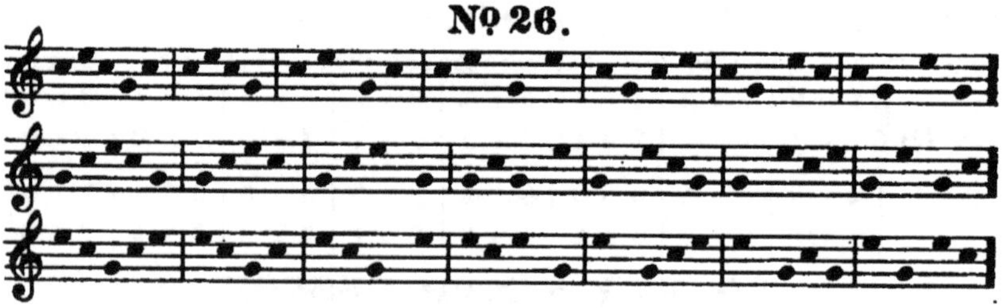

Solfa.

KEY OF SOL. (5-5.)

Nº 32. ‖ *f* 1 5 | 5 1 | 2 5 | 5 2 | 3 5 | 5 3 | 4 . | . . | *p* 3 5 | 5 3 |

| 2 5 | 5 2 | 1 7 | . 6 | 7 1 | 2 3 | *f* 1 5 | . 1 | 2 5 | . 2 | 3 . 5 |

| . 3 | 4 . | . . | *p* 3 5 | . 3 | 2 5 | . 2 | 4 3 | 2 3 | 1 . | . 0 ‖

Duett.

KEY OF SOL.

Nº 20.

3 2 3	5 . 3	2 3 4	3 . 0	5 4 3	2 . 2	1 3 2	1 . .
1 7 1	3 . 1	7 6 5	5 . 0	3 2 1	5 . 5	6 5 5	1 . .

Intonation.

Review Nos. 142 & 143.

KEY OF RÉ.

Pupils being in-
clined to sing the
FA too high, I will
take the following
exercise slowly.

No 149.

```
1 2 3 4 5 5 6 7 7 6 5 5 4 3 2
  2 3 4 5 5 6 7 7 6 5 5 4 3 2
  2 3 4 5 5 6 7 7 6 5 5 4 3 2
  2   5 5   7 7   5 5     2
  2   5     7 7     5     2
  2   5     7       5     2
```

No 150.

```
1 7 7 6 5 5 4 3 2 2 3 4 5 5 6 7
  7 6 5 5 4 3 2 2 3 4 5 5 6 7
  7 6 5 5 4 3 2 2 3 4 5 5 6 7
  7   5 5     2 2     5 5   7
  7   5       2 2       5   7
  7   5       2         5   7
```

No 151.

```
2   5 7   5 2
2   5 7   5
2   5 7 5 2
2   5 2 5 7
2 5 7 5   2
2 5 7 5   7
2 5 7 2   5
```

No 152.

```
5 7   5   2 5
5 7   5   2
5 7 5 2   5
5 7 5 2 5 7
5 2   5   7
5 2 5 7   5
5 2 5 7 5 2
```

No 153.

```
7   5   2 5 7
7   5   2 5
7   5   2 5 7
7   5   7 5 2
7 5 2   5   7
7 5 2   5   2
7 5 2 5 7   5
```

Dictation.

1st - Nos. 127 & 129. (page 52.)

2nd - No. 56, Second col. down & up beginning with DO, RE, MI, to make pupils recognize the MI (3) on which the dictation starts. (p. 17.)

Time.

KEY OF SOL.

No 45.

```
1 . . | 2 3 4 | 5 4 3 | 2 1 2
1 . . | 2 3 4 | 5 4 3 | 2 . 3
1 . . | 2 3 4 | 5 4 3 | 2 . .
1 . . | 2 3 4 | 5 . 4 | 3 2 3
1 . . | 2 3 4 | 5 . 4 | 3 . 2
1 . . | 2 3 4 | 5 . 4 | 3 . .
1 . . | 2 3 1 | 3 . . | 2 1 2
1 . . | 2 3 1 | 3 . . | 2 . 3
1 . . | 2 3 1 | 5 . . | 5 . .
```

No 46.

```
1 0 0 | 2 3 4 | 5 4 3 | 2 1 2
1 0 0 | 2 3 4 | 5 4 3 | 2 0 3
1 0 0 | 2 3 4 | 5 4 3 | 2 0 0
1 0 0 | 2 3 4 | 5 0 4 | 3 2 3
1 0 0 | 2 3 4 | 5 0 4 | 3 0 2
1 0 0 | 2 3 4 | 5 0 4 | 3 0 0
1 0 0 | 2 3 1 | 3 0 0 | 2 1 2
1 0 0 | 2 3 1 | 3 0 0 | 2 0 3
1 0 0 | 2 3 1 | 5 0 0 | 5 0 0
```

Staff.

P. name first, then sing. T. gives the sound of SOL for DO.

Nº 27.

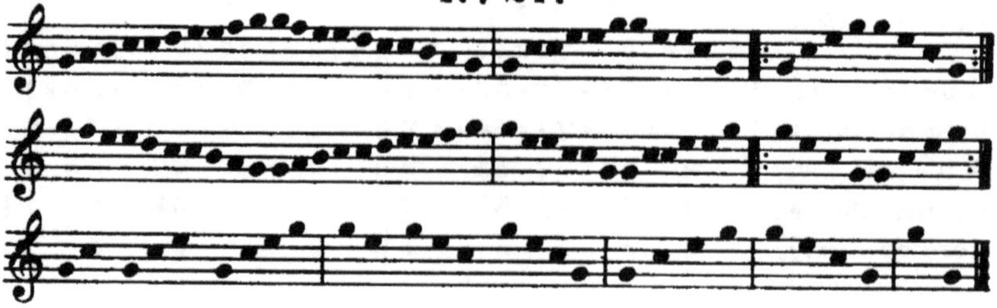

Solfa.

KEY OF SOL. (5 - 5)

Nº33.	1 5	5 3	1 5	5 3	(5) 2 3	1 3	2 1	6 7	(9) 1 5	5 3	1 5	5 3
	(13) 2 3	1 3	2 .	1 .	(17) 2 5	5 3	2 5	5 3	(21) 2 5	6 1	7 5	7 6
	(25) 2 5	5 3	2 5	5 3	(29) 2 5	6 1	6 .	5 .	(33) 1 5	5 3	1 5	5 3
	(37) 2 3	1 3	2 1	6 7	(41) 1 5	5 3	1 5	5 3	(45) 2 3	1 3	2 .	1 0

Duett.

KEY OF MI.

Nº21.	111	777	671	5 . .	444	333	222	1 . 0	123	123
	333	555	444	3 . .	222	111	777	1 . 0	171	171
	123	4 . .	434	234	234	5 . .	176	543	217	1 . 0
	171	2 . .	212	712	712	3 . .	354	321	765	1 . 0

THIRTY EIGHTH LESSON.

Intonation.

Review Nos. 146, 147 and 148.

KEY OF FA.

Nº 154.

5 4 3 2	2 1 7	7 1 2	2 3 4 5
5 4 3 2	2 1 7	7 1 2	2 3 4 5
5 4 3 2	2 1 7	7 1 2	2 3 4 5
5 2	2 7	7 2	2 5
5 2	7	7 2	5
5 2	7	2	5

Nº 155.

7 1 2	2 3 4 5	5 4 3 2	2 1 7
7 1 2	2 3 4 5	5 4 3 2	2 1 7
7 1 2	2 3 4 5	5 4 3 2	2 1 7
7 2	2 5	5 2	2 7
7 2	5	5 2	7
7 2	5	2	7

Nº 156.   Nº 157.   Nº 158.

Nº 156.				Nº 157.				Nº 158.			
5	2	7	2 5	2 5	2	7 2		7	2	5	2 7
5	2	7	2	2 5	2	7		7	2	5	2
5	2	7 2 5		2 5 2	7	2		7	2	5 2 7	
5	2	5 2 7		2 5 2	7 2 5			7	2	7 2 5	
5 2 7	2	5		2 7	2	5		7 2 5	2	7	
5 2 7	2	7		2 7 2 5	2			7 2 5	2	5	
5 2 7 2 5	2			2 7 2 5 2 7				7 2 5 2 7	2		

Dictation.

1st - Nos. 130 & 132 . (page 54.)

2nd - Nos. 57 & 58 beginning with DO so pupils can recognize the *Sol.* (page 19.)

Time.

KEY OF SOL.

Nº 47.   Nº 48.

Nº 47.				Nº 48.			
1 ..	3 . 5	5 4 3	2 1 2	1 0 0	3 0 5	5 4 3	2 1 2
1 ..	3 . 5	5 4 3	2 . 3	1 0 0	3 0 5	5 4 3	2 0 3
1 ..	3 . 5	5 4 3	2 ..	1 0 0	3 0 5	5 4 3	2 0 0
1 ..	3 . 5	5 . 3	2 1 2	1 0 0	3 0 5	5 0 3	2 1 2
1 ..	3 . 5	5 . 3	2 . 3	1 0 0	3 0 5	5 0 3	2 0 3
1 ..	3 . 5	5 . 3	2 ..	1 0 0	3 0 5	5 0 3	2 0 0
1 ..	3 . 5	5 ..	2 3 2	1 0 0	3 0 5	5 0 0	2 3 2
1 ..	3 . 5	5 ..	2 . 3	1 0 0	3 0 5	5 0 0	2 0 3
1 ..	3 . 5	5 ..	5 ..	1 0 0	3 0 5	5 0 0	5 0 0

Staff.

P. Name first, then sing. T. gives the sound of *LA* for *DO*.

Nº 28.

Solfa.

Nọ 34. |1 . 1|3 . 3|535|i . i|23i|23i|255|5 . .|

|1 . 1|3 . 3|535|i . 3|2i7|656|555|5 . .|2 . 2|2i2|

|3 . 3|32i|255|255|3ii|3ii|2.2|2i2|3 . 3|32i|

|2i7|656|543|212|1 . 1|3 . 3|535|i . i|23i|23i|

|255|5 . .|12i|12i|i . i|234|3 . .|2 . .|i . .|. . .|

Duett.

Review last duett and have it sung on *la*.

THIRTY NINTH LESSON.
Intonation.

Review Nos. 146, 147, and 148, then No. 159, singing the small notes lightly and repeating first line three or four times when reading the two col. in succession. KEY OF DO.

Nọ 159. Nọ 160. Nọ 161.

i3 i5i	72 757	5 i3i5	567 275	3 i 5 i3	2 7 572
i3 i5 i	72 7 5	5 i3 i	567 2 7	3 i 5 i	2 7 572
i3i5i	7275 7	5 i3i5	567 275	3 i 5 3	2 7 5,2
i3i5i3i	72757 2	5 i5i3	567 57 2	3 i 3i567	2 7 275
i5 i 3i	75 7 2	5i3i 5	572 7 5	3i5 i 3	275 7 2
i5i3i	757 2 7	5i3i 3	572 7 2	3i5 i 5i	275 7 5
i5i3i5i	7572 75	5i35 i	572 75 7	3i5i3 i	2757 2 7

Dictation.

1st - Nos. 131 & 133. (page 54.)

2nd - No. 59 both col. by small arrows, line divided in two. When coming to the second col. T. will tell the P. to be watchful as they will not begin to go up with the same note as the one on which they ended. This is the first time they will have had such dictation, the previous instruction having always been given in such case by dictating the line without cutting it in two. T. will understand the difference between the two ways of dictating - that one sound helps to get the next one, this be- ing the reason they dictated heretofore a line at a time, while now by dividing in two P. have to listen to a run of notes and after a pause re- member the starting sound . (see page 19.)

Time .

(see page 19.)

KEY OF SOL .

N.º 49.				N.º 50.			
1 . .	3 . .	5 3 5	5 2 5	1 0 0	3 0 0	5 3 5	5 2 5
1 . .	3 . .	5 3 5	5 . 5	1 0 0	3 0 0	5 3 5	5 0 5
1 . .	3 . .	5 3 5	5 . .	1 0 0	3 0 0	5 3 5	5 0 0
1 . .	3 . .	5 . 3	2 1 2	1 0 0	3 0 0	5 0 3	2 1 2
1 . .	3 . .	5 . 3	2 . 3	1 0 0	3 0 0	5 0 3	2 0 3
1 . .	3 . .	5 . 5	5 . .	1 0 0	3 0 0	5 0 5	5 0 0
1 . .	3 . .	5 . .	2 3 2	1 0 0	3 0 0	5 0 0	2 3 2
1 . .	3 . .	5 . .	2 . 3	1 0 0	3 0 0	5 0 0	2 0 3
1 . .	3 . .	5 . .	5 . .	1 0 0	3 0 0	5 0 0	5 0 0

Staff.

T. gives the sound of DO for DO- and prepares for the interval($\dot{2}$- 7)be. before singing.

N.º 29.

KEY OF RÉ .(1_$\dot{2}$)

Solfa .

N.º 35. | 1 . 3 | 5 . 3 | 1 . 3 | 5 . 3 | 2 3 1 | 2 . . | 2 3 1 | 2 . . | 1 . 3 |
5 . 3	1 . 3	5 . 3	2 3 1	2 . 3	2 1 1	1 . .	5 . 6	7 . 6	5 . 6
7 . 5	6 i 7	6 i 7	6 i 7	6 5 6	5 . 6	7 . 6	5 . 6	7 . 5	2 i 7
6 5 6	5 4 3	2 1 2	1 . 3	5 . 3	1 . 3	5 . 3	2 3 1	2 3 1	2 5 5
4 3 2	1 . 3	5 . 3	1 . 3	5 . i	5 3 5	i 5 3	1 . .	. . . ∎

Duett .

KEY OF SOL . The two parts at first reading.

N.º 22. | 5 5 5 | 1 1 1 | 2 2 2 | 3 . . | 5 5 5 | 5 4 3 | 2 1 7 | 1 . . |
| 5 5 5 | 1 1 1 | 7 7 7 | 1 . . | 3 3 3 | 3 2 1 | 7 6 5 | 1 . . |

(Repeat this duett with syllables from memory .)

FORTIETH LESSON.
Intonation.

Do not take this exercise unless the previous one is *perfectly mas-tered by every pupil*. It is advisable to stop the best ones, once in a while, in order to be sure that the others can sing it as well.

KEY OF RÉ.

Nº 162.		Nº 163.		Nº 164.	
5671 535	5 6 75s25	3 5i 53	2s457 5 2	i 535 i	7 5 2 57
5671 5 3	5 6 7 5s32	3 5i 5s3	2 57 5 s3	i 535 i	7 5 2 5s7
5s71s3 5	5 6 7s2 5	3 5i 8	2s4575s2	i 58i	7 5 2s7
5s671s3 i	5 6 75s2s7	3 535is3	2s452s7 54	i 5i3s5i	7 5 7s2
5 s 3 5 i	5s3s2 5. 7	3s5i5 8	2 s75 2	is35i	7s2s5 7
5 s 3s i 5	5s3s2s7 5	3s5i5 is3	2 s75 7	is353s5i	7s2 5 2
5 s 3s is3	5s3s2s75s2	3s5i3 5	2 s72 5	is3i5 i	7s2s7 5

Dictation.

1st No. 134 - Watch the FA (4) (page 56)

2nd No. 60 both col. by single col. dividing the line in two. (page 19.

KEY OF SOL.

Time.

Nº 51.				Nº 52.			
1 2 3	3 2.	5 3 1	3 2.	1 2 3	3 2 0	5 3 1	3 2 0
1 2 3	3 2.	5 . 3	3 2.	1 2 3	3 2 0	5 0 3	3 2 0
1 2 3	3 2.	5 ..	3 2.	1 2 3	3 2 0	5 0 0	3 2 0
1 . 3	3 2.	5 3 1	3 2.	1 0 3	3 2 0	5 3 1	3 2 0
1 . 3	3 2.	5 . 3	3 2.	1 0 3	3 2 0	5 0 3	3 2 0
1 . 3	3 2.	5 ..	3 2.	1 0 3	3 2 0	5 0 0	3 2 0
1 ..	3 2.	5 3 1	3 2.	1 0 0	3 2 0	5 3 1	3 2 0
1 ..	3 2.	5 . 3	3 2.	1 0 0	3 2 0	5 0 3	3 2 0
1 ..	3 2.	5 ..	3 2.	1 0 0	3 2 0	5 0 0	3 2 0

Staff. Nº 30.

KEY OF DO.   (*Time Practice*.) always end with DO.

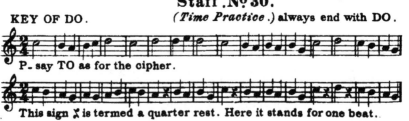

P- say TO as for the cipher.

This sign X is termed a quarter rest. Here it stands for one beat.

KEY OF MI.(5-i)

Solfa.

N?36. |5.5 | 543 | 4.4 | 432 | 313 | 313 | 234 | 234 | 5.5 |
543	4.4	432	313	2..	1..	...	2.2	234	5.5
543	424	313	255	5..	2.2	234	5.6	543	425
315	231	234	5.5	543	4.4	432	313	313	231
234	5.5	i.i	i..	.76	543	212	1..	...

Duett.

Sing the notes only; the words at the next lesson.
KEY OF MI.(5-i) M.M. 160.

5.4	3.4	5..	1.0'	2.3	4.3	2..	..0'
Now the	sun is	sink -	ing,	In the	gol-den	west;	
And the	mer-ry	stream -	let,	As it	runs a-	long,	
3.2	1.2	3..	1.0'	7.1	2.1	5..	..0'

N?23.

3.4	5.6	5..	1.0'	5.4	3.2	1..	..0
Birds and	bees and	chil -	dren	All have	gone to	rest.	
With a	voice of	sweet -	ness	Sings it's	ev'-ning	song.	
1.2	3.4	3..	3.0'	3.2	1.7	1..	..0

FORTY FIRST LESSON.
Intonation.

Review - Nos. 162, 163 & 164. After singing by single col. No. 165 repeat three or four times the first line of the first two columns.

KEY OF FA.

N? 165. N? 166. N? 167.

(intonation exercise tables)

Dictation.

1st Nos. 135 and 136. In dictating No.136 *accent* the low Mi(3) in ascending. The 3,1,5,3. in descending. (page 57.)
2nd Nos. 61 & 62. (page 21.)

KEY OF SOL.

Time.

Nº 53. Nº 54.

1 2 .	3 4 2	5 3 .	3 2 5̣	1 2 0	3 4 2	5 3 0	3 2 5̣
1 2 .	3 4 2	5 3 .	3 . 2	1·2 0	3 4 2	5 3 0	3 0 2
1 2 .	3 4 2	5 3 .	2 . .	1 2 0	3 4 2	5 3 0	2 0 0
1 2 .	3 . 2	5 3 .	3 2 5̣	1 2 0	3 0 2	5 3 0	3 2 5̣
1 2 .	3 . 2	5 3 .	3 . 2	1 2 0	3 0 2	5 3 0	3 0 2
1 2 .	3 . 2	5 3 .	2 . .	1 2 0	3 0 2	5 3 0	2 0 0
1 2 .	3 . .	5 3 .	3 2 5̣	1 2 0	3 0 0	5 3 0	3 2 5̣
1 2 .	3 . .	5 3 .	3 . 2	1 2 0	3 0 0	5 3 0	3 0 2
1 2 .	3 . .	5 3 .	2 . .	1 2 0	3 0 0	5 3 0	2 0 0

Staff.

T. gives an illustration of the transposition of a dotted half note into figures explaining that the half note being equal to two beats, the dot after it means half the value of the preceding note or half of two which is one. To indicate this new kind of time on the staff the sign $\frac{3}{4}$ is set after the clef by which is understood that each measure should contain the *value* of three quarter notes and to count three between each bar.

T. gives the sound of RÉ for DO.

Nº 31.

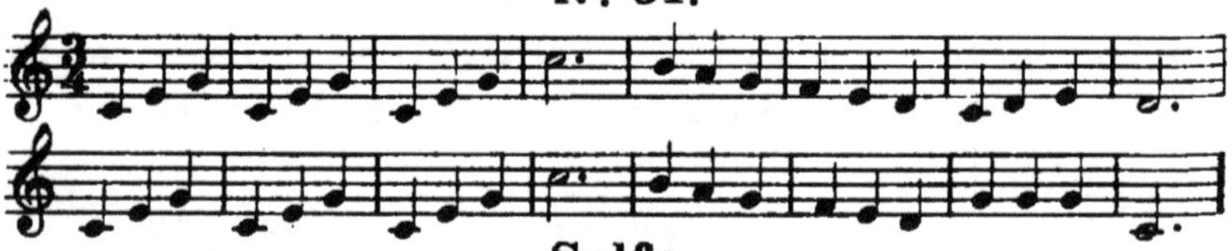

Solfa.

KEY OF SI. (1-4̇)

Lively.

Nº 37. | 5 1 5 | 3 . 3 | 3 5 3 | 1 . 1 | 2 3 1 | 2 3 1 | 1̇ 7 6 | 7 . 5 |
5 1̇ 5	3 . 3	3 5 3	1 . 1̇	7 6 5	6 7 1̇	7 . 6	5 . .
5 6 5	7 . 5	5 6 5	1̇ . 2̇	1̇ 7 1̇	7 6 7	6 5 3	5 . .
5 6 5	2̇ . 5	5 6 5	3̇ . 3̇	4̇ 3̇ 2̇	1̇ 5 3̇	2̇ . .	1̇ . .

Duett.

Review last duett by notes then on *la* then add the words.

FORTY SECOND LESSON.

Intonation.

Review by large arrows Nos. 159, 160, 161, 162, 163 & 164.

Dictation.

1st No. 136 T_ will read remarks made in last lesson. (page 57.)
2nd Nos. 63 & 64. (page 21.)

Time.

KEY OF SOL.

Nº 55.				Nº 56.			
1 2 3	3 2 .	5 3 .	3 2 5̣	1 2 3	3 2 0	5 3 0	3 2 5̣
1 2 3	3 2 .	5 3 .	3 . 2	1 2 3	3 2 0	5 3 0	3 0 2
1 2 3	3 2 .	5 3 .	2 . .	1 2 3	3 2 0	5 3 0	2 0 0
1 . 3	3 2 .	5 3 .	3 2 5̣	1 0 3	3 2 0	5 3 0	3 2 5̣
1 . 3	3 2 .	5 3 .	3 . 2	1 0 3	3 2 0	5 3 0	3 0 2
1 . 3	3 2 .	5 3 .	2 . .	1 0 3	3 2 0	5 3 0	2 0 0
1 . .	3 2 .	5 3 .	3 2 5̣	1 0 0	3 2 0	5 3 0	3 2 5̣
1 . .	3 2 .	5 3 .	3 . 2	1 0 0	3 2 0	5 3 0	3 0 2
1 . .	3 2 .	5 3 .	2 . .	1 0 0	3 2 0	5 3 0	2 0 0

Staff.

Review last melody in $\frac{3}{4}$ and see that all understand the way of writing duration with the dot following the half note.

P_ name first, then sing. T_ gives sound of DO for DO.

Nº 32.

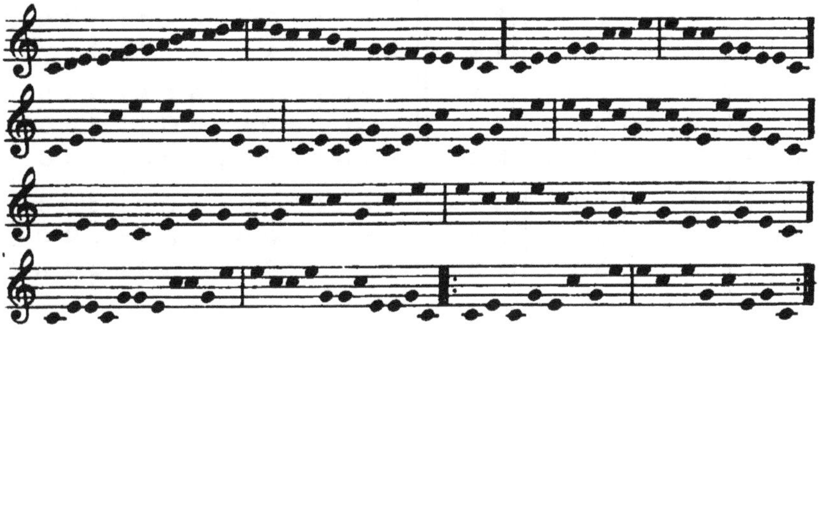

KEY OF RÉ .(1 - 2) **Solfa.**

%*Lively.*

Nọ 38. | 3 . 5 | 2 . 5 | 2 . 5 | 1 . 5 | 1 . 5 | 3 2 1 | 2 5 5 | 5 1̇ 5 |

Fine.

| 3 . 5 | 2 . 5 | 2 . 5 | 1 . 5 | 1 . 5̇ | 3 5 3 | 2 . . | 1 . . ▮

| 5 . 6 | 7 . 1̇ | 7 6 5 | 6 . 5 | 6 . 7 | 5 . 5 | 6 . 7 | 5 . . |

| 5 . 6 | 7 . 1̇ | 7 6 5 | 6 . 5 | 6 7 1̇ | 2̇ 1̇ 7 | 6 . . | 5 . . ▮

%

Duett.

Key of MI. The two parts together at first reading.

Nọ 24. | 1 . 2 | 3 . 3 | 4 5 4 | 3 . 2 | 3 . 4 | 5 . 5 | 4 3 4 | 3 . 0 |
| 1 . 7 | 1 . 1 | 2 3 2 | 1 . 7 | 1 . 2 | 3 . 3 | 2 1 2 | 1 . 0 |

| 2 . 3 | 4 . 5 | 6 6 6 | 6 . 5 | 5 . 6 | 5 . 5 | 5 6 7 | 1̇ . 0 ▮
| 7 . 1 | 2 . 3 | 4 4 4 | 4 . 3 | 3 . 4 | 3 . 3 | 3 4 2 | 3 . 0 |

FORTY THIRD LESSON.

Intonation.

Review Nos . 162, 163, 164, 165, 166 & 167 .

Dictation.

1st- No . 137 and first col . of No . 139 . Repeat last line . (page 58.)
2nd- No . 66 down and up . (page 23.)

KEY OF SOL . **Time.**

Nọ 57. Nọ 58.

1 2 .	3 4 2	5 3 1	3 2 .		1 2 0	3 4 2	5 3 1	3 2 0
1 2 .	3 4 2	5 . 3	3 2 .		1 2 0	3 4 2	5 0 3	3 2 0
1 2 .	3 4 2	5 . .	3 2 .		1 2 0	3 4 2	5 0 0	3 2 0
1 2 .	3 . 2	5 3 1	3 2 .		1 2 0	3 0 2	5 3 1	3 2 0
1 2 .	3 . 2	5 . 3	3 2 .		1 2 0	3 0 2	5 0 3	3 2 0
1 2 .	3 . 2	5 . .	3 2 .		1 2 0	3 0 2	5 0 0	3 2 0
1 2 .	3 . .	5 3 1	3 2 .		1 2 0	3 0 0	5 3 1	3 2 0
1 2 .	3 . .	5 . 3	3 2 .		1 2 0	3 0 0	5 0 3	3 2 0
1 2 .	3 . .	5 . .	3 2 .		1 2 0	3 0 0	5 0 0	3 2 0

Up to the present time we have not mentioned anything about letters, fearing confusion. Supposing the pupils have learned their alphabet the teacher will write in figures 6 7 1 2 3 4 5 placing underneath in corresponding order A.B.C.D.E.F.G. then have the P. repeat the first seven letters several times . T. will then state that seven let. ters will be used to distinguish the pitch on the staff; When wishing to express higher sounds we will start again from A .

Ex :
6 7 1 2 3 4 5   6 7 1̇ 2̇ 3̇ 4̇ 5̇ 6̇
A B C D E F G   A B C D E F G A

Solfa.

KEY OF MI .(♭-♮)

Duett.

KEY OF SOL . P. sing by syllables first , then on *la* .

Nº 25.

1 . 5	1 . 2	3 . . '	3 . 5	4 . 3	2 . .
Let's sing	do _ re _	mi	My dear	lit _ tle	friends
1 . 5	1 . 2	3 . . '	1 . 3	2 . 1	5 . .

1 . 2	3 . 1	3 . . '	5 . 4	3 . 2	1 . .
do _ re _	mi . do	mi	My dear	lit _ tle	friends
1 . 2	3 . 1	3 . . '	3 . 2	1 . 7	1 . .

FORTY FOURTH LESSON .
Intonation .   Nº 168.

KEY OF FA .

We recommend the T. to carefuL ly watch the interval 1-4 as some P. experience trouble in singing it .

1 2 3	3 4 3	3 4 3	3 2 1
1 2 3	4 3	3 4 3	2 1
1 2 3	4 3	3 4 3	2 1
1 2 3	4 3	3 4 3	2 1
1	4 3	3 4	1

KEY OF FA.

Nº 169.	Nº 170.	Nº 171.	Nº 172.
1 2 3 4 4 5 6 6 5 4 4 3 2 1	14641	46414	64146
1 2 3 4 4 5 6 6 5 4 4 3 2 1	1464	4641	6414
1 2 3 4 4 5 6 6 5 4 4 3 2 1	14641	46414	64146
1 4 4 6 6 4 4 1	14146	464146	64641
1 4 6 6 4 1	14641	4146	64146
1 4 6 4 1	14646	41464	64141
	14614	414641	641464

Dictation.

1st. Nº 138 and 2nd col. of Nº 139. (page 58.)
2nd. Nº 67 down & up. (page 28.)

Time.

KEY OF FA. **Nº 59.** **Nº 60.**

Nº 59.				Nº 60.			
1 2 3	3 2 1	5 3 .	3 2 .	1 2 3	3 2 1	5 3 0	3 2 0
1 2 3	3 . 2	5 3 .	3 2 .	1 2 3	3 0 2	5 3 0	3 2 0
1 2 3	2 . .	5 3 .	3 2 .	1 2 3	2 0 0	5 3 0	3 2 0
1 . 3	3 2 1	5 3 .	3 2 .	1 0 3	3 2 1	5 3 0	3 2 0
1 . 3	3 . 2	5 3 .	3 2 .	1 0 3	3 0 2	5 3 0	3 2 0
1 . 3	2 . .	5 3 .	3 2 .	1 0 3	2 0 0	5 3 0	3 2 0
1 . .	3 2 1	5 3 .	3 2 .	1 0 0	3 2 1	5 3 0	3 2 0
1 . .	3 . 2	5 3 .	3 2 .	1 0 0	3 0 2	5 3 0	3 2 0
1 . .	2 . .	5 3 .	3 2 .	1 0 0	2 0 0	5 3 0	3 2 0

Staff.

Repeat the illustration of the use of the letters, but this time draw a staff thus: 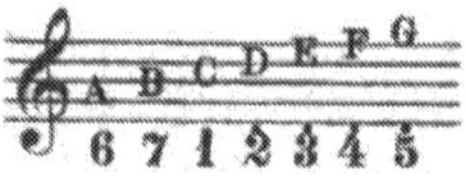
A B C D E F G
6 7 1 2 3 4 5
Impress the pupils' minds with the position of the first letter A

Nº 33. KEY OF DO.

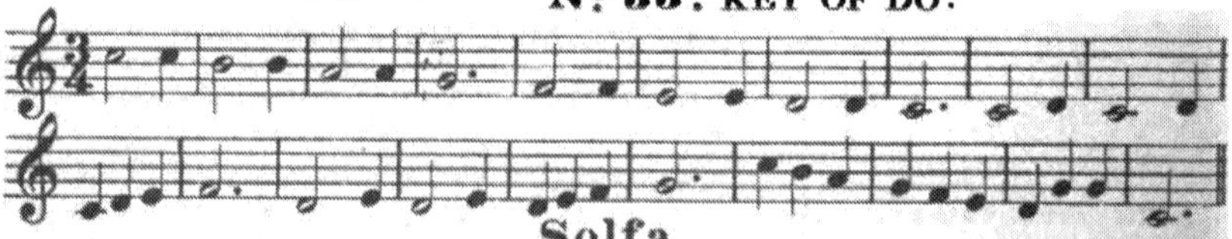

Solfa.

In the following Solfa call attention to bar Nº 31, the *la* (6̣) is difficult for some pupils to intone especially after do-mi-sol but by accenting the first notes after bars Nos. 26 and 28 it will help to surmount this difficulty. Also, accent strongly the *RÉ* at bars 17 & 19. Be sure to get the RÉ at bar N° 25 and the LA at bar N° 31.

KEY OF SOL . (5-5)

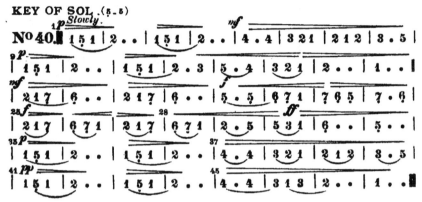

Duett.

Review last duett by syllables, then on lä, then the words.

FORTY FIFTH LESSON
Intonation.

Review Nos. 169, 170, 171, & 172.

KEY OF RÉ.

N° 173.				N° 174.	N° 175.	N° 176.
i 7 6	6 5 4	4 5 6	6 7 i	i 6 4 6 i	6 i 6 4 6	4 6 i 6 4
i 7 6	6 5 4	4 5 6	6 7 i	i 6 4 6	6 i 6 4	4 6 i 6
i 7 6	6 5 4	4 5 6	6 7 i	i 6 4 6 i	6 i 6 4 6	4 6 i 6 4
i 6	6 4	4 6	6 i	i 6 i 6 4	6 i 6 4 3 i	4 6 4 6 i
i 6	4	4 6	i	i 6 4 6 i	6 4 6 i	4 6 i 6 4
i 6	4	6	i	i 6 4 6 4	6 4 6 i 6	4 6 i 6 i
				i 6 4 6 i 6	6 4 6 i 6 4	4 6 i 6 4 6

Dictation.

First, Nos. 140 and 141. Begin with the last line and repeat each twice; then the third line also repeating it twice, stop at each group and accent every note but the *SOL*. (page 60.)

Second, Nos. 68 69 70 & 71 by single col. (page 25.)

Time .

KEY OF SOL .

Nº 61.				Nº 62.			
1 2 .	3 2 .	5 3 1	3 2 5	1 2 0	3 2 0	5 3 1	3 2 5
1 2 .	3 2 .	5 3 1	3 . 2	1 2 0	3 2 0	5 3 1	3 0 2
1 2 .	3 2 .	5 3 1	2 . .	1 2 0	3 2 0	5 3 1	2 0 0
1 2 .	3 2 .	5 . 3	3 2 5	1 2 0	3 2 0	5 0 3	3 2 5
1 2 .	3 2 .	5 . 3	2 . 5	1 2 0	3 2 0	5 0 3	2 0 5
1 2 .	3 2 .	5 . 3	2 . .	1 2 0	3 2 0	5 0 3	2 0 0
1 2 .	3 2 .	5 . .	3 2 5	1 2 0	3 2 0	5 0 0	3 2 5
1 2 .	3 2 .	5 . .	3 . 2	1 2 0	3 2 0	5 0 0	3 0 2
1 2 .	3 2 .	5 . .	5 . .	1 2 0	3 2 0	5 0 0	5 0 0

Staff.

Illustrate on the black board the letters corresponding to the pitch on the staff thus :

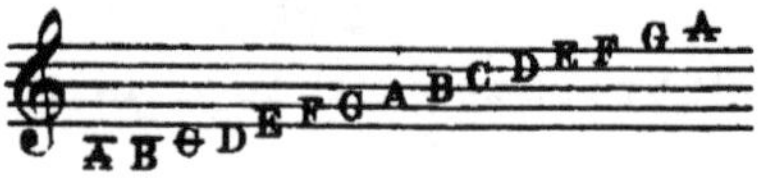
A B C D E F G A B C D E F G A

Call attention to the A which is placed on the ***second leger line below*** the staff and first line above it , also on the second space .

Staff (Time) Nº 34.

T- gives the sound of RÉ for DO .

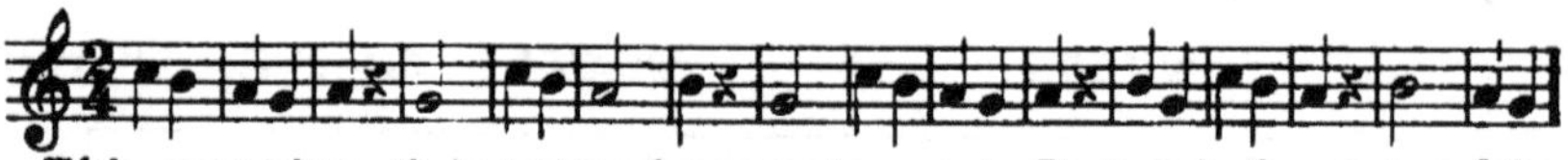

This new sign 𝄽 is termed a quarter rest . It stands for a stop of the duration of one beat . For the present we will say "To" as we did for the cipher.

Solfa .

KEY OF MI . (5 - i)

5 9
Nº41. 1 7 1 | 2 1 2 | 3 2 3 | 4 3 4 | 5 . i | i . 5 | i . . | 5 6 5 | 4 5 4 |

13 17
| 3 4 3 | 2 3 2 | 1 2 1 | 7 . 7 | 7 . 7 | 7 . . | . . . | 1 5 1 | 2 5 2 | 3 2 3 | 4 3 2 |

21 25 29
| 5 . i | i . 5 | i . . | . . . | 7 i 7 | 7 i 7 | 7 6 5 | 6 7 i | 7 . . | 6 5 6 | 5 . . |

33 37 41
| . . 4 | 3 2 1 | 2 3 4 | 3 2 1 | 2 3 4 | 3 2 1 | 2 . 3 | 5 . . | . . . | 6 5 4 | i 7 6 |

45 49 53
| 5 4 3 | i 7 6 | 5 4 5 | 4 3 4 | 3 2 1 | 2 5 4 | 3 2 1 | 2 3 4 | 3 2 1 | 2 3 4 | 3 2 1 |

57 61
| 3 . 5 | 6 . . | . . . | 7 6 7 | 6 5 i | 7 6 7 | 6 5 i | 5 4 5 | 4 3 5 | 2 . . | 1 . . ||

N°26. | 3 2 3 | 5 . 3 | 2 3 4 | 3 . 0 | 5 4 3 | 2 . 2 | 1 3 2 | 1 . 0 |
| 1 7 1 | 3 . 1 | 7 6 5 | 5 . 0 | 3 2 1 | 5 . 5 | 6 5 5 | 1 . 0 |

FORTY SIXTH LESSON.
Intonation.

Review Nos. 174, 175 & 176.

KEY OF LA.

N° 177.					N° 178.			N° 179.		N° 180.		
1234	4321	176	671	1234	4	1	614	14	161	6	1 416
	4321	176	671	1234	4	1	61	14	16	6	1 41
	4321	176	671	1234	4	1	614	14161	6	1 416
	4	116	6 11	4	4	1	416	141614	6	1 614
	4	1	6 6 1	4	416	1 1	16 14	6 1 1 6
	4	1	6 1	4	416	1 6	1614 1	614 1 4
					41614 1	161416	61416 1

Dictation.

1st. Repeat N° 140 following same instruction as that given at last lesson; then N° 142 beginning with last line & dictating from bottom to top always by small groups. (page 60.)

2nd. Nos. 70, 71, 72 & 73. (p. 25)

Time.

KEY OF FA. N° 63. ✓　　　　　N° 64. ✓

1 2 3	. 2 1	2 5 2	4 3 2	1 2 3	0 2 1	2 5 2	4 3 2
1 2 3	. 2 1	2 5 5	5 . 2	1 2 3	0 2 1	2 5 5	5 0 2
1 2 3	. 2 1	2 5 5	5 2 .	1 2 3	0 2 1	2 5 5	5 2 0
1 2 3	. 2 1	2 5 5	5 . .	1 2 3	0 2 1	2 5 5	5 0 0
1 2 3	. 2 1	2 5 .	4 3 2	1 2 3	0 2 1	2 5 0	4 3 2
1 2 3	. 2 1	2 5 .	5 . 2	1 2 3	0 2 1	2 5 0	5 0 2
1 2 3	. 2 1	2 5 .	5 2 .	1 2 3	0 2 1	2 5 0	5 2 0
1 2 3	. 2 1	2 5 .	5 . .	1 2 3	0 2 1	2 5 0	5 0 0
1 2 3	. 2 1	2 . 5	4 3 2	1 2 3	0 2 1	2 0 5	4 3 2
1 2 3	. 2 1	2 . 5	5 . 2	1 2 3	0 2 1	2 0 5	5 0 2
1 2 3	. 2 1	2 . 5	5 2 .	1 2 3	0 2 1	2 0 5	5 2 0
1 2 3	. 2 1	2 . 5	1 . .	1 2 3	0 2 1	2 0 5	1 0 0

Staff.

Now that the pupils are sure of the position of the first letter A on the staff it can be remarked that the teacher will remove all letters except the four on the spaces F, A, C, E - that these four letters make a word well known by all - "FACE", and that pupils should not forget it as it will be the means of recognizing the names of the spaces .

T - gives the sound of MI for DO. **N⁰ 35.**

Solfa.

KEY OF FA .(5 - i)

N⁰42.▌123 | 52. | 123 | 52. . . | 123 | 4 . 1 | 3 . . | . . . | 545 | 43 . |
| 323 | 21 . | 176 | 6 . 7 | 7 . . | . . . | 123 | 52 . | 123 | 52 . | 123 |
| 4 . 1 | 5 . . | . . . | 176 | 17 . | 654 | 65 . | 432 | 43 . | 252 | 1 . .▌

Duett.

KEY OF SOL .

Lively.

N⁰27.▌555 | 1 . 1 | 3 . 3 | 5 . . | 444 | 3 . 1 | 5 . 3 | 2 . . | 222 | 2 . 3 | 1 . 1 | 1 . 3⌐
▌555 | 1 . 1 | 1 . 1 | 3 . . | 222 | 1 . 1 | 7 . 1 | 5 . . | 555 | 5 . 5 | 1 . 1 | 1 . 1⌐

| 1 . 1 | 1 . 3 | 2 . 5 | 5 . . | 5 . . | 3 . . | 1 . . | 5 . . | 333 | 2 . 2 | 5 . 5 | 1 . .▌
| 1 . 1 | 1 . 1 | 5 . 5 | 5 . . | 3 . . | 1 . . | 1 . . | 5 . . | 111 | 5 . 5 | 5 . 5 | 1 . .▌

FORTY SEVENTH LESSON.
Intonation.

Review Nos . 170, 171, 172, 174, 175, 176, 178, 179 & 180 .

Dictation .

1st - Nos. 141 & 143 as per instruction given at last lesson . (page 60.)
2nd - Nos. 72, 73, 74 & 75 . (page 25) large notes only.

Time .

KEY OF RÉ . T - calls attention to the variation made in the third col. at every fourth line. **N⁰ 65.✓**   **N⁰ 66.✓**

5 . 5	. 1̇ 5	3 1 3	2 5 5	5 0 5	0 1̇ 5	3 1 3	2 5 5
5 . 5	. 1̇ 5	3 1 3	3 . 2	5 0 5	0 1̇ 5	3 1 3	3 0 2
5 . 5	. 1̇ 5	3 1 3	3 2 .	5 0 5	0 1̇ 5	3 1 3	3 2 0
5 . 5	. 1̇ 5	3 1 2	1 . .	5 0 5	0 1̇ 5	3 1 2	1 0 0
5 . 5	. 1̇ 5	3 1 .	2 5 5	5 0 5	0 1̇ 5	3 1 0	2 5 5
5 . 5	. 1̇ 5	3 1 .	2 . 5	5 0 5	0 1̇ 5	3 1 0	2 0 5
5 . 5	. 1̇ 5	3 1 .	3 2 .	5 0 5	0 1̇ 5	3 1 0	3 2 0
5 . 5	. 1̇ 5	3 2 .	1 . .	5 0 5	0 1̇ 5	3 2 0	1 0 0
5 . 5	. 1̇ 5	3 . 5	5 2 5	5 0 . 5	0 1̇ 5	3 0 5	5 2 5
5 . 5	. 1̇ 5	3 . 5	5 . 2	5 0 5	0 1̇ 5	3 0 5	5 0 2
5 . 5	. 1̇ 5	3 . 5	2 5 .	5 0 5	0 1̇ 5	3 0 5	2 5 0
5 . 5	. 1̇ 5	3 . 2	1 . .	5 0 5	0 1̇ 5	3 0 2	1 0 0

Questions about the four spaces - F,A,C,E, - What is the name of the
pitch of the first space? Second space? Third space? Fourth space?

Staff (Time) № 36.

This new sign ▬ is termed a half rest and is equal to the half note and
two beats will be observed for it . T_ gives the sound of RÉ for DO .

KEY OF SOL .(s_s)

Solfa .

No 43. ∎3i. |765|3i. |765| 3i5|3i. |3i5|3i.|4̇2̇. |765|
|4̇2̇.|765|4̇3̇2̇|2̇i7|765|675|3i.|765|3i.|765|3i.|
|3i.|3i.|3i5|4̇2̇.|765|4̇2̇.|765|5..|...|4̇2̇3̇|i.0∎

Duett .

T _ will make use of two pointers one white and one black and extem_
porize two part singing on chart recommending that the first division
follow the white stick, the second division the black one. Of course
the T. will limit the difficulty to the knowledge mastered, using easy
intervals such as thirds and sixths .(*Thirds,intervals embracing three
degrees; sixths,six degrees.*)

FORTY EIGHTH LESSON.
Intonation .

Review quickly Nos. 174, 175, 176, 178, 179, & 180, then take the follow_
ing by small arrows only, accenting MI (3) FA (4) SOL (5) LA (6) espec_
ially on the last lines. P_ should take great care in singing the MI (3)
and FA (4) as they are so close to each other that the ear can easily be
disturbed. KEY OF RÉ. **№ 181.** **№ 182.**

31	341	451	561	651	541	143
3.1	34.	145.	156.	165.	154.	143
31	341	451	561	651	541	43
31	341	451	561	651	541	43
31	341	451	561	651	541	43
31	41	51	61	51	41	3

№ 183. **№ 184.**

Dictation.

1st Nos. 140 & 141 all across, following large arrows, dictating second line thus: 15_ 125_ 235 (page 60.)

2nd Nº 76 the first and second col. (page 29.) large notes.

KEY OF SOL.

Time.

T- calls attention to the variation made in the third col- at every fourth line.

Nº 67. **Nº 68.**

Nº 67				Nº 68			
5 5 .	. 3 1	2 3 4	3 2 1	5 5 0	0 3 1	2 3 4	3 2 1
5 5 .	. 3 1	2 3 4	3 . 2	5 5 0	0 3 1	2 3 4	3 0 2
5 5 .	. 3 1	2 3 4	3 2 .	5 5 0	0 3 1	2 3 4	3 2 0
5 5 .	. 3 1	2 3 2	1 . .	5 5 0	0 3 1	2 3 2	1 0 0
5 5 .	. 3 1	2 4 .	3 2 5	5 5 0	0 3 1	2 4 0	3 2 5
5 5 .	. 3 1	2 4 .	3 . 2	5 5 0	0 3 1	2 4 0	3 0 2
5 5 .	. 3 1	2 4 .	3 2 .	5 5 0	0 3 1	2 4 0	3 2 0
5 5 .	. 3 1	2 3 .	1 . .	5 5 0	0 3 1	2 3 0	1 0 0
5 5 .	. 3 1	2 . 4	3 2 5	5 5 0	0 3 1	2 0 4	3 2 5
5 5 .	. 3 1	2 . 4	3 . 2	5 5 0	0 3 1	2 0 4	3 0 2
5 5 .	. 3 1	2 . 3	2 5 .	5 5 0	0 3 1	2 0 3	2 5 0
5 5 .	. 3 1	2 . 3	1 . .	5 5 0	0 3 1	2 0 3	1 0 0

Staff. Nº 37.

Question about the four spaces skipping from first to third, (etc)

T- gives the sound of RÉ for DO.

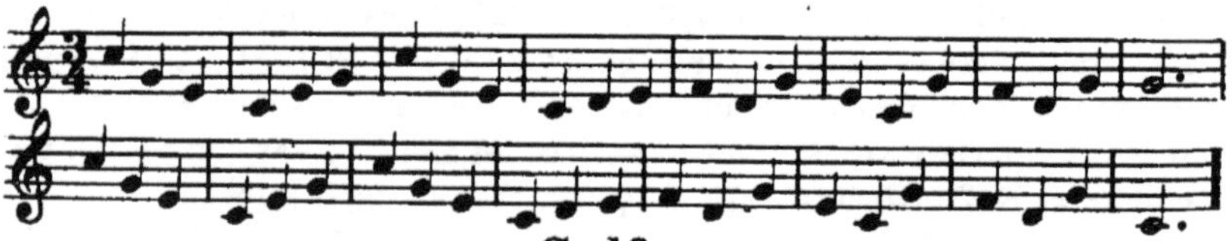

Solfa.

KEY OF RÉ. The slur ‿ indicates that the voice should pass smoothly from one tone to the next. (1_2̇)

Nº 44 ‖ 123 | 32. | 53. | 325 | 6.5 | 543 | 52. | 2.. | 123 | 32. | 53. | 325 |
| 1̇.5 | 435 | 2.. | 1.. | 356 | 77. | 67. | 653 | 1̇76 | 1̇7. | 1̇76 | 1̇7. |
| 556 | 77. | 67. | 653 | 1̇76 | 1̇76 | 1̇76 | 542 | 123 | 32. | 531 | 325 |
| 6.5 | 543 | 52. | 2.. | 123 | 32. | 53. | 325 | 1̇.5 | 435 | 2.. | 1.0 ‖

Duett.

T. will again make use of the two pointers as at last lesson extemporizing easy exercises.

FORTY NINTH LESSON
Intonation.

Review Nos. 181,182,183 & 184 following large arrows, then the next four numbers by small arrows. Remember to accent MI(3)FA(4)SOL (5)LA(6)

KEY OF RÉ.

N? 185.

3̄1̄	3̄4̄1̇	4̄5̄1̄	5̄6̄1̇	6̄5̄1̄	5̄4̄1̇	4̄3̇
3.134.145.156.165.154.143
31 34̇ 451 56̇ 651 54̇ 43
31 ₃4̇ 451 ₅6̇ ₆51 ₅4̇ 43
31 ₃4̇ 451 ₅6̇ ₆51 ₅4̇ 43
31 4̇ 51 6̇ 51 4̇ 3

N? 186.

3̇1̄	3̄4̄1̇	4̄5̄1̇	5̄6̄1̇	6̄5̄1̇	5̄4̄1̄	4̄3
3.134.145.i56.165.i54.143
3̇1 341 45̇1 561 65̇1 541 43
3̇1 ₃41 ₄5̇1 ₅61 ₆5̇1 ₅41 43
3̇1 ₃41 ₄5̇1 ₅61 ₆5̇1 ₅41 43
3̇1 41 ₅̇1 61 5̇1 41 3

N? 187.

3̄1̄	3̄4̄1̄	4̄5̄1̄	5̄6̄1̄	6̄5̄1̄	5̄4̄1̄	4̄3
3̄1̄	₃4̄1̇	4̄5̄1̇	₅6̄1̇	₆5̄1̇	₅4̄1̇	4̄3
3̄1̄	₃4̄1̇	4̄5̄1̇	₅6̄1̇	₆5̄1̇	₅4̄1̇	4̄3
31̇ 41̇1 51̇ 61̇1 51̇1 41̇1 3

N? 188.

3̇1̄	3̄4̄1̄	4̄5̄1̄	5̄6̄1̄	6̄5̄1̄	5̄4̄1̇	4̄3
3̇1̇	₃4̄1̇	₄5̄1̇	₅6̄1̇	₆5̄1̇	₅4̄1̇	4̇₃
3̇1̇	₃4̄1̇	₄5̄1̇	₅6̄1̇	₆5̄1̇	₅4̄1̇	4̇₃
3̇1̇1 41̇1 51̇1 61̇1 5̇1̇1 41̇1 3

Dictation.

1st-Nos. 142 & 143 following large arrows dictating by groups thus: 1 5 _ 2 5 5 _ 3 5 5 accenting the notes DO, RE, MI. (page 60)

2nd- N? 76 first, second and third col. singly. (page 29) large notes.

KEY OF RÉ.

N? 69.   Time.   N? 70.

5 · ·	· 1̇ 5	3 1 3	2 5 5 || 5 0 0	0 1̇ 5	3 1 3	2 5 5
5 · ·	· 1̇ 5	3 1 3	2 · 5	5 0 0	0 1̇ 5	3 1 3	2 0 5
5 · ·	· 1̇ 5	3 1 3	2 5 ·	5 0 0	0 1̇ 5	3 1 3	2 5 0
5 · ·	· 1̇ 5	3 1 2	1 · ·	5 0 0	0 1̇ 5	3 1 2	1 0 0
5 · ·	· 1̇ 5	3 1 ·	2 5 5	5 0 0	0 1̇ 5	3 1 0	2 5 5
5 · ·	· 1̇ 5	3 1 ·	2 · 5	5 0 0	0 1̇ 5	3 1 0	2 0 5
5 · ·	· 1̇ 5	3 1 ·	2 5 ·	5 0 0	0 1̇ 5	3 1 0	2 5 0
5 · ·	· 1̇ 5	3 2 ·	1 · ·	5 0 0	0 1̇ 5	3 2 0	1 0 0
5 · ·	· 1̇ 5	3 · 1	2 5 5	5 0 0	0 1̇ 5	3 0 1	2 5 5
5 · ·	· 1̇ 5	3 · 1	2 · 5	5 0 0	0 1̇ 5	3 0 1	2 0 5
5 · ·	· 1̇ 5	3 · 1	2 5 ·	5 0 0	0 1̇ 5	3 0 1	2 5 0
5 · ·	· 1̇ 5	3 · 2	1 · ·	5 0 0	0 1̇ 5	3 0 2	1 0 0

Question about spaces as before . Remark that being sure of the names
of the pitch of the spaces the pupils can easily tell the names of the
lines . For instance: the second space is A, the line next will be B ac_
cording to alphabetical order; and so on with the others. T. illustrates
only for the first line . Ask what letter precedes F. By starting from A
and naming the letters in succession (A, B, C, D, E, F,) we will find it is E,
the letter wanted for the first line . Also, by remembering the phrase,
Every Good Boy Does Finely,   which can be written on lines of
the staff, starting with the first word on the first line, etc . Call the pu_
pils attention to the fact that the first letter of each word is the letter
intended for the line .

Time .

T_ gives the sound of DO for DO.   T_ says TO for the rests.

N.º 38.

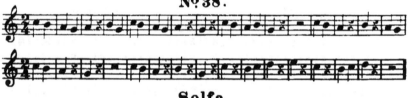

Solfa .

KEY OF FA . (5 - i)   9

N.º 45. | 1 2 . | 3 4 2 | 5 3 1 | 3 2 . | 1 2 . | 2 3 1 | 2 3 5 | 3 . 2 |
1 2 .	3 4 2	5 3 1	3 2 .	5 1 .	2 3 4	2 . .	1 . 0	2 5 .	3 2 1
2 5 .	3 2 1	7 1 .	7 1 .	7 1 7	7 . .	2 5 .	3 2 1	2 5 .	3 2 1
7 1 7	1 7 6	5 . .	. . .	1 2 .	3 4 2	5 3 1	3 2 .	1 2 .	2 3 1
2 3 5	3 . 2	1 2 .	3 4 2	5 3 1	3 2 5	1 1 .	2 3 4	2 . .	1 . 0

KEY OF RÉ .

Round .

A			
5 6	7 i	7 6	5 .
Kind words	speak and	kind deeds	plan
B			
3 4	2 3	5 4	3 .
Help each	oth _ er	when you	can
C			
1 .	1 .	1 .	1 .
Kind	words	kind	deeds

FIFTIETH LESSON.

Intonation.

Nº 189.

KEY OF FA. *

1.23.3.45.5.43.3.21.	1.234.4.56.6.54.4.321.
1.23.3.45.5.43.3.21.	1.234.4.56.6.54.4.321.
1.23.3.45.5.43.3.21.	1.234.4.56.6.54.4.321.
1. 3.3. 5.5. 3.3. 1.	1. 4.4. 6.6. 4.4. 1.
1. 3 5.5. 3. 1.	1. 4. 6.6. 4. 1.
1. 3 5. 3. 1.	1. 4. 6. 4. 1.

* Review Nos. 185,186, 187 & 188 following large arrows; then Nº 189 which cannot be passed before every one is able to
make this new transition; even if neccessary to take it again at the next lesson.
When satisfactorily done then begin 190.

Nº 190.

123 5 31	123456 4321
123 5 3	1234 6 4
123 531	1234 641
123 135	1234 146
135 3 1	14 641
135 3 5	14 646
135 31 3	14 641 4

Dictation.

1st- Nº 95 the three col. dictating all across the same as though a
large arrow extended over them, of course making a stop at each vertical line. and without small notes. (see page 38.)

2nd- Nº 76 the three col. the same as though a large arrow extended over them. Tell pupils you change the note in beginning each
dictation. Do not give more than five notes at a time. large notes p.29

Time.

KEY OF RÉ. Nº 71.   Nº 72.

5 . .	. . 1	5 4 3	3 2 1	5 0 0	0 0 1	5 4 3	3 2 1
5 . .	. . 1	5 4 3	3 . 2	5 0 0	0 0 1	5 4 3	3 0 2
5 . .	. . 1	5 4 3	3 2 .	5 0 0	0 0 1	5 4 3	3 2 0
5 . .	. . 1	5 3 2	1 . .	5 0 0	0 0 1	5 3 2	1 0 0
5 . .	. . 1	5 3 .	3 2 1	5 0 0	0 0 1	5 3 0	3 2 1
5 . .	. . 1	5 3 .	3 . 2	5 0 0	0 0 1	5 3 0	3 0 2
5 . .	. . 1	5 3 .	3 2 .	5 0 0	0 0 1	5 3 0	3 2 0
5 . .	. . 1	5 5 .	1 . .	5 0 0	0 0 1	5 5 0	1 0 0
5 . .	. . 1	5 . 3	3 2 1	5 0 0	0 0 1	5 0 3	3 2 1
5 . .	. . 1	5 . 3	3 . 2	5 0 0	0 0 1	5 0 3	3 0 2
5 . .	. . 1	5 . 3	3 2 .	5 0 0	0 0 1	5 0 3	3 2 0
5 . .	. . 1	5 . 5	1 . .	5 0 0	0 0 1	5 0 5	1 0 0

Staff.

Questions about pitch - names of lines and spaces.
T - gives the sound of MI for DO.

N⁰ 39.

Solfa.

After having given key note let pupils practice intervals 3̇-7.
KEY OF LA.(5-5̇)

N⁰46.|565|i̇.2̇|3̇2̇3̇|i̇..|2̇3̇2̇|i̇.6|71̇2̇|5..|565|i̇.2̇|

|3̇2̇3̇|i̇..|3̇1̇3̇|7.5|676|5..|52̇.|2̇..|51̇.|i̇..|567|

|676|5.6|6..|52̇.|2̇..|51̇.|i̇..|55̇4̇|2̇3̇1̇|6.7|i̇..|

Duett.

Sing the notes first, then on *lä*

The Sleigh Ride. KEY OF SOL. (5̣-5) M.M.184.

	3 1 3	5 . 0	3 1 3	5 . 0	5 4 2	3 . 1
N⁰ 28.	Swiftly we	go,	O-ver the	snow,	And the bells	tin - kle
	1 1 1	3 . 0	1 1 1	3 . 0	3 2 7	1 . 1

5 4 2	3 . 1	3 2 3	4 . 0	2 3 2	1 . 0
And the sleighs	jin - gle;	Lightly we	go,	O-ver the	snow.
3 2 7	1 . 1	1 7 1	2 . 0	7 5̣ 5̣	1 . 0

———✳———

Part II.

FIFTY FIRST LESSON.

Intonation.

KEY OF MI. If Nº 190 can be sung without the small notes, then the following can be attempted, if small notes are used then two col. can be sung across.

Nº 191.		Nº 192.		Nº 193.	
13531	$1_{23}4_{5}641$	3531 3	$464_{32}14$	5313 5	$6\,4_{32}146$
$1_{2}353$	$1_{23}4_{5}64$	3531_{23}	$464_{32}1$	5313_{45}	6 4 1 4
$1_{2}351$	$1_{23}4_{5}6_{4}1$	$35_{3}1\,3$	$46_{4}\,1\,4$	5315	6 4 1 6
$1_{2}315$	$1_{23}41_{4}6$	$35_{3}1\,5$	$46_{4}\,1\,_{4}6$	5351_{23}	$_{45}646_{4}1$
$1_{3}531$	$1_{4}\,641$	3135	4146	$5_{3}135$	$6_{4}\,146$
$1_{3}535$	$1_{4}\,646$	$31_{3}5\,3$	$41_{4}\,6\,4$	$5_{3}131\,_{23}$	$_{45}6_{4}\,141$
$1_{3}513$	$1_{4}\,6_{4}14$	$31_{3}5\,1_{23}$	$41_{4}\,6\,_{4}1$	$5_{3}153\,_{45}$	$6_{4}1_{4}64$

Dictation.

1st - Nº 104, the three columns straight across as though a large arrow covered all. (page 41.)

2nd Nº 76, the same as last lesson. (page 29.)

Time.

Review Nº 71 & 72. The four beats measure coming at the next lesson it is well to prepare for it by showing how it should be done. The first beat is *down*, the second *left*, the third *right*, the fourth *up*. Pupils should begin to beat slowly but move together promptly,

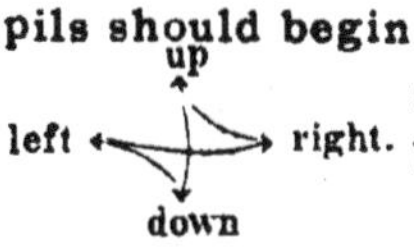
up
left
right.
down

saying the words down, left, right, up, keeping the hand steady at each place.

Staff.

Questions about the names of pitches as before.
(TIME) T - gives the sound of DO for DO.

Nº 39.

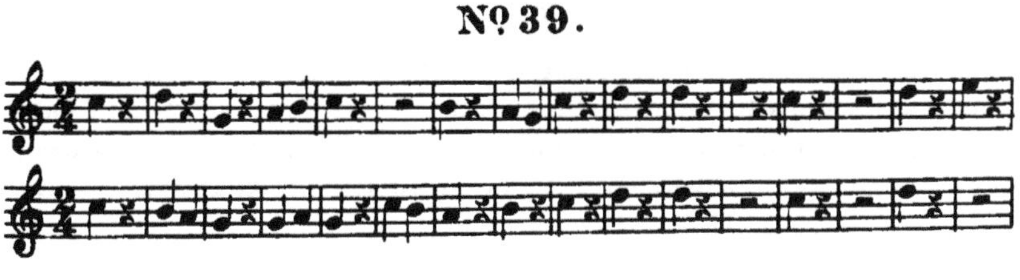

KEY OF SOL. (7-6)

Solfa.

Nº 47. ‖ 5 1 . | 2 3 2 | 5 2 . | 3 4 3 | 5 1 . | 2 3 2 | 5 2 . | 2 3 2 | 5 5 . | 6 4 . | 2 3 4 |
| 5 3 . | 1 2 3 | 4 2 . | 7 1 2 | 3 1 . | 6 4 . | 2 3 4 | 5 3 . | 1 2 3 | 4 2 . | 5 6 5 | 1 . . ‖

Duett.

T- will point first five notes of the scale up and down requesting pupils to sing *ah* on every note according to the pitch; (Teacher illustrates) then bringing the two sticks together on the same note. Teacher will show how to make the swell, stating that when wishing to increase the volume of sound, T- opens the two sticks thus ＜ If wishing to decrease the sound, do the opposite thus ＞ that is bring the two sticks together. For the first time the teacher must be satisfied to experiment with the latter exercise, the decrease of sound: that is, starting loudly then gradually becoming soft.

FIFTY SECOND LESSON.

Intonation.

Review Nos. 191, 192, & 193.

KEY OF LA. **Nº 194.** **Nº 195.**

Nº 194		Nº 195	
1 2̇ 3̇ 1̇ 5 1	1̇ 2̇ 3̇ 4̇ 1 7 6 1̇	5 1̇ 3̇ 1̇ 5	6 1̇ 2̇ 3̇ 4̇ 1̇ 6
1 2̇ 3̇ 1̇ 5	1̇ 2̇ 3̇ 4̇ 1 7 6	5 1̇ 3̇ 1̇ 7	6 1̇ 2̇ 3̇ 4̇ 1̇ 7 6
1 2̇ 3̇ 1̇ 5 1	1̇ 2̇ 3̇ 4̇ 1̇ 6 1̇	5 1̇ 3̇ 1̇ 5	6 1̇ 2̇ 3̇ 4̇ 1̇ 6
1 2̇ 3̇ 1̇ 5 1̇ 3̇	1 2̇ 3̇ 4̇ 1̇ 6 1̇ 4̇	5 1̇ 5 1̇ 3̇ 1̇ 7	6 1̇ 6 1̇ 4̇ 1̇ 6
1 7 6 5 1̇ 3̇	1̇ 7 6 1 2̇ 3̇ 4̇	5 1̇ 3̇ 1̇ 5	6 1̇ 4̇ 1̇ 6
1 7 6 5 1̇ 3̇ 1	1 7 6 1̇ 4̇ 1̇	5 1̇ 3̇ 1̇ 3̇ 1̇ 7	6 1̇ 4̇ 1̇ 4̇ 1̇ 6
1 7 6 5 1̇ 3̇ 1̇ 5	1 7 6 1̇ 4̇ 1̇ 6	5 1̇ 3̇ 1̇ 5 1̇	6 1̇ 4̇ 1̇ 6 1̇

Dictation.

1st - Nos. 159 & 160, dictating the *whole line of the two col*. thus:
1̇ 3̇ 1̇ 5̇ 1̇ — 7 2̇ 7 5 7 — making a stop at each vertical line. (page 66)
2nd - Nos. 78, 79, 80 & 81 by small arrows. (page 33) large notes only

Time.

Practice beating as at last lesson, pupils saying down, left, right, up. Then, if satisfied with the movement, take the following. The difficulty being in the change of beating new time, the intonation of these exercises is made easy in order to take up one difficulty at a time. Let P- still accent the duration.

No.73.		No.74.		No.75.		No.76.	
1234	5432	123·	4543	1·23	4543	1·2·	3455
1234	543·	123·	4-55·	1·23	455·	1·2·	345·
1234	5·43	123·	4·55	1·23	4·55	1·2·	3·45
1234	5·5·	123·	4·5·	1·23	4·5·	1·2·	3·2·
1234	5···	123·	2···	1·23	2···	1·2·	3···

Staff.

Before singing the following, have pupils name notes by letters thus:
C,E,G (etc)   No.41. T - gives the sound of RÉ for DO.

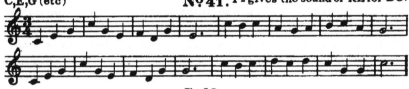

Solfa.

After having given the key note have pupils practice both skips 6-8
and 7-3. before starting, always making use of the missing consecu_
tive sounds between the skips.

KEY OF LA. (5 - 3).

No.48. |560|560|517|765|670|670|631|176|
|710|710|732|317|630|630|765|100|

Duett.

T - will repeat similar exercises as at last lesson.

FIFTY THIRD LESSON.
Intonation. No.196.

KEY OF LA.

Review No 194 & 195.
Take 196 slowly and
sing it twice.

3	15	13		431	176	14
3	15	1	23	4	16	1 2
3	15 1	3		431	614	
3	13 5	61	4	1	416 1 2	
3 1 51	3		4 1	6 1	4	
3 1 51	5	61	4 1	6 1	6 1	
3 1 53	1	23	4 1	6 4	1	

Dictation.

1st - Nos. 160 & 161. (page 66) see instruction at last lesson.
2nd Nos. 81,82,83 & 84. (page 33.)

KEY OF MI.

Time.

N.º 77.		N.º 78.		N.º 79.		N.º 80.	
1 2 3 4	5 4 3 2	1 2 3 0	4 5 4 3	1 0 2 3	4 5 4 3	1 0 2 0	3 4 5 5
1 2 3 4	5 4 3 0	1 2 3 0	4 5 5 0	1 0 2 3	4 3 2 0	1 0 2 0	3 4 5 0
1 2 3 4	5 0 4 3	1 2 3 0	4 0 3 2	1 0 2 3	4 0 5 5	1 0 2 0	3 0 4 5
1 2 3 4	5 0 5 0	1 2 3 0	4 0 5 0	1 0 2 3	4 0 5 0	1 0 2 0	3 0 2 0
1 2 3 4	5 0 0 0	1 2 3 0	2 0 0 0	1 0 2 3	2 0 0 0	1 0 2 0	3 0 0 0

Staff (Time.)

The curved line ⌒ in the next exercise is termed a tie. It is used for the prolongation of a sound, when the same note is tied on the staff it is generally used to cross over a bar. It is held according to its value. If, as in the following example : ♩|♩ there be a quarter note which we know requires one count we will hold the preceding note one more beat sustaining the same sound and giving a little accent on the vowel of the name of the note as heretofore done when singing by the figures.

N.º 42.

T- gives the sound of DO for DO.

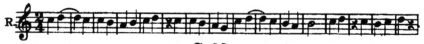

Solfa.

Before singing the following T- will see that P- experience no more trouble with the skips (2-4) (6-1) and when neccessary using as a help the missing notes in the skip.

KEY OF MI .(5-1)

N.º 49. |1 . 3 | 3 2 . | 5 3 1 | 3 2 . | 4 . 6 | 6 5 . | 1 4 3 | 3 2 5 |
1 . 3	3 2 .	5 3 1	3 2 .	4 . 6	1 5 .	5 2 3	2 1 .	7 . 1	1 7 .
7 2 1	1 7 .	1 . 3	5 2 .	2 1 7	6 . .	7 . 1	1 7 .	1 3 1	1 7 .
1 3 5	5 2 1	7 1 6	5 . .	1 . 3	3 2 .	5 3 1	3 2 .	4 . 6	6 5 .
1 4 3	3 2 5	1 . 3	3 2 .	5 3 1	3 2 .	4 . 6	1 5 .	2 5 2	1 . . ▮

Duett.

Now T- will reverse the exercise of the swell, remarking how nicely and softly was the *piano* made, stating that the difficulty now would be to begin with this piano as well and increase it to a loudness which is named FORTE. This experiment will not succeed as quickly as the first. The trouble lies in the fact that the fuller the breath the more difficult it is to control it.

FIFTY FOURTH LESSON.

Intonation.

Review Nos. 194, 195, & 196.

KEY OF RÉ. **Nº 197.** **Nº 198.**

5 i 5 3 5	6 i 6 4 6	3 5 i 5 3	4 6 i 6 4
5 i 5 3 4 5	6 i 6 4	3 5 i 5	4 6 i 6 5 4
5 i 5 3 5	6 i 6 4 6	3 5 i 5 3	4 6 i 6 4
5 i 5 3 5 i 7	6 i 6 4 6 i 7 6	3 5 3 5 i 7 6 5	4 6 4 6 i
5 4 3 5 i 7	6 5 4 6 i 7 6	3 5 i 5 3	4 6 i 6 4
5 3 5 i 5	6 5 4 6 i 6	3 5 i 5 i 7 6 5	4 6 i 6 i 6 4
5 3 5 i 5 3 4 5	6 5 4 6 i 6 4	3 5 i 5 3 5	4 6 i 6 4 6

Dictation.

1st - Nos. 162 & 163. (page 68.)

2nd - Nos. 80, 81, 85 & 86 following large arrows. (page 83.)

Time.

P. say first, down, left, right, up, for a few seconds.

KEY OF MI.

Nº81.		Nº82.		Nº83.		Nº84.		Nº85.	
1234	5432	1230	4543	1023	4543	102.	3455	1...	2345
1234	5430	1230	455.	1023	432.	102.	3450	1..0	232.
1234	5043	1230	4.32	1023	4.55	102.	3045	1.00	2032
1234	505.	1230	405.	1023	405.	102.	302.	1000	203.
1234	5.00	1230	2.00	1023	2.00	1020	3.00	1...	2.00

Staff.

Give the sound of MI for DO. **Nº43.**

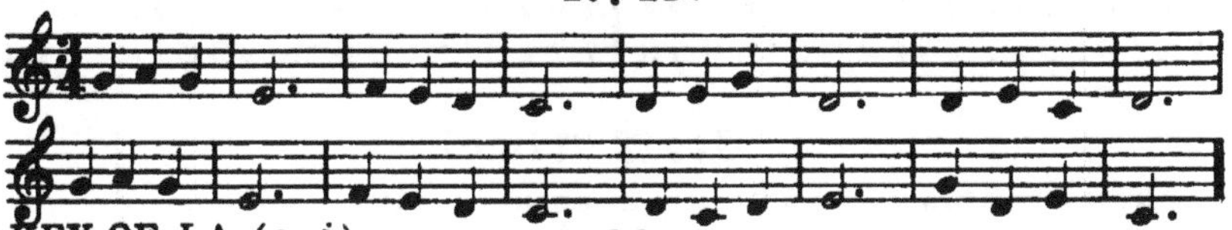

KEY OF LA. (2.5)

Solfa.

Nº 50. *p* 3 . 5 | . 24 | 3 . 5 | . 24 | *crescendo* 3 . 5 | . 3 i | . 76 | . 54 | *p* 3 . 5 | . 24 |
| 3 . 5 | . 24 | 3 3 2 | . i 7 | 6 . . | 5 . 0 | *mf* 5 . i | . 75 | 5 . i | *crescendo* . 75 | *f* 5 . 5 |
| . 43 | . 2i | 7 i 2 | *dim.* 5 . i | . 75 | *mf* 5 . i | . 75 | *p* 5 5 3 | i 5 i | 2 . . | i . 0 ‖

Duett.

Repeat, as at last lesson, the swell from a *piano* to a forte.

FIFTY FIFTH LESSON.

Intonation.

Nᵒ 199.

Review Nos. 197 & 198.

P. Sing 199 twice.

These exercises as chord suc.
cessions serve as the base to mod.
ern music and therefore should
not be neglected .There should be
no hesitation in the transition .

i	7 6	5	3	5 i	i	7	6	5	4	6 i
i	7 6	5	3	5	i	7	6	5	4	6
i	7 6	5	3	5 i	i	7	6	5	4	6 i
i	7 6	5	1	5 3	i	7	6	1	6	4
i 7 6 5 4 3		5		i	i 7 6 5 4		6		1
i 7 6 5 4 3		5		3	i 7 6 5 4		6		4
i 7 6 5 4 3	5	i		5	i 7 6 5 4	6	i		6

Dictation.

1st - Nos. 163 & 164 (page 68)

2nd - Nos. 87, 88, 89, 90, 91, & 92 following large arrows. T. begins
with i 7 6 5 to make P. recognize the 5 . (page 37)

Time.

By *small arrows only* .

KEY OF SOL .

Nᵒ 86.		Nᵒ 87.		Nᵒ 88.		Nᵒ 89.	
1 2 . 3	2 1 2 3	1 2 0 3	4 3 2 3	1 2 . 3	2 3 2 3	1 2 0 3	5 3 2 3
1 2 . 3	5 1 2 .	1 2 0 3	5 1 2 0	1 2 . 3	5 2 2 0	1 2 0 3	5 2 2 .
1 2 . 3	5 2 . .	1 2 0 3	5 2 0 0	1 2 . 3	5 2 0 0	1 2 0 3	5 2 . 0
1 2 . 3	2 . 5 3	1 2 0 3	2 0 5 2	1 2 . 3	2 0 5 3	1 2 0 3	2 . 5 2
1 2 . 3	2 . 5 .	1 2 0 3	5 0 2 0	1 2 . 3	2 0 5 0	1 2 0 3	5 0 2 .
1 2 . 3	5 . . 2	1 2 0 3	5 0 0 2	1 2 . 3	5 0 0 2	1 2 0 3	5 . . 2
1 2 . 3	5 . . .	1 2 0 3	5 0 0 0	1 2 . 3	5 . 0 0	1 2 0 3	5 . . 0

Staff (Time)

T- should remind P. what was said about the tie .

T- gives the sound of DO for DO.

Nᵒ 44 .

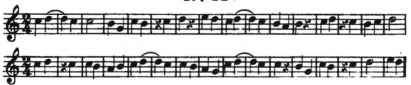

Solfa.

KEY OF RÉ.$\binom{5-\acute{1}}{(Slowly.)}$

N⁰ 51. | 5̣ 5 . | . 3 1 | 5̣ 5 . | . 3 1 | 1 2 3 | 4 5 6 | i̇ 5 . | . . . |
7 6 .	6 5 3	7 6 .	6 5 3	5 6 7	6 . i̇	7 5 6	5 . .
5̣ 5 .	. 3 1	5̣ 5 .	. 3 1	1 2 3	4 5̀ 6	i̇ 5 .	. . .
2̇ i̇ 7	. i̇ 5	6 5 4	. 5 3	4 3 2	. 3 1	2̣ 5̣ 5	1 . .

Duett.

Repeat the same exercise as at the last lesson for the swell.

FIFTY SIXTH LESSON.
Intonation.

Review Nos. 197, 198 & 199.

Dictation.

1ˢᵗ- Nos. 165 & 166. (page 69)

2ⁿᵈ- Nos. 91, 92, 93 & 94 following large arrows; beginning as at the last lesson with i̇ 7 6 5. (page 37)

Time.

Review Nos. 86, 87, 88, 89 by large arrows.

Staff.

How happy would the pupils be if they knew a language that could be understood in every country! This is a similar case.

The scale or language of DO we have partly learned is all that is ne-cessary to sing fourteen foreign scales; but we will have to do work that at first will seem very difficult but which will not be so after studying the new exercises in the manner in which they are present ed. We will have to name the first line of the staff DO and the follow-ing spaces and lines in regular order RE, MI etc. T- writes on the blackboard the staff with the seven numerals as a temporary help thus: ≡≡≡≡≡≡≡ then erasing 2 and 4, keep pointing on the staff the ≡≡≡≡≡≡ scale ascending & descending, P- naming do, ré, mi, etc. following the pointer. Erase 6 and 7 leaving only 1 3 5 i̇ and let P- practice in the same manner.

KEY OF LA.(5-5)   **Solfa.**

No 52. | 500 | 035 | 424 | 310 |⁵200 | 072 | 161 | 750 |⁹
Crescendo.
| 100 | 051 | 200 | 052 |¹³ 300 | 053 | 231 | 234 |¹⁷
f
| 5 .. | .35 | 424 | 31. |²¹ 2 .. | .72 | 161 | 75. |²⁵
| 1 .. | .31 | 2 .. | .42 |²⁹ 353 | 212 | 151 | 1 .. |

Duett.

T. will now proceed both ways. First increasing the sound from a piano to forte, P. breathing deeply, then from forte to piano always using the syllable *Ah* on every sound of the first five notes.

FIFTY SEVENTH LESSON.
Intonation.

KEY OF FA. **No 200.**   **No 201.**

1	3	5	3	1	1	23	4	6	4	1	1	2	3	5	3	1	7 2 5 2 7		
1	3	5	3		1	23	4	6	4		1	2	3	5	3	1	7 2 5 2		
1	3	5	1		1		4	6	1		1		3	5	1		7 2 5 7		
1	3	1	5		1		4	1	6		1		3	1	5	31	7 2 7 5 2 27		
1	5	3	1		1		6	4	1		1		5	3	1		7 5 2 7		
1	5	3	5		1		6	4	6		1		5	3	5	31	7 5 2 5 27		
1	5	1	3		1		6	1	4		1		5	1	3	1	7 5 7 2		

Dictation.

1st- Nos 166 & 167. (page 69.)
2nd- Nos. 91, 92, 93 & 94. Begin as heretofore with 1765.(page 87)

Time.

Following small arrows only.
KEY OF FA.

No 90.		No 91.		No 92.		No 93.	
1234	25.3	1235	3203	1235	52.3	1235	5203
123.	25.3	1230	2502	123.	2502	1230	25.2
15..	25.2	1500	2502	15.0	2502	1500	25.2
1.53	25.2	1053	2502	1.53	2502	1053	25.2
1.5.	25.2	1050	2502	1.50	2502	105.	2502
1..3	25.2	1008	2502	1.03	2505	1003	25.5
1...	25.2	1000	2502	1..0	2505	1000	25.5
13.1	25.2	1301	2502	13.1	2505	1301	25.5

Similar work on *transposition* as at previous lesson, leaving the
figures 1 3 5 i̇ on the staff P. naming notes as soon as pointed.

Solfa.

KEY OF LA.(¡ . s̱) P. practice first the skip (6.2)

№53.|0 0 5 | 3 3 5 | 5 2 5 | 5 . 6 | 5 . 3 | 1 . 1 | 2 . 2 | 3 . . |
| 1 . 5 | 5 3 5 | 5 2 5 | 5 . i̇ | 5 . 3 | 1 . 1 | 2 3 2 | 1 . . | . . 2 | *f*
2 5 2	2 5 2	2 . 5	6 5 6	7 . 7	2̇ . 2̇	7 . .	. . 5	i̇ . .
3̇ . 3̇	2̇ 3̇ 2̇	7 . 2̇	i̇ . i̇	7 . 7	6 . .	. . 2	2 5 2	2 5 2
2 . 5	6 5 6	7 . 7	2̇ . 2̇	2̇ . .	. . 5	3̇ . .	5̇ . 3̇	2̇ . 5	6 7 i̇
7 . .	6 . .	5 . .	. . 5	5 3 5	5 2 5	5 . i̇	5 . 3	1 . 1	2 1 2
3 . .	1 . 5	5̇ i̇ 5	5 2̇ 5	5 . i̇	5 . i̇	3̇ 4̇ 3̇	2̇ i̇ 2̇	i̇ . .	. . . ∎

Duett.

Sing notes first, then on *la*.

Good-Bye to Summer. KEY OF RÉ(s̱ - i) M.M. 160.

№ 29.	1	1 . 2	3 . 1	3 . 4	5 . '5	1 . 5	6 5 5
	Good .	bye Good . bye	to	Sum .	mer Cool	blow the	bree.zes
	1	1 . 5	1 . 1	1 . 2	3 . '5	3 . 3	4 3 3

1 . 5	6 5'5	4 . 5	3 . 5	6 . 7	1 . 0
in the	sun For	sum . mer	now is	near . ly	done.
3 . 3	4 3'3	2 . 2	1 . 3	4 . 5	3 . 0

FIFTY EIGHTH LESSON.

Intonation.

Review Nos. 200 and 201.

KEY OF FA. №202.   №203.

3 5 3 1 3	4 6 4 1 4	3 5 3 1 3	2 5 2 7 2
3 5 3 1 3	4 6 4 1 4	3 5 3 1	2 5 2 7 2
3 5 3 1 3	4 6 4 1 4	3 5 3 1 3	2 5 3 7 2
3 5 3 1 3 5	4 6 4 1 4 6 4	3 5 3 1 3 5 3	2 5 3 7 3 5
3 1 3 5	4 1 4 6 4	3 1 3 5 3	2 7 2 5
3 1 3 5 3	4 1 4 6 4	3 1 3 5 3	2 7 2 5 2
3 1 3 5 3 1	4 1 4 6 4 1	3 1 3 5 3 1	2 7 2 5 2 7

Dictation.

1st - Nos. 181 & 182. 1st, 3rd, & 6th lines in this manner: 3 1 1 3-4 1 1 4-5 1 1 5 etc. (page 79)

2nd - Nos. 96, 97, 98 & 99. (page 39)

Time.

Nos. 90, 91, 92, & 93 following large arrows.

Staff.

T - states that one-three-five, the odd numerals representing DO-MI-SOL, are for the present set on the three first lines and that the three even numerals, two-four-six, representing RÉ-FA-LA: are on the spaces. T - can now remove the figure 3 representing the MI from the staff leaving 1 5 i and pointing ascending and descending, P - still *naming* the notes.

KEY OF MI. (6̣ - i)

Solfa.

Fine.

Nº 54. ‖ 345. | 67i. | 345. | 652. | 345. | 67i. | 123. | 421. ‖

| 232. | 565. | 232. | 17̣6̣. | 232. | 567. | 656. | 765. ‖ *D.C.*

Duett.

Repeat last one by notes, on *la*, then with words.

FIFTY NINTH LESSON.

Intonation.

Review Nos. 202 & 203 following large arrows.

KEY OF FA. **Nº 204.** **Nº 205.**

5 3 1 3 5	6 4 1 4 6	5 3 1 3 5	5 2 7̣ 2 5
5 3 1 3 5	6 4 1 4	5 3 1 3	5 2 7̣ 2
5 3 1 3 5	6 4 1 4 6	5 3 1 3 5	5 2 7̣ 2 5
5 3 5 3 1 35	6 4 6 4 1 46	5 3 5 3 1 3	5 2 5 2 7̣ 2
5 3 1 3 5	6 4 1 4 6	5 3 1 3 5	5 2 7̣ 2 5
5 3 1 3 1 35	6 4 1 4 1 46	5 3 1 3 1 3	5 2 7̣ 2 7̣
5 3 1 3 5 3 5	6 4 1 4 6 4	5 3 1 3 5 3	5 2 7̣ 2 5 2

Dictation.

1st - Nos. 183 & 184 by small groups, thus: 3 1 i - 4 1 i - 5 1 i etc. Only the last two lines. (page 79)

2nd - Nos. 100, 101, 102 & 103. Begin from high DO so P. can recognize the MI. (page 40)

Time.

Follow small arrows first, then the large ones.

KEY OF FA.

Nº 94.		Nº 95.		Nº 96.		Nº 97.	
1 2 . .	3 4 3 2	1 2 0 0	3 4 3 2	1 2 . 0	3 5 3 2	1 2 0 0	3 5 3 2
1 2 . .	3 5 2 .	1 2 0 0	3 5 2 0	1 2 . 0	3 1 5 0	1 2 0 0	3 1 5 .
1 2 . .	3 . 5 2	1 2 0 0	3 0 5 2	1 2 . 0	3 0 2 5	1 2 0 0	3 . 2 5
1 2 . .	3 . 5 .	1 2 0 0	3 0 5 0	1 2 . 0	3 . 5 0	1 2 0 0	3 0 5 .
1 2 . .	5 . . .	1 2 0 0	5 0 0 0	1 2 . 0	5 . 0 0	1 2 0 0	5 . . 0

Staff.

In the following exercise the signs intended for the notes should only be *named*, not sung.

Nº 45.

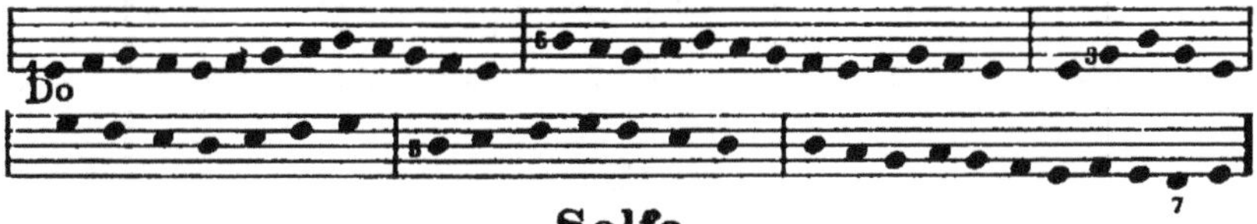

Do
7

Solfa.

KEY OF FA. (5̣ - 5)

Nº 55. ‖ 1 5̣ 1 3 | 1 5̣ 1 3 | 5 3 5 3 | 1 2 2 . |[5] 1 5̣ 1 3 | 1 5̣ 1 3 |
| 5 1̇ 5 3 | 1 2 1 . |[9] 2 5̣ 2 5̣ | 1 3 2 . | 3 1 5 3 | 1 7̣ 6̣ . |
[13] | 5̣ 5̣ 2 5̣ | 1 3 2 . | 3 1 5 3 | 2 2 2 . |[17] 1 5̣ 1 3 | 1 5̣ 1 3 |
| 5 3 5 3 | 1 2 2 . |[21] 1 5̣ 1 3 | 1 5̣ 1 3 | 5 3 5 3 | 2 . 1 . ‖

KEY OF MI. **Round for three voices.**

Nº 30. ‖ (A) 5 6 5 | 5 . 1̇ | 5 4 3 | 3 4 3 | (B) 3 2 1 | 3 2 1 | 1 . 1 | (C) 1 7̣ 6̣ | 5̣ 5̣ 1 |

SIXTIETH LESSON.

Intonation.

Review by large arrows Nos. 204 & 205.

KEY OF LA.

Nº 206.		Nº 207.	
1̇ 2̇ 3̇ 1̇ 5 1̇	1̇ 2̇ 3̇ 4̇ 1̇ 6 1̇	1̇ 2̇ 3̇ 1̇ 5 1̇	7 2̇ 7 5 7
1̇ 2̇ 3̇ 1̇ 5	1̇ 2̇ 3̇ 4̇ 1̇ 6	1̇ 2̇ 3̇ 1̇ 5 1̇	7 2̇ 7 5 7
1̇ 2̇ 3̇ 1̇ 5 1̇	1̇ 2̇ 3̇ 4̇ 1̇ 6 1̇	1̇ 2̇ 3̇ 1̇ 5 1̇	7 2̇ 7 5 7
1̇ 2̇ 3̇ 1̇ 5 1̇ 3̇	1̇ 2̇ 3̇ 4̇ 1̇ 6 1̇ 4̇	1̇ 2̇ 3̇ 1̇ 5 1̇ 3̇ 1̇	7 1̇ 2̇ 7 5 7 2̇
1̇ 5 1̇ 3̇	1̇ 7 6 1̇ 4̇	1̇ 7 6 5 1̇ 3̇ 1̇	7 5 7 2̇
1̇ 5 1̇ 3̇ 1̇	1̇ 7 6 1̇ 4̇ 1̇	1̇ 7 6 5 1̇ 3̇ 1̇	7 5 7 2̇ 7
1̇ 5 1̇ 3̇ 1̇ 5	1̇ 7 6 1̇ 4̇ 1̇ 6	1̇ 7 6 5 1̇ 3̇ 1̇ 5 6	7 5 7 2̇ 5

Dictation.

1st- Nos. 185 & 186 taking care to dictate first line thus: 3 1 1 3_
4 1 1 4 _ 5 1 1 5 _ etc. third and sixth lines by little groups as printed p.81

2nd- Nos. 105 & 107 making a stop between the notes that are repeated or by small groups. T- begins from 1 7 6 5 (page 42.)

Time.

KEY OF FA.

No. 98.		No. 99.		No. 100.		No. 101.	
1235	32..	1235	3200	1235	3200	1235	32.0
123.	52..	1230	5200	123.	2500	1230	25.0
1.23	52..	1023	5200	1.23	2500	1023	25.0
1.2.	35..	1020	3500	1.20	3200	1020	32.0
1...	52..	1000	2500	1..0	5200	1.00	25.0
12..	52..	1200	5200	12.0	52.0	1200	55.0

Staff.

A few minutes can be spent on the names of pitches as before.

P- only name the following with syllables. T- will remark that the
lower DO is on the line while the upper one is on the space and that
DO-MI-SOL are on the first three lines.

No. 46.

KEY OF RÉ (1_2).

Solfa.

No. 56. *mf* | 1235 | 6.5. | 1535 | 2.3. *f* | 3567 | 617. | 6567 | 653. |
| 564. | 564. | 51.2 | 2.1. | 17.6 | 1143 *p* | 2... | 1..0 ∎

KEY OF SOL.

Duett. No 30.

1.3.	5..0	5432	1..0	232 1	5531
Do mi,	sol............	Little birdie	sing.........	In the trees oh	sing! oh sing and
1.3.	5..0	3217	1..0	555 1	3311

2321	553.	1234	5..0	5432	1..0
with a sweetly	charming voice	do, re, mi, fa,	sol.........	Lit_tle bird_ie	sing.........
5551	331.	1234	5..0	321 5	1..0

SIXTY FIRST LESSON.

Intonation.

Review Nos. 206 & 207.

KEY OF LA. **Nº 208.** **Nº 209.**

Nº 208		Nº 209	
5 1̇ 3̇ 1̇ 5	6 1̇ 2̇3̇ 4̇ 1̇ 6	5 1̇ 3̇ 1̇ 5	5 6 7 2̇ 7 5
5 1̇ 3̇ 1̇ 7	6 1̇ 2̇3̇ 4̇ 1̇ 7 6	5 1̇ 3̇ 1̇	5 6 7 2̇ 7
5 1̇ 3̇ 1̇ 5	6 1̇ 4̇ 1̇ 6	5 1̇ 3̇ 1̇ 5	5 6 7 2̇ 7 5
5 1̇ 5 1̇ 3̇ 1̇ 7	6 1̇ · 6 1̇ 4̇ 1̇ 6	5 1̇ 5 1̇ 3̇	5 6 7 5 7 2̇
5 1̇ 3̇ 1̇ 5	6 1̇ 4̇ 1̇ 6	5 1̇ 3̇ 1̇ 5	5 7 2̇ 7 5
5 1̇ 3̇ 1̇ 3̇ 1̇ 7	6 1̇ 4̇ 1̇ 4̇ 1̇ 6	5 1̇ 3̇ 1̇ 3̇	5 7 2̇ 7 2̇
5 1̇ 3̇ 1̇ 5 1̇ 7	6 1̇ 4̇ 1̇ 6 1̇ 7 6	5 1̇ 3̇ 1̇ 5 1̇	5 7 2̇ 7 5 7

Dictation.

1st - Nos. 187 & 188. The last two lines by small groups, accenting the notes MI, FA, SOL, LA, whenever they are met. (page 81)
2nd - Nos. 106 & 108. (page 42)

KEY OF FA.

Time.

Nº 102.		Nº 103.		Nº 104.		Nº 105.	
1 . . 2	3 5 3 2	1 0 0 2	3 5 3 2	1 . 0 2	3 5 3 2	1 0 0 2	3 5 3 2
1 . . 2	3 5 2 .	1 0 0 2	3 5 5 0	1 . 0 2	3 5 2 0	1 0 0 2	3 5 5 .
1 . . 2	3 2 . .	1 0 0 2	3 5 0 0	1 . 0 2	3 2 0 0	1 0 0 2	3 5 0 0
1 . . 2	3 . 5 2	1 0 0 2	3 0 5 2	1 . 0 2	3 0 5 2	1 0 0 2	3 . 5 2
1 . . 2	3 . 5 .	1 0 0 2	3 0 5 0	1 . 0 2	3 . 5 0	1 0 0 2	3 0 5 .
1 . . 2	5̣ . . .	1 0 0 2	5 0 0 0	1 . 0 5̣	5̣ . 0 0	1 0 0 5	5 . . 0

Staff.

P. should be asked where DO, MI, SOL, and RE, FA, LA, are located.
NAME only (slowly)

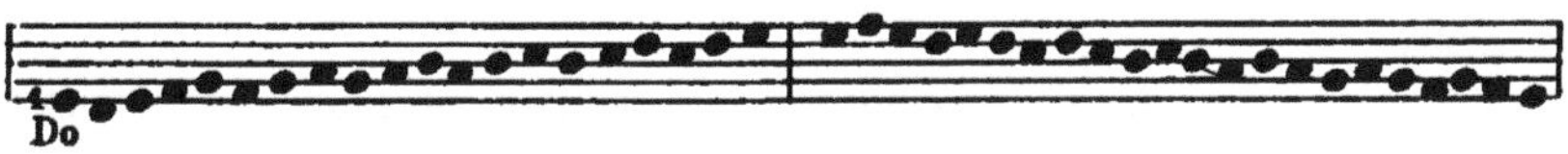

Do

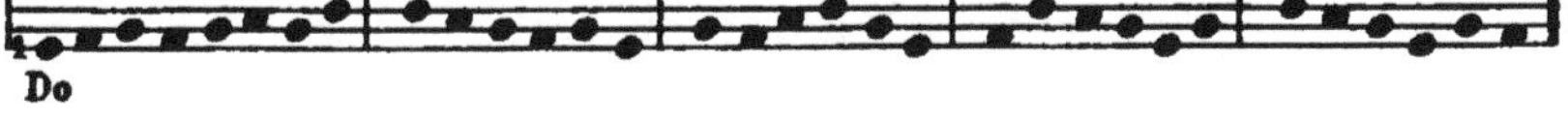

Do

KEY OF DO .(1 - 3)   **Solfa.**

NO 57.$ p$ 3 | 2 1 2 3 | 2 . 1 5 | 4 3 4 5 | mf 5 4 . 3 1 | 7 6 7 1 | 5 4 5 6 | 5 3 1 2 | 3 . . 3 | p 9

| 2 1 2 3 | 2 . 1 5 | 4 3 4 5 | f 13 4 . 3 1 | 7 6 7 1 | 3 2 7 1 | 6 . . . | 5 . . 0 | 17

| 5 6 7 1 | 1 . 7 5 | 5 6 7 1 | 21 1 . 7 5 | 5 6 7 1 | 7 6 5 6 | 5 2 3 4 | 3 . . 5 | mf 25

| 5 6 7 1 | 1 7 7 5 | 5 6 7 1 | 29 1 7 2 5 | 5 1 2 3 | 3 2 1 6 | 2 . . . | 1 . . 0 |

KEY OF DO .
    A B   **Round .**

NO 31.$ 3355 | 1 . 2 . | 3 . 2 . | 1 1 5 5 | 6 . 7 . | 1 . 3 2 | 1 5 5 4 | 3 3 5 5 | 1 1 2 7 | 1 . . 0 |

SIXTY SECOND LESSON.
Intonation .

Review Nos . 208 & 209 .

KEY OF LA . **NO 210.**   **NO 211.**

3	1	5	1 3	4 3 2 1	6	1 4	3	1 5	1	3	2	7	5	7 2
3	1	5	1 2 3	4 3 2 1	6	1 2	3	1 5	1		2	7	5	7 2
3	1	5 1 3		4 3 2 1	6 1 4		3	1 5 1 3			2	7	5 7 2	
3	1	3 i 5	1 3	4 3 2 1	4 i 6	1	3	1 3 1 5	1		2	7	2 7 5 7 2	
3 i 5	1	3		4 i 6	1	4	3 i 5 1	3			2 7 5	7	2	
3 i 5	1	5 1 3		4 i 6	1	6 i	3 i 5 1	5 1			2 7 5	7	5 7 2	
3 i 5 1 3	1	3		4 i 6 1 4	1 2		3 i 5 3	1			2 7 5 7 2	7		

Dictation .

1st - Nos 191 & 192 . (page 85)

2nd - Nos . 109 & 111 .(p . 43) **Staff (Time .)**

T - gives the sound of DO for DO .

    T - will tell P - that the new sign ♭ is named a flat . Why they are used will be explained in the next book in which will be begun the theory of music .

NAME first , keeping time ; then P - sing . T - gives the sound of RÉ for DO .

NO 48.

№ 58. ｆ₃ |2015|403ｉ|76ｉ6|655ｉ|5045|403ｉ|767ｉ|2̇753|

| 2.15| 4.3ｉ | 76ｉ6 | 6553̇ | 2̇.ｉ2̇ | ｉ.7ｉ | 6 . . . | 5 . . 0 |

| 305ｉ | ｉ750 | 345ｉ | ｉ750 | 351̇3̇ | 2̇ｉ76 | 5234 | 4.30 |

| 3.5ｉ | ｉ75. | 353̇ｉ | ｉ75. | 5̇.3̇ｉ | 766ｉ | 2̇ . . . | ｉ . . 0 ᴨ

Recreation.

Review exercises on the swell, piano to forte and forte to piano.

SIXTY THIRD LESSON.
Intonation.

Review Nos. 210 & 211 following large arrows.

KEY OF RÉ. № 212.   № 213.

5 ｉ	5 3 5	6 ｉ 6 4 6		5 ｉ	5 3 5	5 7	5 2 5
5 ｉ	5 3 ₅	6 ｉ 6 4		5 ｉ	5 3	5 7	5 2
5 ｉ ₅ 3 5		6 ｉ ₆ 6 4 6		5 ｉ ₅ 3 5		5 7 ₅ 2 5	
5 ｉ ₅ 3 5 ｉ ₇		6 ｉ ₆ 6 4 ₆ ｉ		5 ｉ ₅ 3 ｉ		5 7 ₅ 2 ₅ 7	
5 3 5 ｉ ₇		6 4 6 ｉ ₆		5 3 5 ｉ		5 2 5 7	
5 3 ₅ ｉ 5		6 4 ₆ ｉ 6		5 3 ₅ ｉ 5		5 2 ₅ 7 5	
5 3 ₅ ｉ ₅ 3 ₅		6 4 ₆ ｉ ₆ 4		5 3 ₅ ｉ ₅ 3		5 2 ₅ 7 ₅ 2	

Dictation.

1ˢᵗ - Nos. 192 & 193. (page 85)

2ⁿᵈ - Nos. 110 & 112.(page 43)

KEY OF FA.

№ 106.   № 107. **Time.** № 108.   № 109.

1 2 3 5	3 . . 2	1 2 3 5	3 0 0 2	1 2 3 5	3 . 0 2	1 2 3 5	3 0 0 2
1 2 3 .	2 . . 5	1 2 3 0	2 0 0 5	1 2 3 .	2 . 0 5	1 2 3 .	2 0 0 5
1 2 . .	5 . . 2	1 2 0 0	5 0 0 2	1 2 . 0	5 . 0 2	1 2 . 0	5 0 0 2
1 . 2 3	2 . . 5	1 0 2 3	2 0 0 5	1 . 2 3	2 . 0 5	1 . 2 3	2 0 0 5
1 . 3 .	2 . . 5	1 0 3 0	2 0 0 5	1 . 3 .	2 . 0 5	1 . 3 0	2 0 0 5
1 . . .	5 . . 2	1 0 0 0	5 0 0 2	1 . . 0	5 . 0 2	1 . 0 0	5 0 0 2
1 . . 3	2 . . 5	1 0 0 3	5 0 0 5	1 . 0 3	2 0 0 5	1 . 0 3	5 . 0 5

P_ Name first, then sing . T_ gives the sound of RÉ for DO.

N⁰ 49.

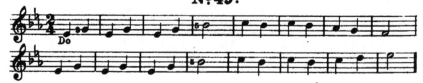

KEY OF DO. (1 . ȧ)   **Solfa.**

N⁰ 59.|5.6,|5.6.|51 35|1 23.|⁵4.3,|4.3.|54.3|1 ƒ 2.|⁹

|5.6.|5.76|5176|6.7.|¹³ ȧ 13i|1765|2...|5...|¹⁷

ᵐᶠ|5 ȧ.5|5i.5|57.5|51 ȧ 3|5 ȧ.5|5i.i|1717|1765|²⁵

ƒ|3.4.|3.4.|3i53|123.|²⁹54.3|54.3|2154|3.2.|³³

|54.3|3.4.|67.i|1.7.|³⁷71.ȧ|3i.5|4325|2.i.■|

KEY OF LA.   **Duett.**

N⁰ 32.|5.67|i..i|ȧ176|6.50|i.ȧ3|ȧ..i|7.6.|5..0|
|3.45|3..3|4354|4.30|3.45|4..3|5.4.|3..0|

|5.67|i..5|17iȧ|3.ȧ0|ȧ.ȧ4|5..5|6.7.|i..0|
|3.45|3..3|3535|i.50|5.iȧ|ȧ..3|4.4.|3..0|

SIXTY FOURTH LESSON.

Intonation.

Review Nos. 212 and 213 following large arrows.

KEY OF RÉ.

N⁰ 214.   N⁰ 215.

3 5 i 5 3	4 6 i 6 4	3 5 i 5 3	2 5 7 5 2
3 5 i 5	4 6 i 6 ₄	3 5 i 5 ₃	2 5 7 5
3 5 i ₅ 3	4 6 i 6 4	3 5 i ₅ 3	2 5 7 ₅ 2
3 5 3 ₅ i ₅₃	4 6 4 ₆ i	3 5 3 ₅ i ₅₃	2 5 2 ₅ 7
3 ₅ i 5 3	4 ₆ i 6 4	3 ₅ i 5 3	2 ₅ 7 5 2
3 ₅ i 5 i ₅	4 ₆ i 6 i ₆₄	3 ₅ i 5 i ₅₃	2 ₅ 7 5 7
3 ₅ i ₅ 3 5	4 ₆ i ₆ 4 6 4	3 ₅ i ₅ 3 5	2 ₅ 7 ₅ 2 5

Dictation.

1st - Nos. 194 & 195 . (page 86.)

2nd - No - 113 following large arrow and first column of No 115 .(p. 45.)

Staff (Time.)

T - gives the sound of DO for DO.

P - name first, then sing . T - gives the sound of RÉ for DO.

P

No. 50.

sol

51

KEY OF SOL .(5 - i)   **Solfa .**

No 60. |ı̇50ı̇|750ż|ı̇567|ı̇żȧ.|ż50ı̇|ż50ı̇|żȧı̇ȧ|żı̇67|ı̇50ı̇|750ż|

|ı̇575|ı̇5ı̇ȧ|ȧż05|ȧż07|żı̇76|6.5.|5607|7ı̇0ȧ|ȧż04|4ȧ0ȧ|ȧżoȧ|

|żı̇oı̇|7ı̇6ı̇|7...|5607|7ı̇0ȧ|ȧż04|4ȧ5.|.4ȧż|4ȧżı̇|5.ż.|ı̇...∎

Duett.

KEY OF DO .   *Fine.*

No 33. | 5 |ı̇5ı̇ż|ȧ.0ȧ|żı̇żȧ|ı̇.0 | ı̇ |żżı̇5|ȧ.ı̇ı̇|żżı̇5|ȧ.ı̇5|
        | 5 |ȧ5ȧ5|5.0ı̇|7655|ı̇.0 | ı̇ |5535|ı̇.ı̇ı̇|5535|ı̇.ı̇5|

SIXTY FIFTH LESSON.
Intonation.

Review Nos. 214 & 215.

KEY OF RE . **No 216.**   **No 217.**

ı̇	76	5	3	5	ı̇		ı̇	7	6	4	6	ı̇		ı̇	76	5	3	5	ı̇
ı̇		5	3	5			ı̇		6	4	6			ı̇		5	3	5	
ı̇		5	3	ı̇			ı̇		6	4	ı̇			ı̇		5	3	ı̇	
ı̇		5	ı̇5ȧ				ı̇		6	ı̇6·4				ı̇		5	ı̇	3	5ı̇
ı̇	5	ȧ	5	ı̇			ı̇	6	4	6	ı̇			ı̇	5	ȧ	5	ı̇	
ı̇	5	ȧ	5	ȧ			ı̇	6	4	6	4			ı̇	5	ȧ	5	ȧ	5ı̇
ı̇	5	ȧ	ı̇	5			ı̇	6	4	ı̇	6			ı̇	5	ȧ	ı̇	5	

7	5	2	5	7
7	5	2	5	
7	5	2	7	
7	5	7ı̇ż	57	
7ı̇ż	5	7		
7ı̇ż	5	2	57	
7ı̇ż	7	5		

Dictation.

1st - Nos . 195 and 196 . (page 86 & 87)
2nd - N° 114 following large arrow and second column of N° 115 . (p. 45)

KEY OF FA .

Time .

N° 110.		N° 111.		N° 112.		N° 113.	
1 2 3 5	. 3 2 3	1 2 3 5	0 3 2 3	1 2 3 5	. 3 2 3	1 2 3 5	0 3 2 3
1 2 3 5	. 3 2 .	1 2 3 5	0 2 2 0	1 2 3 5	. 3 2 0	1 2 3 5	0 2 2 .
1 2 3 .	. 5 3 2	1 2 3 0	0 5 2 3	1 2 3 .	0 5 3 2	1 2 3 .	0 5 2 3
1 2 3 .	. 5 2 .	1 2 3 0	0 2 5 0	1 2 3 .	0 5 2 0	1 2 3 0	0 2 5 .
1 . 2 .	. 5 2 3	1 0 2 0	0 5 2 3	1 . 2 0	0 5 2 3	1 0 2 .	0 5 2 3
1 . 2 .	. 5 2 .	1 0 2 0	0 5 2 0	1 . 2 0	0 5 2 0	1 0 2 .	. 5 2 .
1 . . .	. 2 5 2	1 0 0 0	0 2 5 2	1 . . .	0 2 5 2	1 . . 0	0 2 5 2
1 . . .	. 2 5 .	1 0 0 0	0 2 5 0	1 . . .	0 2 5 0	1 . . 0	0 2 5 .

Staff .

P - first name , then sing . T - gives the sound of RÉ for DO .

N° 51.

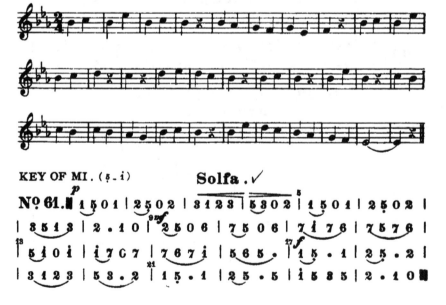

KEY OF MI . (5 - i)

Solfa . ✓

N° 61. | 1 5 0 1 | 2 5 0 2 | 3 1 2 3 | 5 3 0 2 | 1 5 0 1 | 2 5 0 2 |
| 3 5 1 3 | 2 . 1 0 | 2 5 0 6 | 7 5 0 6 | 7 1 7 6 | 7 5 7 6 |
| 5 1 0 1 | 1 7 0 7 | 7 6 7 1 | 5 6 5 . | 1 5 . 1 | 2 5 . 2 |
| 3 1 2 3 | 5 3 . 2 | 1 5 . 1 | 2 5 . 5 | 1 5 3 5 | 2 . 1 0 ∎

Duett.

Sing by syllables first, then on *la*.

KEY OF MI.   **N? 34.**

1 2 3 4	5..0	6 6 i 6	5..0	4 4 6 4	3 3 5 3
Children all will	tell,	They like candy	well,	But these words I	give in warning
1 7 1 2	3..0	4 4 6 4	·3..0	2 2 4 2	1 1 3 1

2 2 4 2	1 . 1 3	5 . 1 3	5 . 1 3	5 5 6 7	i .. O
little should they	take if too	much they don't	touch, Healthy	boys and girls they'll	make
7 7 6 7	4 . 1 1	3 . 1 1	3 . 1 1	3 3 4 4	3..O

SIXTY SIXTH LESSON
Intonation.
Review Nos. 214, 215, 216, 217 following large arrows.
Dictation.

1st – Nos. 197 and 198. (page 89.)

2nd – N? 116. (page 46.)

Staff (Time.)

T – gives the sound of SI for DO.

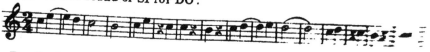

Pupils first name in time then sing - Teacher will explain that $\frac{2}{4}$ which is placed at the beginning of a piece of music means each meas-ure should contain the value of three quarter notes, and that three beats should be counted therein also reminding P- of the value of the dotted half note.

T- gives the sound of MI for DO.

N? 52.

KEY OF RÉ. (5 _ i)   **Solfa.**

N?62. |5i07|5i07|7605|5433|5i07 5i07 4717 4050
|5605|5i03|4345|4030|5605 5i0i 7737 7....
|5i·7|5i·7|76·5|5432|5i·7 74·5 i255 2·10

Duett.

Review last one as before, then add the words

SIXTY SEVENTH LESSON

Intonation.

KEY OF SOL.

Nº 218.

4 3 2 2 1 7	7 1 2 2 3 4
4 3 2 2 1 7	7 1 2 2 3 4
4 2 2 7	7 2 2 4
4 2 7	7 2 4

Nº 219.

7 1 2 2 3 4	4 3 2 2 1 7
7 1 2 2 3 4	4 3 2 2 1 7
7 2 2 4	4 2 2 7
7 2 4	4 2 7

Nº 220.

4 2 7 7 2 4	4 2 7 7 2 4
4 2 2 4	4 2 2 4
4 2 2 4	4 2 4

Nº 221.

7 2 4 4 2 7	7 2 4 4 2 7
7 2 2 7	7 2 2 7
7 2 2 7	7 2 7

Nº 222.

4 2 4 4 2 7 4	7 2 7 7 2 4 7
4 2 4 2 7	7 2 7 2 4

Nº 223.

7 2 7 7 2 4 7	4 2 4 4 2 7 4
7 2 7 2 4	4 2 4 2 7

Nº 224.

4 2 2 4 2 7	7 2 2 7 2 4
4 2 2 4 2 7	7 2 2 7 2 4
4 2 2 4 2 7	7 2 2 7 2 4
4 2 4 2 7	7 2 7 2 4

Nº 225.

7 2 2 7 2 4	4 2 2 4 2 7
7 2 2 7 2 4	4 2 2 4 2 7
7 2 7 2 4	4 2 4 2 7
7 2 7 4	4 2 4 7

Dictation.

1st - Nos. 198 & 199. (page 89 & 90)

2nd - Nos. 119 & 120. (page 48)

Time.

KEY OF SOL.

Nº 114.		Nº 115.		Nº 116.		Nº 117.	
1 2 . .	. 5 2 3	1 2 0 0	0 5 2 3	1 2 . .	0 5 2 3	1 2 . 0	0 5 2 3
1 2 . .	. 5 2 .	1 2 0 0	0 5 2 0	1 2 . .	0 5 2 0	1 2 . 0	0 5 2 .
1 . 2 3	. . 5 2	1 0 2 3	0 0 5 2	1 . 2 3	. 0 5 2	1 0 2 3	. . 5 2
1 . 2 3	. . 2 .	1 0 2 3	0 0 5 0	1 . 2 3	. 0 2 0	1 0 2 3	. 0 5 .
1 2 3 5	. . . 2	1 2 3 5	0 0 0 5	1 2 3 5	. . 0 2	1 2 3 5	. 0 0 5
1 3 2 .	. . . 5	1 3 5 0	0 0 0 5	1 3 2 .	. . 0 5	1 3 5 .	. 0 0 5
1 . 2 .	. . . 5	1 0 5 0	0 0 0 5	1 . 2 .	. 0 0 5	1 0 5 .	. 0 0 5
1 . . .	. . . 5	5 0 0 0	0 0 0 5	1 . . .	. 0 0 5	5 . . 0	0 0 0 5

P_ name first then sing. T_ gives the sound of MI for DO.

N⁰ 53.

Solfa. N⁰ 63.✓

$\dfrac{4}{2}$

KEY OF SOL. (5 _ 5)

| 5505 | 3303 | 4404 | 2202 | 5101 | 5203 | 5803 | 4202 |
| 5505 | 3303 | 4404 | 2202 | 5101 | 5203 | 5803 | 2510 |

Round.

This round can be sung in two, three or four voices _ according to the number of pupils in the class. In order to be sure of keeping correct time P_ must say either mentally or softly *"TO"* when coming to the rests.

KEY OF LA.

A
| 1 | 2 | 3 | 1 | 2 | 7 | 1 | 5 |
| Though to | us | our | sing ing's | play ing |

B
| 3 | 4 | 5 | 3 | 4 | 2 | 3 | 1 |
| Yet | our | thoughts must not be | straying |

C
| 0 | 0 | 0 | 0 | 5 | 5 | 1 | 1 |
| | | Fix'd at _ | ten_tion |

D
| 0 | 0 | 0 | 0 | 5 | 5 | 5 | 3 |
| | | Must be | gi _ ven. |

SIXTY EIGHTH LESSON.
Intonation.

Review Nos. 218, 220, 222 & 224.

KEY OF SOL. N⁰ 226.

T_ will strictly watch the *FA* as P_ have a tendency to sing it too high. If the *FA* is correctly sung watch the *SI* which sometimes is sung too low.

4 2 7 2 4	2 7 2 4 2	7 2 7 2 4
4 2 7 2 4	2 7 2 4 2	7 2 7 2 4
4 2 7	2 7 2 4 2	7 2 4
4 2 7 2	2 7 2 4 7	7 2 4 2
4 2 4 2 7	2 7 2 4 2	7 2 4 7
4 2 7 2 4	2 4 2 7	7 2 4 2 7 2
4 2 7 2 7	2 4 2 7 2	7 2 4 2 7
4 2 7 2	2 4 2 7	7 2 4 2
4 2 7 2 4 2	2 4 2 7 4	7 2 4 2 4

Dictation.

1st _ Nos. 200 & 201, following large arrows, stopping at the vertical line.
2nd _ Nos 121, 122, 123 & 124. (page 49)   (p. 92)

Time.

When the voice utters several sounds for one beat each sound re-presents a fraction of the beat.

Writing must therefore express the division of beat.

As young children grasp with difficulty the idea of the word fraction the T_ will make it plain by drawing a circle on the board with a di-ametrical line, showing if half was taken away half would be left, impressing on the minds of the P_ that each side is called a half, and that two halves make a whole or one. Thus far P_ have only produced one sound to a beat_ they have executed beats that were not divided. (Explain what is meant by divided.)

We will now have to produce two sounds to each motion that is, for each beat. They will now execute beats divided by two that will be known as the "Binary" division _

BINARY DIVISION OF THE BEAT. When in the beat are found two sounds of equal duration each sound represents half of a beat. To express this division we group the two halves under a small horizontal dash, thus _ |$\overline{12}$ $\overline{34}$ |$\overline{54}$ $\overline{32}$| Each group represents a beat.

LANGUAGE OF DURATION. To express with precision the divisions of beats AIMÉE PARIS invented a language for duration applicable to every system of notation_

Two vowels $\ddot{a}$ and $\bar{a}$ mark the division of the beat by two. If the sound is expressed by a figure the vowel is preceded by the conso-nant t_ if a duration the vowel alone is used_ the rest by the word "to".

BINARY DIVISION OF TIME.

Ex.No 1. ‖$\overset{1}{1}$ $\overline{23}$ |$\overset{2}{1}$. $\overline{2}$ |$\overset{3}{3}$ $\overline{0}$ $\overline{02}$ |$\overset{4}{34}$. $\overline{5}$ |$\overset{5}{1}$. $\overline{0}$‖

tä ä tä tä   tä ä ä tä   tä to to tä   tä tä ä tä   tä ä ä to

Although not divided we know that a unit is the equal of two halves and it is for this reason we write the two syllables "tä ä" under the first beat of bars 1, 2 and 5.

Staff. (Time)

T_ gives the sound of SI for DO.

No 54.

Solfa. Nº 64.

KEY OF SOL. (5 - 5)

‖ 5305 | 5205 | 5101 | 7607 | 1203 | 3203 | 2000 | 5000 |

| 5305 | 5205 | 5101 | 7607 | 1302 | 4305 | 6005 | 1000 ‖

Practice the exercise on *ah* on the chart with the two pointers making the crescendo and decrescendo in a single breath _ of course it must be short at first.

SIXTY NINTH LESSON.

Intonation.

Review Nº 226 by single col.

KEY OF RÉ.

Nº 227.

2 3 4	4 5 6	6 5 4	4 3 2
2 3 4	4 5 6	6 5 4	4 3 2
2 4	4 6	6 4	4 2
2 4	6	6 4	2

Nº 228.

6 5 4	4 3 2	2 3 4	4 5 6
6 5 4	4 3 2	2 3 4	4 5 6
6 4	4 2	2 4	4 6
6 4	2	2 4	6

Nº 229.

2 4 6	6 4 2	2 4 6	6 4 2
2 4 6	4 2	2 4	4 2
2 4	4 2	2 4	2

Nº 230.

6 4 2	2 4 6	6 4 2	2 4 6
6 4 2	4 6	6 4	4 6
6 4	4 6	6 4	6

Nº 231.

2 4 2	2 4 6 2	6 4 6	6 4 2 6
2 4	2 4 6	6 4	6 4 2

Nº 232.

6 4 6	6 4 2 6	2 4 2	2 4 6 2
6 4	6 4 2	2 4	2 4 6

Nº 233.

2 4	4 2 4 6	6 4	4 6 4 2
2 4	4 2 4 6	6 4	4 6 4 2
2 4	2 4 6	6 4	6 4 2
2 4	2 6	6 4	6 2

Nº 234.

6 4	4 6 4 2	2 4	4 2 4 6
6 4	4 6 4 2	2 4	4 2 4 6
6 4	6 4 2	2 4	2 4 6
6 4	6 2	2 4	2 6

Dictation.

1st _ Nos 202 and 203 following large arrows and stopping at each vertical line. (page 93)

2nd _ Nº 125. (page 51)

Remind P— of what has been said about the division of the beat in previous lesson. Then have all P— move their hands down and up saying the two syllables *tä tä* at each beat the motion to take place on tä.

Staff.

P— name first then sing. T— gives the sound of MI for DO.

Nº 55.,

Fine.

D.C.

KEY OF RÉ. (7 — ż)   **Solfa.** ✔

p
Nº 65. | 3̄2̄05 | 3̄2̄05 | 6531 | 2504 | 3̄2̄05 | 3̄2̄05 | 5175 | 6.50 |

mf
| 5̄6̄05 | 5̄4̄05 | 4343 | 3.2, | 4504 | 4305 | 7̣103 | 2... |

f
| 3̄2̄.5 | 3̄2̄.5 | 6531 | 7̣5̄.4 | 4̣3̄,1 | 2̣1̣,6 | 65.7̣ | 7.10 ‖

KEY OF FA.   **Duett. Nº 35.**

1 3 4	5 6 5	4 3 2	3 . 0	1 3 4	5 6 5	4 3 2	3 0 5
1 1 2	3 4 3	2 1 7	1 . 0	1 1 2	3 4 3	2 1 7	1 0 3
5 0 3	2 0 4	6 0 5	3 0 1	3 0 1	6 5 4	3 4 2	1 . 0
3 0 1	7 0 2	4 0 3	1 0 1	1 0 1	4 3 3	1 2 7	1 . 0 ‖

SEVENTIETH LESSON.
Intonation.

Review Nos. 227, 229, 231 & 233.

KEY OF FA. **Nº 235.**

It is with intention that the following exercise comes after Nº 218 although much easier. Had it come first the P— having slightly memorized the perfect minor chord 2— 4—6 would never have sung the *FA* perfectly in the chord 7—2—4. They would always have sung *FA* sharp.

2 4 2 4 6	4 2 4 6 4	6 4 2 4 6
2 4 2 ₄ 6	4 2 4 6	6 4 2 ₄ 6
2 4 6 4	4 2 ₄ 6	6 4 2
2 4 6	4 2 ₄ 6 2	6 4 2 4
2 4 6 ₄ 2	4 2 ₄ 6 4	6 4 6 2
2 6 2 4	4 6 4 2	6 2 4 6
2 6 4 2	4 6 ₄ 2	6 2 4 2
2 6 4	4 6 ₄ 2 4	6 2 4
2 6 4 6	4 6 ₄ 2 6	6 2 6 4

Dictation.

1st _ Nos. 204 and 205 following large arrows. (page 94.)

2nd _ Nos. 126 and 128 starting from *DO* so P_ can recognize the *MI*, and following large arrows. (page 52.)

Time.

T_ writes on black-board the following_

P_ say time - name.

‖ 1̅ 2̅ 3̅ 4̅ | 5̅ 4̅ 3 ‖ 1̅ 2̅ 3 | 4̅ 3̅ 2 ‖ 1 2̅ 3̅ |

tä tä tä tä   tä tä tä ä   tä tä tä ä   tä tä tä ä   tä ä tä tä

| 4̅ 5̅ 4̅ 3̅ ‖ 1 2̅ 3̅ | 4̅ 3̅ 2 ‖ 1 2 | 3̅ 4̅ 5 ‖

tä tä .tä tä   tä ä tä tä   tä tä tä ä   tä ä tä ä   tä tä tä ä

Call attention to the "tä ä" when meeting a note by itself. Repeat each couple of measures several times then after this the ten measures straight forward.

Staff. No 56.

T_ explains that in $\frac{4}{4}$ time each measure should contain the value of four quarter notes.

Count four beats to each measure.

P_ name first then sing T_ gives the sound of MI for DO.

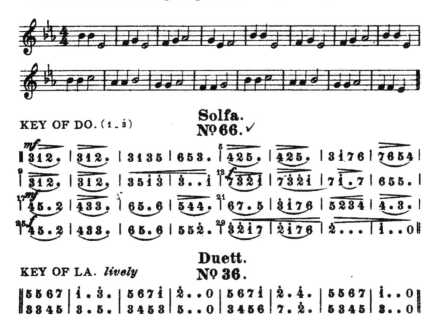

KEY OF DO. (1 _ 3)

Solfa.
No 66. ✓

mf

‖ 3̅1̅2 . | 3̅1̅2 . | 3135 | 653 . | 4̅2̅5 . | 4̅2̅5 . | 3̅1̅76 | 7̅6̅54 |

9 ‖ 3̅1̅2 , | 3̅1̅2 , | 3513 | 3 . . 1 | 7̅3̅2̇1 | 7̇3̅2̇1 | 7̇1̇ . 7 | 655 . |

17 *mf* ‖ 4̅5 . 2 | 4̅3̅3 , | 65 . 6 | 5̅4̅4 . | 67 . 5 | 3̅1̅76 | 5234 | 4 . 3 . |

25 ‖ 4̅5 . 2 | 4̅3̅3 , | 65 . 6 | 55̇2̇ . 7 | 3̅2̇1̇7 | 2̇1̇76 | 2 . . . | 1 . . 0 ‖

Duett.
No 36.

KEY OF LA. *lively*

‖ 5567 | 1̇ . 3̇ . | 567̇1̇ | 2̇ . . 0 | 567̇1̇ | 2̇ . 4̇ . | 5567 | 1̇ . . 0 ‖

‖ 3345 | 3 . 5 . | 3453 | 5 . . 0 | 3456 | 7 . 2̇ . | 5345 | 3 . . 0 ‖

SEVENTY FIRST LESSON.
Intonation.

Review N? 235._

After having sung N? 236 and before taking N? 237 sing last column FA-RÉ-SI-RÉ-FA by itself.

Repeat first line of each N?, three or four times.

KEY OF FA. N? 236.   N? 237.

5	3	1	3	5	6	4	2	4	6	5	3	1	3	5	4	2	7	2	4
5	3	1	3	5	6	4	2	4	6	5	3	1	3	5	4	2	7	2	4
5	3	1	3	5	6	4	2	4	6	5	3	1	3		4	2	7	2	
5	3	1	3	5	6	4	2	4	6	5	3	1	3		4	2	7	2	
5	3	5	1	3 5	6	4	6	2	4	5	3	5	1	3	4	2	4	7	
5	1	3	5		6	2	4	6		5	1	3	5		4 2 7	2	4		
5	1	3	1 3 5		6	2	4	2	4	5	1	3	1	3	4 2 7	2	7		
5	1	3	5		6	2	4			5	1	3			4 2 7	2			
5	1	5	3	5	6	2	6	4		5	1	5	3		4 2 7 2	4	2		

Dictation.

1st _ Nos. 206 and 207 following large arrows. (page 95.)

2nd _ Nos. 127 and 129 starting with *DO, RÉ, MI* following large arrows. (page 52.)

Time.

T_ writes on board the following_

Call attention to the two vowels ä ä under the dot, then proceed as before pointing the first two measures several times, then the next two and so on until all are named _ then sing every two measures several times, then across the entire line.

Staff.(Time)

N? 57.

T_ gives the sound of SI for DO.

Nº 67. ‖5i..│5i..│5i3i│76i.│i6..│i5..│i543│52..│
│5i..│5i..│322i│i7..│67i6│567i│6...│5..0│
│52..│52..│5i23│532i│52..│52..│5i23│5...│
│432i│32i7│2i76│i765│i654│35i3│2...│i...‖

Duett.

KEY OF LA _ to be sung the two parts together at first reading.

Nº 37.
│5│3.2│i.7│7.6│5.5│i.i│2.2│3..│
│5│i.7│6.5│4..│3.5│6.6│7.7│i..│

│.05│4.3│2.i│7.6│5.i│3.3│2.2│i.│
│.05│2.i│7.6│5.4│3.3│5.5│4.4│3.‖

SEVENTY SECOND LESSON.

Intonation.

Review Nos. 236 and 237 following large arrows.

KEY OF FA. Nº 238.   Nº 239.

3	1	3	5	3		4	2	4	6	4		3	1	3	5	3		2	7	2	4	2	
3	1	3	5	3		4	2	4	6	4		3	1	3	5	3		2	7	2	4	2	
3	1	3	5			4	2	4	6			3	1	3	5	3		2	7	2	4		
3	1	3	5	1		4	2	4	6	2		3	1	3	5	1		2	7	2	4	7	2
3	1	3	5	3		4	2	4	6	4		3	1	3	5	3		2	7	2	4	2	
3	5	3	1	3		4	6	4	2			3	5	3	1			2	4	2	7	2	
3	5	3	1			4	6	4	2			3	5	3	1			2	4	2	7	2	
3	5	3	1	3		4	6	4	2	4		3	5	3	1	3		2	4	2	7	2	
3	5	3	1	5		4	6	4	2	6		3	5	3	1	5	3	2	4	2	7	2	4

Dictation.

1st _ Nos. 208 and 209 following large arrows. (page 97.)

2nd _ Nos. 130 and 132 following large arrows. (page 54.)

Time.

T_ writes on board the same exercise as at previous lesson but this time omitting the time-name syllables which before were written under the figures.

Ex. |1̄ 2̄ 3̄ 4̄ | 5 . ‖ 1̄ 2̄ etc. P― to place the syllables according to the time― tä tä whenever two signs of articulation are grouped under one dash $\left(\begin{smallmatrix}\overline{1\ 2}\\ t\ddot{a}\ t\ddot{a}\end{smallmatrix}\right)$ tä ä $\left(\begin{smallmatrix}1\\ t\ddot{a}\ \ddot{a}\end{smallmatrix}\right)$ for one single sign of articulation and ä ä for the one beat duration: $\left(\begin{smallmatrix}\cdot\\ \ddot{a}\ a\end{smallmatrix}\right)$

Staff.

T― will remind the P― of the half rest(▬) and its value in $\frac{4}{4}$ time.
P― name first then sing, T― gives the sound of MI for DO.

№ 58.

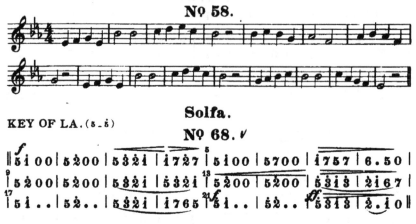

KEY OF LA.(5.5̣)

Solfa.
№ 68. ✔

f
‖5̇1 00|5̇200|5̇3̇2̇1̇ |1̇727|5̇100|5̇700|1̇757|6 . 50|
|5̇200|5̇200|5̇3̇2̇1̇|5̇3̇2̇1̇|5̇200|5̇200|5̇3̇1̇3̇|2̇1̇67|
|5̇1..|5̇2..|5̇3̇2̇1̇|1̇765|5̇1..|5̇2..|5̇3̇1̇3̇|2̇.1̇0‖

KEY OF SOL.

Duett.

First part should rehearse the skip (3─6) before starting.

№38.‖005̣|1.3|5.3|5.3|2.3|1.3|653|653|2.2|321|
‖005̣|1.1|3.1|3.1|5.5̣|1.1|171|171|5ˣ5̣|176|

|5.2|321|5.2|321|542|321|5.5̣|1.3|653|2..|1.0‖
|5.5̣|176|5.5̣|171|327|176|5.5̣|1.1|171|5..|1.0‖

SEVENTY THIRD LESSON.
Intonation.

Review Nos. 238 and 239.
If necessary take each col. separately before taking two.
The first line should be repeated two or three times when taking two col.

KEY OF FA. **Nº 240.** **Nº 241.**

1 3 5 3 1	2 4 6 4 2	1 3 5 3 1	7 2 4 2 7
1 3 5 3 1	2 4 6 4 2	1 3 5 3 1	7 2 4 2 7
1 3 5 3	2 4 6 4 2	1 3 5 3 1	7 2 4 2
1 3 5 3	2 4 6 4 2	1 3 5 3 1	7 2 4
1 3 5 3 1 3	2 4 6 4 2 4	1 3 5 3 1 3	7 2 4 2 7 2
1 3 5 3 1	2 4 6 4 2	1 3 5 3 1	7 2 4 2 7
1 3 5 3 5 3	2 4 6 4 6 4 2	1 3 5 3 5	7 2 4 2 4
1 3 5 3	2 4 6 4 2	1 3 5 3	7 2 4 2

Dictation.

1st _ Nos. 210 and 211. (page 98.)

2nd _ Nos. 131 and 133 following large arrows starting with *DO, RÉ, MI.* (page 54.)

Time.

Nº 118 will now be read by P_ with the time-name speaking *tä tä* etc._ Then sing following the first arrow. Do the same work with the next one; first, time name, then sing and so on until the whole exercise has been spoken with time name and sung.

KEY OF SOL. **Time. Nº 218.**

1234	5432	123	4543	1 23	4543	1 2	3432	1 .	2345
1234	543	123	432	1 23	432	1 2	345	1 .	232
1234	5 43	123	4 32	1 23	4 32	1 2	3 45	1 .	2 32
1234	3 2	123	4 5	1 23	4 5	1 2	3 2	1 .	2 3
1234	5 .	123	2 .	1 23	2 .	1 2	3 .	1 .	2 .

Staff.

T_ remind P_ the value of the whole note.

P_ name first then sing, T_ gives the sound of RÉ for DO.

Nº 59.

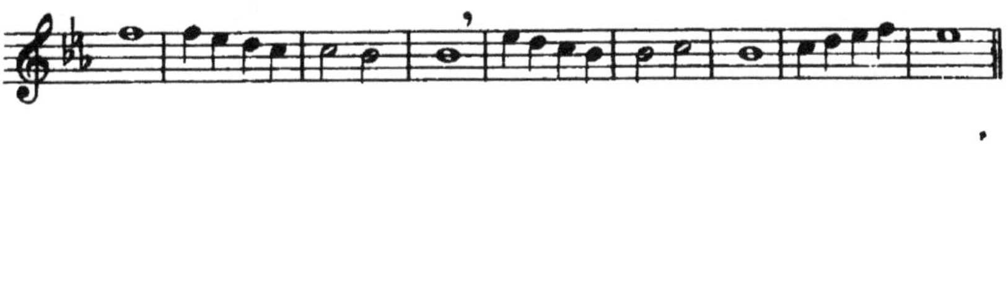

KEY OF LA. (1 . 5) **Solfa.** ✓

No 69. *mf*
|1 . . 3 |2 . . 4 |3 5 i 6 |6 5 5 . |4 . . 5 |3 . . i |i 5 4 3 |5 2 2 . |

|1 . . 3 |2 . . 4 |3 5 i 6 |6 7 7 . |i . . 3 |2 5 5 i |6 . . 7 |6 5 5 . |

|5 . . i |i 7 7 . |5 . . i |i 7 2 . |5 . . i |7 6 5 6 |5 2 3 4 |4 . 3 . |

|5 . . i |i 7 7 . |5 . . i |i 7 2 . |i 5 4 3 |2 i 7 6 |i . 2 . |i . . 0 |

KEY OF MI. **Duett. No 39.** (without words)

Let us cheer the stars and stripes. *Lively with spirit*

f
1 3	3 .	2 4	4 .	3 5	3 5	2 2	2 .
Let us	sing!	shout our	praise!	to the	land we	love, Hur-	rah!!
1 1	1 .	7 2	2 .	1 3	1 7	5 5	5 .

1 3	3 .	2 4	4 .	5 5	6 7	i i	i .	*Fine.*
Flags we	bring!	Banners	raise!	Cheer the	stars and	stripes Hur-	rah!!
1 1	1 .	7 2	2 .	3 3	4 5	3 3	3 .

mf
1 3	5 5	6 6	6 .	5 6	5 6	5 4	3 .
All our	hearts are	filled with	pride	Dear-est	land of	lib - er -	ty
1 1	3 3	4 4	4 .	3 4	3 4	3 2	1 .

1 3	5 5	6 6	6 .	5 6	5 6	5 4	3 .	*D.C.*
And what	e - ver	ill be -	tide,	We shall	al - ways	stand by	thee.
1 1	3 3	4 4	4 .	3 4	3 4	3 2	1 .

SEVENTY FOURTH LESSON.

Intonation.

Review Nos. 236, 237, 238, 239, 240 & 241 following large arrows.

Dictation.

1st _ Nos. 212 and 213. (page 99)

2nd _ Nos. 135 and 136 by large arrows _ begin with *DO, RÉ, MI.*
(page 57)

Time.

Review time Nos. 118 to 122 by single numbers without the time-name.

Staff. Nº 60. (Time).

T_ gives the sound of DO for DO.

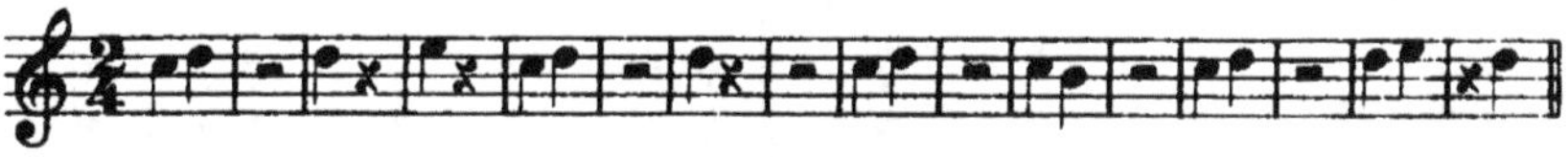

Solfa. Nº 70.

KEY OF SOL. (5_5)

|3131|4004|3131|2002|3131|4004|3213|5000|5353|4242|

|3543|2000|3216|7020|3020|1650|1235|4003|2003|1000‖

Duett.

Review last duett, adding the words to it.

SEVENTY FIFTH LESSON.

Intonation.

STUDY OF THE CHORD OF SEVENTH OF DOMINANT.

Though this chord has been already prepared by the chords 5 7 2 and 7 2 4 P_ generally experience a certain difficulty on account of having in their mind the chord 5 7 2 5. It is therefore important that T_ should go slowly and carefully watching the *FA* which is generally intoned too high. This chord is one of the bases of the modern musical system and its mastery is of the greatest importance.

KEY OF LA.

Nº 242.

567 712 234	432 217 765
567 712 234	432 217 765
5 7 7 2 2 4	4 2 2 7 7 5
5 7 2 2 2 4	4 2 2 7 7 5
5 7 2 4	4 2 7 5

Nº 243.

432 217 765	567 712 234
432 217 765	567 712 234
4 2 2 7 7 5	5 7 7 2 2 4
4 2 2 7 7 5	5 7 7 2 2 4
4 2 7 5	5 7 2 4

Nº 244.

5724 4275	5724 4275
572 275	572 275
57 75	57 75

Nº 245.

4275 5724	4275 5724
427 724	427 724
42 24	42 24

Nº 246.

575 5725 57245	424 4274 42754
57 572 5724	42 427 4275
57 572 5724	42 427 4275
57 572 5724	42 427 4275
57 52 54	42 47 45

Nº 247.

4 2 4	4 2 7 4	4 2 7 5 4	5 7 5	5 7 2 5	5 7 2 4 5
4 2	4 2 7	4 2 7 5	5 7	5 7 2	5 7 2 4
4 2	4 2 7	4 2 7 5	5 7	5 7 2	5 7 2 4
4 2	4 2 7	4 2 7 5	5 7	5 7 2	5 7 2 4
4 2	4 7	4 5	5 7	5 2	5 4

Dictation.

1st _ Nos. 214 and 215 as before following large arrows. (page 100)

2nd _ Nos. 137 and 138 following large arrows starting with *DO,RÉ,MI.* (page 58)

Time.

Having already an idea of time-name we will not spend so much time on the rest (0), still it is necessary for P_ to familiarize themselves with the new names.

T_ writes the following ‖ 1 0 2 0 (tä to tä to) | 3 0 2 0 (tä to tä to) ‖ 1 2 3 4 (tä tä tä tä) | 3 0 2 0 (tä to tä to) ‖

‖ 1 2 3 0 (tä ta tä to) | 2 0 0 (tä to to-o) ‖ 1 0 (tä-ā to-o) | 2 0 (tä ā to-o) ‖

Study every two measures separately as before then the whole line. (time-name only)

Staff.

We will now place our first degree of the scale on the second line announcing the change to P_ and of the necessity for great attention. T_ will illustrate on black-board.

T_ will then use the Meloplast with pointer taking the first degree or *DO* on the second line placing the figures 1, 3, 5, on the three middle lines showing that the next spaces are *RÉ, FA, LA*, etc, etc. _ After pointing a little while T_ will erase 2,4 and 6 then proceeding as before point without these figures.

KEY OF LA. (1-6) **Solfa.** ✓

Nº 71. ‖ *mf* 1003 | 500i | i772 | 2ii0 | 5004 | 3003 | 4321 | 2550 |

9 1003 | 500i | i776 | 7i20 | 13 3001 | 327i | 6007 | 6550 |

17 *f* 500i | i765 | 500i | i725 | 21 500i | 2323 | 2i2i | 7676 |

25 5..i | i765 | 5..i | i725 | 29 *ff* 5..3 | i234 | 2... | i..0 ‖

Far away from home. *slowly with feeling.*

p
| 5 . 6 7 | i . 2̇ i | 7 . 6 5 | 5 . 3 . |
NO 40. | Back to my | home to that | land would I · | flee |
p
| 3 . 4 5 | 3 . 4 3 | 2 . 4 4 | 3 . 1 . |

5 . 6 7	i . 2̇ i	7 . 6 7	i . . .	3̇ . i 2̇	3̇ . i 2̇
Un _ der whose	pines my heart	was e_ver	free	My tears fall	fast, shall I
3 . 4 5	3 . 4 3	2 . 4 4	3 . . .	5 . 3 4	5 . 3 4

3̇ . 4 3	3̇ . 2̇ .	2̇ . 7 i	2̇ . 7 i	pp 2̇ 3̇ . 2̇	i . . 0
yet reach my	home	o _ ver the	sea from it	never to	roam.
5 . 6 5	5 . 4 .	4 . 2 3	4 . 2 3	4 5 . 4	3 . . 0

SEVENTY SIXTH LESSON.

Intonation.

These exercises done on the chord of the dominant seventh are more difficult than those done on the perfect chords of *DO, SOL* and *FA* and require greater attention from P_ the interval 7-4̇ being often missed. Review Nos. 242 to 247 inclusive.

KEY OF LA. NO 248.   NO 249.

57	7572̇	2̇72̇4	42̇	2̇42̇7	7275	42̇	2̇42̇7	7275	57	7572̇	2̇72̇4
57	75 2̇	27₂4	42̇	2̇42̇7	72̇75	42̇	2̇42̇7	72̇75	57	7572̇	272̇4
57	75 2̇	272̇4	42̇	2̇42̇7	72̇75	42̇	2̇42̇7	72̇75	57	7572̇	272̇4
57	75 2̇	27 4	42̇	2̇4 7	72̇ 5	42̇	2̇4 7	72̇ 5	57	75 2̇	2̇7 4
57	7 5 2̇	27 4	42̇	2̇42̇7	72̇ 5	42̇	2̇4 7	72̇ 5	57	7 5 2̇	2̇7 4
57	7 5 2̇	27 4	42̇	2̇42̇7	72̇ 5	42̇	2̇4 7	72̇ 5	57	7 5 2̇	2̇7 4
57	5 2̇	7 4	42̇	4 7	2̇ 5	42̇	4 7	2̇ 5	57	5 2̇	7 4

Dictation.

1st _ Nos. 216 and 217 following large arrow. (page 101)

2nd _ NO 139 beginning with DO, RÉ, MI. (page 58)

Time.

Review previous exercise and when satisfactorily done erase the time-name and have the P_ still do the same work speaking time-name only.

T_ will point to the staff illustration given at last lesson leaving only 1 on the second line and 5 on the fourth of course pointing the notes in succession ascending and descending.

KEY OF MI. (5 _ i)   ✓**Solfa.** Look out at bars 16 & 17 for skip
(6-2)

Nọ 72. ‖ 5.50 | 5.50 | 4321 | 1765 | 5.50 | 5.5.| .513 | 2.10 |

| 2.50 | 2.50 | 6535 | 1776 | 7.50 | 7.50 | 6767 | 6..0 |

| 2.50 | 2.50 | 6535 | 1776 | 7.50 | 6.70 | 1135 | 6.50 |

| 5.5.| 5.5.| 4321 | 1765 | 5.5.| 5.5.| .313 | 2167 |

| 5.5.| 5.5.| .432 | 2176 | 5.5.| 1.i.| .153 | 2.10 |

Duett.

Review last duett singing first by notes, then on *la*, then adding words.

SEVENTY SEVENTH LESSON.
Intonation.

Review Nos. 242 to 249 inclusive, following large arrows.

Dictation.

1st _ Nos. 218 to 225 inclusive. (page 104.)
2nd _ Nos. 140 and 141. (page 60.)

Time.

By small arrows only. First, speak the time-name   then sing. While singing do not forget to name the rest in strict time as P_generally make the one beat rest too short.

KEY OF FA. _ Use time-name first.

Nọ 119.

1234	5432	1230	4543	1023	4543	1020	3432	100	2345
1234	5430	1230	4320	1023	4320	1020	3450	100	2320
1234	5043	1230	4032	1023	4032	1020	3045	100	2032
1234	3020	1230	4050	1023	4050	1020	3020	100	2030
1234	500	1230	200	1023	200	1020	300	100	200

If T_ can spare the time it is better to have the following exercise on the board and to remind P_ that DO is on the second line, MI on the third line and SOL on the fourth line; that *DO, MI, SOL* are on the three middle lines. Repeat this exercise several times naming only.

DO

Solfa. ✓

Lookout at bar 24 for the skip from LA to RÉ.

KEY OF RÉ. (₅ - ₂̇)

N.° 73. ‖ 3 1 0 ₅ | 3 1 0 ₅ | 5 3 1 i̇ | . 5 4 3 | ⁵4 2 0 5 | 3 1 0 i̇ | i̇ 7 i̇ 7 | 7 6 5 4 |

| 3 1 0 ₅ | 3 1 0 ₅ | 5 3 1 i̇ | . 6 6 . | . 7 i̇ 2̇ . | 2̇ i̇ 0 5 | 6 5 0 2 | 3 . . . ‖

¹⁷| 2 5 0 7 | 7 6 0 i̇ | 7 6 5 6 | 6 7 0 2̇ | 2̇ i̇ 0 i̇ | i̇ 7 0 7 | 7 6 7 6 | 6 . . . |

²⁵| 2 5 0 7 | 7 6 0 i̇ | 7 6 7 i̇ | 2̇ . . . | ²⁹. i̇ . 6 | i̇ 7 . 5 | 7 6 . 7 | 5 . . . ‖

Duett. N.° 41.

This duett can be sung in the two parts together without rehearsing each line.

KEY OF FA.

‖| 1 . 1 | 3 . 3 | 2 1 2 | 1 . 0 | 3 . 3 | 5 . 5 | 4 3 4 | 3 . 0 |
‖| 1 . 1 | 1 . 1 | 7 6̣ 7 | 1 . 0 | 1 . 1 | 3 . 3 | 2 1 2 | 1 . 0 |
| 2 . 2 | 4 . 4 | 2 3 4 | 5 . . | 4 . 2 | 1 . 1 | 2 3 2 | 1 . 0 ‖|
| 7 . 7 | 2 . 2 | 7 1 2 | 3 . . | 2 . 7 | 1 . 1 | 7 6̣ 7 | 1 . 0 ‖|

SEVENTY EIGHTH LESSON.
Intonation.

Review Nos. 248 and 249 accent notes 1-2-3-4-3-2-1-7.

KEY OF FA.

N.° 250.

1 5	1 2 5	2 3 5	3 4 5	4 3 5	3 2 5	2 1 5	1 7 5	7 1
1 5	1 2 5	2 3 5	3 4 5	4 3 5	3 2 5	2 1 5	1 7 5	7 1
1 5	₁ 2 5	₂ 3 5	₃ 4 5	₄ 3 5	₃ 2 5	₂ 1 5	₁ 7 5	₇ 1
1 5	₁ 2 5	₂ 3 5	₃ 4 5	₄ 3 5	₃ 2 5	2 1 5	₁ 7 5	₇ 1
R.₋1 5	2 5	3 5	4 5	3 5	2 5	1 5	7 5	1

No 251.

```
1 5    1 2 5    2 3 5    3 4 5    4 3 5    3 2 5    2 1 5    1 7 5    7 1
1 5    1 2 5    2 3 5    3 4 5    4 3 5    3 2 5    2 1 5    1 7 5    7 1
1 5    1 2 5    2 3 5    3 4 5    4 3 5    3 2 5    2 1 5    1 7 5    7 1
1 5    1 2 5    2 3 5    3 4 5    4 3 5    3 2 5    2 1 5    1 7 5      1
R_1 5    2 5    3 5    4 5    3 5    2 5    1 5    7 5    1
```

Dictation.

1st _ No 226 following large arrow. (page 105)
2nd _ Nos. 142 and 143 by small groups. (page 60)

Time.

Review No 119.

Staff. (No 62.)

Repeat several times.

DO

KEY OF SOL. P_name first. **Solfa.** ∨
(1_5)
No 74. ‖ 1̄7̄1 | 2̄3̄2 | 3̄3̄5̄3 | 2̄3̄2 | 1̄7̄1 | 2̄2̄2 | 3̄3̄5̄4 | 3̄2̄1 ‖ Fine

| 2̄4̄3 | 4̄3̄2 | 3̄1̄5̄3 | 2̄2̄2 | 2̄4̄3 | 2̄7̄2 | 1̄2̄3̄7 | 5̄5̄5̄ ‖ D.C.

KEY OF DO. **Duett.**

No 42.
| 534 | 5.i | 7.6 | 6.5 | 563 | 4.4 | 5.2 | 3.0 | 534 | 5.i |
| 312 | 3.3 | 5.4 | 4.3 | 311 | 2.2 | 7.7 | 1.0 | 312 | 3.3 |

| 7.6 | 6.5 | 535 | i.i | 2̇. 2̇ | 3̇.. | 535 | i.i | 2̇.3 | i00 ‖
| 5.4 | 4.3 | 313 | 3.3 | 5. 5 | 5... | 313 | 3.3 | 5.5 | 300 ‖

SEVENTY NINTH LESSON.
Intonation.

Review Nos. 250 and 251 as if they were written in a single number,
then take Nos. 252 and 253.

```
 1 5   5 1₂5   5 2 3 5   5 3 4 5   5 4 3 5   5 3 2 5   5 2 1 5   5 1 7 5   5 7 1
 1 5   5 ₁2 5   5 ₂ 3 5   5 ₃ 4 5   5 ₄ 3 5   5 ₃ 2 5   5 ₂ 1 5   5 ₁ 7 5   5 7 1
 1 5   5 ₁2 5   5 ₂ 3 5   5 ₃ 4 5   5 ₄ 3 5   5 ₃ 2 5   5 ₂ 1 5   5 ₁ 7 5   5 7 1
R.1 5   5   2 5   5   3 5   5   4 5   5   3 5   5   2 5   5   1 5   5   7 5   5   1
```

Nº 253.

```
 1 5   5 1 2 5   5 2 3 5   5 3 4 5   5 4 3 5   5 3 2 5   5 2 1 5   5 1 7 5   5 7 1
 1 5   5 ₁ 2 5   5 ₂ 3 5   5 ₃ 4 5   5 ₄ 3 5   5 ₃ 2 5   5 ₂ 1 5   5 ₁ 7 5   5 7 1
 1 5   5 ₁ 2 5   5 ₂ 3 5   5 ₃ 4 5   5 ₄ 3 5   5 ₃ 2 5   5 ₂ 1 5   5 ₁ 7 5   5 7 1
R.1 5   5   2 5   5   3 5   5   4 5   5   3 5   5   2 5   5   1 5   5   7 5   5   1
```

Dictation.

1ˢᵗ- Nos. 227 to 234 inclusive following large arrows. (page 107)

2ⁿᵈ- Nos. 144 and 145 beginning with DO_RÉ_MI_FA_SOL. (page 61)

Time Nº 120.

KEY OF FA. First use time_name.

1234	5432	1230	4543	1023	4543	1 20	3432	1 0	2345
1234	5430	123	4320	1 23	4320	102	3450	1 .	2320
1234	5 43	1230	4 32	1023	4 32	1 20	3 45	1 .0	2032
1234	3 20	123	405	1 23	4 50	102	302	100	2 30
1234	5 0	1230	2 .0	1023	2 0	1 20	3.0	1	. 20 0

Staff Nº 63.

Repeat the following several times, naming only. T_asks_If second
line is named DO what will the third line be named? The fourth? etc.

Do.

Solfa.

Take slowly the teacher pointing at *first* reading. Voices must not
weaken on prolongation.

KEY OF SOL. (₅_5) ⌄

Nº 75. ‖ 1̄5̄ 1̄2̄ | 3 . | 2̄3̄ 4̄3̄ | 2 . ' | 3̄4̄ 3̄2̄ | 1 . | 2̄3̄ 2̄1̄ | 2 . ' |
| 1̄5̄ 1̄2̄ | 3 . | 2̄3̄ 4̄3̄ | 5 . ' | 5̄4̄ 3̄2̄ | 1 . | 2̄1̄ 2̄3̄ | 1 . ∎

Recreation.

EXERCISES ON THE SLUR. At first detached, then smoothly.
KEY OF DO (1-2)

N°43. | 1 2 1 2 | 1 . | 2 3 2 3 | 2 . | 3 4 3 4 | 3 . | 4 5 4 5 | 4 . |
       Ha   Ha   Ha   Ha

| 5 6 5 6 | 5 . | 6 7 6 7 | 6 . | 7 i 7 i | 7 . | i 2 i 2 | i . |
  Ha   Ha   Ha   Ha

EIGHTIETH LESSON.
Intonation.

Review Nos. 252 and 253 as though they were a single number, that is,
P_ sing the first line of N° 252 continuing with first line of N° 253
then second line of 252 followed by second line of 253 (etc.)

KEY OF FA.   **N°254.**

1 5	5 1 2 5	5 2 3 5	5 3 4 5	5 4 3 5	5 3 2 5	5 2 1 5	5 1 7 5	5 7 1
1 5	5 1 2 5	5 2 3 5	5 3 4 5	5 4 3 5	5 3 2 5	5 2 1 5	5 1 7 5	5 7 1
1 5	5 1 2 5	5 2 3 5	5 3 4 5	5 4 3 5	5 3 2 5	5 2 1 5	5 1 7 5	5 7 1
1 5	5 2 5	5 3 5	5 4 5	5 3 5	5 2 5	5 1 5	5 7 5	5 1

N°255.

1 5	5 1 2 5	5 2 3 5	5 3 4 5	5 4 3 5	5 3 2 5	5 2 1 5	5 1 7 5	5 7 1
1 5	5 1 2 5	5 2 3 5	5 3 4 5	5 4 3 5	5 3 2 5	5 2 1 5	5 1 7 5	5 7 1
1 5	5 1 2 5	5 2 3 5	5 3 4 5 ,	5 4 3 5	5 3 2 5	5 2 1 5	5 1 7 5	5 7 1
1 5	5 2 5	5 3 5	5 4 5	5 3 5	5 2 5	5 1 5	5 7 5	5 1

Dictation.

(p. 108.)

1st_ N° 235 following large arrow accenting first note of each line.
2nd_ N° 146 starting with *DO_RÉ_MI_FA_SOL*. (page 61)
T_ calls attention to the note on which the dictation starts.

Time.

P_ speak time_name first, then sing following the small arrows of
N° 121 only T_ calls attention to the change made in the first column
at the fifth and ninth lines.

KEY OF FA. **Nº 121.** **Nº 122.**

Nº 121		Nº 122	
1 2 3 1	5 2 5	1 2 3 0 1 0	5 0 2 0 5 0
1 2 3 1	5 • 2	1 2 3 0 1 0	5 0 0 2 0
1 2 3 1	5 2 •	1 2 3 0 1 0	5 0 2 0 0
1 2 3 1	5 • •	1 2 3 0 1 0	5 0 0 0
1 2 3 1	2 5 2	1 0 2 3 1 0	2 0 5 0 2 0
1 2 3 1	2 • 5	1 0 2 3 1 0	2 0 0 5 0
1 2 3 1	2 5 •	1 0 2 3 1 0	2 0 5 0 0
1 2 3 1	5 • •	1 0 2 3 1 0	5 0 0 0
1 2 3 1	5 2 3	1 0 2 0 3 1	5 0 2 0 3 0
1 2 3 1	5 • 2	1 0 2 0 3 1	5 0 0 2 0
1 2 3 1	5 2 •	1 0 2 0 3 1	5 0 2 0 0
1 2 5 5	1 • •	1 0 2 0 5 5	1 0 0 0

Staff (Nº 64.)

P - name first, then sing. T - gives sound of *Sol* for *Do*

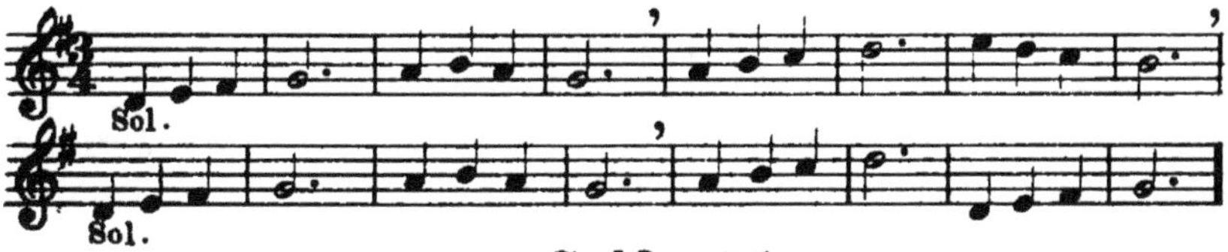
Sol.
Sol.

Solfa. ✓

T - at first reading will speak the rest *TO* as a help for the pupils to keep perfect time.

KEY OF SOL. *Slowly*. (1 - 5)

Nº 76. ‖ 5 4 | 3 0 | 2 3 4 2 | 1 0 | 3 4 5 3 | 2 3 4 2 | 3 4 5 3 | 2 3 4 2 | 5 4 | 3 0 | 2 3 4 2 | 1 0 ‖

Round for four voices.

KEY OF SOL.

Nº 40.

A				B			
1 2	3 1	1 2	3 1	3 4	5 •	3 4	5 •
O-pen	our ears	keep our	mouths closed	A se-	cret	must be	kept

C				D			*D.C.*
5 6 5 4	3 1	5 6 5 4	3 1	1 5	1 •	1 5	1 •
Then our friends will	love us	every one will	trust us	We will	hold	what we're	told

EIGHTY FIRST LESSON.
Intonation.

Review Nos. 254 and 255.

P_ Sing first line of N⁰ 254 followed by first line of 255 etc.

KEY OF FA.

N⁰ 256.

1 5	1 2 5	2 3 5	3 4 5	4 3 5	3 2 5	2 1 5	1 7 5	7 1
1 5	1 2 5	2 3 5	3 4 5	4 3 5	3 2 5	2 1 5	1 7 5	7 1
1 5	1 2 5	2 3 5	3 4 5	4 3 5	3 2 5	2 1 5	1 7 5	7 1
1 5	1 2 5	2 3 5	3 4 5	4 3 5	3 2 5	2 1 5	1 7 5	7 1
1 5	2 5	3 5	4 5	3 5	2 5	1 5	7 5	1

N⁰ 257.

1 5	1 2 5	2 3 5	3 4 5	4 3 5	3 2 5	2 1 5	1 7 5	7 1
1 5	1 2 5	2 3 5	3 4 5	4 3 5	3 2 5	2 1 5	1 7 5	7 1
1 5	1 2 5	2 3 5	3 4 5	4 3 5	3 2 5	2 1 5	1 7 5	7 1
1 5	1 2 5	2 3 5	3 4 5	4 3 5	3 2 5	2 1 5	1 7 5	7 1
1 5	2 5	3 5	4 5	3 5	2 5	1 5	7 5	1

Dictation.

1st_ N⁰s 236 & 237 following large arrows. (page 110)

2nd-N⁰ 147 beginning as before with *DO, RÉ, MI, FA, SOL* and dictat_
ing first line of N⁰ 146 the T_ calling attention to the note with which
the dictation starts. (page 61)

Time.

Review N⁰ 121 of preceding lesson, then start with N⁰ 122 slowly not
forgetting to first apply time-name and to sing the *TO* when using sylla_
bles.

Staff (Time.)

T_ gives the sound of *SI* for *DO*.

P_ name first then T_ gives the sound of *SOL* for *DO*.

N⁰ 65.

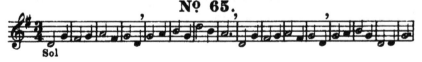

Sol

Nº 77. ‖3̄ 1̄ 3̄ 1̄ |2 2| 3̄ 1̄ 3̄ 1̄ |7̣ . ˈ1̄ 7̣ 1̄ 3̄ |5 5 |6̄ 5̄ 4̄ 3̄ |2 . ˈ|
|3̄ 1̄ 3̄ 1̄ |2 2 |3̄ 1̄ 5̄ 3̄ |2 . ˈ|1̄ 2̄ 3̄ 4̄ |5 5 |6̄ 5̄ 4̄ 2̄ |1 . ‖

Round for three voices.

KEY OF RE. (1 1) M.M. 120.

Nº 45.   **A** ‖1 2 |3 1 **B** |3 4 |5 . **C** |1̄ 1̄ 7̄ 7̄ |1̄ 5̄ 3̄ 1̄ |5 5 |1 0 |

EIGHTY SECOND LESSON.
Intonation.

In Nº 258 care should be taken that the first and second col. are sung separately then the two together, also the third and fourth col. separately then together, and at last the four col. together entirely across as indicated by the large arrow.

KEY OF LA. **Nº 258.**   **Nº 259.**

1̇	5	1̇	3̇	1̇	2̇	5	2̇	4̇	2̇	1̇	5	1̇	3̇	1̇	7	5	7	4̇	7
1̇	5	1̇	3̇		2̇	5	2̇	4̇		1̇	5	1̇	3̇	1̇	7	5	7	4̇	
1̇	5	1̇	3̇		2̇	5	2̇	4̇		1̇	5	1̇	3̇	1̇	7	5	7	4̇	
1̇	5		3̇	5	2̇	5		4̇	5	1̇	5		3̇	5	7	5		4̇	5
1̇	5		3̇	1̇	2̇	5		4̇	2̇	1̇	5		3̇	1̇	7	5		4̇	7
1̇	3̇	1̇	5	1̇	2̇	4̇	2̇	5	2̇	1̇	3̇	1̇	5	1̇	7	4̇	7	5	7
1̇	3̇	1̇	5		2̇	4̇	2̇	5		1̇	3̇	1̇	5		7	4̇	7	5	
1̇	3̇	1̇	5		2̇	4̇	2̇	5		1̇	3̇	1̇	5		7	4̇	7	5	
1̇	3̇		5	1̇	2̇	4̇		5	2̇	1̇	3̇		5	1̇	7	4̇		5	7
1̇	3̇		5	3̇	2̇	4̇		5	4̇	1̇	3̇		5	3̇	7	4̇		5	4̇

Dictation.

1st. Nos. 238 and 239 following large arrow. (page 111.)

2nd. Nº 148 introducing same means as before to make the pupils recognize the starting sound. (page 61)

Time.

Review time Nos. 121 and 122 following large arrow, letting pupils hum the *TO* and warning them when coming to the one beat rest not to hold the preceding note more than its value.

Staff. Nº 66.

P. name first, then sing. Give sound of *SOL* for *DO*.

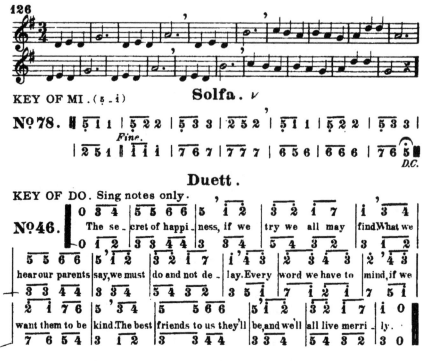

KEY OF MI. (5 _ i)   **Solfa.** ✓

Nº 78. ‖5̄ 1̄ 1 | 5̄ 2̄ 2 | 5̄ 3̄ 3 | 2̄ 5 2 | 5̄ 1̄ 1 | 5̄ 2̄ 2 | 5̄ 3̄ 3 |

Fine.

| 2̄ 5 1 ‖ 1̄ 1̄ 1 | 7̄ 6 7 | 7̄ 7̄ 7 | 6̄ 5 6 | 6̄ 6̄ 6 | 7̄ 6 5 ‖

D.C.

Duett.

KEY OF DO. Sing notes only.

Nº 46.

0 3̄ 4̄	5̄ 5̄ 6̄ 6̄	5 1̇ 2̇	3̇ 2̇ 1̇ 7	1̇ 3̇ 4̇
The se_	cret of happi_	ness, if we	try we all may	find What we
0 1̄ 2̄	3̄ 3̄ 4̄ 4̄	3 3̄ 4̄	5̄ 4̄ 3̄ 2	3 1̄ 2̄

5̄ 5̄ 6̄ 6̄	5 1̇ 2̇	3̇ 2̇ 1̇ 7	1̇ 4̇ 3̇	2̇ 3̇ 4̇ 3̇	2̇ 4̇ 3̇
hear our parents	say, we must	do and not de _	lay. Every	word we have to	mind, if we
3̄ 3̄ 4̄ 4̄	3 3̄ 4̄	5̄ 4̄ 3̄ 2	3 5̄ 1̇	7 1̇ 2̇ 1̇	7 5̄ 1̇

2̇ 1̇ 7 6	5 3̇ 4̇	5̄ 5̄ 6̄ 6̄	5 1̇ 2̇	3̇ 2̇ 1̇ 7	1̇ 0
want them to be	kind. The best	friends to us they'll	be, and we'll	all live merri _	ly.
7 6 5̄ 4̄	3 1̄ 2̄	3 3̄ 4̄ 4̄	3 3̄ 4̄	5̄ 4̄ 3̄ 2	3 0

EIGHTY THIRD LESSON.
Intonation.

Review Nos. 258 and 259 following middle-size arrows. Study Nos. 260 and 261 according to preceding instructions _ first by single col. then two together etc. etc.

KEY OF LA. **Nº 260.**   **Nº 261.**

5 1̇ 5 1̇ 3̇	5 2̇ 5 2̇ 4̇	5 1̇ 5 1̇ 3̇	5 7 5 7 4̇
5 1̇ 5 1̇ 3̇	5 2̇ 5 2̇ 4̇	5 1̇ 5 1̇ 3̇	5 7 5 7 4̇
5 1̇ 3̇ 5	5 2̇ 4̇ 5	5 1̇ 3̇ 5	5 7 4̇ 5
5 1̇ 3̇	5 2̇ 4̇	5 1̇ 3̇	5 7 4̇
5 1̇ 3̇ 1̇	5 2̇ 4̇ 2̇	5 1̇ 3̇ 1̇	5 7 4̇ 7
5 1̇ 3̇ 1̇ 5 1̇	5 2̇ 4̇ 2̇ 5 2̇	5 1̇ 3̇ 1̇ 5 1̇	5 7 4̇ 7 5 7
5 3̇ 1̇ 5 1̇	5 4̇ 2̇ 5 2̇	5 3̇ 1̇ 5 1̇	5 4̇ 7 5 7
5 3̇ 1̇ 5	5 4̇ 2̇ 5	5 3̇ 1̇ 5 1̇	5 4̇ 7 5
5 3̇ 1̇	5 4̇ 2̇	5 3̇ 1̇	5 4̇ 7
5 3̇ 1̇ 3̇	5 4̇ 2̇ 4̇	5 3̇ 1̇ 3̇	5 4̇ 7 4̇

Dictation.

1st - Nos. 240 and 241 following large arrow. (page 113)

2nd - Nos. 149 and 150 - use *small notes first,* then dispense with them. (page 63)

Time.

P - speak time-name first then sing the following by *small arrows only.*

KEY OF FA. **Nº 123.** **Nº 124.**

Nº 123		Nº 124	
1 2 3 4 3	2 5 2	1 0 2 3 4 3	2 0 5 0 2 0
1 2 3 4 3	2 • 5	1 0 2 3 4 3	2 0 0 5 0
1 2 3 4 3	2 5 •	1 0 2 3 4 3	2 0 5 0 0
1 2 3 4 3	5 • •	1 0 2 3 4 3	5 0 0 0
1 2 3 4 3	2 5 2	1 2 3 4 3 0	2 0 5 0 2 0
1 2 3 4 3	2 • 5	1 2 3 4 3 0	2 0 0 5 0
1 2 3 4 3	2 5 •	1 2 3 4 3 0	2 0 5 0 0
1 2 3 4 3	5 • •	1 2 3 4 3 0	5 0 0 0
1 2 3 4 5 6	5 2 3	1 2 3 4 5 6	5 0 2 0 3 0
1 2 3 4 5 6	5 • 2	1 2 3 4 5 6	5 0 0 2 0
1 2 3 4 5 6	5 2 •	1 2 3 4 5 6	5 0 2 0 0
1 2 3 4 5 6	5 • •	1 2 3 4 5 6	5 0 0 0

Staff (Nº 67.)

P - name first saying *TO* in very soft voice. T - gives sound of *SOL* for *DO*. When meeting bars surmounted by letters, the measure 1a is omitted at the second reading and the one marked 2a sung instead.

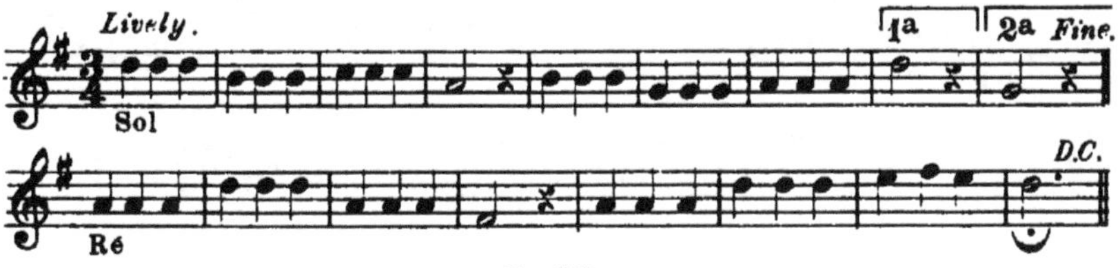
Lively.
1a
2a
Fine.
Sol
Ré
D.C.

Solfa.

KEY OF SOL. (5 - 6)

Nº 79. ‖ 5 5 | 5 4 3 | 2 3 2 | 1 5̣ | 1 7̣ 1 2 | 3 5 4 | 3 2 1 | 2 • |

| 5 5 | 5 4 3 | 6 6 | 5 • | 6 5 4 3 | 4 2 3·4 | 5 5 | 1 • ‖

Duett.

Review preceding duett with syllables and on *la*.

EIGHTY FOURTH LESSON.
Intonation.

Review Nos. 260 and 261 following large arrow.

KEY OF MI. **№ 262.**　　　　　　　　　　　**№ 263.**

1	3	1	3	5		2	4	2	4	5		1	3	1	3	5		7	2	4	7	4	5
1	3	1	5			2	4	2	4	5		1	3	1	5			7	4	7	5		
1	3	5	3	1		2	4	5	4	2		1	3	5	3	1		7	4	5	4	7	
1	3	5	3			2	4	5	4	2		1	3	5	3	1		7	2	4	5	4	
1	3	5				2	4	5				1	3	5	1			7	4	5			
1	3	5	1			2	4	5	2			1	3	5	1			7	4	5	7		
1		5	1	3		2			5	2	4	1		5	1	3		7		5	7	4	
1		5	3	1		2			5	4	2	1		5	3	1		7		5	4	7	
1		5	3			2			5	4		1		5	3			7		5	4		
1		5	3	5		2			5	4	5	1		5	3	5		7		5	4	5	

Dictation.

1st Nos. 242 to 245 inclusive. (page 115)

2nd - No. 151 after having first dictated № 149 as introductory line .
(page 63)

Time.

Review Nos. 123 and 124 by small arrows.

Staff (Time) № 68.

P - name first observing time then sing . T - gives sound of *SOL* for *DO*
and points at first reading.

Solfa.

T _ will see that the sounds on the second beats are well sustained.

KEY OF LA.(5_5)

No 80. ‖ 1 2 3 | 1 7 6 | 7 1 2 | 7 6 5 | 2 3 4 | 3 2 1 | 1 7 6 | 7 1 2 |
| 1 2 3 | 1 7 6 | 7 1 2 | 7 6 5 | 4 3 2 | 5 3 1 5 | 6 2 | 1 . ‖

Duett.

Review last duett first on *la* then with the words.

EIGHTY FIFTH LESSON.
Intonation.

Review Nos. 262 and 263 following large arrow.

KEY OF MI.   **No 264.**   **No 265.**

		No 264					No 265		
3 1 3 5 3		4 2 4 5 4			3 1 3 5 3		4 2 7 4 5 4		
3 1 3 5		4 2 4 5			3 1 3 5		4 2 7 4 5		
3 1 5		4 2 5			3 1 5		4 7 5		
3 1 5 1		4 2 5 2			3 1 5 1		4 7 5 7		
3 1 5 3		4 2 5 4			3 1 5 3		4 7 5 4		
3 5 3 1 3		4 5 4 2 4			3 5 3 1 3		4 5 4 7 4		
3 5 3 1		4 5 4 2			3 5 3 1		4 5 4 7		
3 5 1		4 5 2			3 5 1		4 5 4 7		
3 5 1 3		4 5 2 4			3 5 1 3		4 5 7 4		
3 5 1 5		4 5 2 5			3 5 1 5		4 5 7 5		

Dictation.

1st - Nos. 246 and 247. (page 115 & 116)

2nd - No. 152 first introducing No 149 as before. (page 63)

Time.

Review Nos. 123 and 124 following large arrow.

Staff (Time.)

Review preceding exercise singing only.

Solfa.

KEY OF SI.

No 81. ‖ 1 7 2 | 1 7 2 | 1 1 2 | 3 2 1 | 7 6 1 | 7 6 1 | 7 6 7 | 5 6 7 |
| 1 7 2 | 1 7 2 | 1 1 2 | 3 4 3 | 2 3 2 | 1 7 6 | 5 2 | 1 . ‖

Slur.

Exercise on the slur — first detached, then smoothly. T — must watch that every sound is perfectly accurate, the danger being to intone a shade off very easily.

KEY OF LA.

No.1. |1 3 5 |3 5 1 |5 1 3 |3 1 5 |1 5 3 |5 3 1 ‖
Ha   Ha   Ha   Ha   Ha   Ha

No.2. |1 3 5 3 |1 . |3 5 1 5 |3 . |5 1 3 1 |5 . |1 5 3 5 |1 . ‖
Ha   Ha   Ha   Ha

EIGHTY SIXTH LESSON.
Intonation.

Review Nos. 262, 263, 264 and 265 following large arrows.

Dictation.

1st- No 248 by large arrow. (page 117)
2nd - No 150 then No 153. (page 63)

Time.

Follow small arrows only then the large one slowly.

KEY OF FA. **No 125.** **No 126.**

1 2	1 7	6 7	1 2	3 4	2 3 ‖	1 2	1 7	6 5	1 2	3 5	3 2
1 2	1 7	6 7	1 2	3 4	2	1 2	1 7	6 5	1 2	3 5	2 0
1 2	1 7	6 7	1 2	3	4 2	1 2	1 7	6 5	1 3	5 0	4 2
1 2	1 7	6 7	1	2 3	2 3	1 2	1 7	6 5	1 0	5 4	2 3
1 2	1 7	6 7	1	2	3 5	1 2	1 7	6 5	1 0	5 0	4 2
1 2	1 7	6 7	1	4 3	2	1 2	1 7	6 5	1 0	2 3	5 0
1 2	1 7	6 7	1 2	3	2	1 2	1 7	6 5	1 3	5 0	2 0
1 2	1 7	6 7	1	2	3	1 2	1 7	6 5	5 0	4 0	2 0

Staff.

Repeat several times by small arrows.
P — name first, observing time — then sing.

Nº 69.

KEY OF DO. (1-3) Solfa.

Nº 82. |5 5 |6̅ 5̅ 6̅ 7̅ | i̇ 5 |6̅ 5̅ 6̅ 7̅ | i̇ 5 |6̅ 5̅ 6̅ 7̅ | i̇ 5 |3 4 |

|2 5 |4̅ 3̅ 2̅ 1̅ |2 5 |4̅ 3̅ 2̅ 1̅ |2 5 |6̅ 5̅ 4̅ 3̅ |2̅ 1̅ 2̅ 3̅ |2 5 |

|5 5 |6̅ 5̅ 6̅ 7̅ | i̇ 5 |6̅ 5̅ 6̅ 7̅ | i̇ 5 |6̅ 5̅ 6̅ 7̅ |i̇ 2̇ 3̇ 2̇ |i̅ 7̅ 6̅ 5̅ |

|6 i̇ |5 i̇ |6 i̇ |5 3 |2̇ i̇ 7 6 |5̅ 4̅ 3̅ 2̅ |1 5 | i̇ . ‖

Duett Nº 48.

KEY OF LA.

|5 3̅ 5̅ | i̇ 5̅ 5̅ | i̇ i̇ 2̇ |3 0 |2 2̅ 3̅ |4̅ 3̅ 2̅ | i̇ 7̅ 2̇ 3̇ | i̇ . |

All that we | love even | the smallest | flow'r | Tells to us | the greatness of | the Almighty | Pow'r

|3 1̅ 3̅ |3 3̅ 3̅ |3 3̅ 5̅ |i̇ 0 |7 7̅ 1̅ |6̅ 5̅ 4̅ 3̅ |2̅ 3̅ 4̅ 5̅ |3 . ‖

EIGHTY SEVENTH LESSON.
Intonation.

Review Nos. 264 & 265 following large arrows.

KEY OF DO.

Repeat first line twice or three times.

Nº 266. Nº 267.

5	3	5	i̇	5	5	4	5	2̇	5	5	3	5	i̇	5	5	4	5	7	5
5	3	5	i̇	5	5	4	5	2̇	5	5	3	5	i̇		5	4	5	7	5
5	3	5	i̇	5	5	4	5	2̇	5	5	3	5	i̇	5	5	4	5	7	5
5	3		i̇	3	5	4		2̇	4	5	3		i̇	3	5	4		7	4
5	3		i̇	5	5	4		2̇	5	5	3		i̇	5	5	4		7	5
5	i̇	5	3	5	5	2̇	5	4	5	5	i̇	5	3	5	5	7	5	4	5
5	i̇	5	3	5	5	2̇	5	4	5	5	i̇	5	3	5	5	7	5	4	5
5	i̇	5	3		5	2̇	5	4		5	i̇	5	3		5	7	5	4	
5	i̇		3	5	5	2̇		4	5	5	i̇		3	5	5	7		4	5
5	i̇		3	i̇	5	2̇		4	2̇	5	i̇		3	i̇	5	7		4	7

132

Dictation.

1st - No 249 following large arrow. (page 117)

2nd - Nos. 154 & 155 (page 64)

Time.

Review Nos. 125 & 126 following large arrow.

Staff (Time.)

Review time practice of previous lesson by small and large arrows.

KEY OF MI. (5 - 2)   **Solfa.**

NO 83. ‖ 5 i | 7 6 5 4 | 3 6 | 5 4 3 2 | 1 4 | 3 2 1 7 | 6 7 | 1 5 |
| 2 5 | 6 5 4 3 | 2 5 | 6 5 4 3 | 2 5 | 6 7 1 2 | 1 7 6 7 | 5 . |
| 5 i | 7 6 5 4 | 3 6 | 5 4 3 2 | 1 2 | 3 4 5 6 | 5 i | 1 . |
| 7 5 | 1 5 6 5 | 7 5 | 1 5 6 5 | 7 5 | 1 7 6 5 | 5 4 3 2 | 1 . ∎

KEY OF LA.   **Round.**

A
NO 49. | 5 . 3 . | 5 . 3 . | 5 . 4   3 | 3 . 2 . | 4 . 2 . | 4 . 2 . | 4 . 3 2 | 3 . . . |
Ding, Ding. | Ding, Ding, | hear the bells | ringing | Let's walk | slowly | with smiling | face |

B
| 3 . i . | 3 . i . | 3 . 2   i | i . 7 . | 2 . 7 . | 2 . 7 . | 2 . i 7 | i . . . |
Ding, Ding, | Ding, Ding | Happy mind | bringing | Let us | each one | sit   at his | place |

C
| 5 . 5 . | 5 . 5 . | 5 .   5   5 | 5 . 5 . | 5 . 5 . | 5 . 5 . | 5 . 5   5 | i   5 i . |
Ding, Ding, | Ding, Ding | not with speed | eating | Be_have | and do | not bring dis. | grace disgrace |

EIGHTY EIGHTH LESSON.
Intonation.

Review Nos. 266 & 267 following large arrows.

KEY OF DO.

NO 268.   NO 269.

3 5 3 5 i 5	4 5 4 5 2 54	3 5 3 5 i 5	4 5 4 5 7 54
3 5 3 5 i	4 5 4 5 2 54	3 5 3 5 i 5	4 5 4 5 7
3 5 i 5 3	4 5 2 5 4	3 5 i 5 3	4 5 7 5 4
3 5 i 5	4 5 2 5	3 5 i 5	4 5 7 5
3 5 i	4 5 2 5	3 5 i 5	4 5 7 5
3 5 i 3	4 5 2 4	3 5 i 3	4 5 7 4
3 5 i 3 5	4 5 2 4 5	3 5 i 3 5	4 5 7 4 5
3 i 5 3	4 2 5 4	3 i 5 3	4 7 5 4
3 i 5 3	4 2 5 4	3 i 5 3	4 7 5 4
3 i 5 i 53	4 2 5 2 54	3 i 5 i 53	4 7 5 7

Dictation.

1st - Nos. 250 and 251 following large arrows. (page 119 & 120)
2nd - Nº 156 after having introduced Nº 154. (page 65)

Time.

KEY OF FA. Each small arrow twice before following the large arrow.

Nº 127. **Nº 128.**

Nº 127		Nº 128	
1 2 3 4 2 3	1 2 1 7 6 7	1 0 2 3 2 3	1 2 1 7 6 5
1 2 3 4 2	1 2 1 7 6 7	1 0 2 3 2 0	1 2 1 7 6 5
1 2 3 4 2	1 2 1 7 6 7	1 2 3 0 4 2	1 2 1 7 6 5
1 2 3 2 3	1 2 1 7 6 7	1 0 2 3 2 3	1 2 1 7 6 5
1 2 3 5	1 2 1 7 6 7	1 3 5 0 2 3	1 2 1 7 6 5
1 2 3 2	1 2 1 7 6 7	1 3 5 3 2 0	1 2 1 7 6 5

Staff Nº 70.

P- name first observing the time then sing. T- gives the sound of *SOL* for *DO*. Use pointer at first reading.

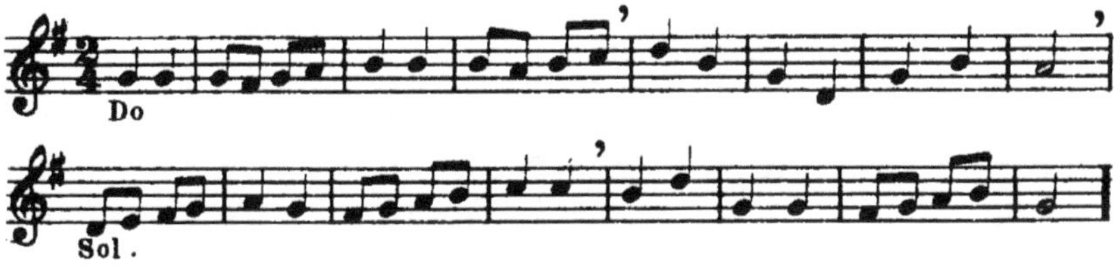
Do
Sol.

Solfa Nº 84.

KEY OF DO. (1 - 3)

mf

| 1 3 5 1 | 1 7 | 1 3 5 1 | 1 7 |5 1 3 5 1 | 7 6 7 6 |

| 54 54 | 32 32 |9 13 51 | 1 7 | 13 51 | 2 . |13 21 21 |

| 17 17 | 76 76 | 5 *f* . |17 56 71 | 1 7 | 56 71 | 1 7 |

21 | 56 71 | 76 56 | 54 34 | 32 34 |25 56 71 | 1 7 |

| 56 71 | 2 . |29 32 21 | 17 65 | 54 32 | 1 . |

KEY OF FA. (⅜-¼) M.M. 104. **Duett.**

The land of the free.

	5	3 .	2	3	1 .	0	5	5 .	4	5	3 . '
Nº 50.	The	land	of	my	birth,		the	land	of	the	free,
	5	1 .	5	5	3 .	0	5	3 .	2	7	1 . '

0	1	6 .	6	6	5 .	3	5	5 4 3	4	5	3 . '
	Oh	land	which I	love		I	will	always sing	praise to	thee.
0	1	4 .	4	4	3 .	1	3	3 2 1	2	7	1 . '

rall.

0	1	6 .	1	6	5 .	3	5	5 4 3	4	2	1 .
	Oh	land	which I	love		I	will	always sing	praise to	thee.
0	1	4 .	3	4	3 .	1	3	3 2 1	2	7	1 .

EIGHTY NINTH LESSON.
Intonation.
Review Nos. 264, 265, 266, 267, 268 & 269.

Dictation.
1st _ Nos. 252 & 253 following large arrows. (page 121)

2nd _ Nº 157 after having introduced Nº 154. (page 65)

Time.

KEY OF FA. **Nº 129.**   **Nº 130.**

1 2 3 2̄1̄	5 5 5 5	1̄0̄ 2̄0̄ 3̄0̄ 2̄1̄	5̄0̄ 5̄0̄ 5̄0̄ 5̄0̄
1 2 3 2̄1̄	5 . 2 3	1̄0̄ 2̄0̄ 3̄0̄ 2̄1̄	5̄0̄ 0 2̄0̄ 3̄0̄
1 2 3 2̄1̄	5 2 . 3	1̄0̄ 2̄0̄ 3̄0̄ 2̄1̄	5̄0̄ 2̄0̄ 0 3̄0̄
1 2 3 2̄1̄	5 5 1 .	1̄0̄ 2̄0̄ 3̄0̄ 2̄1̄	5̄0̄ 5̄0̄ 1̄0̄ 0
1 2̄3̄2 1	5 5 5 5	1̄0̄ 2̄3̄ 2̄0̄ 1̄0̄	5̄0̄ 5̄0̄ 5̄0̄ 5̄0̄
1 2̄3̄2 1	5 . 2 3	1̄0̄ 2̄3̄ 2̄0̄ 1̄0̄	5̄0̄ 0 2̄0̄ 3̄0̄
1 2̄3̄2 1	5 2 . 3	1̄0̄ 2̄3̄ 2̄0̄ 1̄0̄	5̄0̄ 2̄0̄ 0 3̄0̄
1 2̄3̄2 1	5 5 1 .	1̄0̄ 2̄3̄ 2̄0̄ 1̄0̄	5̄0̄ 5̄0̄ 1̄0̄ 0

Staff. Nº 71.

P_ name first observing the time, then sing. T_ gives the sound of FA
for DO and point at first reading.

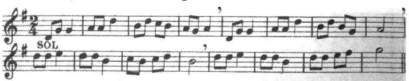

KEY OF LA. (5 - 5)

Solfa. No 85.

𝄋 56 71	17 70	56 71	17 20	[5] 56 71	67 12	71 23	21 76
mf 56 71	17 70	56 71	17 20	[13] 56 71	67 12	71 *f* 23	1 0 *Fine* ‖
[17] *mf* 71 71	70 20	17 67	56 70	[21] 10 70	30 20	32 21	17 76
[25] 71 71	70 20	17 67	65 5	[29] 53 13	23 21	7 6	5 . 𝄋 ‖

Duett.

Review the preceding duett with the syllables, then on *la*.

NINETIETH LESSON.

Intonation.

Repeat each line twice, the last one three times.

KEY OF FA. **No 270.** **No 271.**

No 270				No 271			
5 6 7	7 1 2	2 3 4	4 5 6	6 5 4	4 3 2	2 1 7	7 6 5
5 6 7	7 1 2	2 3 4	4 5 6	6 5 4	4 3 2	2 1 7	7 6 5
5 7	7 2	2 4	4 6	6 4	4 2	2 7	7 5
5 7	. 2	. 4	. 6	6 4	. 2	. 7	. 5
5 7	2	4	6	6 4	2	7	5

No 272				No 273			
575	5725	57245	5724665	646	6426	64276	6427565
57.	572.	5724.	57246.	64.	642.	6427.	64275
57.	572.	5724.	57246.	64.	642.	6427.	64275
57.	572.	5724.	57246.	64.	642.	6427.	64275
57.	5 2.	5 4.	5 6.	64.	6 2.	6 7.	6 5

Dictation.

1st _ Nos. 254 to 255 inclusive. (page 122)

2nd _ No 158 after having introduced No 154. (page 65)

Time.

KEY OF FA. **No 131.** **No 132.**

No 131								No 132							
1	2	32	1	5	5	5	5	10	20	32	10	50	50	50	50
1	2	32	1	5	.	2	3	10	20	32	10	50	0	20	30
1	2	32	1	5	2	.	3	10	20	32	10	50	20	0	30
1	2	32	1	5	5	1	.	10	20	32	10	50	50	10	0
12	3	2	1	5	5	5	5	12	30	20	10	50	50	50	50
12	3	2	1	5	.	2	3	12	30	20	10	50	0	20	30
12	3	2	1	5	2	.	3	12	30	20	10	50	20	0	30
12	3	2	1	5	5	1	.	12	30	20	10	50	50	10	0

Staff. Nº 72.

P_ name first observing time, then sing. T_ gives the sound of SOL for DO. P_ only read by small arrows. T_ may point at *first* reading.

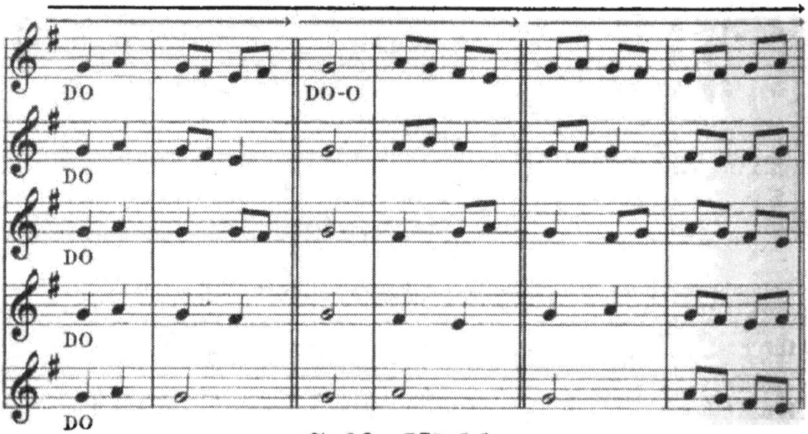
DO
DO-O
DO
DO
DO
DO

KEY OF RÉ. (1 - 1̇)

Solfa. Nº 86.

| 12 3 4 | 5 1̇ 76 | 54 3 2 | 1 . . | 2 32 1 | 4 . 3 | 23 2 2 | 5 . . |
| 12 3 4̇ | 5 1̇ 76 | 54 3 2 | 1 . . | 2 32 1 | 6 . 5 | 61̇ 1̇ 7 | 1̇ . 0 |

NINETY FIRST LESSON

Intonation.

Review Nos. 270, 271, 272 & 273.

Repeat each line twice, the last one three times.

KEY OF FA.

Nº 274.	Nº 275.
5 7 7 5 7 2 2 7 2 4 4 2 4 6	6 4 4 6 4 2 2 4 2 7 7 2 7 5
5 7 7 5 7 2 2 7 2 4 4 2 4 6	6 4 4 6 4 2 2 4 2 7 7 2 7 5
5 7 . 5 2 . 7 4 . 2 6	6 4 . 6 2 . 4 7 . 2 5
5 7 5 2 7 4 2 6	6 4 6 2 4 7 2 5

Dictation.

1st_ Nos. 256 & 257. (page 124)

2nd_ Nº 159. (large arrows page 66)

KEY OF FA. **Nọ 133.** **Time.** **Nọ 134.**

5	4̄3̄	3	2̄1̄	2	5	2	5	5	4̄3̄	3̄0̄	2̄1̄	2̄0̄	5̄0̄	2̄0̄	5̄0̄
5	4̄3̄	3	2̄1̄	2	.	5	5	5	4̄3̄	3̄0̄	2̄1̄	2̄0̄	0	5̄0̄	5̄0̄
5	4̄3̄	3	2̄1̄	2	5	.	5	5	4̄3̄	3̄0̄	2̄1̄	2̄0̄	5̄0̄	0	5̄0̄
5	4̄3̄	3	2̄1̄	2	5	1	.	5	4̄3̄	3̄0̄	2̄1̄	2̄0̄	5̄0̄	1̄0̄	0
5̄4̄	3	3̄2̄	1	2	5	2	5	5̄4̄	3̄0̄	3̄2̄	1̄0̄	2̄0̄	5̄0̄	2̄0̄	5̄0̄
5̄4̄	3	3̄2̄	1	2	.	5	5	5̄4̄	3̄0̄	3̄2̄	1̄,0̄	2̄0̄	0	5̄0̄	5̄0̄
5̄4̄	3	3̄2̄	1	2	5	.	5	5̄4̄	3̄0̄	3̄2̄	1̄0̄	2̄0̄	5̄0̄	0	5̄0̄
5̄4̄	3	3̄2̄	1	2	5	1	.	5̄4̄	3̄0̄	3̄2̄	1̄0̄	2̄0̄	5̄0̄	1̄0̄	0

Staff.

Review previous time exercise following small arrows then following the large arrow.

Solfa. Nọ 87.

KEY OF LA. (1 - 5)

12	34	56	5	1	.	53	2	.	53	1	.	12	34	56
5	3	.	21	6	.	27	5	.	53	21	51	2	5	.
53	21	71	2	5	.	54	32	17	67	12	34	3	.	2	1	.	.

Exercise on the Slur.

To be sung at first detached, then quite smoothly.

KEY OF DO. (1 - 3) **Nọ 51.**

| 1 | 23 | 43 | 21 | 2 | 34 | 54 | 32 | 3 | 45 | 65 | 43 | 4 | 56 | 76 | 54 |
| Ha | | | | Ha | | | | Ha | | | | Ha | | | |

| 5 | 67 | 17 | 65 | 6 | 71 | 21 | 76 | 7 | 12 | 32 | 17 | 1 | . | . | 0 |
| Ha | | | | Ha | | | | Ha | | | | | | | |

NINETY SECOND LESSON.

Intonation.

Repeat each col. twice before following the large arrow.

KEY OF DO. **Nọ 276.**

1	7	6	5	5	6	7	1	7	1₇	6	5	6	7	1	5
1	7₆5	6		5	6₇1	7		7	1	5	6	6	7₆5	1	
1₇	6	7	5	5₆7	1	6		7	6	5	1	6₇1	7	5	
1	6	5₆7		5	7	6	1	7	6₇1	5		6	1	5₆7	
1	5	6	7	5	1	7	6	7₆5	6	1		6	5₆7	1	
1	5	7	6	5	1	6	7	7	5	1	6	6	5	1	7

Dictation.

1st_ Nos. 258 & 259 accenting RÉ-FA-SI. (page 125)
2nd_ Nº 160. following large arrow (page 66)

KEY OF FA. Nº 135.　　**Time.**　　Nº 136.

1	5	4̄3̄	2̄1̄	2	5	2	5	1̄0̄	5̄0̄	4̄3̄	2̄1̄	2̄0̄	5̄0̄	2̄0̄	5̄0̄
1	5	4̄3̄	2̄1̄	2	.	5	5	1̄0̄	5̄0̄	4̄3̄	2̄1̄	2̄0̄	0	5̄0̄	5̄0̄
1	5	4̄3̄	2̄1̄	2	5	.	5	1̄0̄	5̄0̄	4̄3̄	2̄1̄	2̄0̄	5̄0̄	0	5̄0̄
1	5	4̄3̄	2̄1̄	2	5	1	.	1̄0̄	5̄0̄	4̄3̄	2̄1̄	2̄0̄	5̄0̄	1̄0̄	0
5̄4̄	3̄2̄	3	1	2	5	2	5	5̄4̄	3̄2̄	3̄0̄	1̄0̄	2̄0̄	5̄0̄	2̄0̄	5̄0̄
5̄4̄	3̄2̄	3	1	2	.	3	5	5̄4̄	3̄2̄	3̄0̄	1̄0̄	2̄0̄	0	3̄0̄	5̄0̄
5̄4̄	3̄2̄	3	1	2	5	.	5	5̄4̄	3̄2̄	3̄0̄	1̄0̄	2̄0̄	5̄0̄	0	5̄0̄
5̄4̄	3̄2̄	3	1	5	5	1	.	5̄4̄	3̄2̄	3̄0̄	1̄0̄	5̄0̄	5̄0̄	1̄0̄	0

Staff.

P_ review time-exercise Nº 72 singing and following large arrow _ then *name* syllables of Nº 73 observing time; thereafter T_ gives the sound of SOL for DO and letsP_sing.

Nº 73.

KEY OF DO. (1_4)　　**Solfa. Nº 88.**

p
1 . 3̄1̄ | 5 . 6̄7̄ | i . 7̄6̄ | 5 . 6̄5̄ | 5 . 6̄5̄ | 5 . 6̄5̄ |

mf
5 . 4̄3̄ | 5 2 . | i . 3̄4̄ | 5 . 6̄7̄ | i . 2̄i̇̄ | 7 . 1̄7̄ | 6 . 7̄1̄ |

f
3̄2̄ 1̄7̄ 6̄5̄ | 6 . . | 5 . 0 | 5 . 1̄2̄ | i . 7̄6̄ | 5 . 1̄2̄ |

ff
i . 7̄6̄ | 5 . 1̄2̄ | i 7 3̇ | 3̇ 2̇ 6 | 2̇ . . | 3̇ . 4̄3̄ | 2̇ . 1 |

pp
7 . 2̄i̇̄ | 7 . 6 | 6 . 7̄i̇̄ | 3̄2̄ 1̄7̄ 1̄7̄ | 6 2̇ . | i . 0 ‖

Round for Five Voices.
KEY OF SOL. (5-6) M. M. 144.　　**Nº 52.**

A
1 1̄2̄ | 3 1 | 2 7 | 1 0 | B 3 3̄4̄ | 5 3 | 4 2 | 3 0 | C 5̄5̄ 5̄5̄ | 5 6̄5̄ |

4 5̄4̄ | 3 0 | D 3̄3̄ 3̄3̄ | 3 4̄3̄ | 2 3̄2̄ | 1 0 | E 1̄1̄ 1̄1̄ | 1 1̄1̄ | 5 5 | 1 0 ‖

NINETY THIRD LESSON.

Intonation.

Review Nº 276.

P_ sing each col. twice before following large arrow.

KEY OF FA. **Nº 277.**

1 2 3 4 5	1 3 2 3 4 5	1 2 3 4 3 2 5	1 5 4 3 2
1 2 3 4 5 4	1 3 2 3 4 5 4	1 4 3 5 4 3 2	1 5 4 2 3
1 2 3 4 3 5	1 2 3 4 5 4 3 2	1 4 5 4 3 2	1 5 3 4 2
1 2 4 5 3	1 3 4 3 2 5	1 4 5 4 3 2 3	1 5 3 2 4
1 2 3 4 5 4 3	1 3 5 4 2	1 4 2 3 5	1 5 4 3 2 3 4
1 2 5 3 4	1 3 5 4 3 2 4	1 4 2 5 3	1 5 4 3 2 4 3

Dictation.

1st_ Nos. 260 & 261 following large arrow accenting RÉ-FA-SI. (p.126.)
2nd_ Nº 161. following large arrow (page 66)

Time.

KEY OF MI. **Nº 137.** **Nº 138.**

Nº 137		Nº 138	
5 65 54 3	2 3 1 5	50 65 54 30	20 30 10 50
5 65 54 3	2 . 7 5	50 65 54 30	20 0 70 50
5 65 54 3	2 5 . 5	50 65 54 30	20 50 0 50
5 65 54 3	2 3 1 .	50 65 54 30	20 30 10 0
56 5 i 54	3 1 2 5	56 50 10 54	30 10 20 50
56 5 i 54	3 . 2 5	56 50 10 54	30 0 20 50
56 5 i 54	3 2 . 5	56 50 10 54	30 20 0 50
56 5 i 54	3 2 1 .	56 50 10 54	30 20 10 0

Staff.

P_ name first then sing T_ gives the sound of RÉ for DO.

Nº 74. *Fine.*

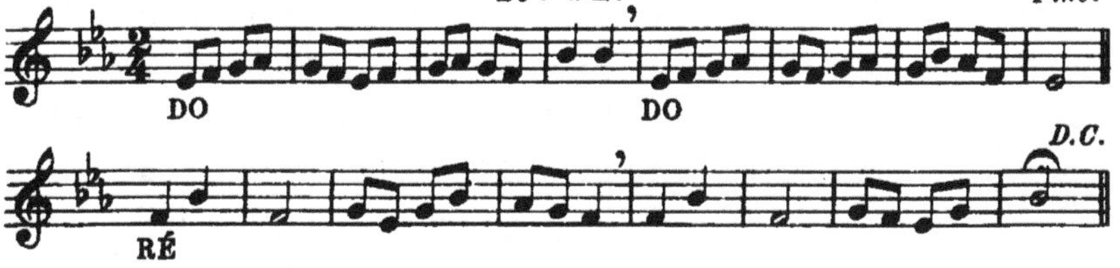
DO
DO
D.C.
RÉ

KEY OF MI.(1 - i) **Solfa. NO 89.**

‖1 2 3 $\overline{21}$ | 5 6 7 $\overline{65}$ | i 5 6 $\overline{54}$ | 3 2 1 . | 2 5 3 $\overline{21}$ |
| 2 5 3 $\overline{21}$ | 2 5 6 $\overline{71}$ | 7 6 5 . | 5 $\overline{67}$ 6 5 | 5 $\overline{67}$ 6 5 |
| 5 $\overline{67}$ 6 5 | 5 3 5 . | 4 $\overline{56}$ 5 4 | 3 $\overline{45}$ 4 3 | 2 . . . | 1 . . 0 ‖

Duett.

KEY OF SOL.

	1	3	5 0	$\overline{5\ \ 4}$	$\overline{3\ \ 2}$	1 0	$\overline{2\ \ 2}$	$\overline{7\ \ 5}$	$\overline{5\ \ 5}$	$\overline{3\ \ 1}$
NO 53.	Haste!Haste!Haste!		Time you must not	waste		Failure will be		sure to come
	1	1	3 0	$\overline{3\ \ 2}$	$\overline{1\ \ 7}$	1 0	$\overline{5\ \ 5}$	$\overline{5\ \ 5}$	$\overline{3\ \ 3}$	$\overline{1\ \ 1}$

$\overline{2\ \ 2}$	$\overline{7\ \ 5}$	$\overline{5\ \ 5}$	$\overline{3\ \ 1}$	$\overline{1\ \ 2}$	$\overline{3\ \ 4}$	5 0	$\overline{5\ \ 4}$	$\overline{3\ \ 2}$	1 0
If your work is		not well done		You must work with		speed	If you would suc	ceed.
$\overline{5\ \ 5}$	$\overline{5\ \ 5}$	$\overline{3\ \ 3}$	$\overline{1\ \ 1}$	$\overline{1\ \ 7}$	$\overline{1\ \ 2}$	3 0	$\overline{3\ \ 2}$	$\overline{1\ \ 7}$	1 0 ‖

NINETY FOURTH LESSON.
Intonation.

Review NO **277** in the Key of SOL instead of FA first following small arrows then the large one. Repeat each col. twice before following the large arrow of the following.

KEY OF. FA. **NO 278.**

5 4	3 2 1	5 3 2	1 2 3 4	5 4 3 2 3 4	1	5 1	2 3 4
5 4 3 2 1 2	5 3 2 3 4 3 2 1	5 2 8	1 2 3 4	5 1	2 4 3
5 4 3 2 3 1	5 3 1	2 3 4	5 2 4	8	1	5 1	3 4 2
5 4	2 1 3	5 3 1 2 3 4	2	5 2 4 3 2 1	3	5 1	3 2 4
5 4 3 2 1 2 3	5 3 4	2	1	5 2 1	3	4	5 1 2 3 4 3 2
5 4	1 3 2	5 3 4 3 2 1	2	5 2 1 2 3 4	3	5 1	4 2 3

1st _ Nos. **262 & 263.**(p 128) **Dictation.**

2nd _ NO **162** begin with DO-SI-LA-SOL. large arrow (p. 68)

Time.

Review Nos **137 & 138** following large arrow.

KEY OF RÉ. **NO 139.** **NO 140.**

5	$\overline{67}$	$\overline{15}$	$\overline{31}$	2 5 2 5	$\overline{50}$	$\overline{67}$	$\overline{15}$	$\overline{31}$	$\overline{20}$	$\overline{50}$	$\overline{20}$	$\overline{50}$
5	$\overline{67}$	$\overline{15}$	$\overline{31}$	2 . 5 5	$\overline{50}$	$\overline{67}$	$\overline{15}$	$\overline{31}$	$\overline{20}$	0	$\overline{50}$	$\overline{50}$
5	$\overline{67}$	$\overline{15}$	$\overline{31}$	2 5 . 5	$\overline{50}$	$\overline{67}$	$\overline{15}$	$\overline{31}$	$\overline{20}$	$\overline{50}$	0	$\overline{50}$
5	$\overline{67}$	$\overline{15}$	$\overline{31}$	5 5 1 .	$\overline{50}$	$\overline{67}$	$\overline{15}$	$\overline{31}$	$\overline{50}$	$\overline{50}$	$\overline{10}$	0
$\overline{13}$	$\overline{51}$	5	$\overline{31}$	2 5 2 5	$\overline{13}$	$\overline{51}$	$\overline{50}$	$\overline{31}$	$\overline{20}$	$\overline{50}$	0	$\overline{50}$
$\overline{13}$	$\overline{51}$	5	$\overline{31}$	2 . 5 5	$\overline{13}$	$\overline{51}$	$\overline{50}$	$\overline{31}$	$\overline{20}$	0	$\overline{50}$	$\overline{50}$
$\overline{13}$	$\overline{51}$	5	$\overline{31}$	2 5 . 5	$\overline{13}$	$\overline{51}$	$\overline{50}$	$\overline{31}$	$\overline{20}$	$\overline{50}$	0	$\overline{50}$
$\overline{13}$	$\overline{51}$	5	$\overline{31}$	5 5 1 .	$\overline{13}$	$\overline{51}$	$\overline{50}$	$\overline{31}$	$\overline{50}$	$\overline{50}$	$\overline{10}$	0

P_ *name* first then sing T_ gives the sound of RÉ for DO.

MI

RÉ

RÉ

Fine

D.C.

KEY OF SOL.(5.5)   ## Solfa. No 90.

𝄋 |5 i 7̄6̄ 5 |5 i 7̄6̄ 5 |5 3̇ 2̇1̇ 7̇ |1̄7̄ 6̄ 7̄1̄ 2̄5̄ |5 i 7̄6̄ 5 |5 i 7̄6̄ 5 |

|5 3̇ 4̄3̄ 2̇ |1̄7̄ 6̄ 7̄ i̇. *Fine* |7̄1̄ 2̇ i̇ 7̇ |6̄7̄ i 7 6 |5̄6̄ 7 6 5 |6̄5̄ 6̄7̄ 6. |

|6̄7̄ i 2̇ 3̇ |3̄2̄ 5̇ i̇ 7̇ |6̄7̄ 6 6̄7̄ 6 |6̄7̄ 8̄7̄ 6. |7̄1̄ 2̇ i̇ 7̇ |6̄7̄ i 7 6 |

|5̄6̄ 7 i 2̇ |3̇...|3̄3̄ 3̇ 3̇ 3̇ |5̄3̄ 4̄3̄ 2̇. |5̄6̄ 7̄1̄ 6. |5. . .|𝄋

P_ sing notes only.
KEY OF FA.

Duett.
No 54.

3	3̄2̄	1 1	2 2	3 1 '	5	5̄4̄	3 3	2̄1̄ 2̄ 3̄	1 1
Well do our	best to	learn our	lesson	Then will our	teacher	praises kindly	give us
1	1̄7̄	1 1	5̱	5̱	1.1'	3	3̄2̄	1 1	5̄5̄ 5̄5̄	1 1

Fine.

3	3̄4̄	5 5	6	1̄6̄	5. .'	3	3̄4̄	5 5	6	1̄6̄	5. .
In our	class lets	try our	best	If once we	fail we	must never	rest.
1	1̄2̄	3 3	4	6̄4̄	3.'	1	1̄2̄	3 3	4	6̄4̄	3. .

D.C.

NINETY FIFTH LESSON.
Intonation.

Review Nos. **276, 277 & 278** following large arrows.

Dictation.

1ˢᵗ_ Nos. **264 & 265.** (page **129**)

2ⁿᵈ_ No **163** begin with DO-RE-MI. (page **68**)

No 141								No 142							
13	5	15	31	2	5	2	5	13	50	15	81	20	50	20	50
13	5	15	31	2	.	5	5	13	50	15	81	20	0	50	50
13	5	15	31	2	5	.	5	13	50	15	31	20	50	0	50
13	5	15	31	5	5	1	.	13	50	15	31	50	50	10	0
51	54	32	1	2	5	2	5	51	54	32	10	20	50	20	50
51	54	32	1	2	.	5	5	51	54	32	10	20	0	50	50
51	54	32	1	2	5	.	5	51	54	32	10	20	50	0	50
51	54	32	1	2	5	5	.	51	54	32	10	20	50	50	0

Staff. No 76.

P_ *name* first then *sing* T_ gives the sound of RÉ for DO.

DO

KEY OF MI.(5_i)   **Solfa. No 91.**

5 65 54 3	2 3 1 .	5 67 12 3	5 2 2 .	5 65 54 3	2 3 1 .
6 71 23 4	3 2 1 . (*Fine*)	23 25 67	1 6 6 .	76 5 5 3	23 23 2 .
23 2 5 67	1 6 6 .	72 7 61 6	57 5 46 4	35 65 54 3	

Duett.

Review last duett with syllable, then on *la*.

NINETY SIXTH LESSON.
Intonation.

P_ sing each single col. twice before following large arrow.

KEY OF RÉ.   **No 279.**

1	3	5	i	i	5	3	1	5	3	1	i	3	1	3	5	i
1	3	5 i	5	i	5 3 1	3	5	3	5 i 5 3 1		3	1 3 5 i	5	
1 3 5	i 5 3			i 5 3	1 3 5		5 3 1	3 5 i		3	5	i 5 3 1	
1 3 5	3 5 i			i 5 3	5 3 1		5 3	1 3 5 i 5 3		3	5 3 1 3 5 i		
1 3 5 i	5	3		i 5 3 1	3	5		5	i 5 3	1	3 5 i	5 3 1	
1 3 5 i	3	5		i 5 3 1 3 5	3		5	i 5 3 1	3	3 5	i 5 3 1 3 5	

1st_ Nos. 266 & 267.(p. 131) **Dictation.**

2nd_ No 164 (page 68)

KEY OF SOL. **Nº 143.** **Time.** **Nº 144.**

15	15	15	15	2	17	6	5	15	15	15	15	20	17	60	50
15	15	15	15	2	5	5	23	15	15	15	15	20	50	50	23
15	15	15	15	23	2	5	2	15	15	15	15	23	20	50	20
15	15	15	15	2	5	23	1	15	15	15	15	20	50	23	10
15	15	15	13	21	23	2	5	15	15	15	13	21	23	20	50
15	15	15	13	2	5	54	32	15	15	15	13	20	50	54	32
15	15	15	13	25	5	5	23	15	15	15	13	25	50	50	23
15	15	15	13	2	54	32	1	15	15	15	13	20	54	32	10

Staff. Nº 77.

P_ *name first* then sing T_ gives the sound of RÉ for DO.

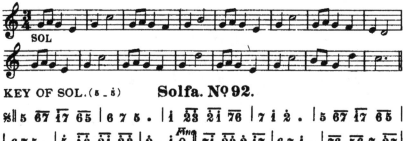

SOL

KEY OF SOL. (5 _ 5) **Solfa. Nº 92.**

%‖ 5 67 17 65 | 6 7 5 . | 1 23 21 76 | 7 1 2 . | 5 67 17 65 |
| 6 7 5 . | 5 43 21 23 | 2 . 1 0 *Fine* ‖ 71 23 2 17 | 6 7 1 . | 76 56 7 27 |
| 6 5 6 . | 71 25 2 17 | 6 7 1 . | 32 32 5 67 | 6 . 5 . ‖ %

Duett.

Review last duett on *la,* then with the words.

NINETY SEVENTH LESSON.

Intonation.

Review Nº 279 following small and large arrows.

P_ sing slowly each col. twice before following large arrow.

KEY OF SOL. **Nº 280.**

5 1 3 5	5 3 1 5	1 3 531 5	3 1 513 5
5 13 5 3	5 31 5 1	1 31 513 5	3 13 531 5
51 3 53 1	53 1 51 3	13 5 31 5	31 5 13 5
51 3 13 5	53 1 31 5	13 531 51 3	31 513 53 1
513 5 3 1	531 5 1 3	1 51 3 5	3 53 1 5
513 53 1 3	531 5 3 1	1 513 5 3	3 531 5 1

Time.

1st _ Nos. 268 & 269 following large arrows. (page 132.)
2nd _ No. 165. (page 69)

No. 145.

KEY OF DO.

12 .1	76 75	1 .2	1 7	1 .	2 2	1 2	1 7
12 .1	71 2	1 .2	1 75	1 .	2 17	1 2	2 .
12 .1	7 5	1 .2	17 67	1 .	21 76	1 2	. .
12 .1	7 67	1 .2	17 7	1 .	21 7	1 2	. 7

Staff. No. 78.

P_ *name first* then sing T_ gives the sound of SOL for DO.

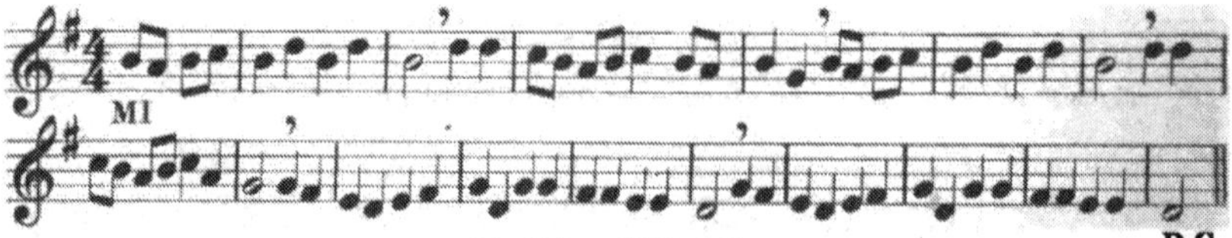
MI

D.C.

KEY OF SOL. (5 _ 5)

Solfa. No. 93.

% 56 71 23 21	17 76 6 5	17 76 6 5	51 23 5 .	56 71 23 21	
17 76 6 5	17 76 6 5	51 23 1 . *Fine*	71 23 32 17	67 67 1 .	
67 67 1 .	71 25 2 .	71 23 32 17	67 67 1 .	67 67 1 .	76 65 5 . %

My country t'is of thee.

This being a national hymn T. must take special pains that children when singing understand fully the meaning of the words and especially the feeling. KEY OF LA.

Moderato.

	1 1 2	7 .1 2	3 3 4	3 .2 1	2 1 7	1 . 0	5 5 5
1.	My country	t'is of thee,	Sweet land of	li-ber-ty,	Of thee I	sing,	Land where my
2.	My native	country thee,	Land of the	no-ble free,	Thy name I	love;	I love thy
	3 3 5	5 .6 7	1 1 2	1 .5 3	4 3 2	3 . 0	3 3 3

5 .4 3	4 4 4	4 .3 2	3 43 21	3 .4 5	64 3 2	1 . 0
fathers died,	Land of the	Pilgrims' pride	From ev'ry	mountain side	Let freedom	ring.
rocks and rills,	Thy woods and	templ'd hills,	My heart with	rapture thrills	Like that a-	bove.
3 .2 1	2 2 2	2 .1 7	1 21 53	1 .2 3	42 1 5	3 . 0

3.

Let music swell the breeze,
And ring from all the trees,
Sweet freedom's song;
Let mortal tongues awake;
Let all that breathe partake;
Let rocks their silence break;
The sound prolong.

4.

Our fathers' God, to Thee,
Author of li-ber-ty,
To Thee we sing;
Long may our land be bright
With freedom's holy light
Protect us by Thy might
Great God our King!

NINETY EIGHTH LESSON.

Intonation.

Review Nos. 279 & 280.

Dictation.

(Page 135)

1st _ Nos. 270, 271, 272, 273. Do not repeat lines which are similar.

2nd _ Nº 166. (page 69)

Time.

Review Nº 145.

Staff. (Time.)

P_ name first then sing T_ gives the sound of RÉ for DO.

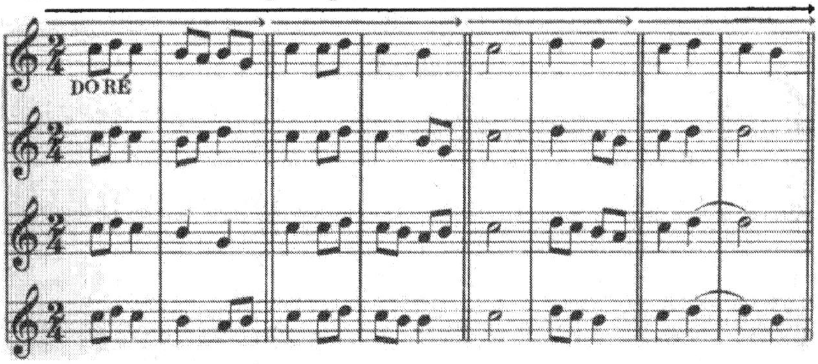

DO RÉ

P_ name first then sing T_ gives the sound of SOL for DO.

Nº 79.

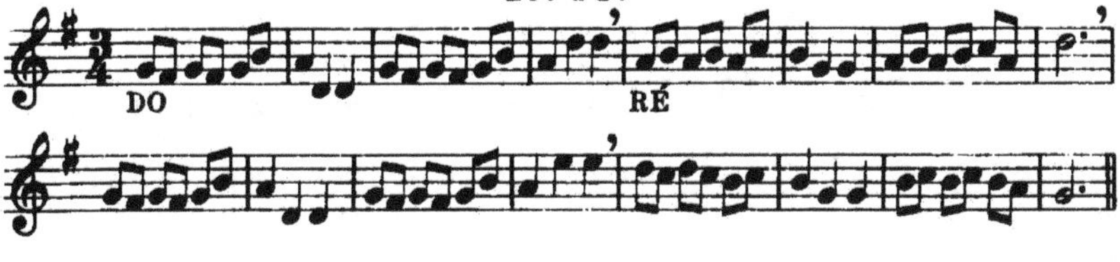

DO
RÉ

KEY of MI. (5-2)

Solfa.

Nº 94. 𝄋| 56 54 32 1 | 23 21 76 5 | 12 31 23 42 | 34 53 25 65 |

| 51 54 32 13 | 23 21 76 57 | 12 31 23 42 | 5 5 1 . Fine ||

| 23 23 25 5 | 23 23 26 6 | 25 67 17 65 | 65 67 6 . |

| 23 23 25 67 | 23 23 26 71 | 21 76 17 65 | 65 67 5 . ||𝄋

Review "My country t'is of thee" by notes then on *la*.

NINETY NINTH LESSON.

Intonation.

Review Nos. 276 & 277.

Dictation.

1st _ Nos. 274 & 275, following large arrows. (page 136)
2nd _ Nº 167. (page 69)

Time.

Review Nº 145.

Staff. (Time)

Review Nº 146.

P_ name first then sing T_ gives the sound of RÉ for DO.

Nº 80.

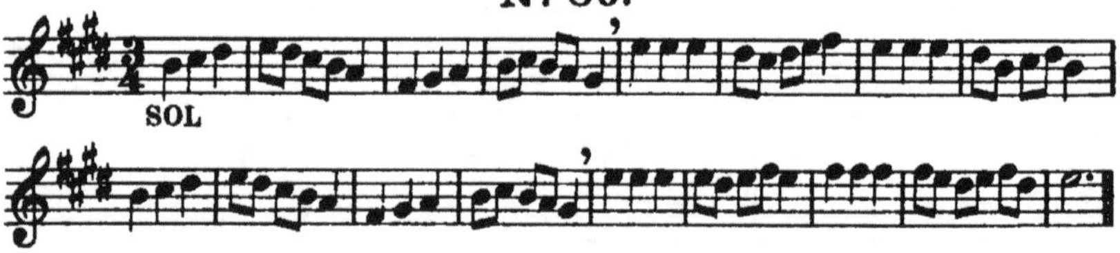
SOL

KEY OF SOL. (5 - 5)

Solfa.

Nº 95. 𝄋‖ 15 13 15 13 | 21 76 52 5 | 15 13 15 13 | 23 23 25 67 |
| 15 13 15 13 | 21 76 55 5 | 15 13 15 13 | 5 5 1 . Fine ‖
| 23 23 21 7 | 12 12 17 6 | 71 71 76 5 | 67 17 6 71 |
| 23 23 21 72 | 12 12 17 61 | 76 57 2 2 | 5 5 6 7 𝄋‖

Review "My country t'is of thee" on lā then add the words to it of 1st verse.

HUNDRETH LESSON.

Intonation.

Study of FA *sharp*.

The acute FA is termed a sharp and is represented by an oblique line crossing the figure going upwards thus: 4, and being intended for a *new sound* a *new name* is given to it FAY. In order to correctly intone this new sound we take as pattern the air DO-SI-DO which we know and we sing SOL-FAY-SOL on the same pitch exactly as if we desired to sing a new verse on the pattern of the first one taking great care *to listen* and be sure to sing SOL-FAY-SOL exactly on the same pitch as DO-SI-DO.

A half dozen repetitions are generally sufficient to enable T_ to proceed with the following exercise.

KEY OF RÉ. **Nº 281.** **Nº 282.**

171 1765 545	545 5671 171	151		171 12345 545	545 54321 171	151
171 176 545	545 671 171	151		171 1234 545	545 4321 171	151
171 17 545	545 71 171	151		171 123 545	545 321 171	151
171 1 545	545 1 171	151		171 12 545	545 21 171	151
				171 1 545	545 1 171	151

Dictation.

1st _ Nº 276 large arrow. (page 137)

2nd _ Nos. 181 & 182. (page 79)

Staff (Time.)

Review Nº 146.

T_ illustrates that for singers the notes on the staff are seldom grouped together and are left to the reader to group them mentally i. e. to see at once in the division of the measure what belongs to the first beat, second beat etc. Ex. Nº 1. 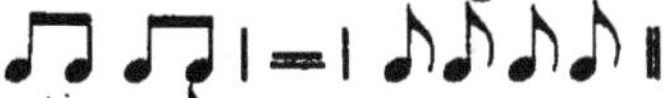

Ex. Nº 2. { Notes on staff / Notes represented by figures } 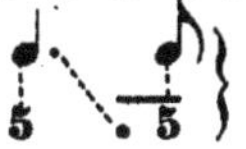

T_ gives the sound of DO for DO.

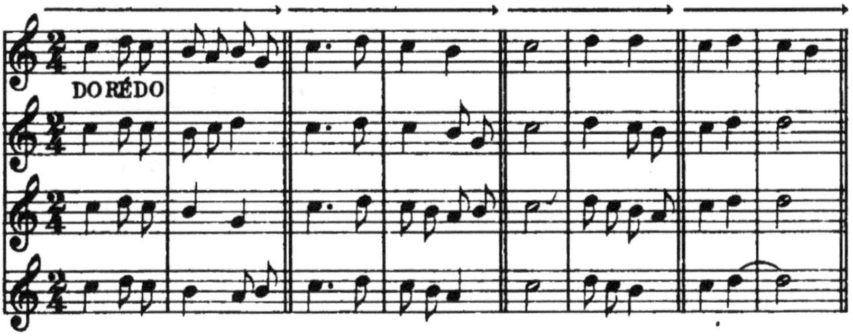
DO RÉ DO

KEY OF RÉ. (5 - 2) **Solfa. Nº 96.**

1 5 6 1 7 2	1 . 3 5	7 . 2 5	1 . 6 5	2 3 4 6 5 4
3 5 1 .	1 7 6 7 1	3 . 2 2	2 3 2 3 2 3	2 . 5 5
2 . 6 6	2 1 7 7	7 1 2 7 5 4	3 6 6 .	5 6 5 6 5 1	1 . 0

T_ will see that the four verses of "My country t'is of thee" are memorized so P_ can sing them at any time without book.

END OF PRIMARY BOOK.

End of the Primary Book.

The SECONDARY book which is in course of publication will treat of the MINOR MODE, the study of CHROMATICS & CHEVE'S THEORY of Music renowned for its clearness and its comprehensive demonstration of the whys and wherefores of things.

Also in course of publication a Series of GRADED Solfas and Duetts for choristers and professionals to be used as a companion to the present manual. *This work making use of staff notation exclusively.*

Note — On account of the feasibility of crowding the EXERCISES, each book will contain six times as much as any other publication known so that when completed they will form a sort of Musical Encyclopedia for the art of teaching the reading of Music at Sight and writing melodies as stenographers do speeches.

Published by

John Zobanaky,

Philadelphia,

Pa.

GALIN-PARIS-CHEVÉ METHOD

AWARDED

GOLD MEDALS at the UNIVERSAL EXHIBITION.

of LONDON 1862, PARIS 1867, 1878, 1889.

EASY POPULAR SIGHT-SINGING MANUAL

BY

John Zobanaky.

THE RECOGNIZED EXPONENT IN AMERICA OF THE

GALIN-PARIS-CHEVÉ METHOD.

Supplement No. 1.

FOR CHORISTERS AND PROFESSIONALS

TO BE USED IN CONJUNCTION

with the

ELEMENTARY BOOK - Part I & II.

REMARKS.

The following series of exercises are to be studied only in conjunction with the first Vol. of the Galin-Paris-Chevé Method in which will be found all instructions to completely master the Major Mode.

As the *Elementary Book,Vol-I* was intended primarily for the use of young children,the staff notation had to be introduced with great care,in order to neither puzzle nor discourage the little ones. This accounts for the publication of this supplement which is intended for choristers and professionals; also for Grammar, High and Normal School pupils, whose mental power being further developed,can be taxed with more difficult work.

The division of study of these exercises can be done in the following manner:

with lessons	1	to	12		staff exercises	1		to	19
,,	,,	13	to	25	,,	,,	20	to	47
,,	,,	26	to	38	,,	,,	48	to	82
,,	,,	39	to	50	,,	,,	83	to	109
,,	,,	51	to	63	,,	,,	110	to	134
,,	,,	64	to	75	,,	,,	135	to	147
,,	,,	76	to	88	,,	,,.	148	to	175
,,	,,	89	to	100	,,	,,	176	to	222
					,,	,,	223	to	270

(*Elementary Book* / *Supplement Book*)

By no means should it be expected or attempted to learn intonation and time by the use of this supplement alone. Each one of the four volumes will have a supplement with the same object in view.

HOW TO TEACH TRANSPOSITION.

The *Meloplast* is a blank staff like the following diagram,and should be made large enough to be seen by every pupil.

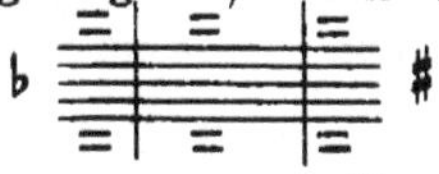

It can be drawn on a black board or still better on cream manilla paper. On this the exercise to be named or sung is indicated by a pointer which the teacher slides up or down at will.When the pointer moves outside of either of the vertical lines the sounds so indicated should be sharped or flatted.In the middle,they remain always naturals.Of course beginners should not attempt sharps and flats, and later, when this step is reached, each sharp should at first always be sung with the note *above*, before and after the sharp and for the flats the note *below* before and after the flat.

When making use of the *Meloplast* and starting with DO on the leger line, the teacher will call attention to the fact that MI will be on the first line and SOL on the second. It should be further impressed on the pupils mind that when DO,MI,SOL,are on lines RE,FA,LA,will be on spaces.This will be exactly reversed in the first octave of these notes either above or below.

The teacher should explain the meaning of an octave(*interval of eight degrees*) and illustrate this point.

No more than three or four weeks should be spent on the study of DO on same line. For the next three or four weeks the DO should be started on the next line,and so on until the DO has been placed on every line.

On reaching the third,fourth and fifth lines,it will be noticed that the DO an octave below will appear on the space. This leaves but one more study—the DO on the second space—which will complete the seven possible positions of the DO. By means of this transposition the pupil will after six or seven months be able to intone any melody in any Major Key.

SOLFAS.

When singing *solfas* the teacher will look first at the compass of the exercises and give a Key suitable for the different voices. B flat to D is a fair range,and one that nearly every one can reach.It is not necessary to adhere strictly to the Key indicated by the signature as the aim is simply to enable pupils to start the DO on any line or space.

The teacher should most carefully observe that during the singing of any exercise perfect pitch is maintained.Sharping and flatting are caused chiefly by carelessness on the part of the pupils. Only pupils who sing accurately can be advised to review lessons at home. Others might only undo the good work done by the teacher. An instrument should *never* be used except to give the key note,or for the verification of a tone, *after* it has been produced.

HINTS FOR HELPING PUPILS TO READ MUSIC.

Pupils should at the outset familiarize themselves thoroughly with the syllables thus:- DO,RÉ,MI,FA,SOL,LA,SI. They should then practice in naming,*not singing*, the syllables of Table No.1 until able to say them from memory very rapidly. Each column should be used separately from bottom to top and top to bottom. After a month Table No.2 should be studied in the same manner -

TABLE No.1.						
DO	RÉ	MI	FA	SOL	LA	SI
SI	DO	RÉ	MI	FA	SOL	LA
LA	SI	DO	RÉ	MI	FA	SOL
SOL	LA	SI	DO	RÉ	MI	FA
FA	SOL	LA	SI	DO	RÉ	MI
MI	FA	SOL	LA	SI	DO	RÉ
RÉ	MI	FA	SOL	LA	SI	DO
DO	RÉ	MI	FA	SOL	LA	SI

TABLE No.2.						
DO	MI	SOL	SI	RÉ	FA	LA
LA	DO	MI	SOL	SI	RÉ	FA
FA	LA	DO	MI	SOL	SI	RÉ
RÉ	FA	LA	DO	MI	SOL	SI
SI	RÉ	FA	LA	DO	MI	SOL
SOL	SI	RÉ	FA	LA	DO	MI
MI	SOL	SI	RÉ	FA	LA	DO
DO	MI	SOL	SI	RÉ	FA	LA

The object of this is to remove all hesitancy in recalling the syllable names,whether they occur at intervals of seconds[a] or thirds[b]

HOME PRACTICE.

Pupils should practice daily at home the *naming* of notes of the exercises corresponding to the study with the teacher;each line several times, then the whole exercise several times.

(a)SECONDS—Interval of two degrees.　　(b)THIRDS—Interval of three degrees.

When taking up the study of a new position of DO, three fourths of the practice time should be allowed for it. The remaining one fourth should be devoted to the previous position. On reaching the next position, pupils will give half of the time to the new position; the remainder to the positions previously learned, and so on through all the seven positions, thus always devoting more time to the newest positions.

By placing DO on successive lines, the pupils are somewhat prepared by preceding exercises, whereas if DO were changed from a line to a space at the outset some confusion would result, and the difficulty be greatly increased.

TIME PRACTICE.

Monsieur Aimée Paris' Time-name is perhaps the only one that has been adopted into the majority of systems and has been recognized as of great value by prominent educators throughout the world; but whether Mons. Paris' time-name is used or not, the syllables and their vowels are absolutely necessary to obtain good results. Thus: ex. 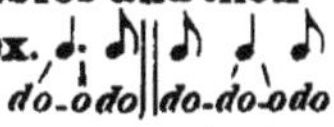
do-odo
do-do-odo

Pupils should practice singing both with and without beating, to obtain a thorough mastery of time. Except when the special need is felt in a complicated passage, beating should be done mechanically, with no thought of the hand, just as walking is accomplished with no thought of the limbs.

PART SINGING.

The instructions in Elementary Book will give all necessary suggestions on this point. The blending of the voices, the phrasing and the shading should be carefully looked after.

HOW TO LOCATE ON THE STAFF

THE FIRST DEGREE OF ANY MAJOR KEY.

Until pupils have studied the formation of scales sufficiently to recognize them by their signatures, some temporary means must be given whereby they may properly locate the DO.

The last sharp added is invariably the seventh degree of the scale *(si)* so that on the next line or space above will be the DO; and in the case of flats the last one added is always the fourth *(fa)* no matter what the clefs are. Pupils may count the syllables in succession either way until the DO is located.

HOW TO MULTIPLY EXERCISES.

Ambitious pupils will find in the following instructions a great resource for increasing their knowledge.

In looking at Exercises Nos. 230 and 231 it will be noticed that between every two bars there are the same number of notes. When such exercises are thoroughly mastered by columns and across without regard to the time, they may be reviewed by columns first, assigning to them one of the following time marks, which are taken as patterns for the whole exercise.

PATTERN No.1. PATTERN No.2. PATTERN No.3.

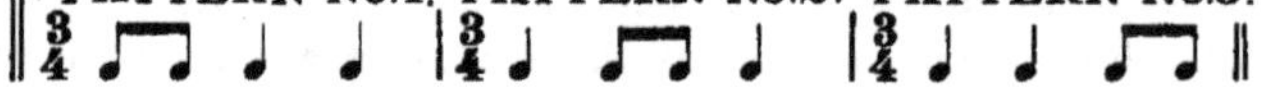

Pupils will sing first Pattern No.1 by column and then all across, then the next pattern and so on. The key may be changed with advantage and the speed increased little by little.

PATTERNS FOR EXERCISES CONTAINING FIVE NOTES.

No.1. No.2. No.3. No.4. No.5. No.6. No.7.

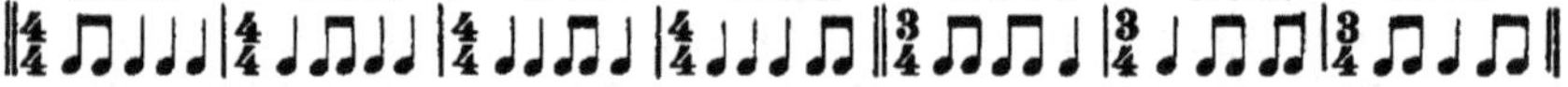

Several weeks may be spent with these exercises thus adapted, and their transposition on the staff in all keys would afford excellent practice in writing.

TABLES SHOWING THE RELATIVE DURATION OF NOTES AND RESTS.

The Whole note
is equal to two half notes
or 4 quarter notes
or 8 eighth notes
or 16 sixteenth notes

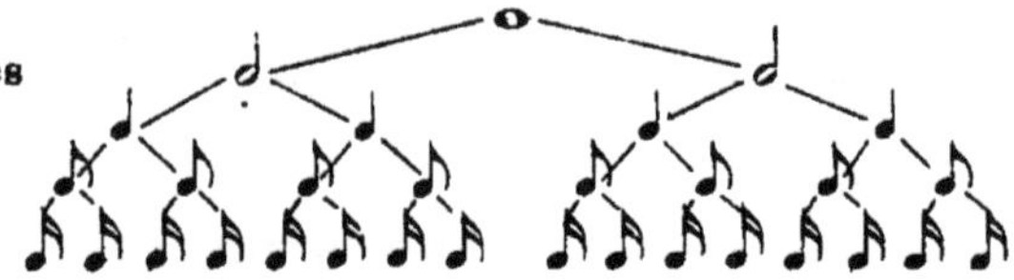

A dot placed after a note increases it by half its length—e.g.
𝅝· = 𝅝 𝅗𝅥 or 𝅗𝅥 𝅗𝅥 𝅗𝅥 or 𝅗𝅥· = 𝅗𝅥 ♩ or ♩ ♩ ♩ ♩· = ♩ ♪ or ♪ ♪ ♪

A second dot adds to the note half the length of the first—e.g. ♩·· = ♩ ♪ 𝅘𝅥𝅯

The whole rest
is equal to 2 half rests
or 4 quarter rests
or 8 eighth rests
or 16 sixteenth rests

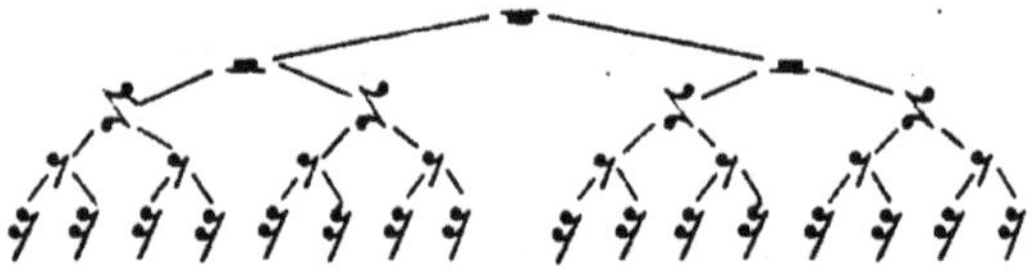

Dots attached to rests effect them as they do notes of sound—e.g.
𝄽· = 𝄽 𝄾 𝄽·· = 𝄽 𝄾 𝄿

TABLE OF TIME MARKS.

The forms marked 2/1, 3/1 are only found in ancient music, and 2/8 and 4/8 are but rarely used.

BINARY DIVISION.			
TWO BEATS.	THREE BEATS.	FOUR BEATS.	VALUE OF EACH BEAT.
2/1 𝅝 𝅝	3/1 𝅝 𝅝 𝅝	4/1 𝅝 𝅝 𝅝 𝅝	𝅝
2/2 or ¢ 𝅗𝅥 𝅗𝅥	3/2 𝅗𝅥 𝅗𝅥 𝅗𝅥	4/2 𝅗𝅥 𝅗𝅥 𝅗𝅥 𝅗𝅥	𝅗𝅥
2/4 ♩ ♩	3/4 ♩ ♩ ♩	4/4 or C ♩ ♩ ♩ ♩	♩
2/8 ♪ ♪	3/8 ♪ ♪ ♪	4/8 ♪ ♪ ♪ ♪	♪

Exercises Nos 1 and 2 to be *named only* by syllables, — not to be sung.

G or SOL clef on the second line.

1

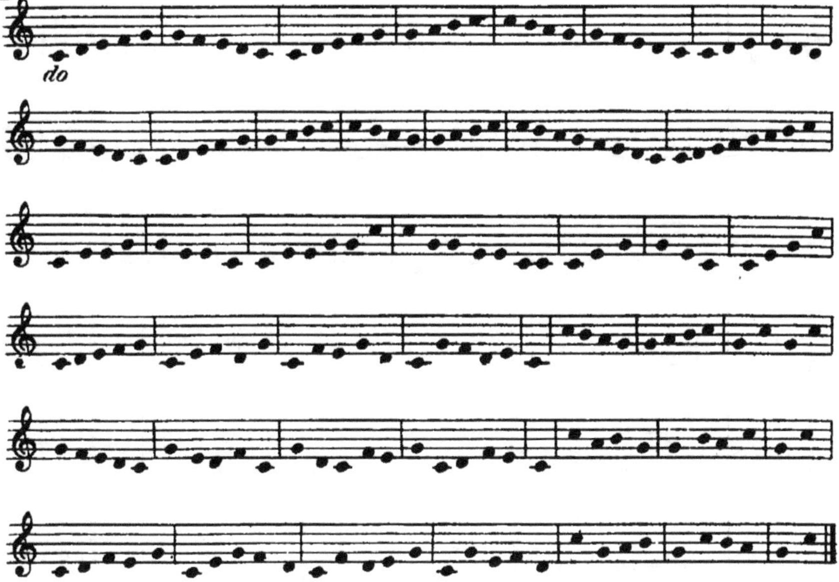
do

2

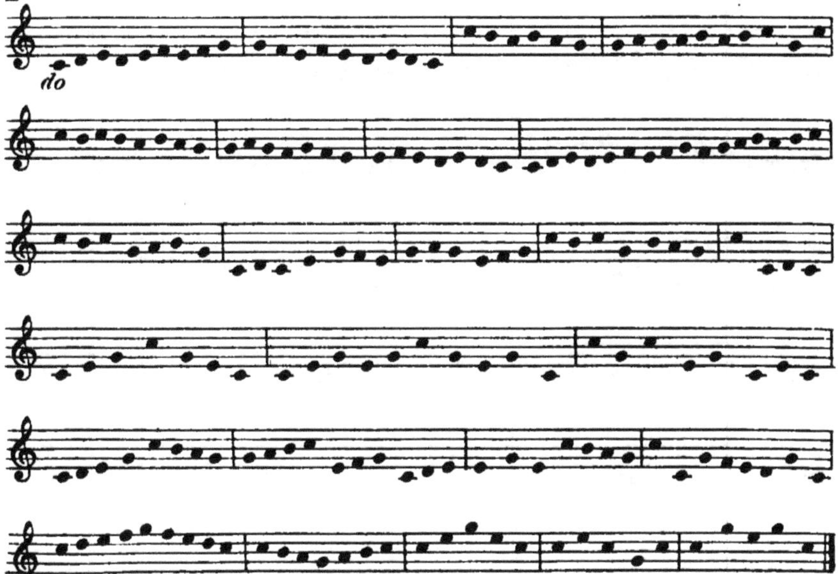
do

Pupils should prepare all exercises at home, *naming* by syllables in strict time, in order to save time at lesson, when they are expected to sing them.

3

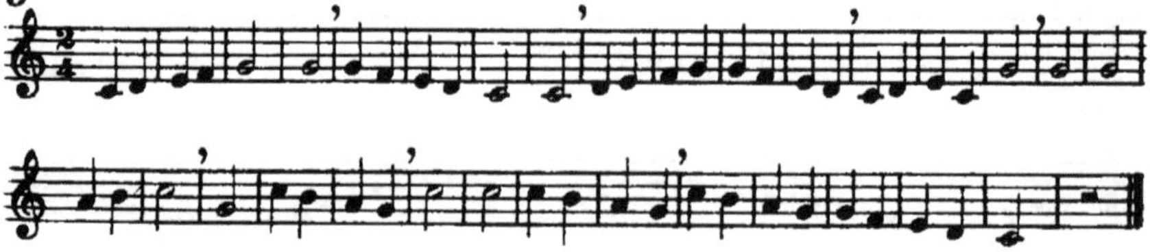

4

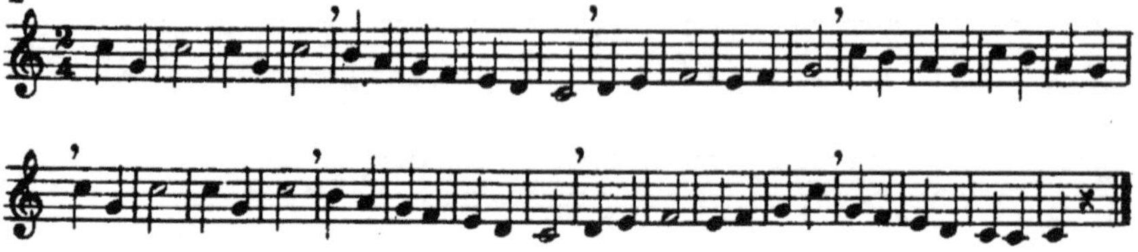

5

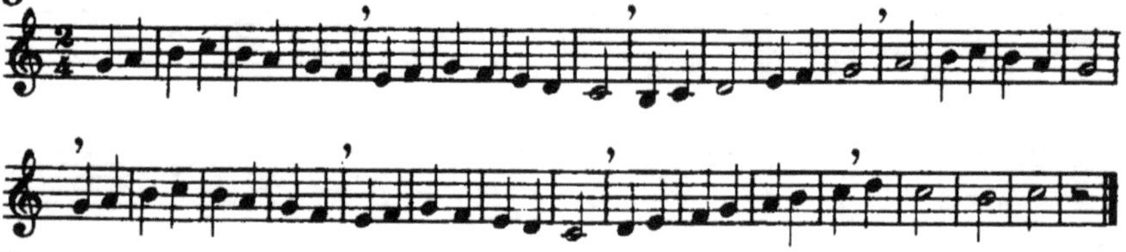

6

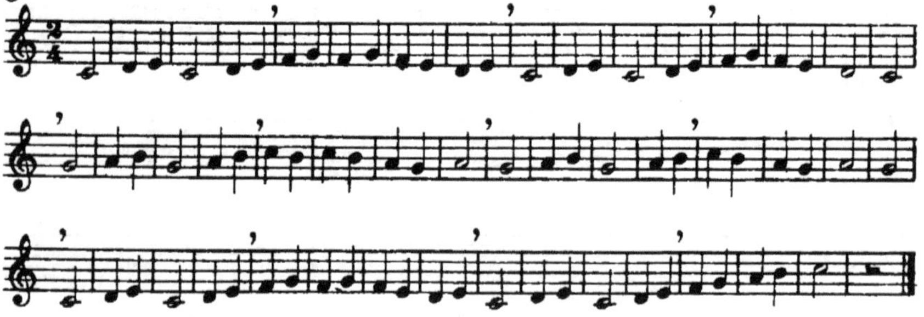

7

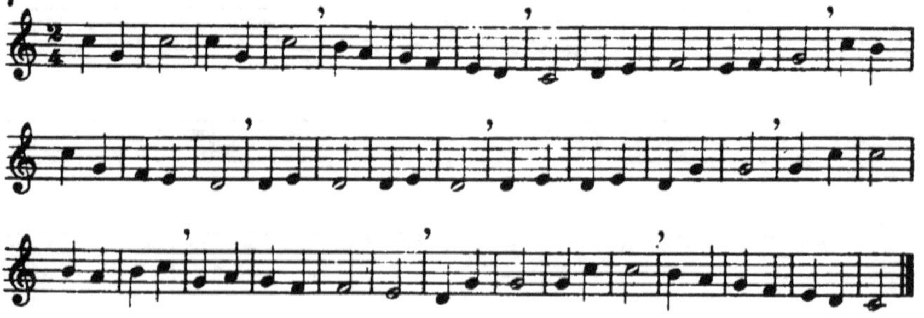

8

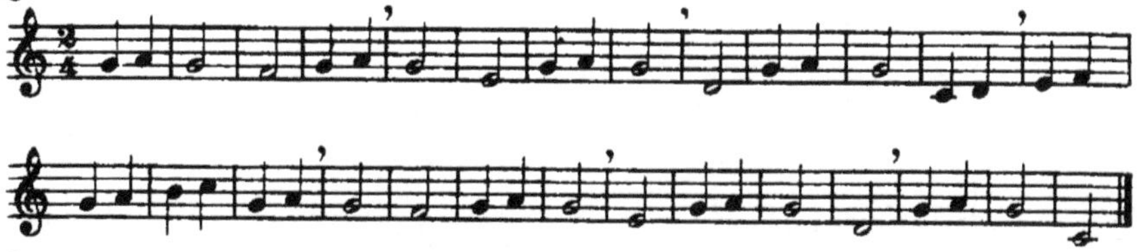

9

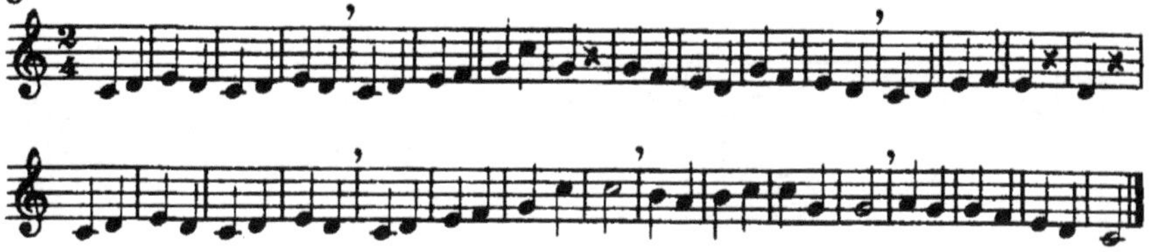

10

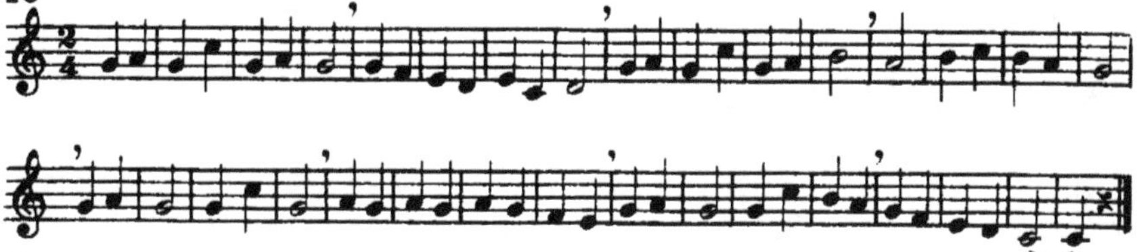

11

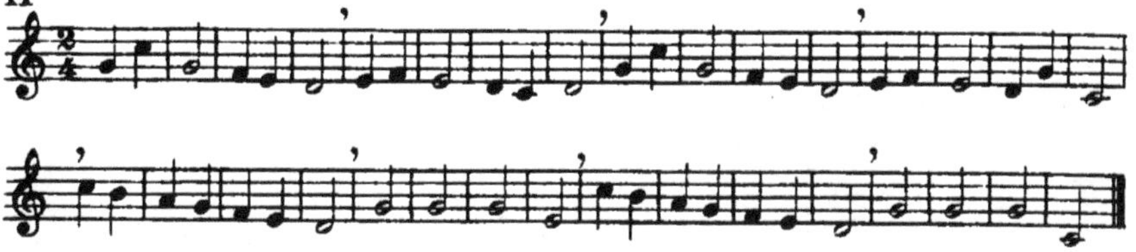

12

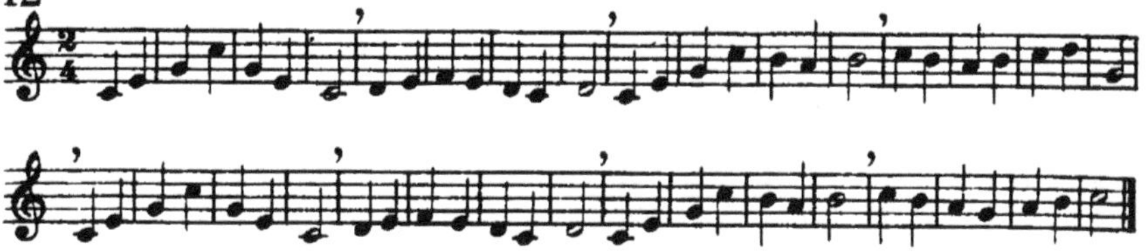

13

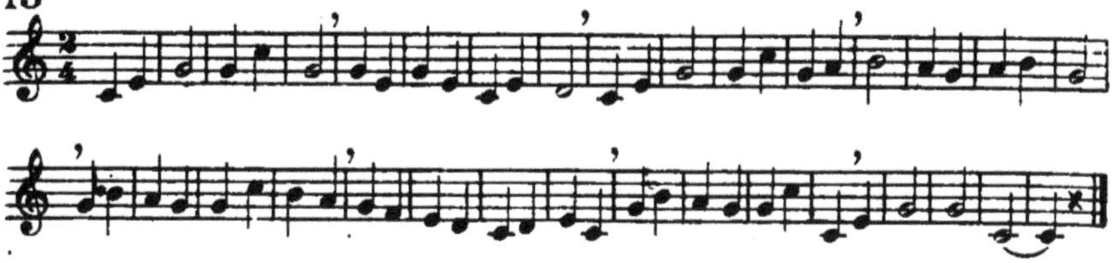

14 Moderato. ♩ = 96

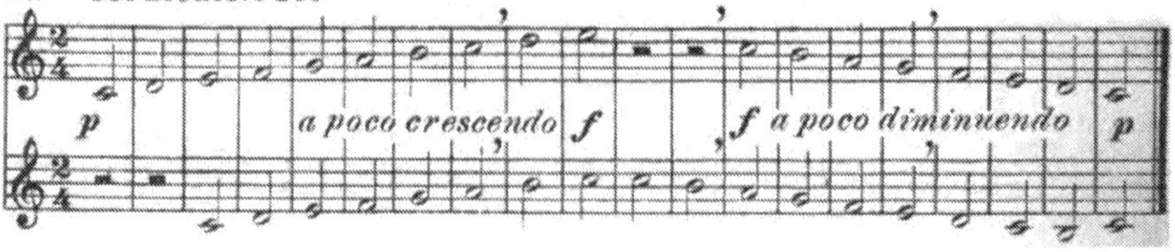
p
a poco crescendo
f
f a poco diminuendo
p

15

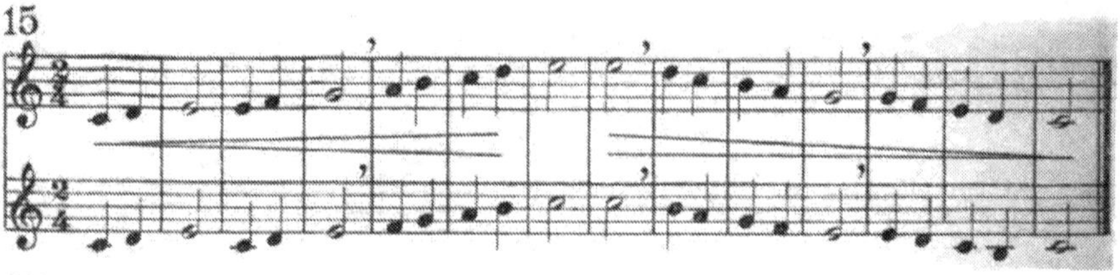

16 Lento. ♩ = 72

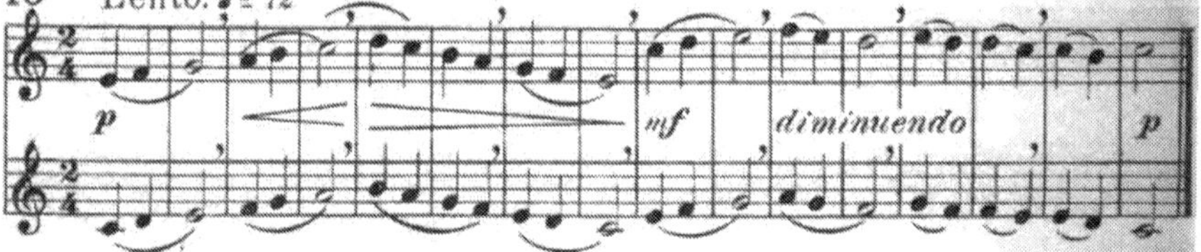
p
mf
diminuendo
p

17

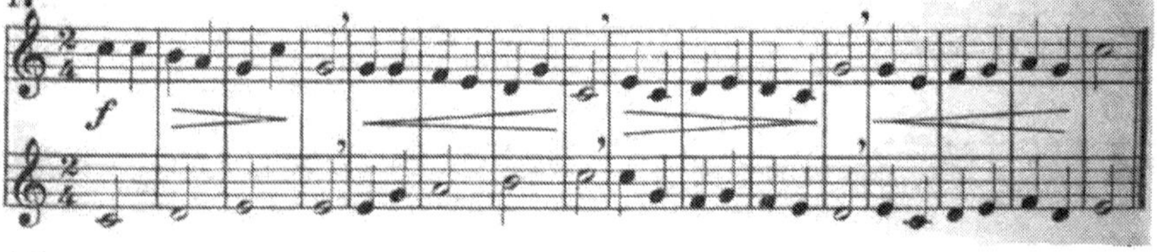
f

18

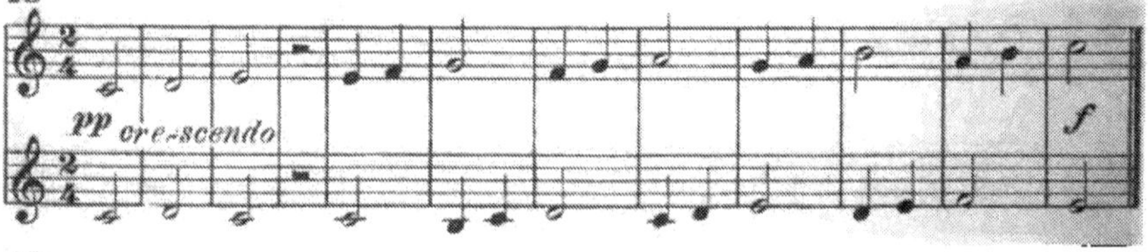
pp cre-scendo
f

19

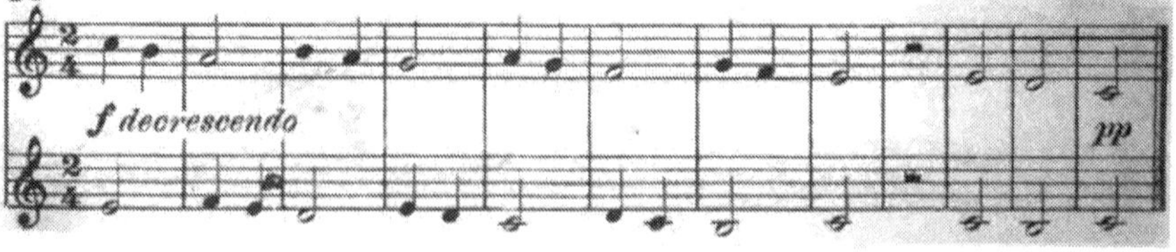
f decrescendo
pp

TIME PRACTICE.

$\frac{2}{4}$ means that every measure should contain the value of two quarter notes — two beats to the measure. *See Elementary Book page 106*

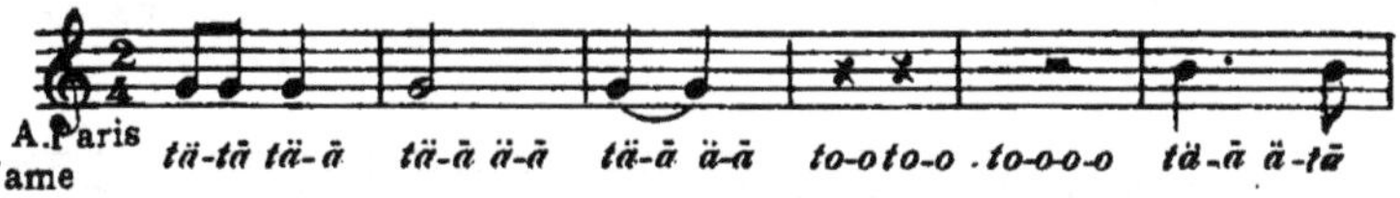
tä-tä tä-ä tä-ä ä-ä tä-ä ä-ä to-o to-o . to-o-o-o tä-ä ä-tä

Monsieur A. Paris
Time Name

Pupils can beat the time, saying in perfectly equal division, *one, two,* for the down beat; *one, two,* for the up beat, before singing the following.

20

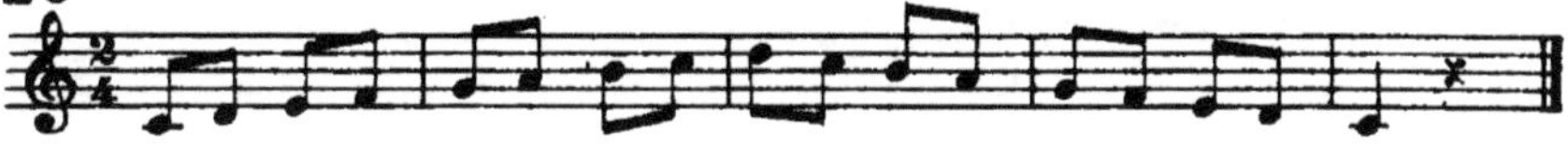

21

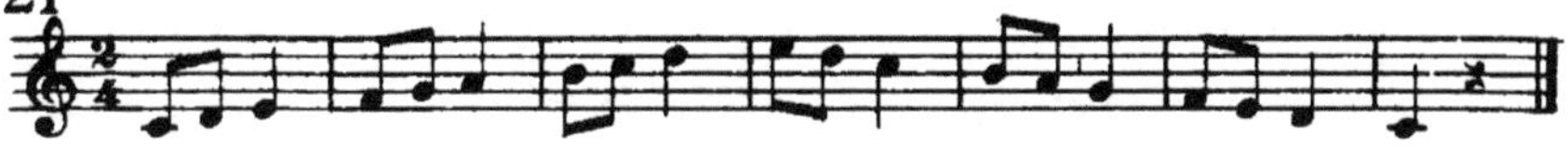

22

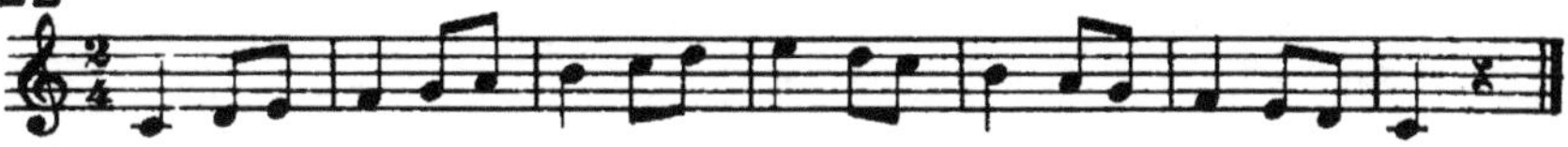

23

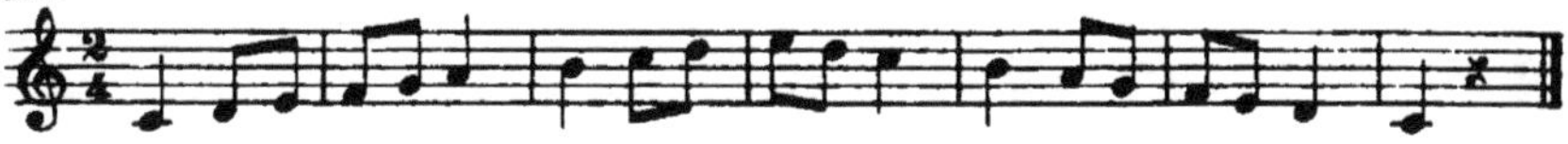

24

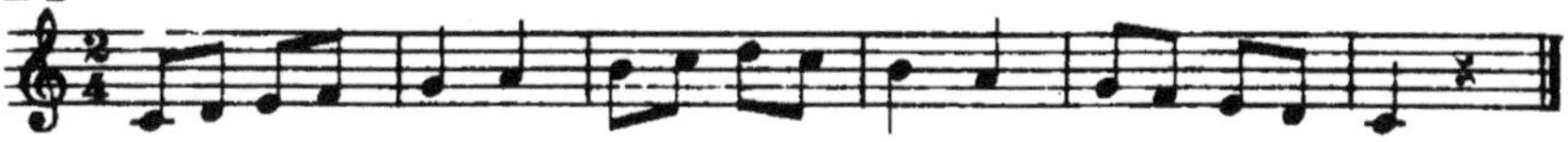

25

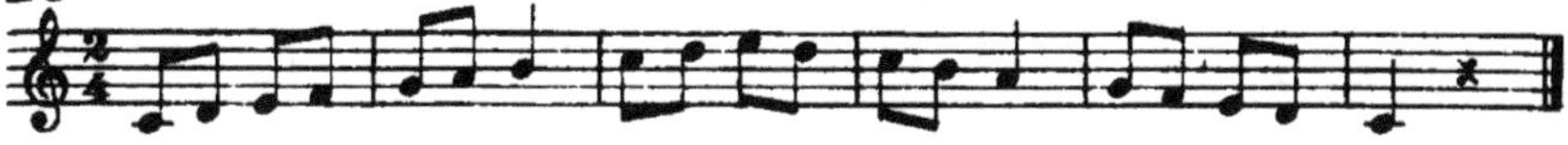

26

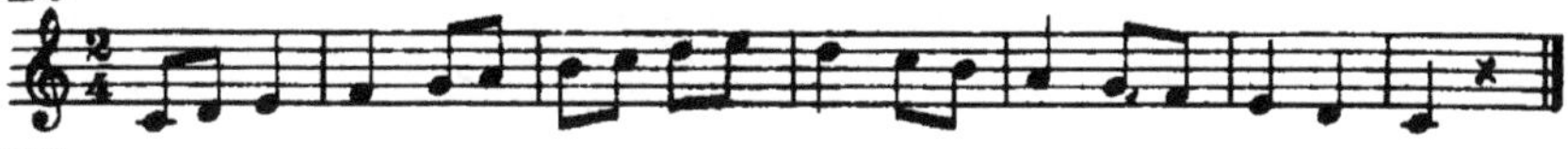

27

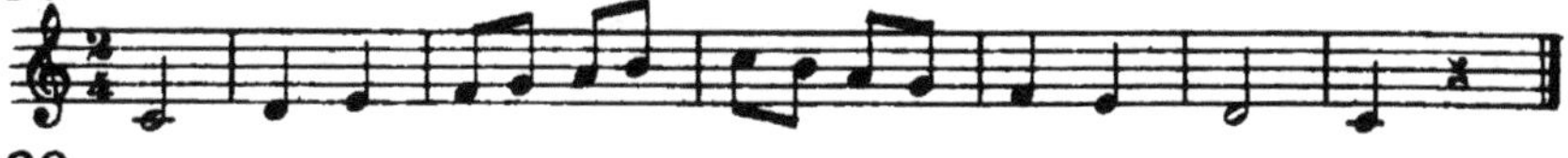

28

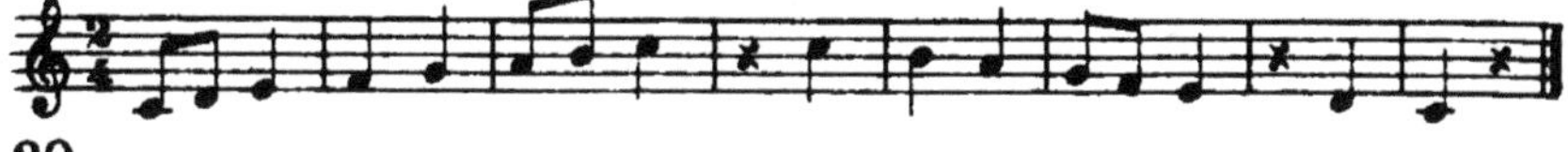

29

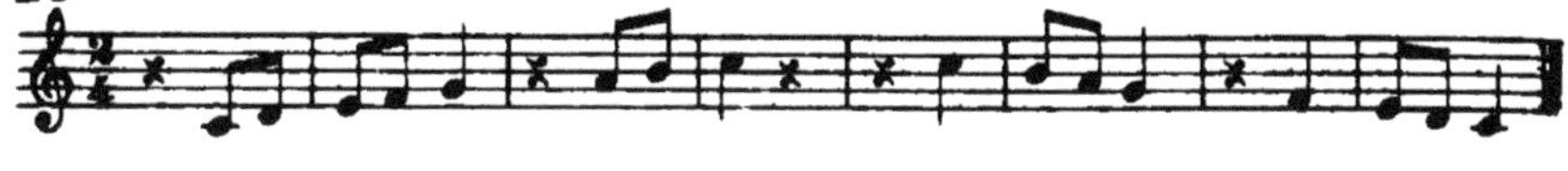

Exercises Nos 30 and 31 to be *named only* by syllables - not to be sung. C or DO clefset on the first line.

30

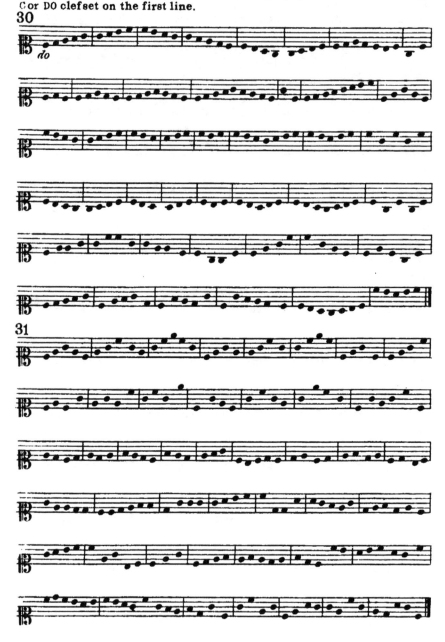

$\frac{3}{4}$ means that each measure should contain the value of three quarter notes - three beats to the measure.

32

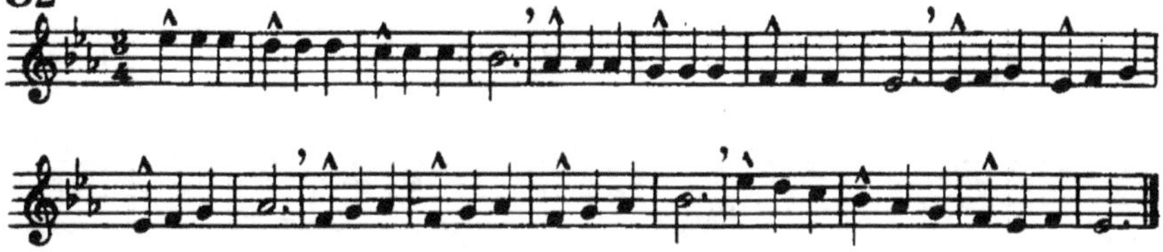

33

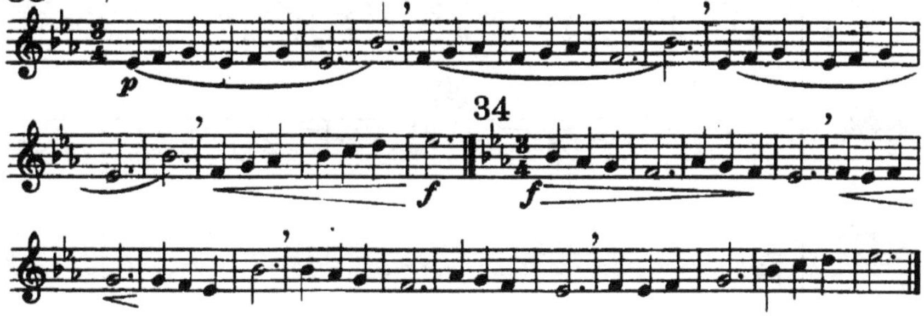
p
34
f
f

35

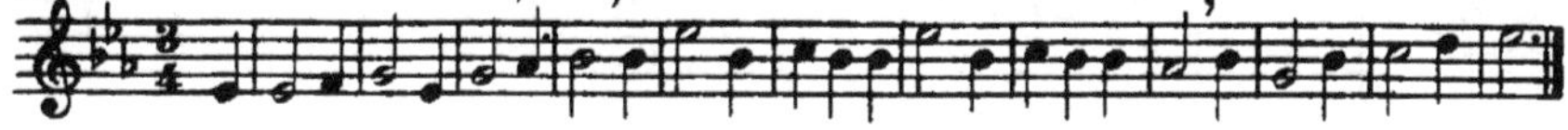

36

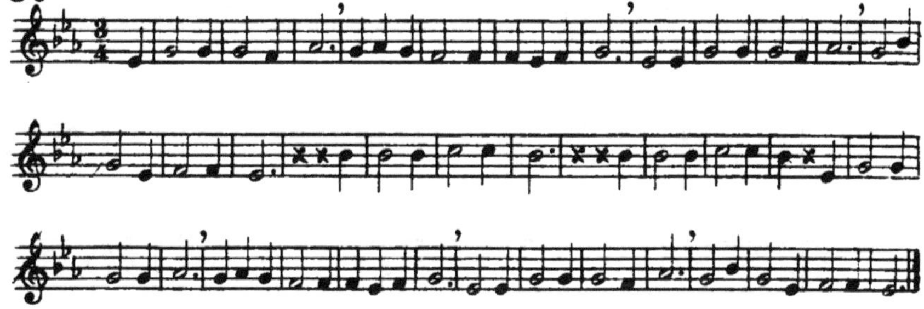

37

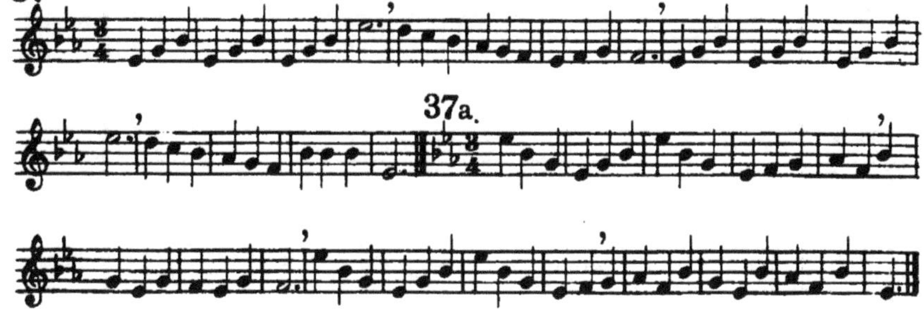
37a.

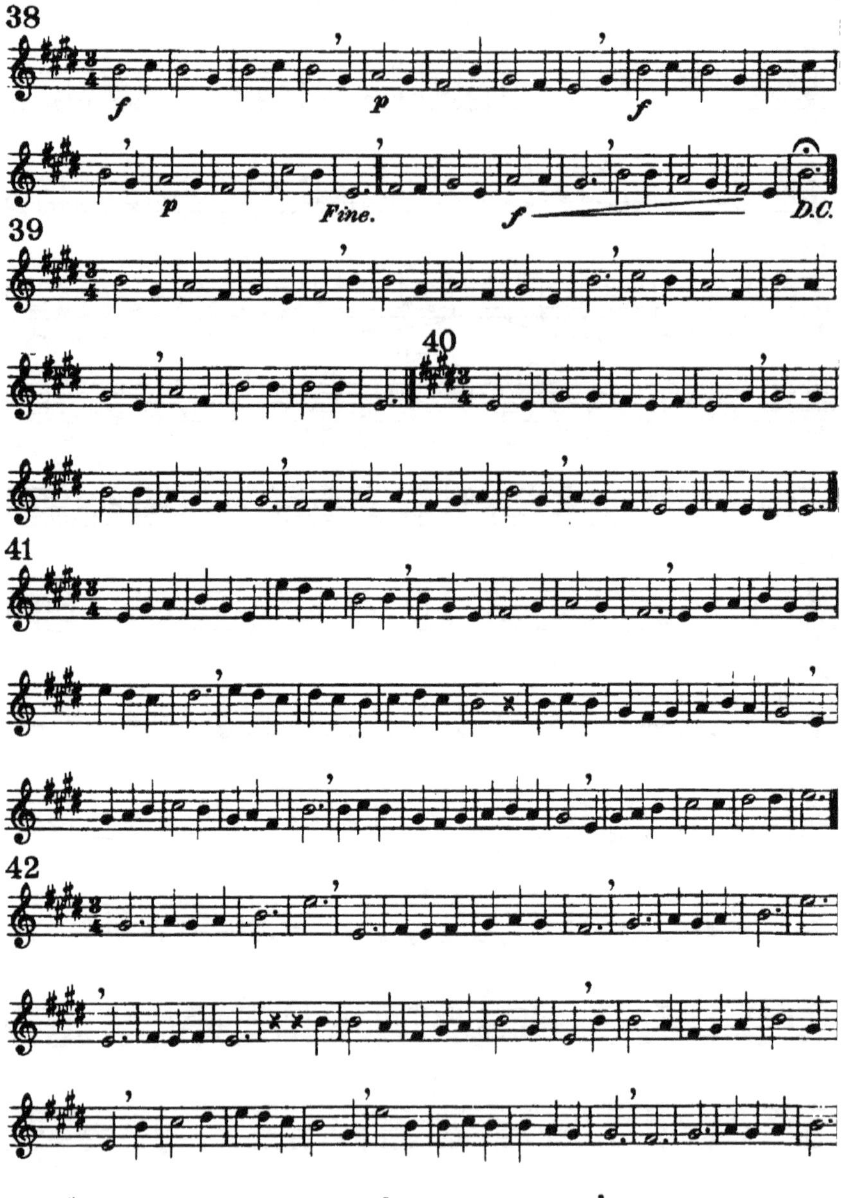
38
f
p
f
p
Fine.
f
D.C.
39
40
41
42

43

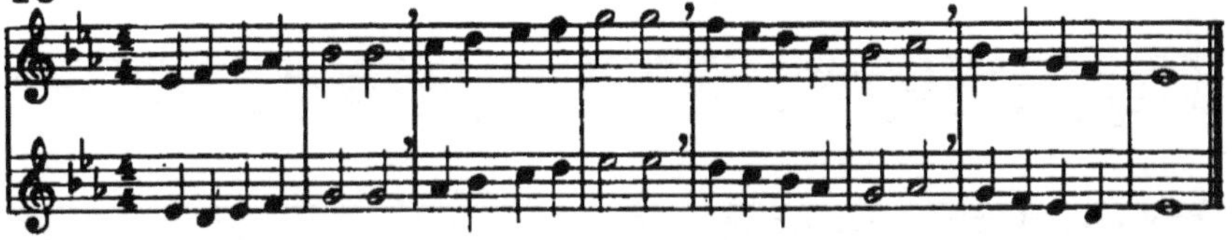

44

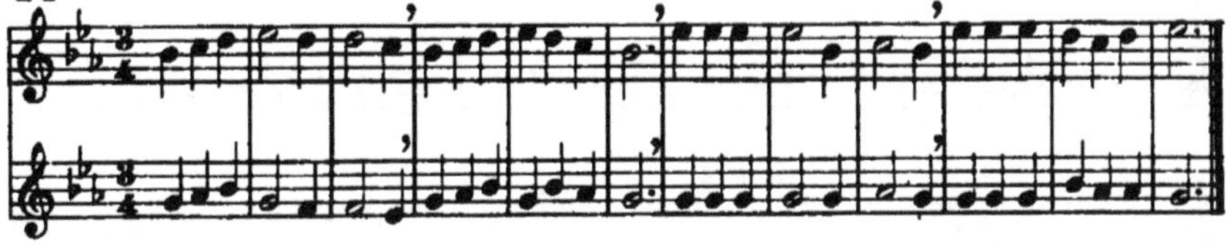

45

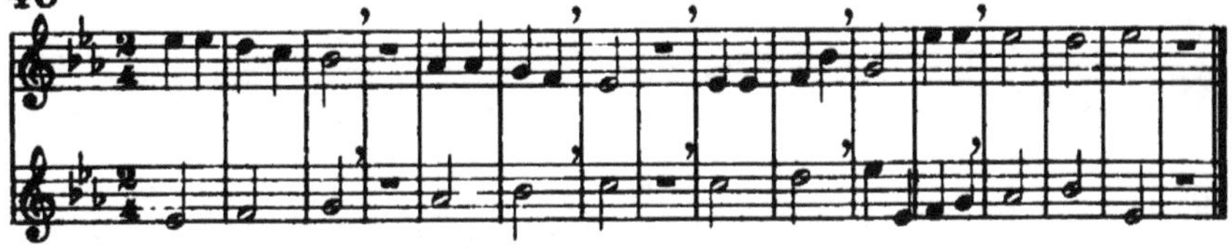

46

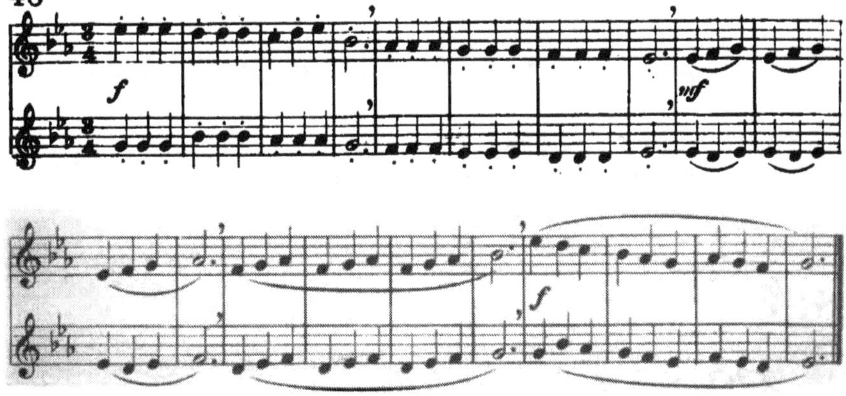
f
mf
f

47

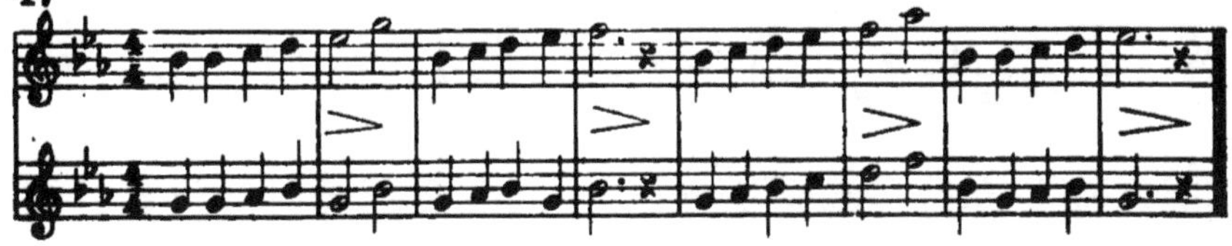

TIME PRACTICE.

$\frac{3}{4}$ means that each measure should contain the value of three quarter notes—three beatsto the measure.

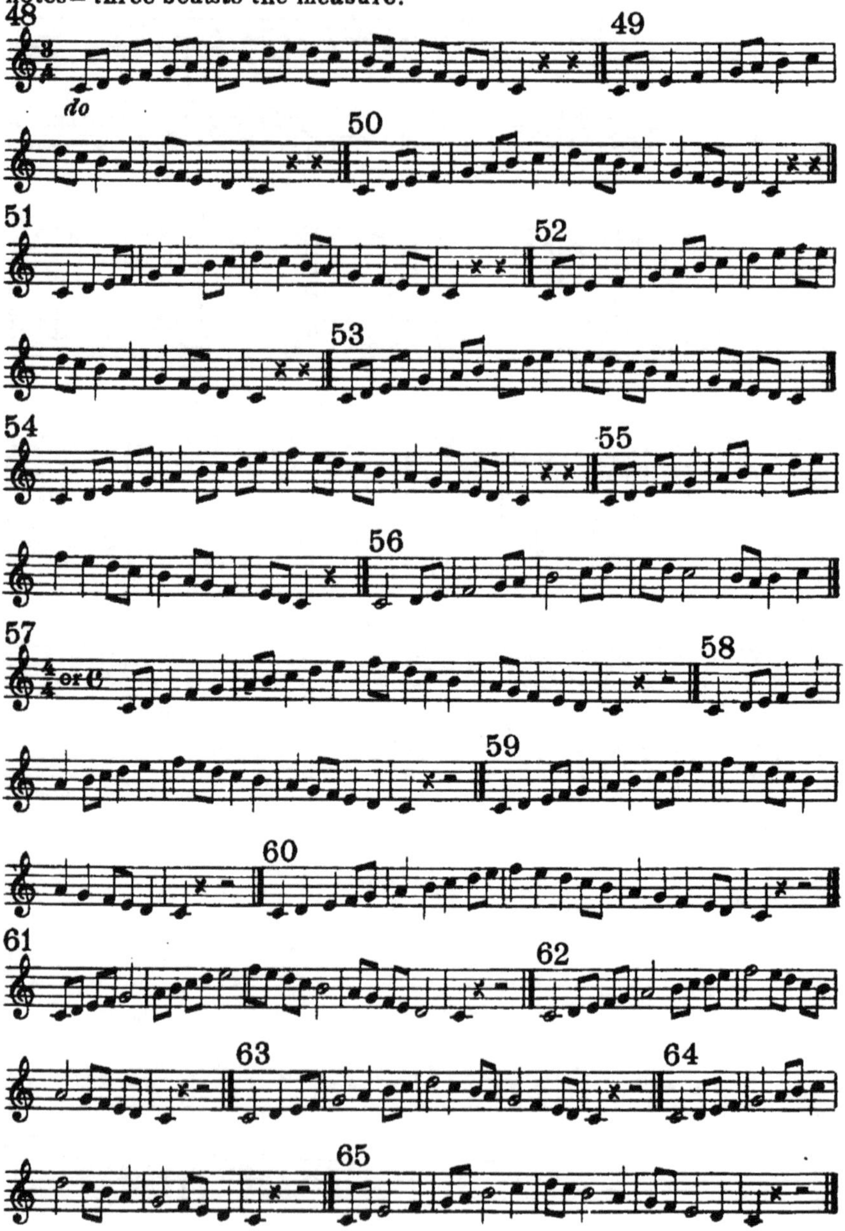
48
do
49
50
51
52
53
54
55
56
57
4/4 or C
58
59
60
61
62
63
64
65

Exercises Nos 66 and 67 to be *named only* by syllables — not to be sung.

66 **C or DO clef on second line.**

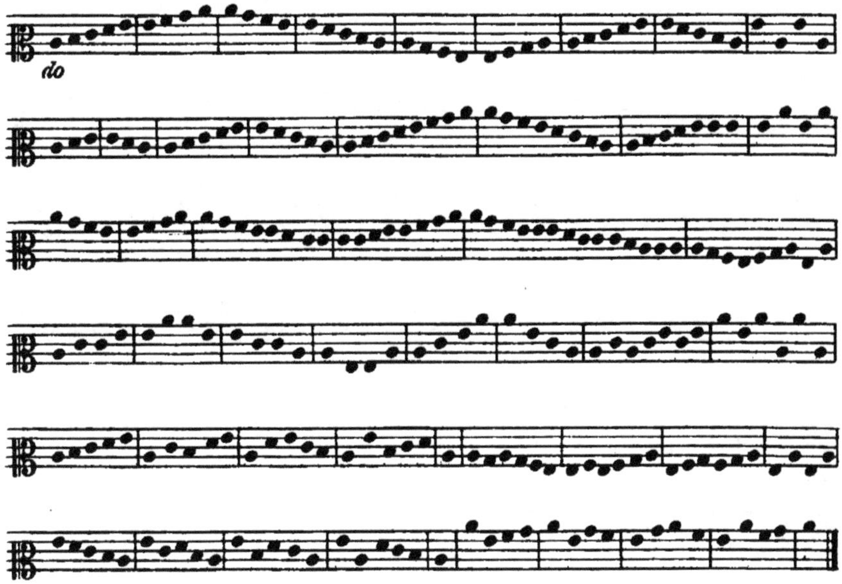
do

67

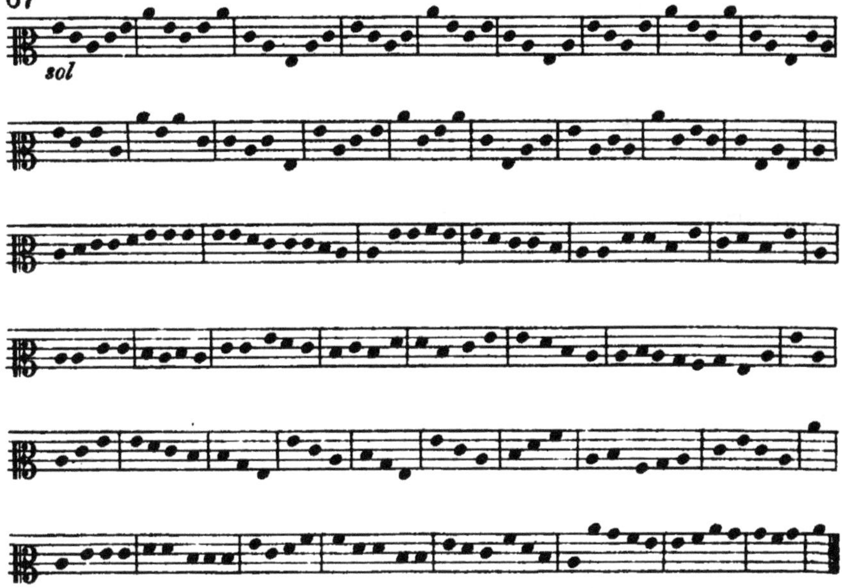
sol

SOLFAS.

68

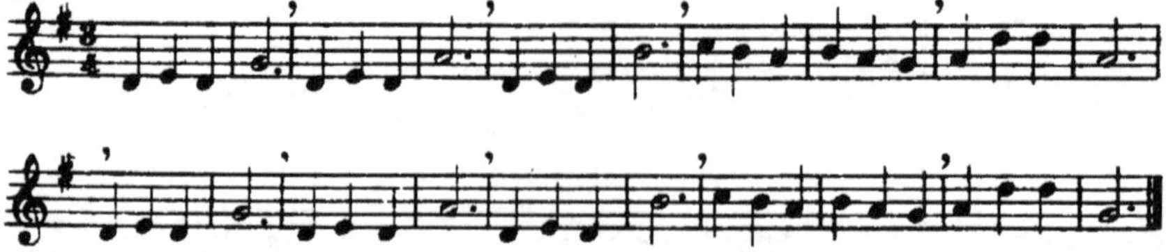

69

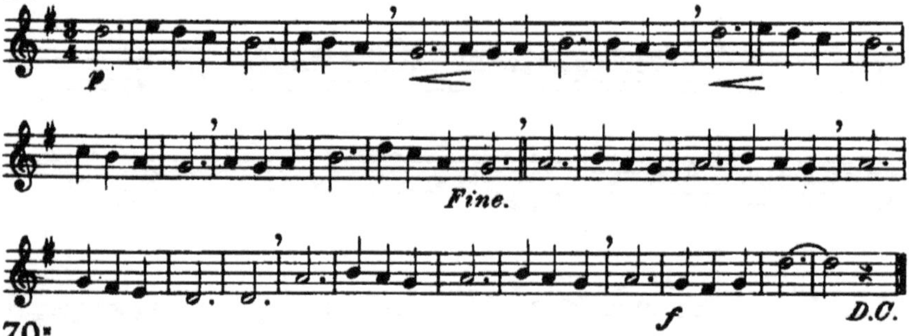
p
Fine.
f
D.C.

70*

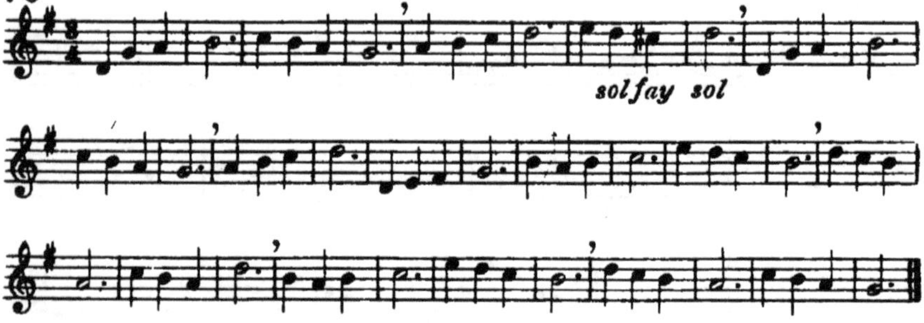
solfay sol

71

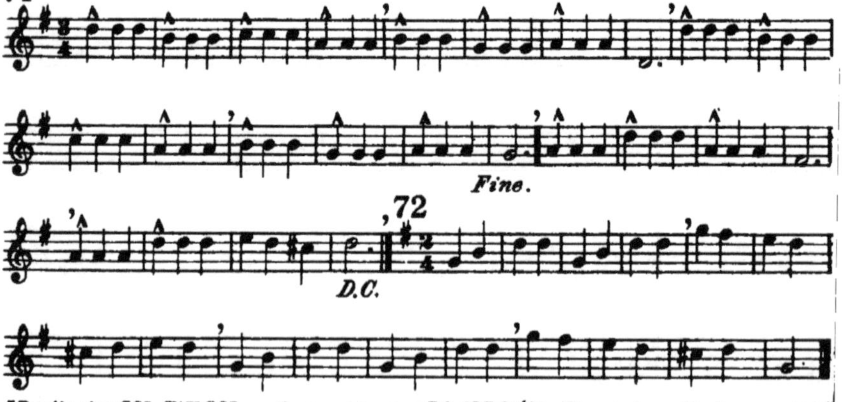
Fine.
D.C.
72

*Pupils sing SOL-FAY-SOL on the same tune as DO-SI-DO. (*See Elementary Book, page 146.*)

73

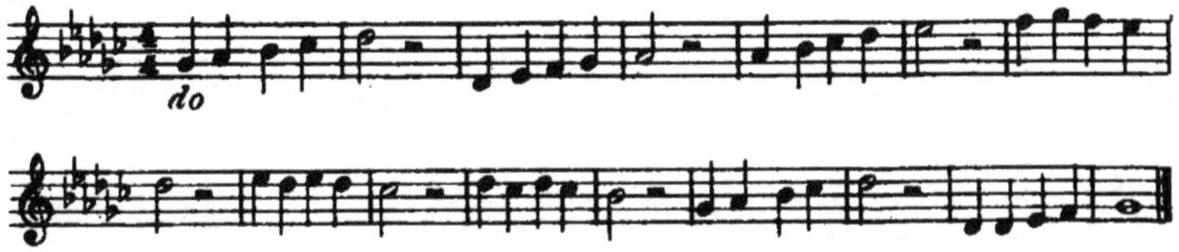
do

74

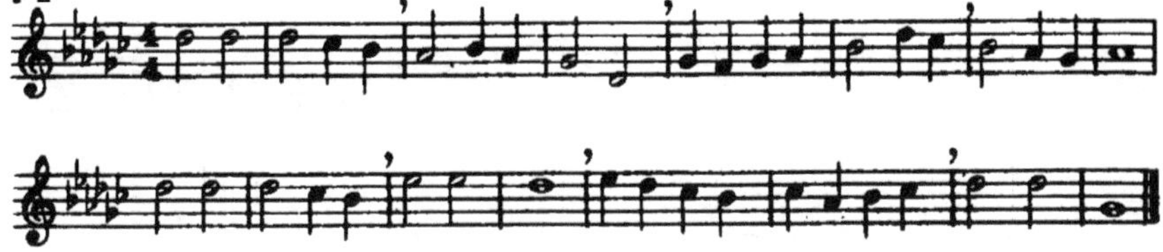

75

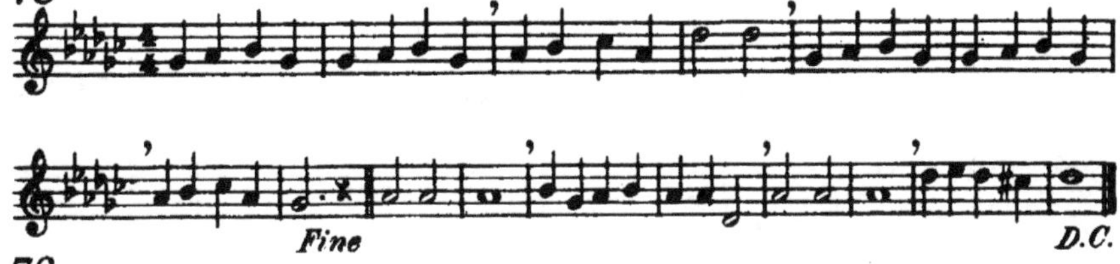
Fine
D.C.

76

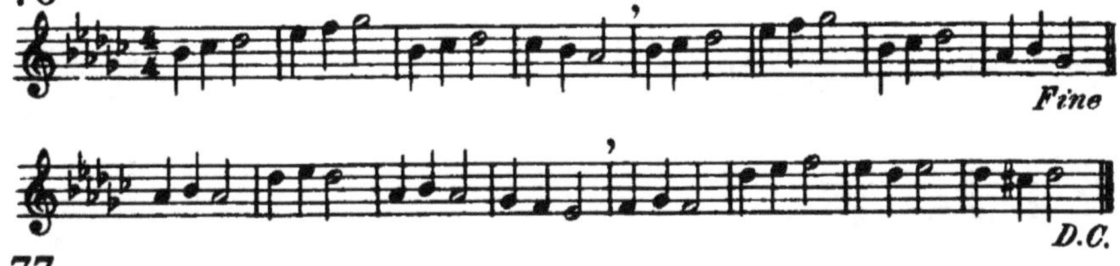
Fine
D.C.

77

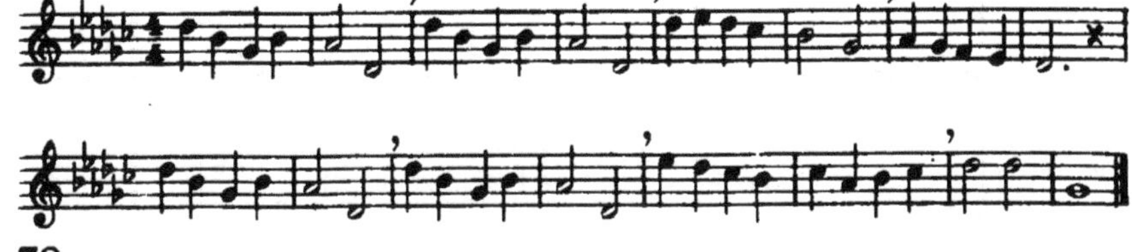

78

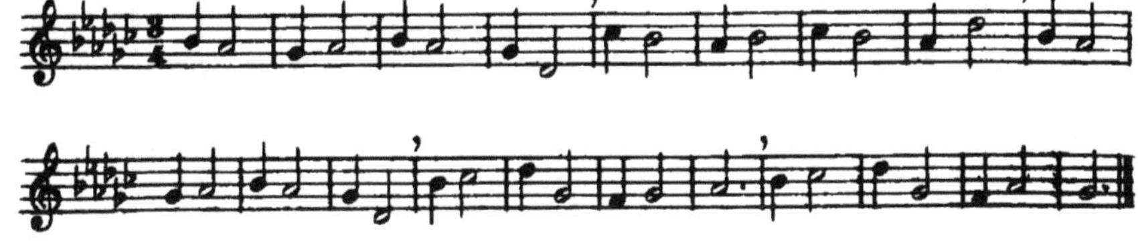

SOLFAS FOR TWO VOICES.

79

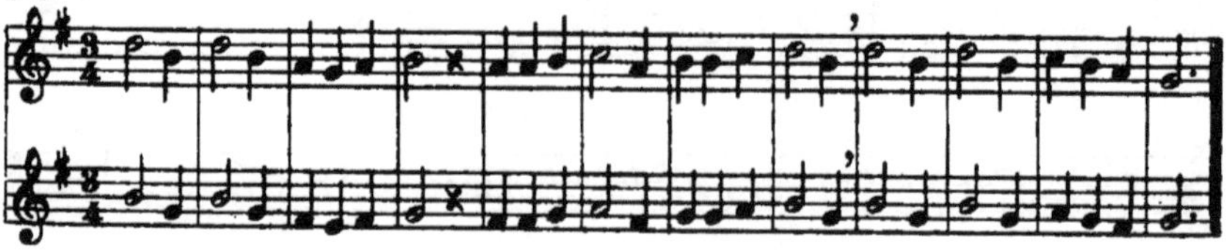

80

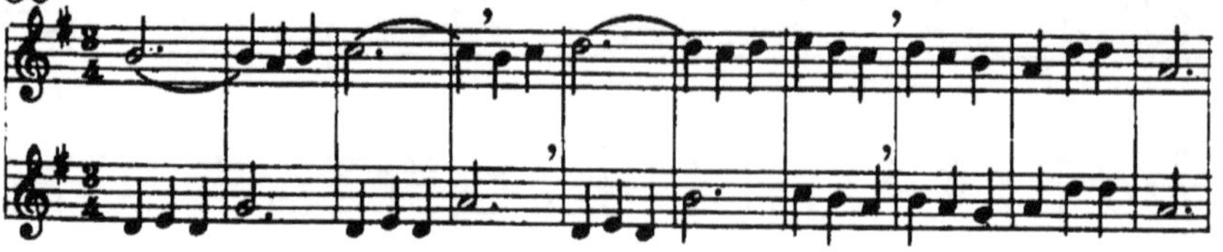

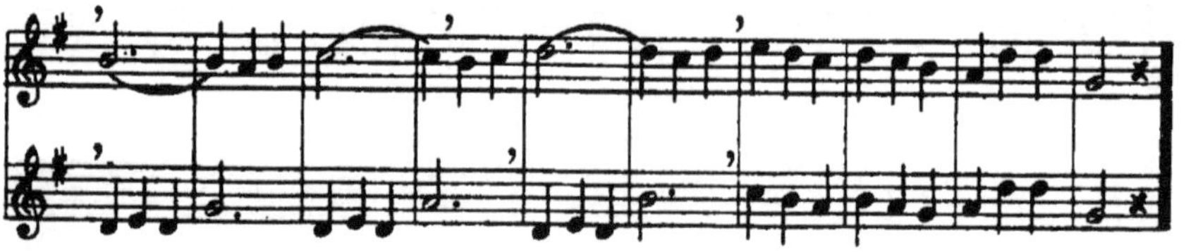

81

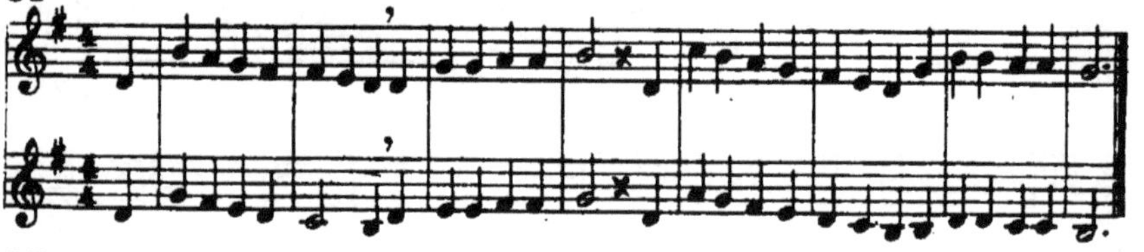

82

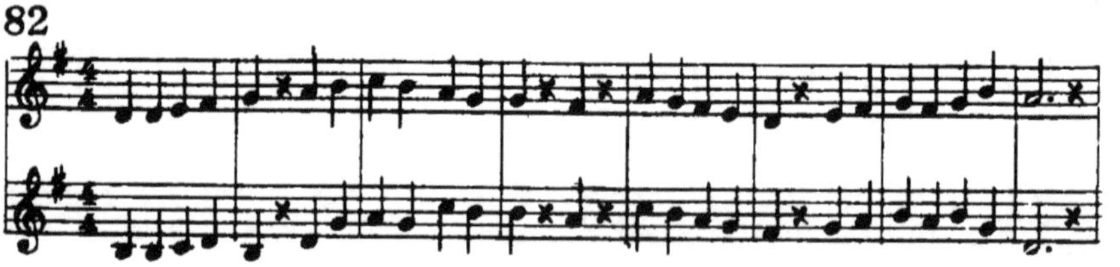

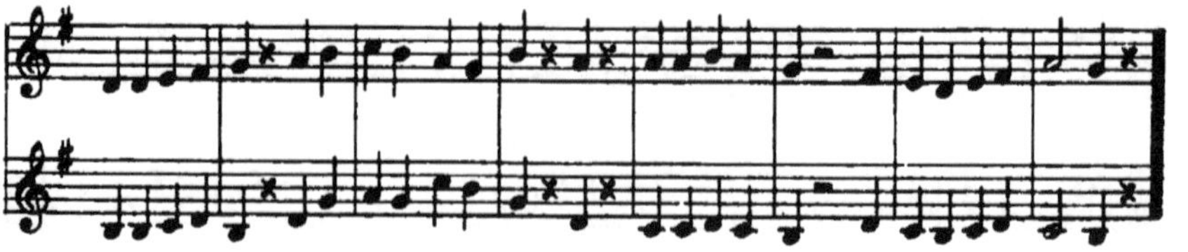

TIME PRACTICE.

Pupils may at first sing the *to* on the pitch of the preceding note after which the teacher may say *to* for the rest until such help is found unecessary.

83

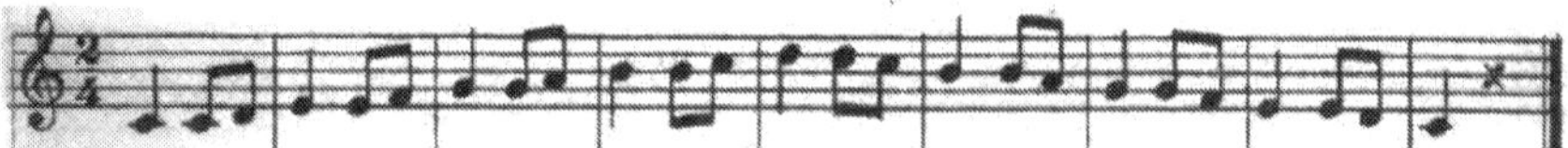

84

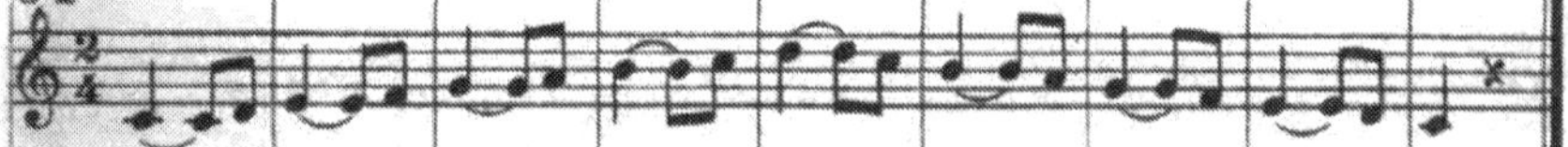

Do - o Ré Mi - i Fa So - ol etc.

85

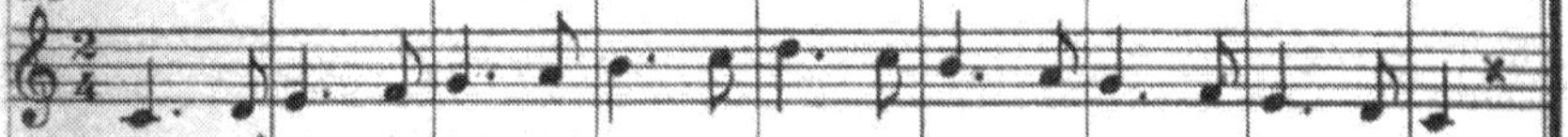

Do - o Ré Mi - i Fa So - ol La

86

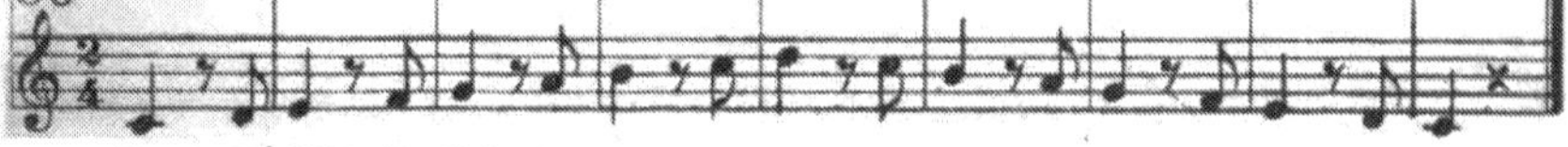

Do to Ré Mi to Fa Sol etc.

87

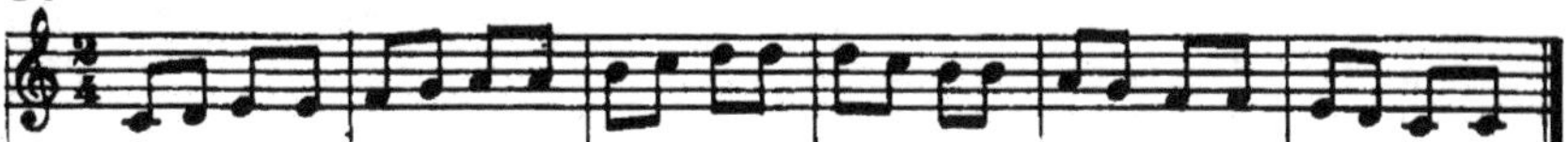

88

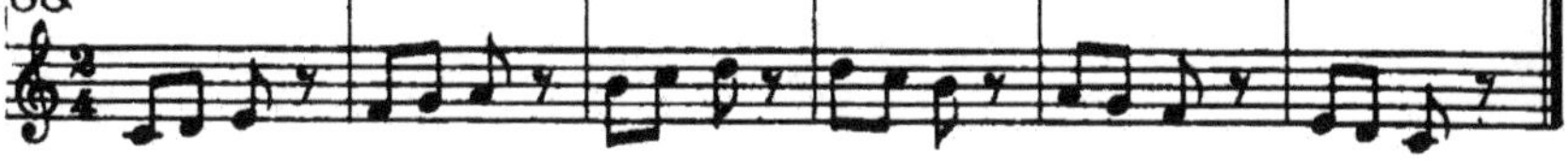

89

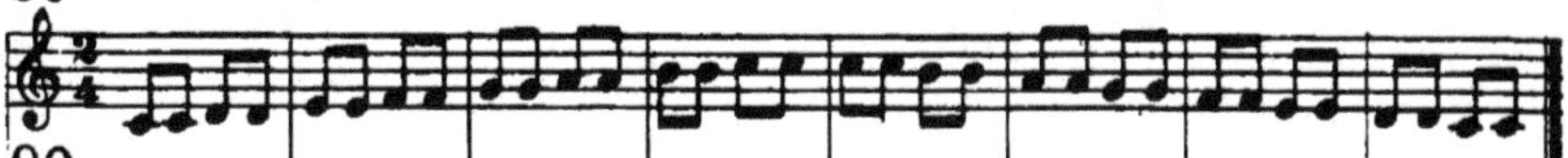

90

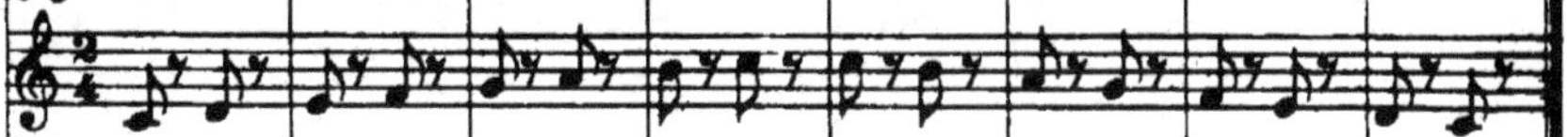

91

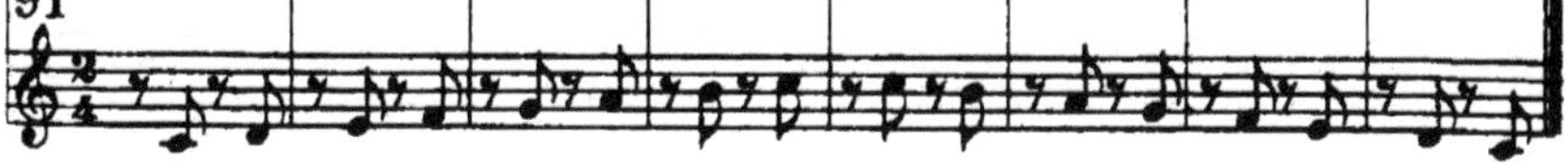

92

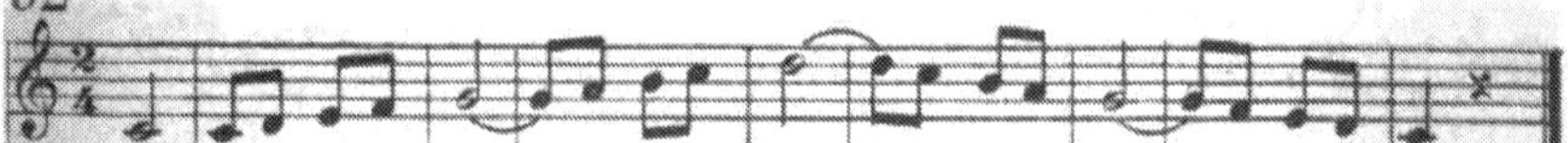

Do - o etc.

93

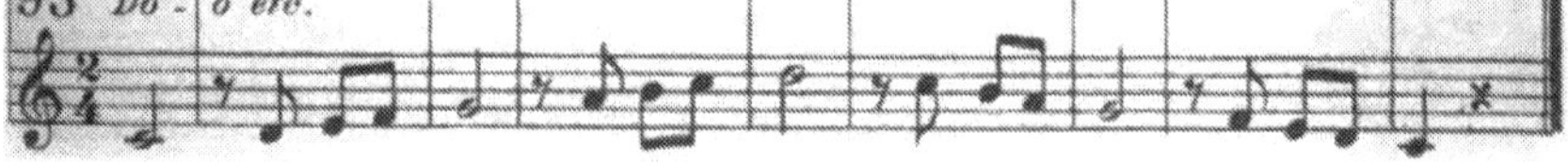

Exercises Nos. 94 and 95 to be *named only* by syllables-not tobe sung.

C or DO clef on the third line.

94

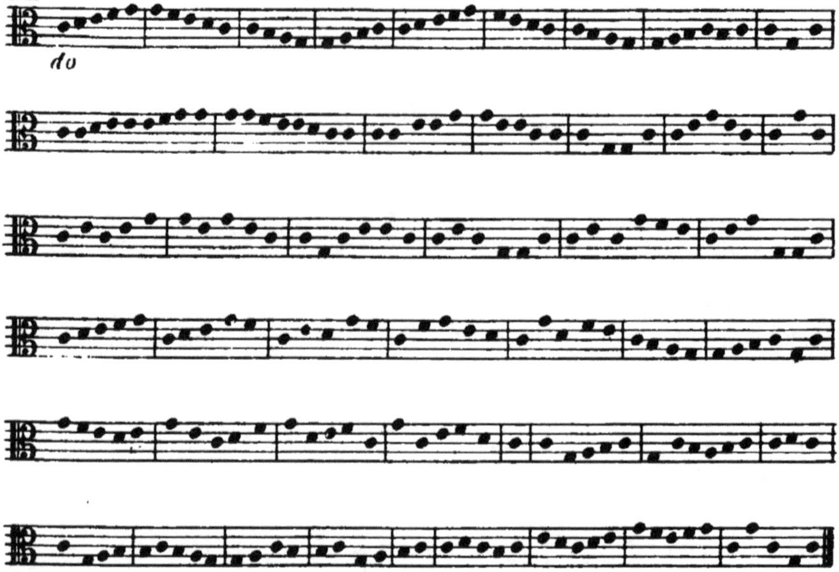
do

95

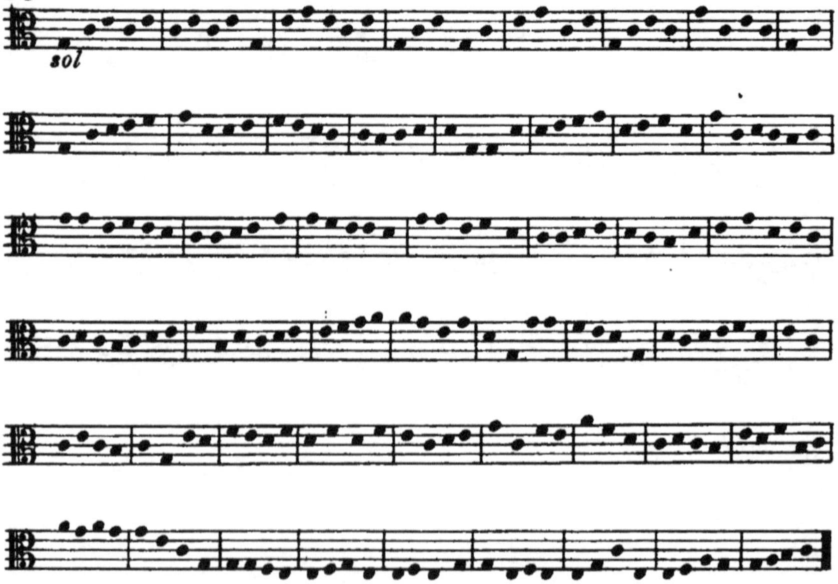
sol

96

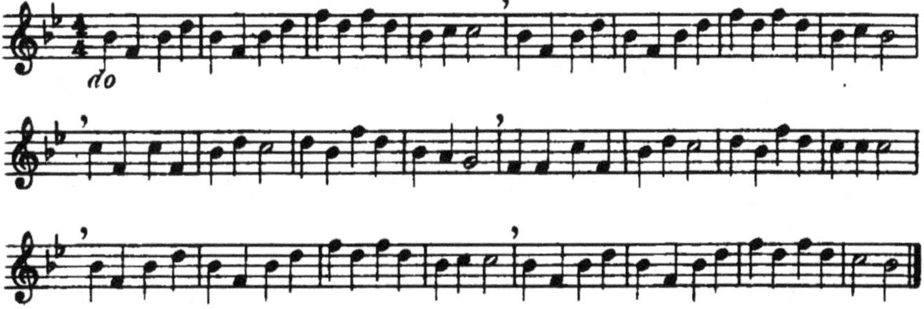
do

97

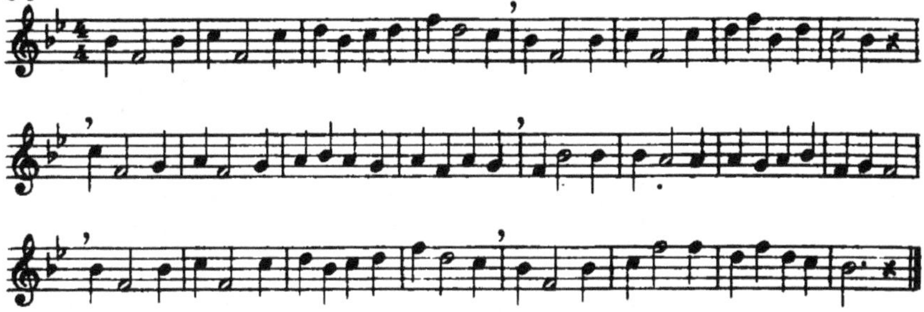

98

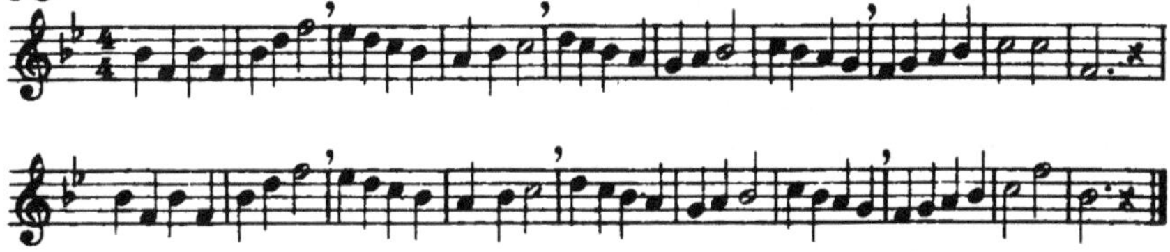

99

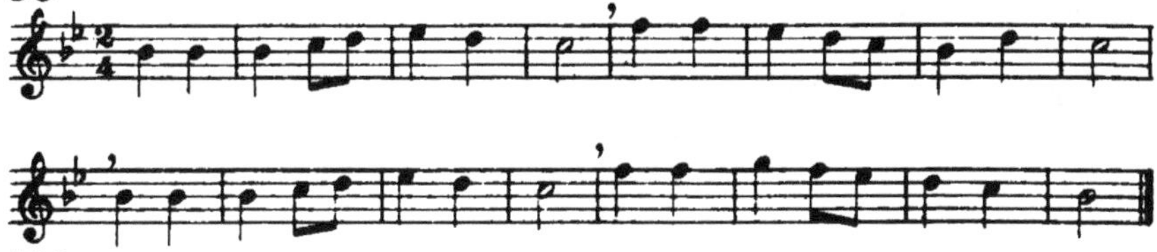

100

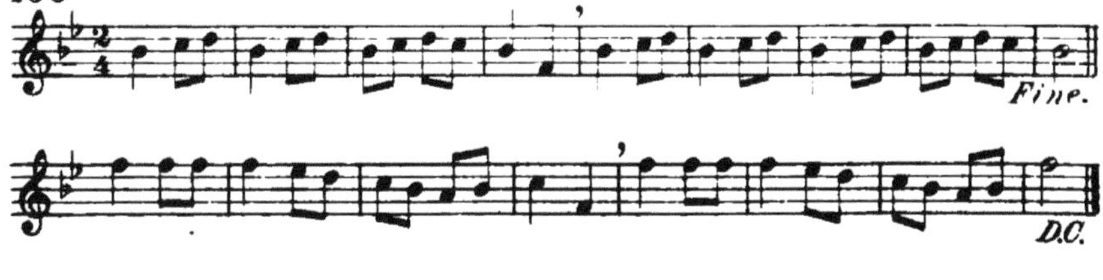
Fine.
D.C.

101

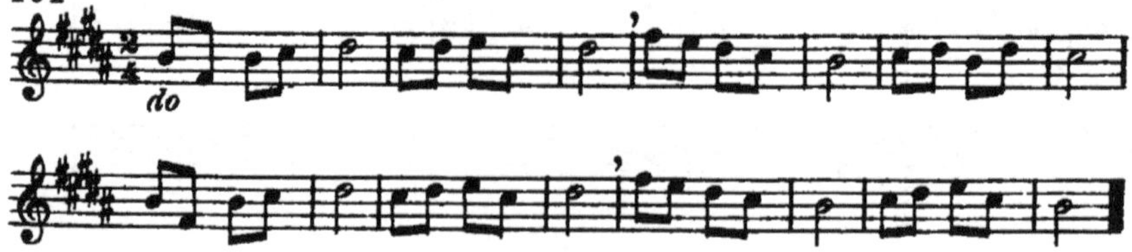
do

102

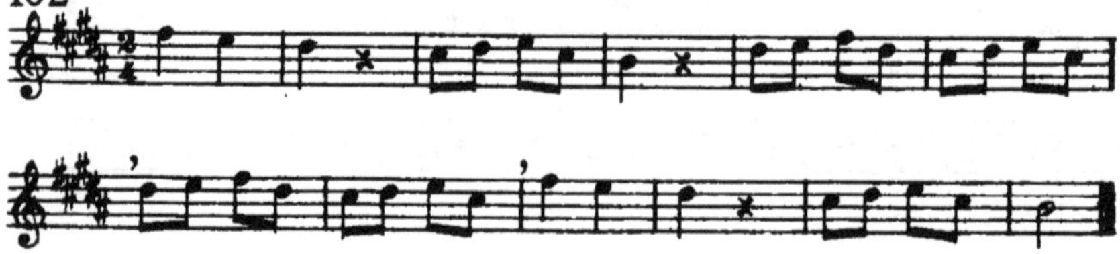

103

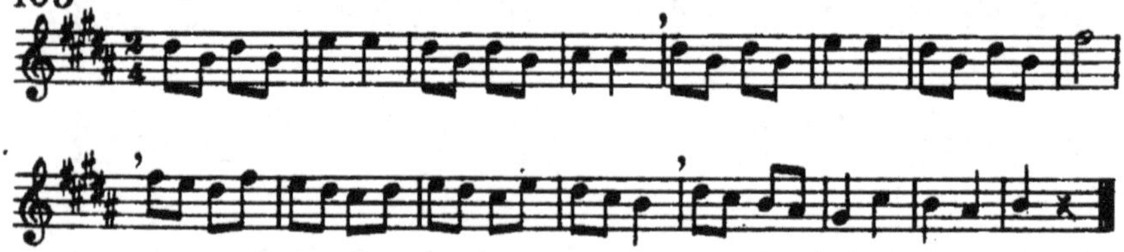

104

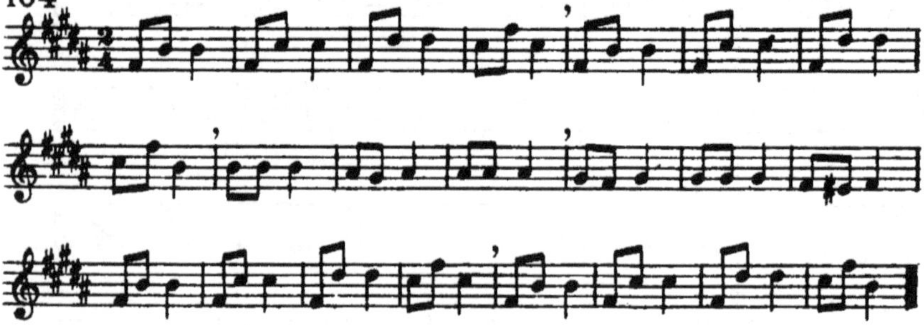

105

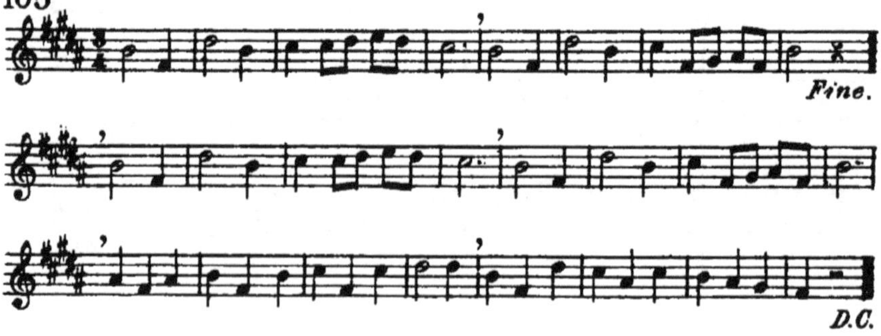
Fine.
D.C.

106

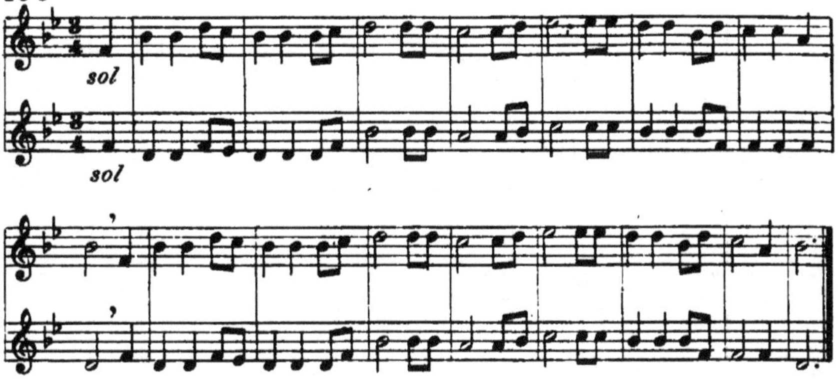
sol
sol

107

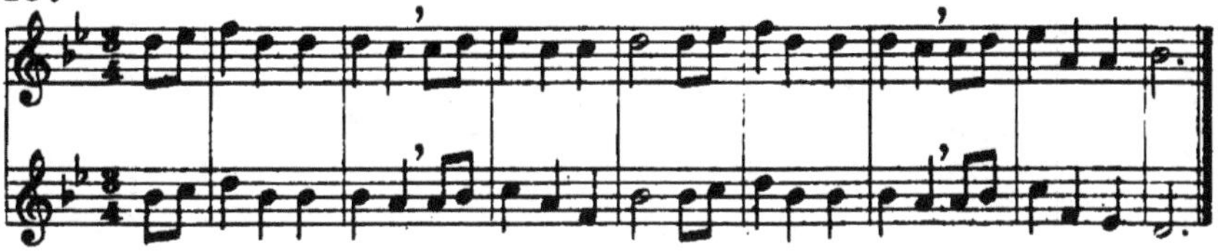

108

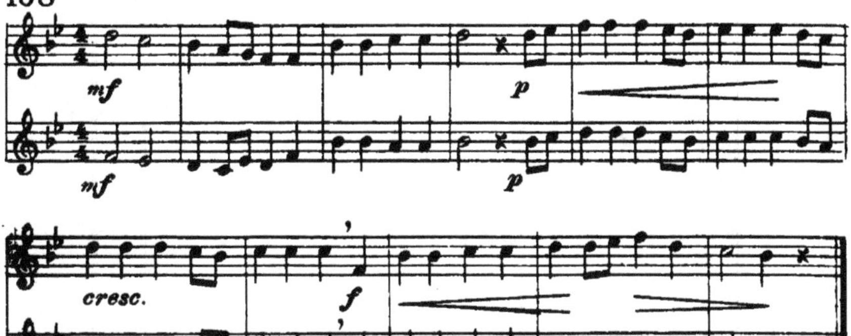
mf
p
mf
p
cresc.
f

109 Slowly.

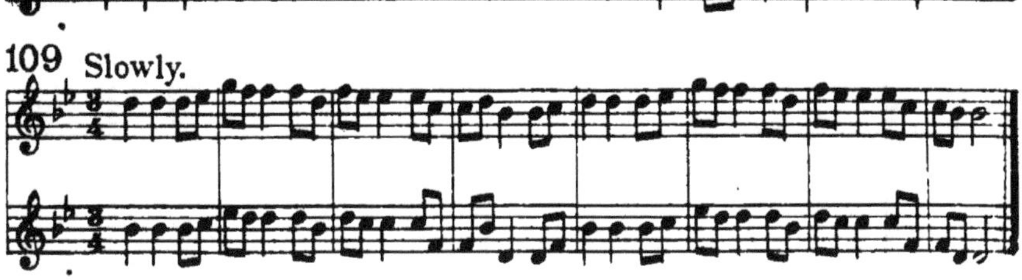

TIME PRACTICE. *Syncopations.*

Teacher will show how to transcribe the following into figures, and direct pupils to do the work at home and sing first from the figures.

110

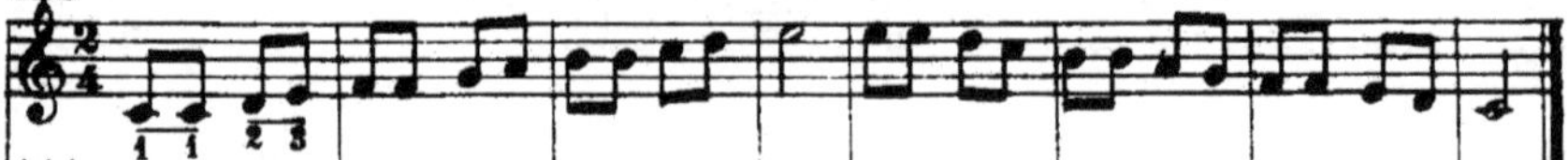
1 1 2 3

111

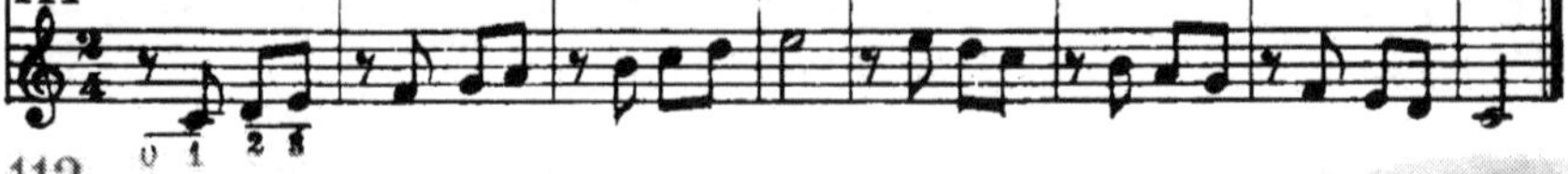
0 1 2 3

112

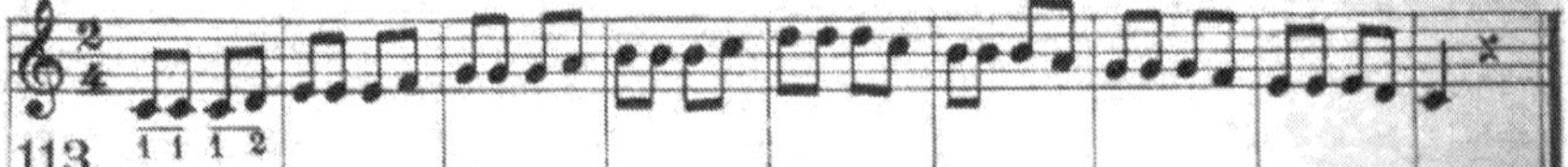
1 1 1 2

113

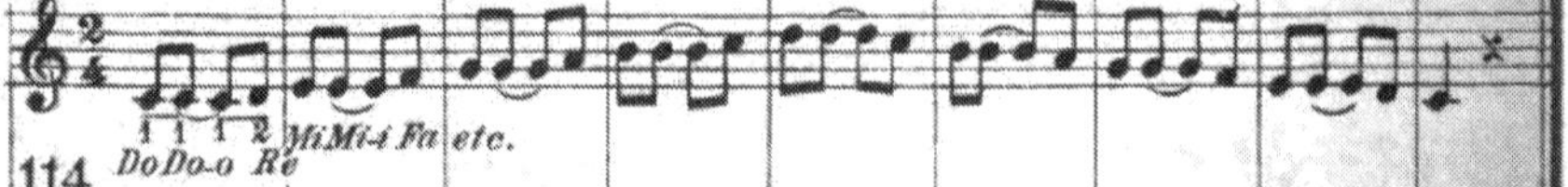
1 1 1 2
DoDo-o Re MiMi-i Fa etc.

114

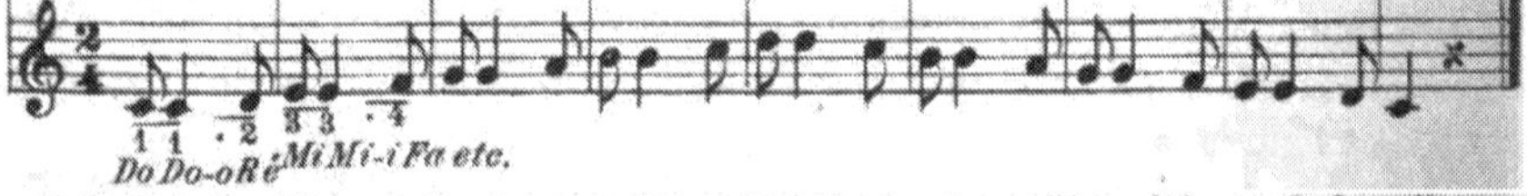
1 1 . 2 3 3 . 4
Do Do-o Re MiMi-i Fa etc.

At first pupil will say *to* for the rest, after which the teacher will say it instead of pupil.

115

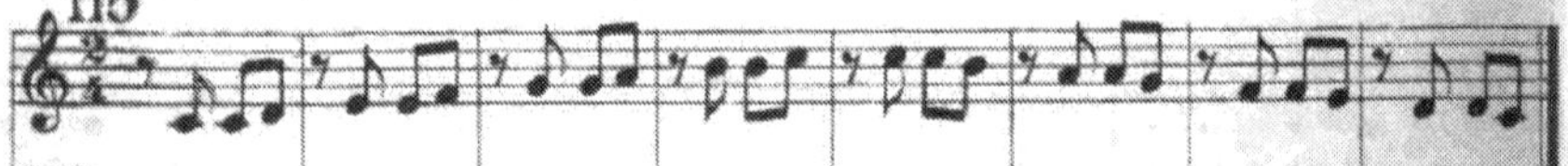

116

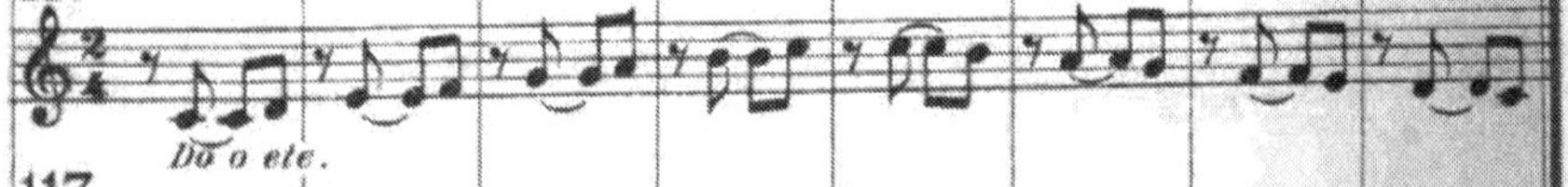
Do o etc.

117

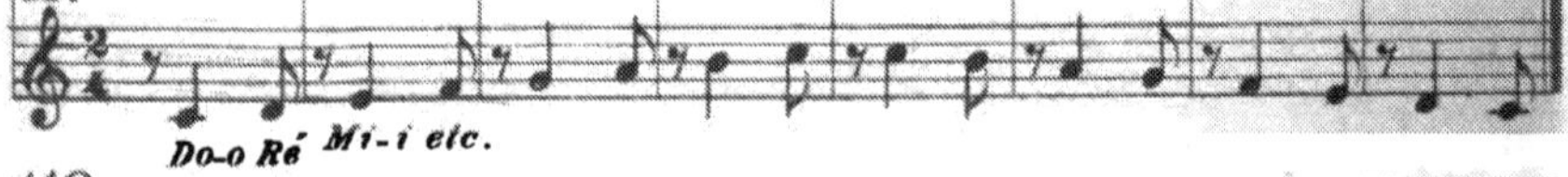
Do-o Ré Mi-i etc.

118

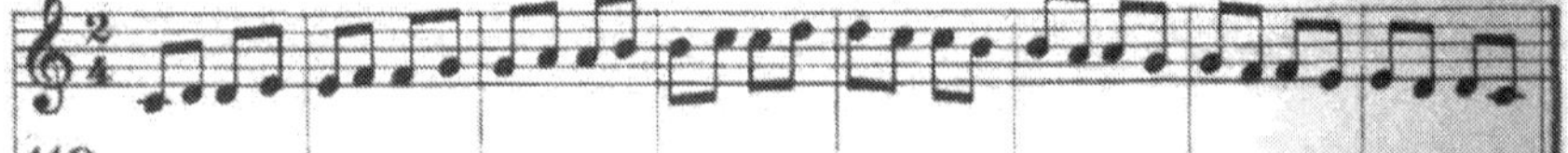

119

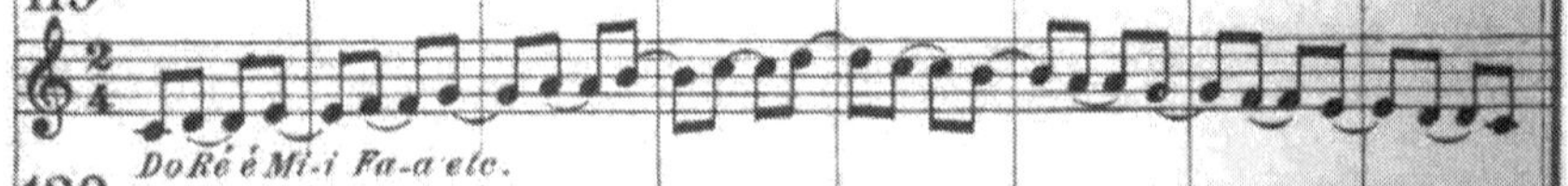
Do Ré é Mi-i Fa-a etc.

120

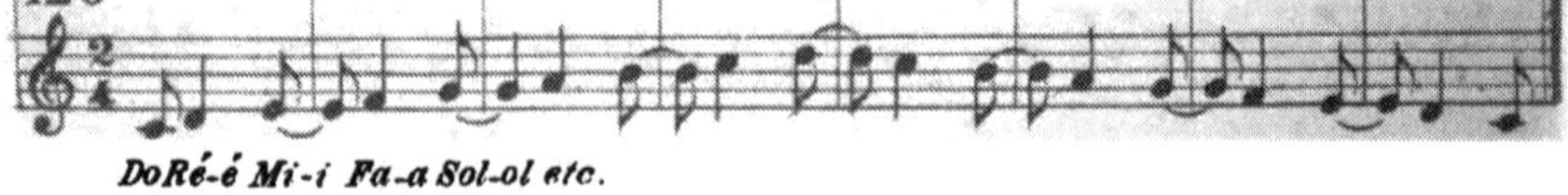
DoRé-é Mi-i Fa-a Sol-ol etc.

Exercises Nos 121 and 122 to be *named only* by syllables - not to be sung.

121 C or DO clef on the fourth line.

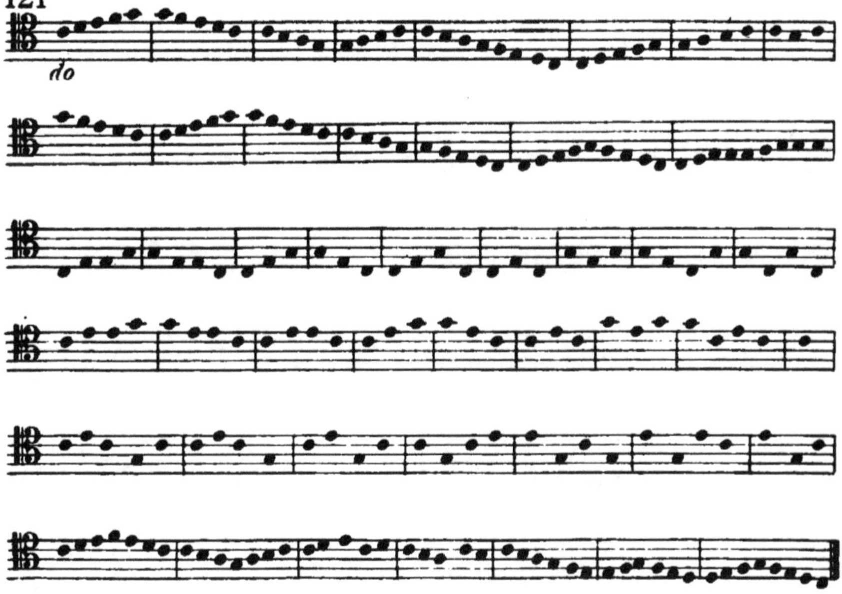
do

122

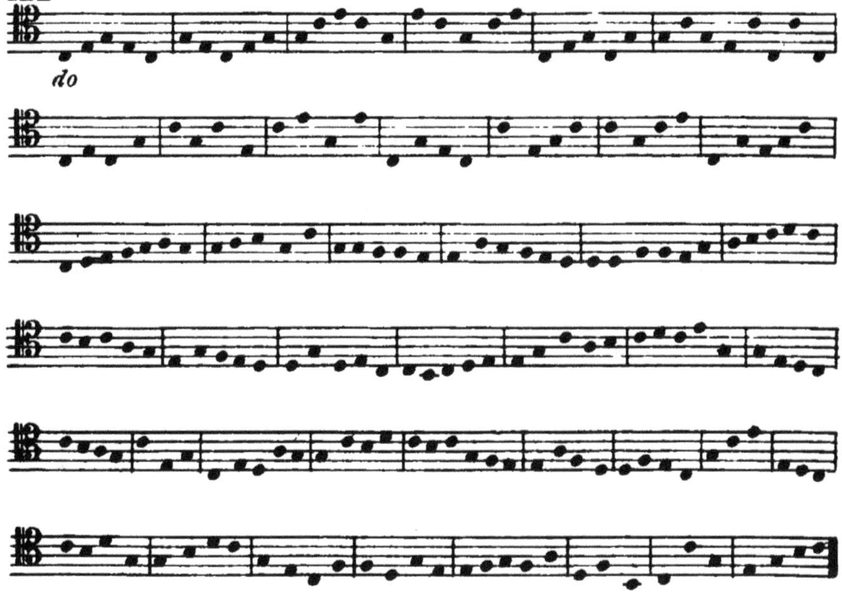
do

SOLFAS.

Prior to singing Exercise No 124 teacher will explain that FA sharp is named FAY- and to intone it correctly, DO-SI-DO should be taken as pattern; that is singing SOL-FAY-SOL on the same air as DO-SI-DO taking care to keep the SOL in the key of the exercise. ***See Elementary Book page 146***

123 Slowly.

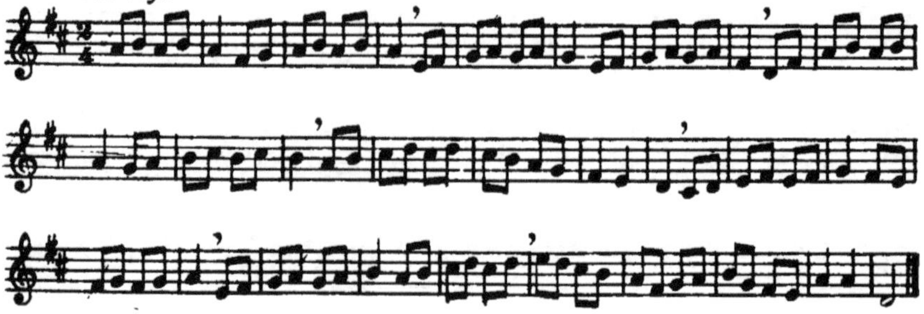

124

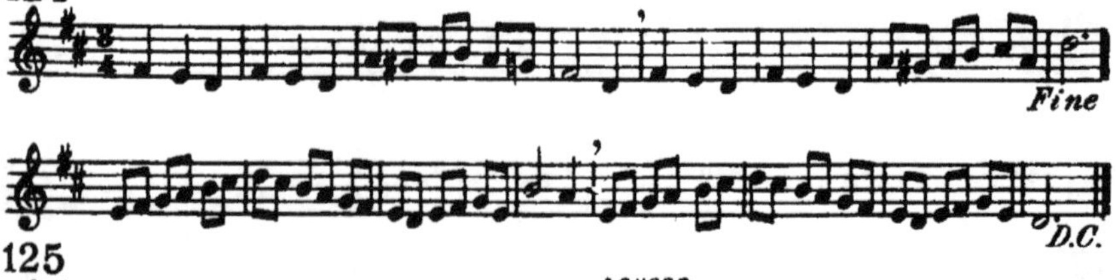
Fine
D.C.

125

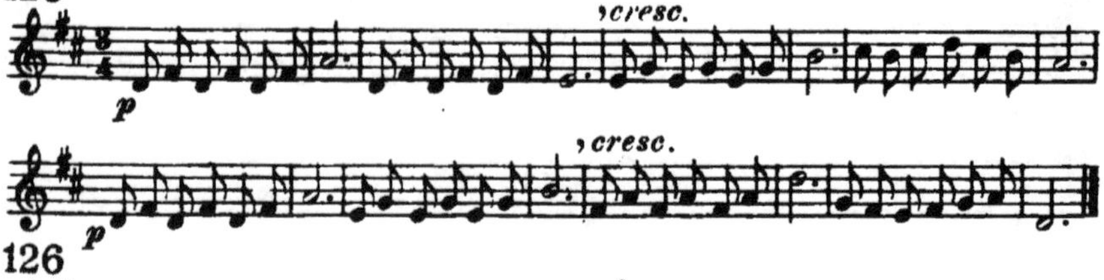
p
cresc.
p
cresc.

126

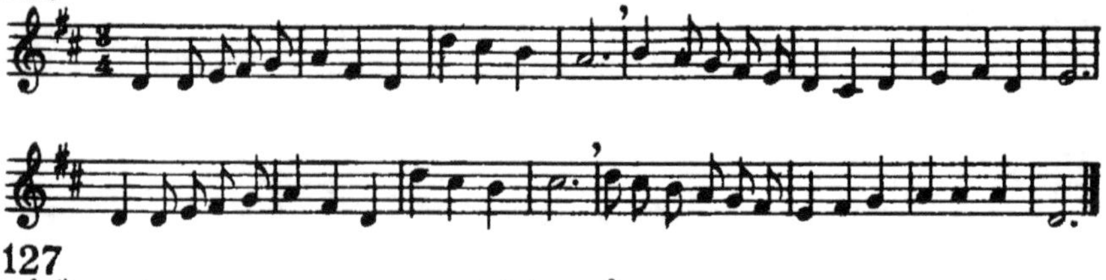

127

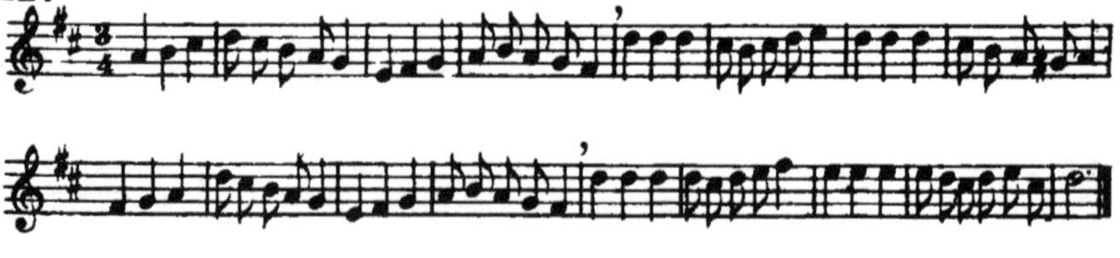

128

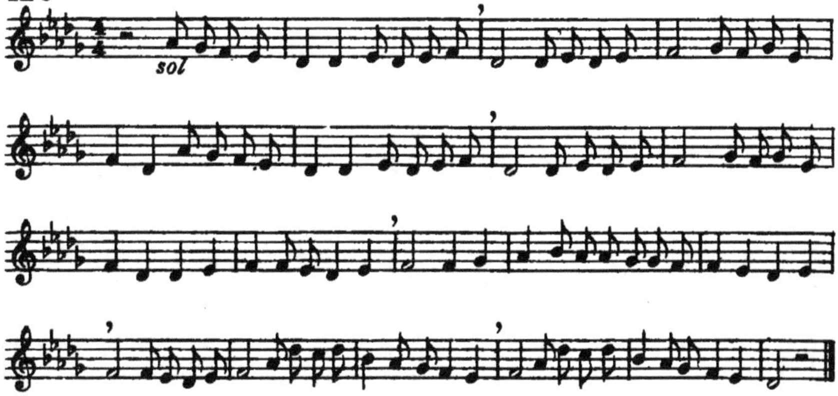
sol

129

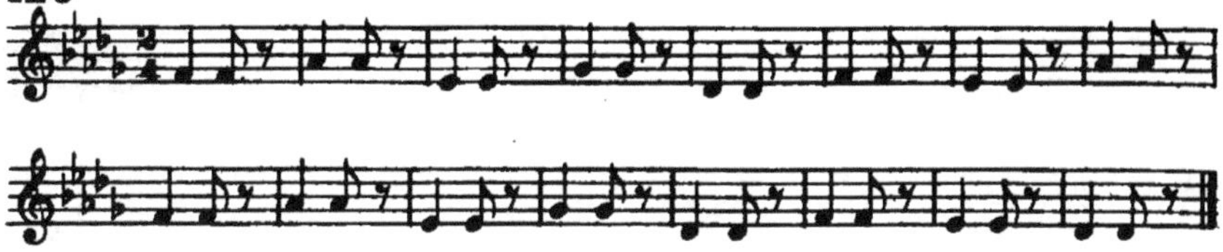

130

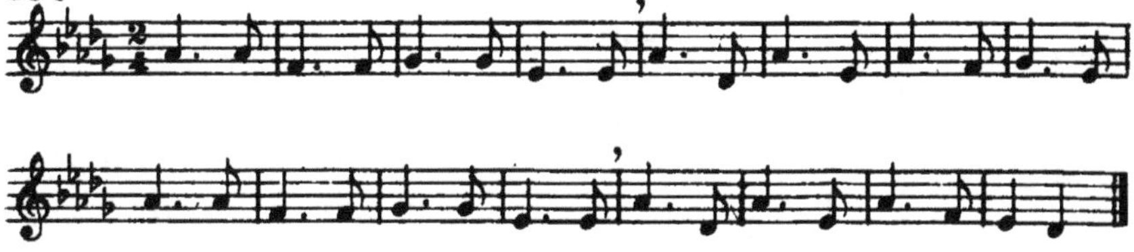

131

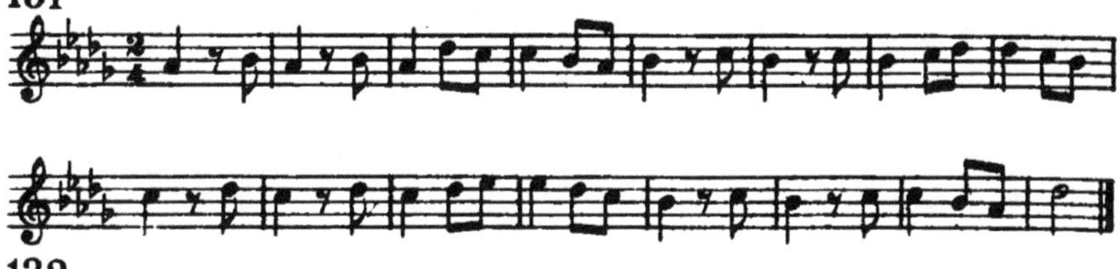

132

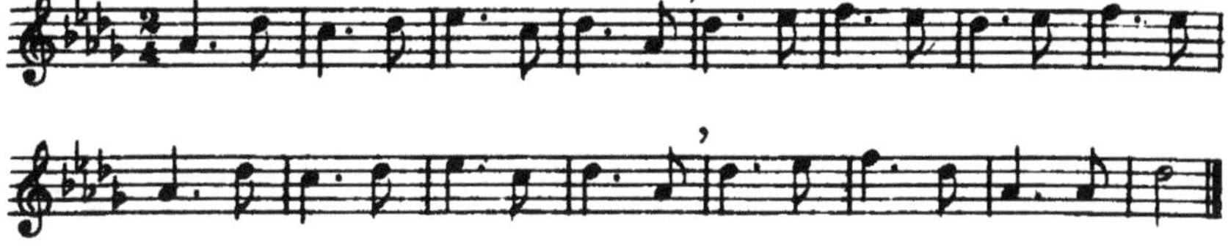

133 Slowly.

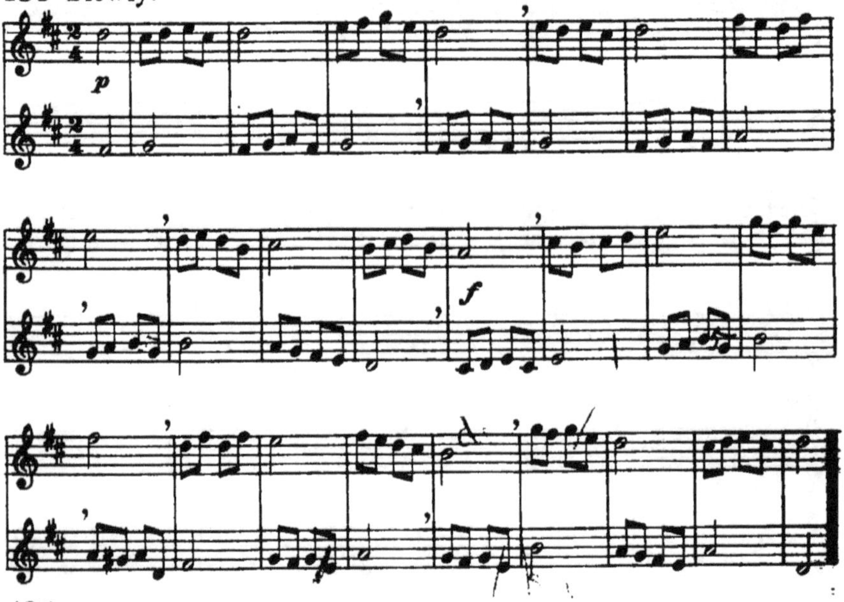

134

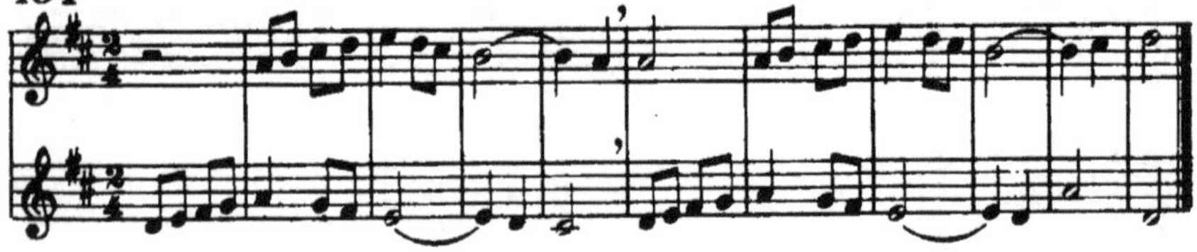

134a

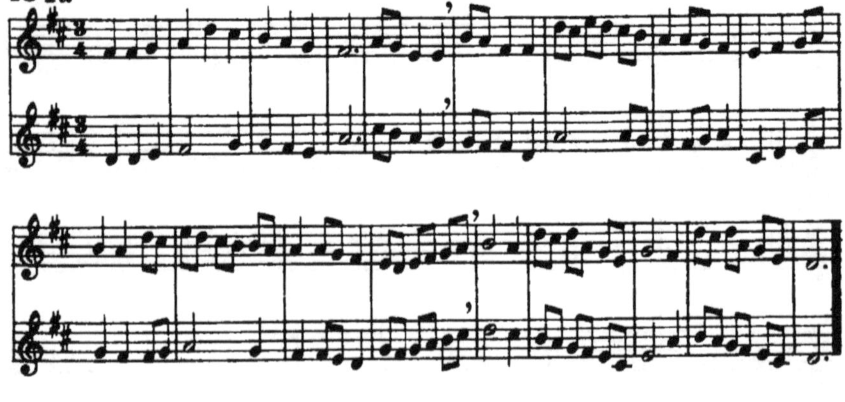

Exercises Nos. 135 and 136 to be *named only* by syllables-not to be sung.

For FA clef on the third line.

135

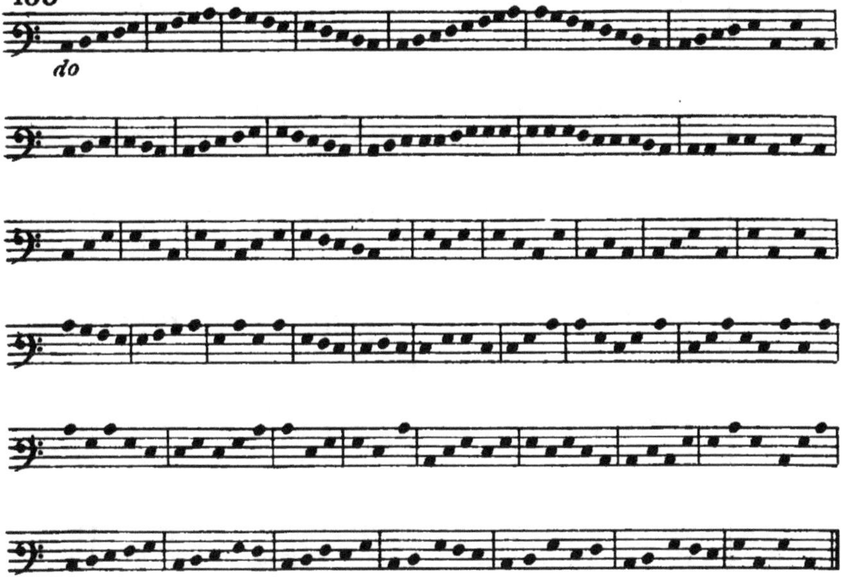
do

136

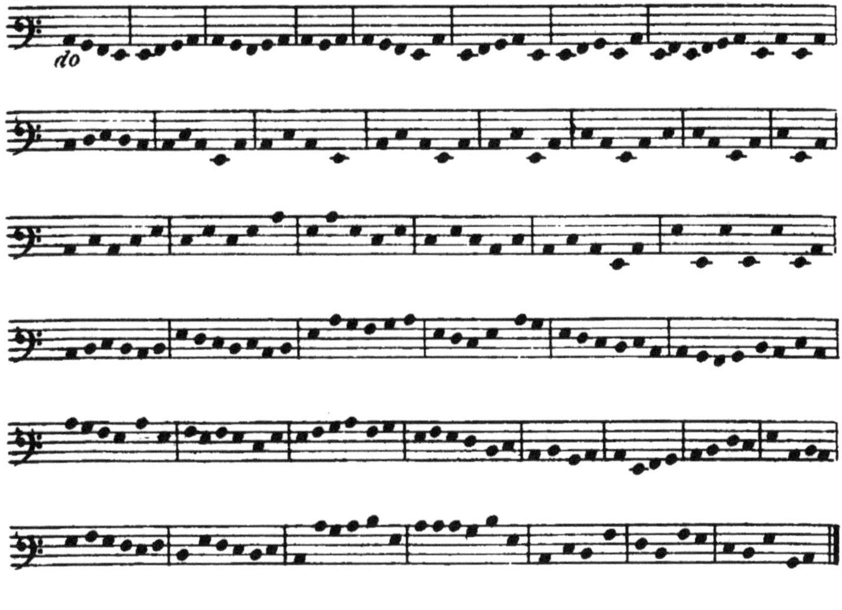
do

SOLFAS.

$\frac{2}{2}$ means that each measure should contain the value of two half notes - Pupils count two beats to the measure.

137

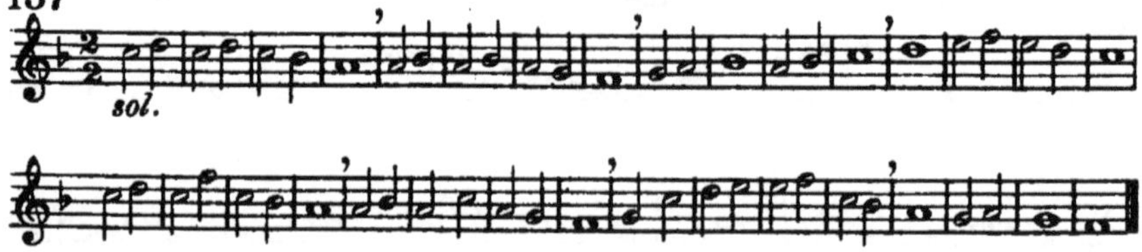
sol.

138

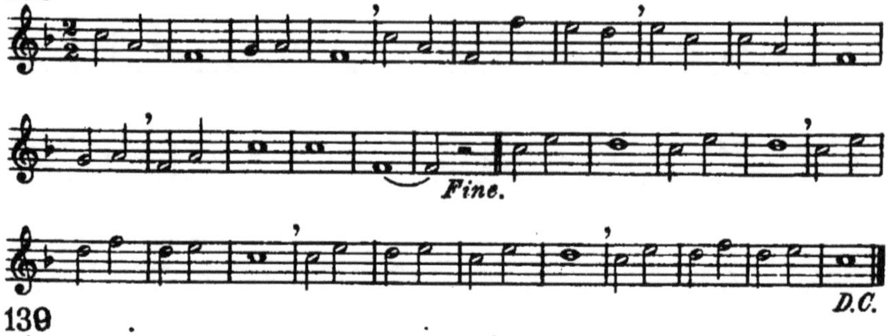
Fine.
D.C.

139

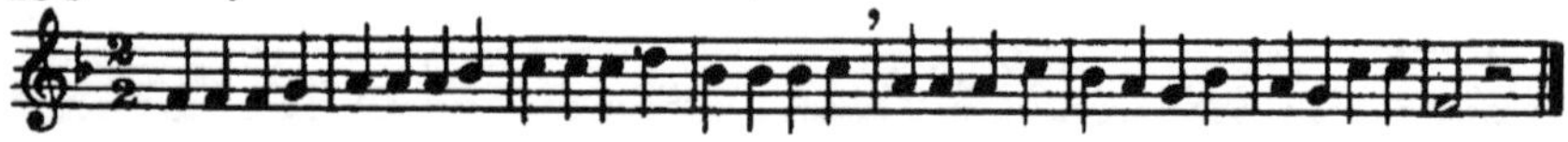

140

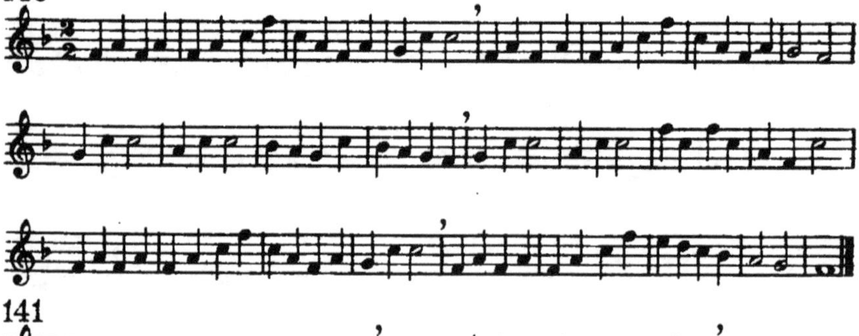

141

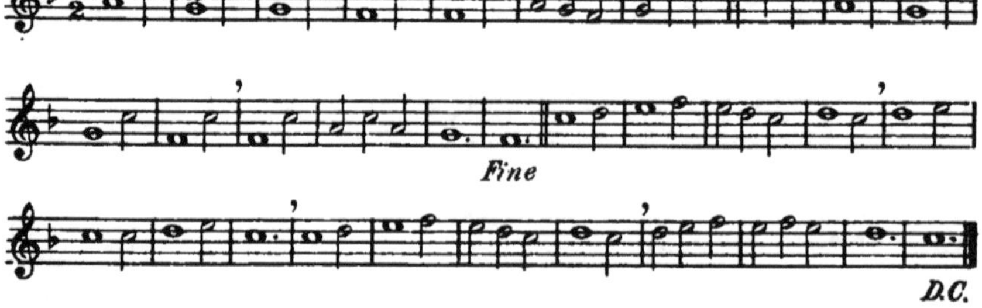
Fine
D.C.

142

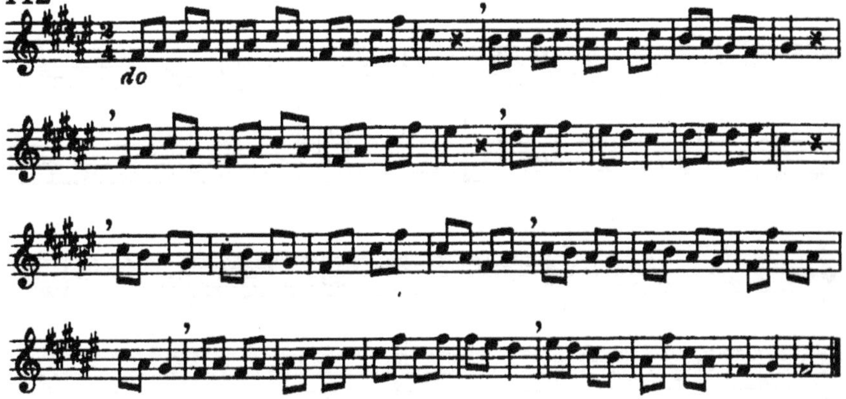
do

143

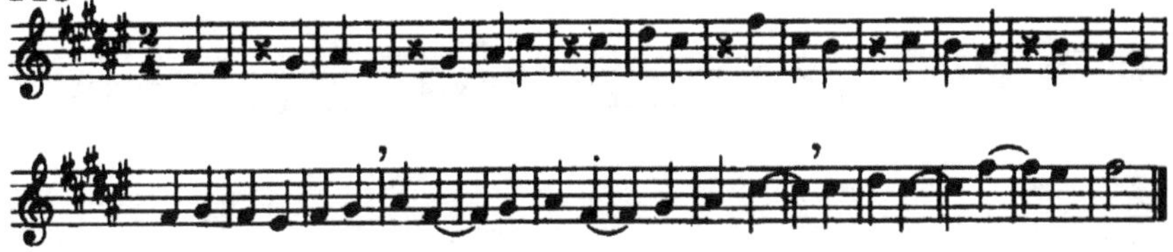

144

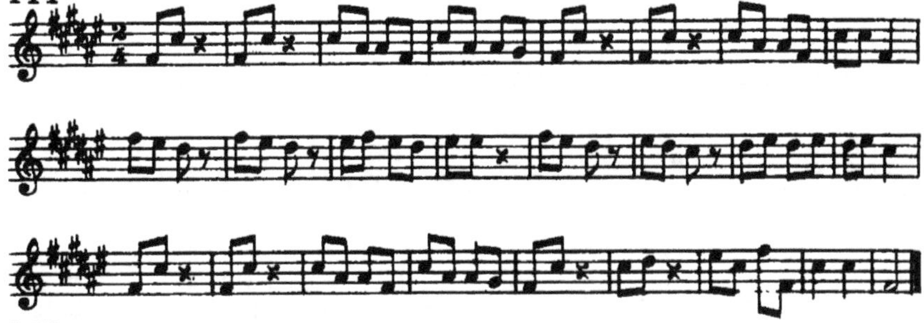

145

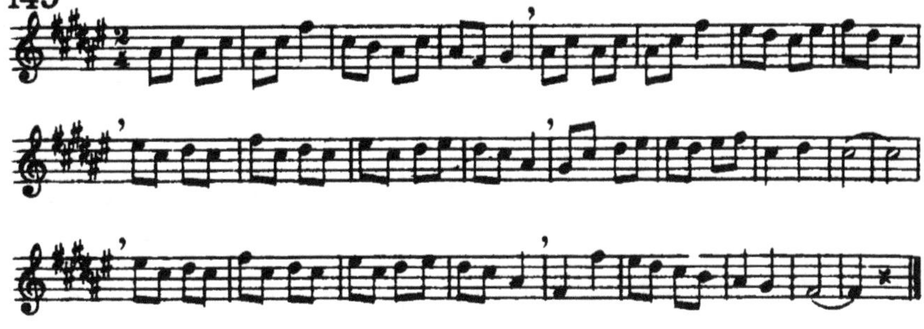

SOLFAS FOR TWO VOICES.

146

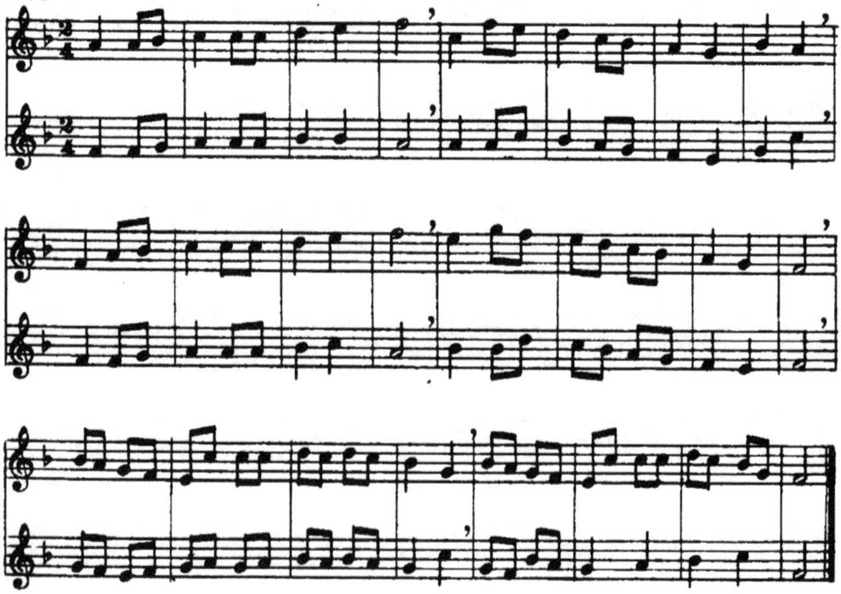

147

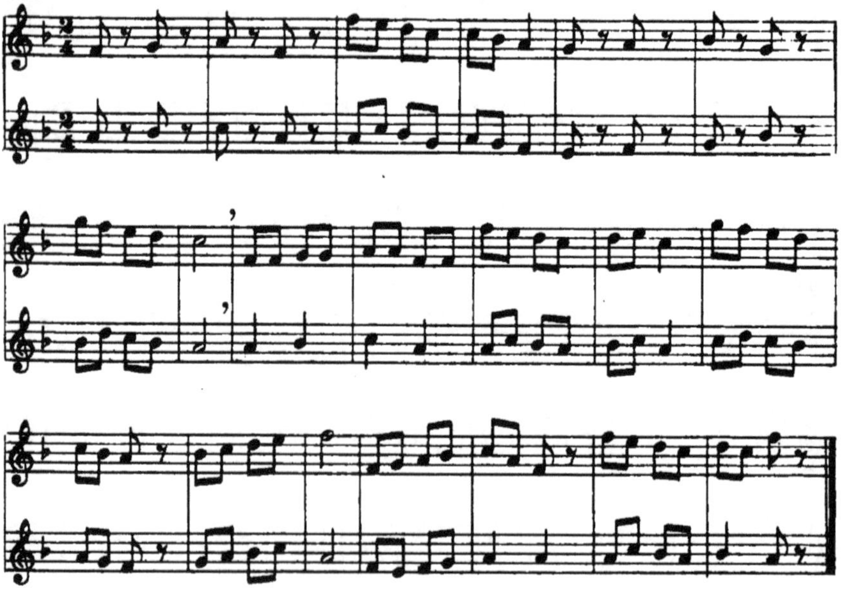

$\frac{3}{8}$ **means that each measure should contain the value of three eighth notes, - three beats to the measure.**

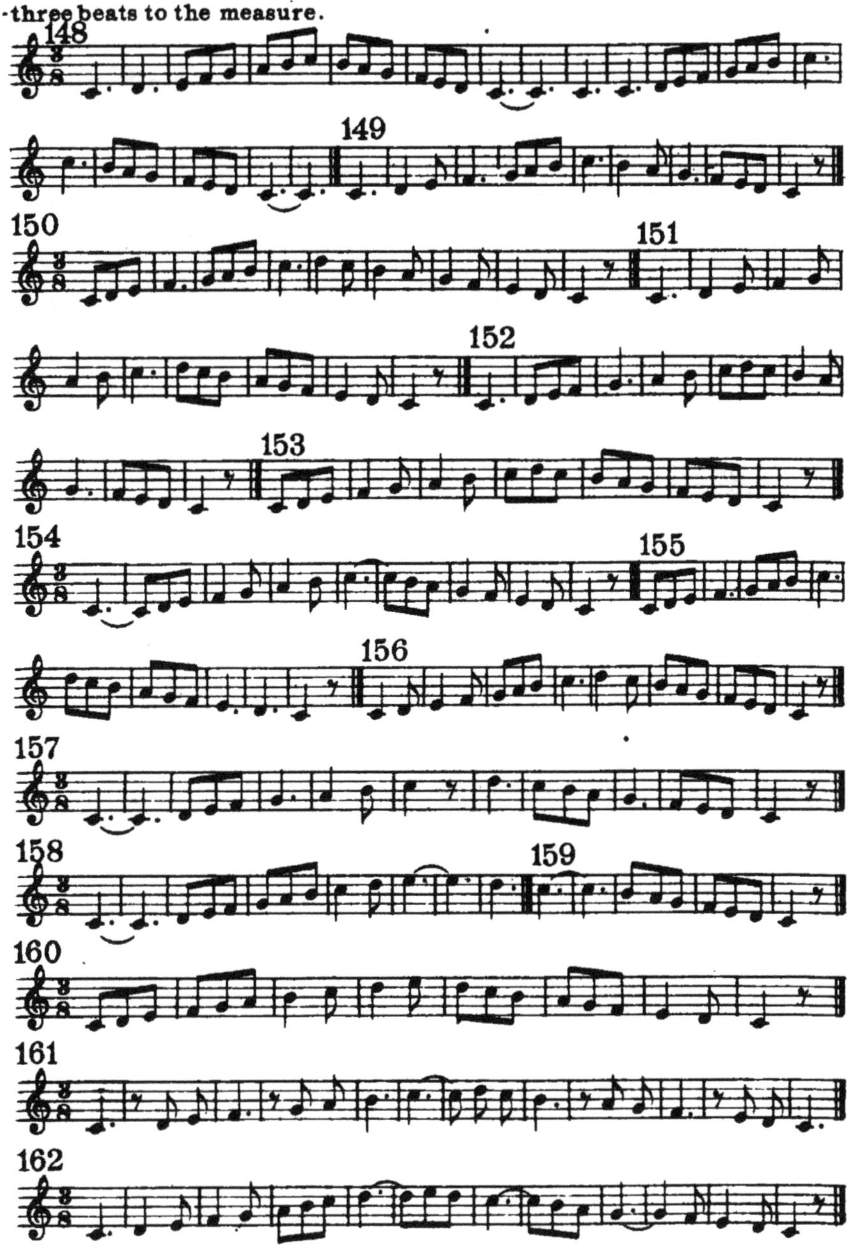
148
149
150
151
152
153
154
155
156
157
158
159
160
161
162

Exercises Nos 163 and 164 to be *named only* by syllables - not to be sung.

163 F or FA clef on the fourth line.

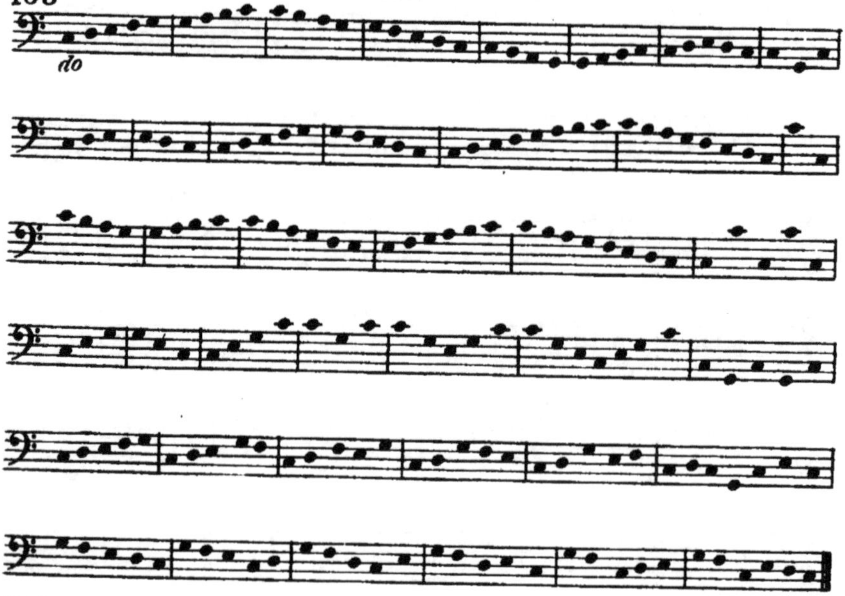
do

164

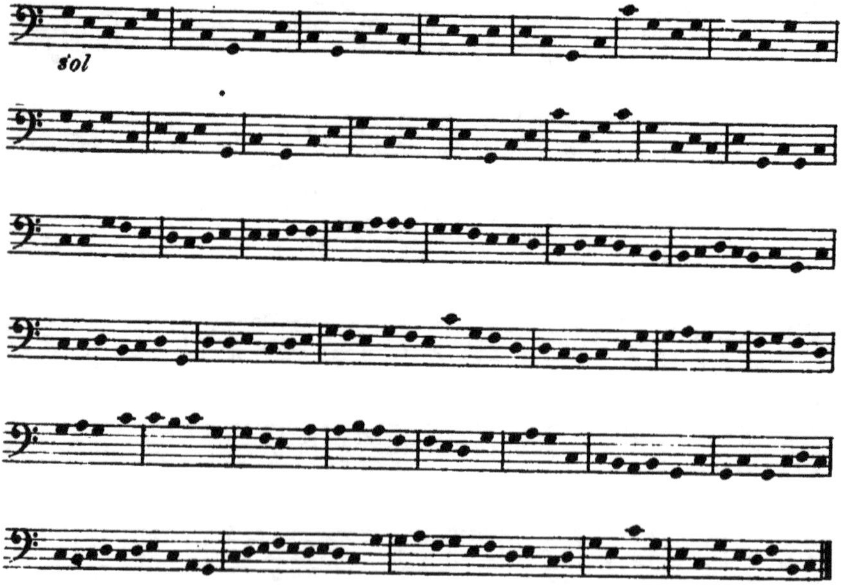
sol

165

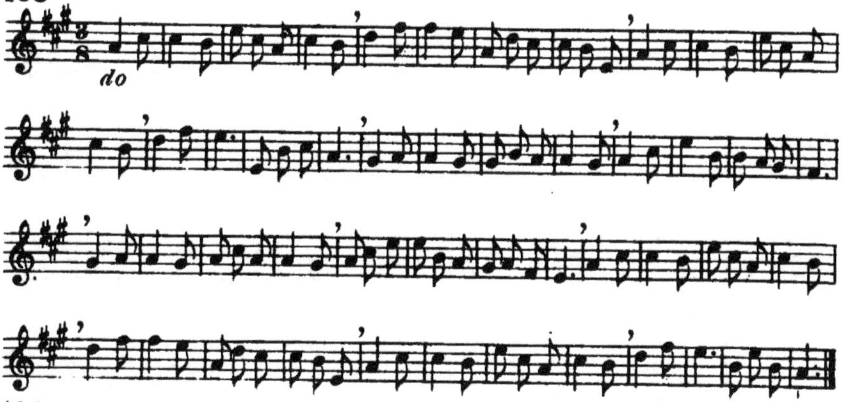
do

166

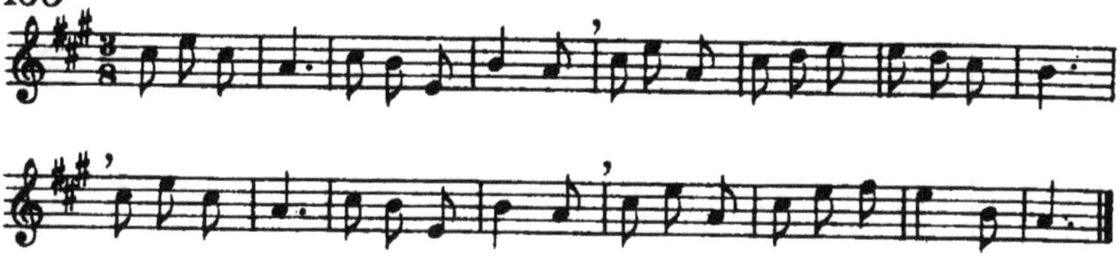

167

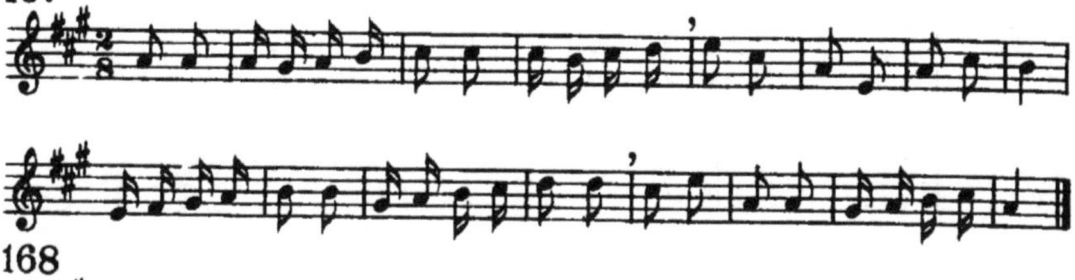

168

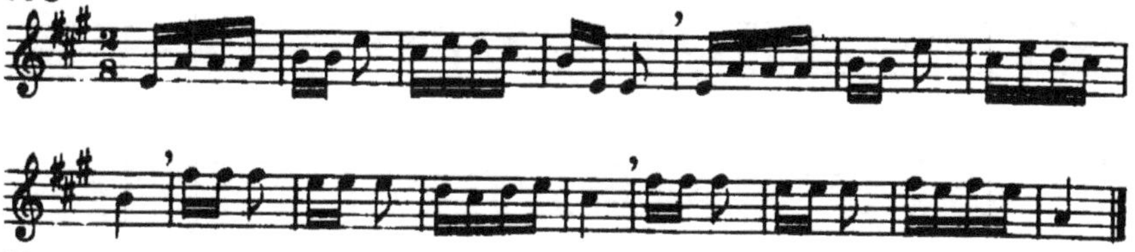

168a

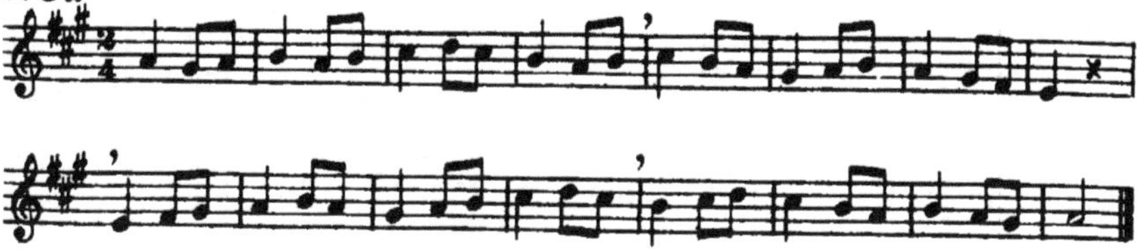

Note—When a natural removes a flat of the signature, pupils sing a sharp.

169

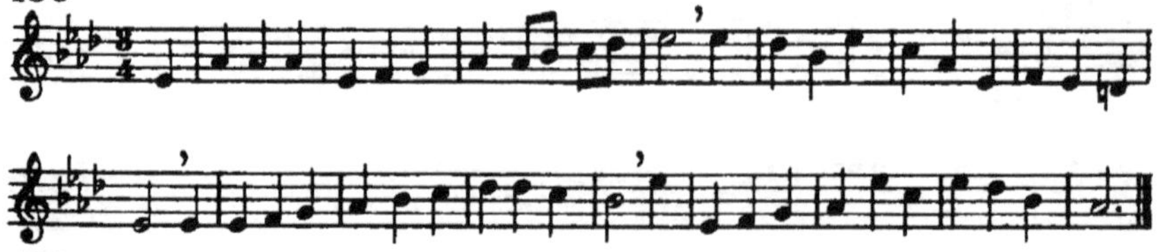

170

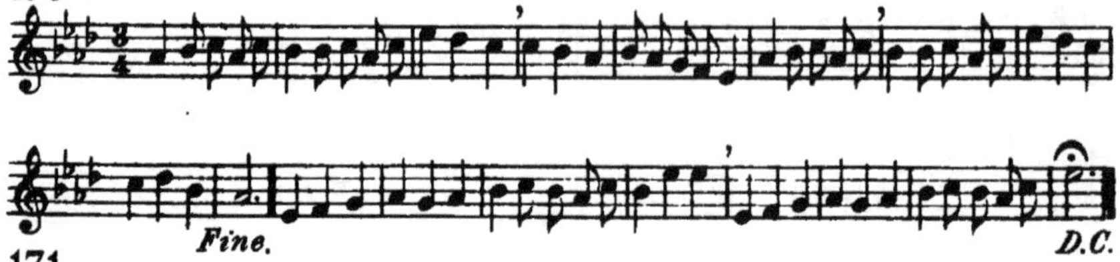
Fine.
D.C.

171

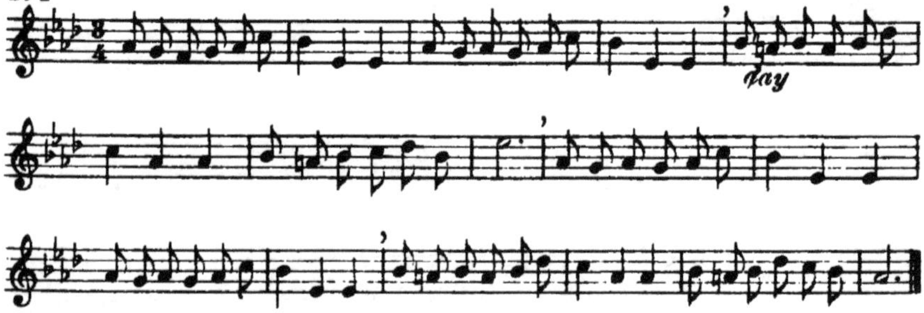
day

172

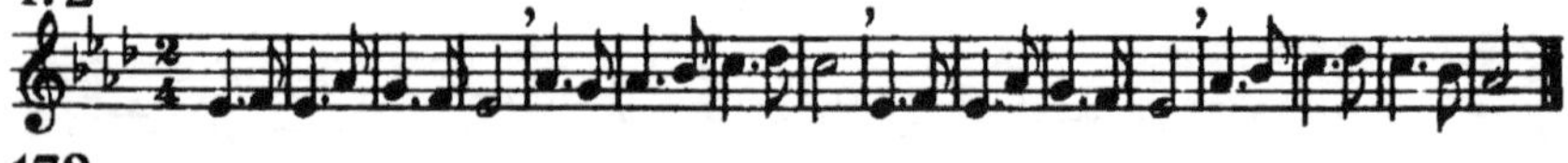

173

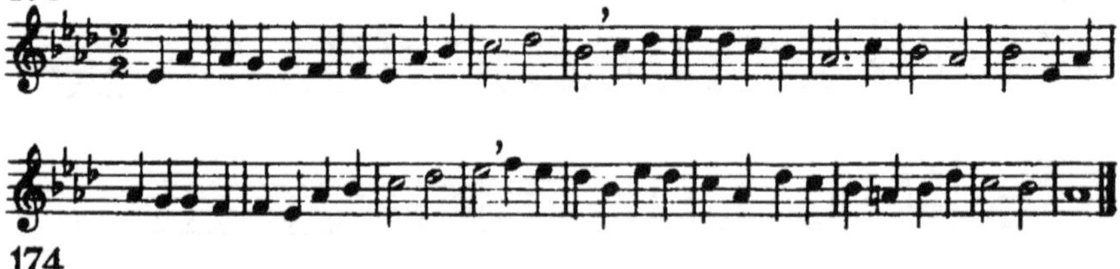

174

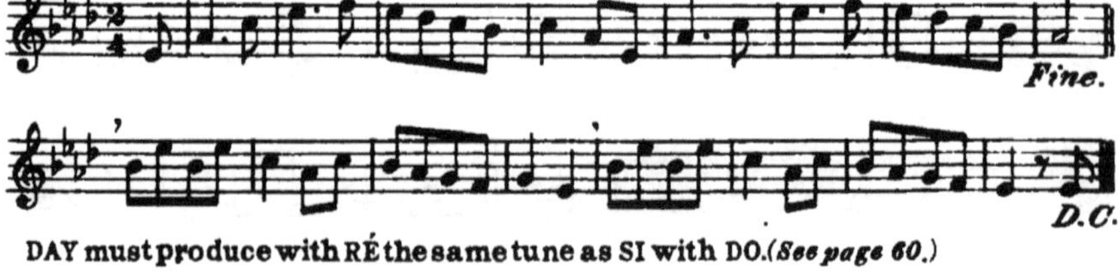
Fine.
D.C.

DAY must produce with RÉ the same tune as SI with DO. (*See page 60.*)

175

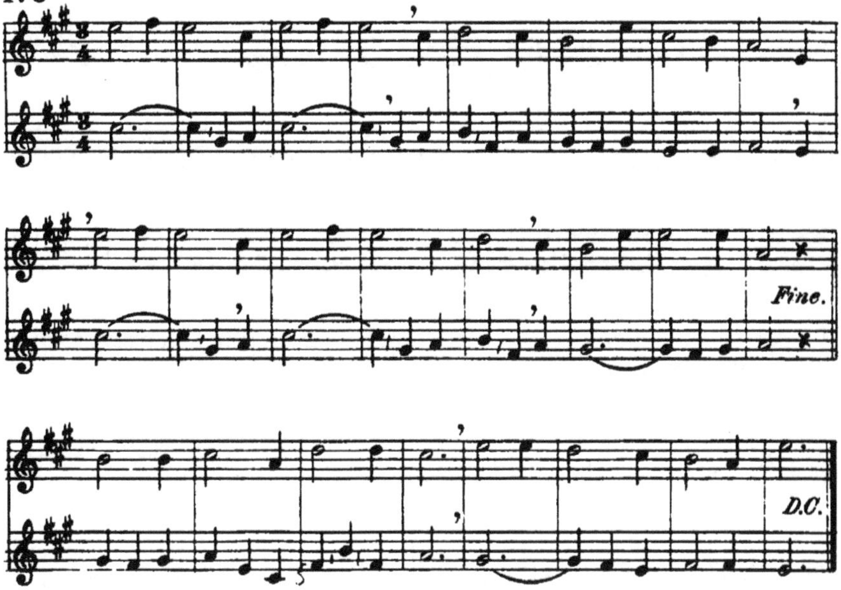
Fine.
D.C.

176

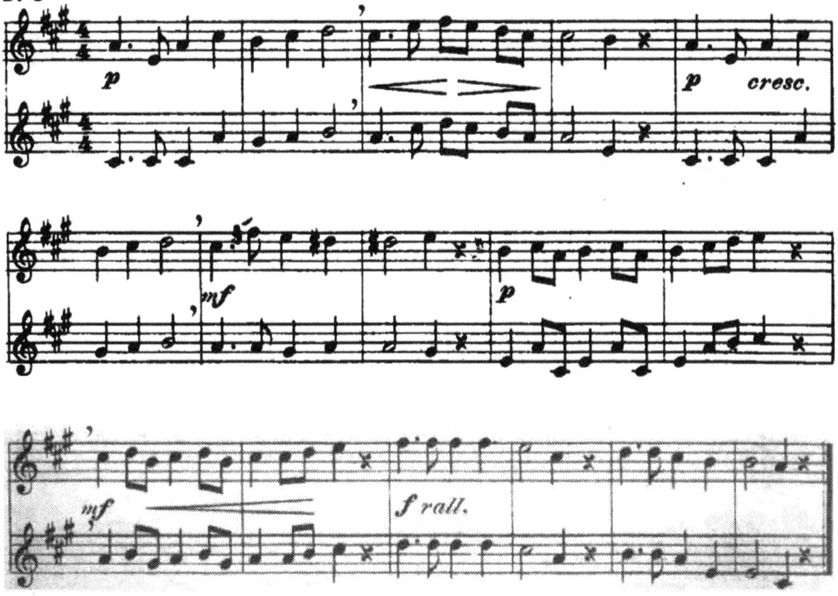
p
p cresc.
mf
p
mf
f rall.

SOLFAS.

177

SOLFAS FOR THREE VOICES.

181 M.M. ♩= 96

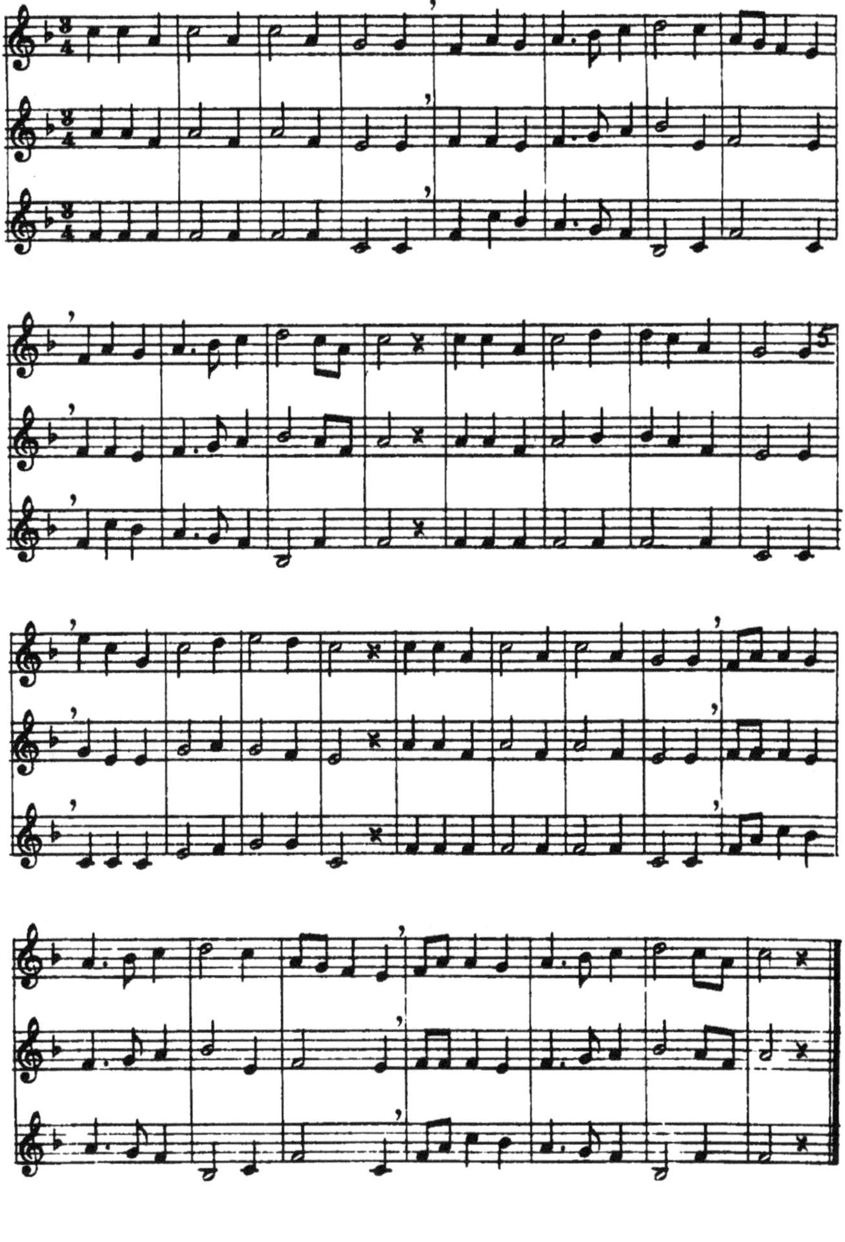
5

SOLFAS.

182

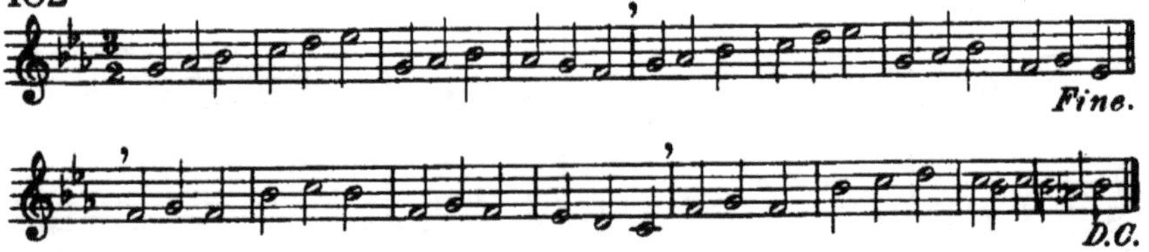
Fine.
D.C.

183

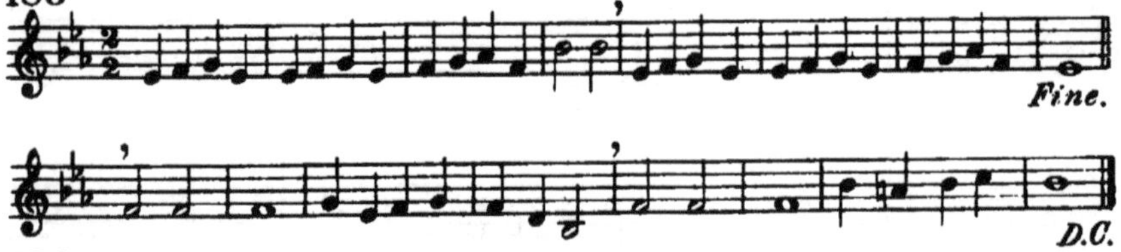
Fine.
D.C.

184

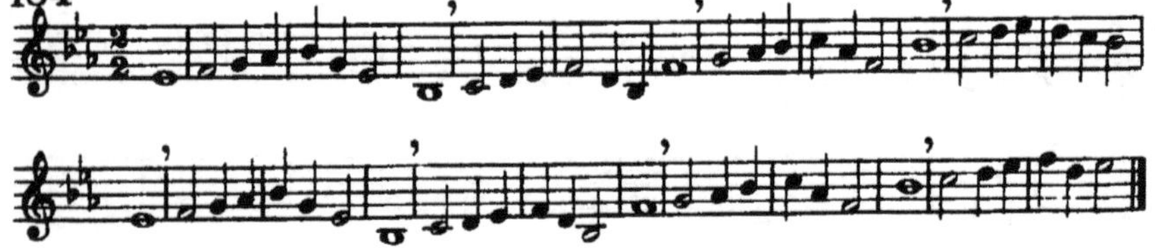

185

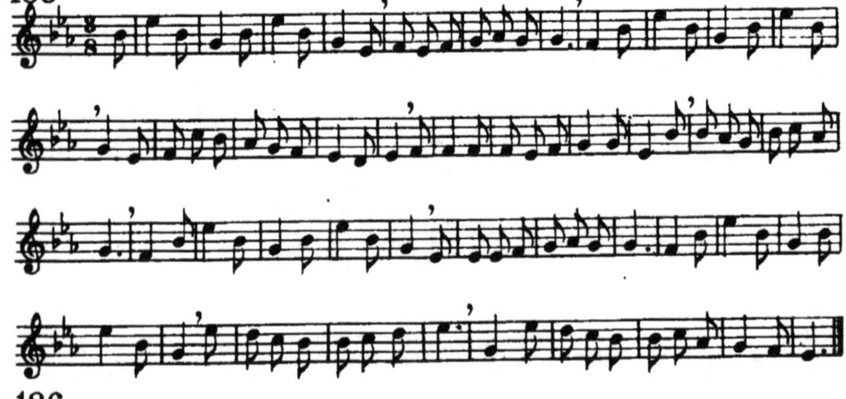

186

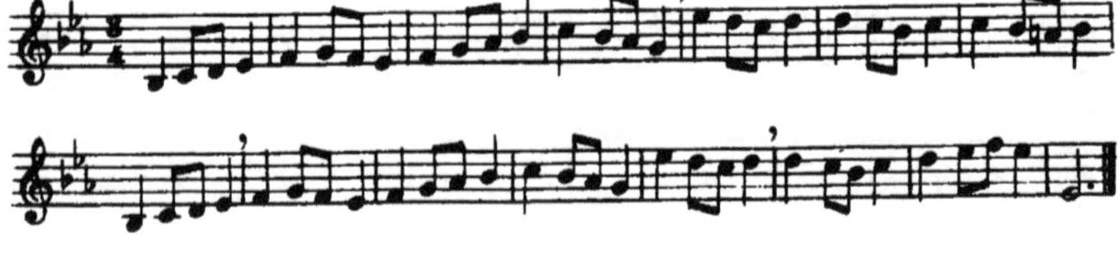

SOLFAS FOR THREE VOICES.

187

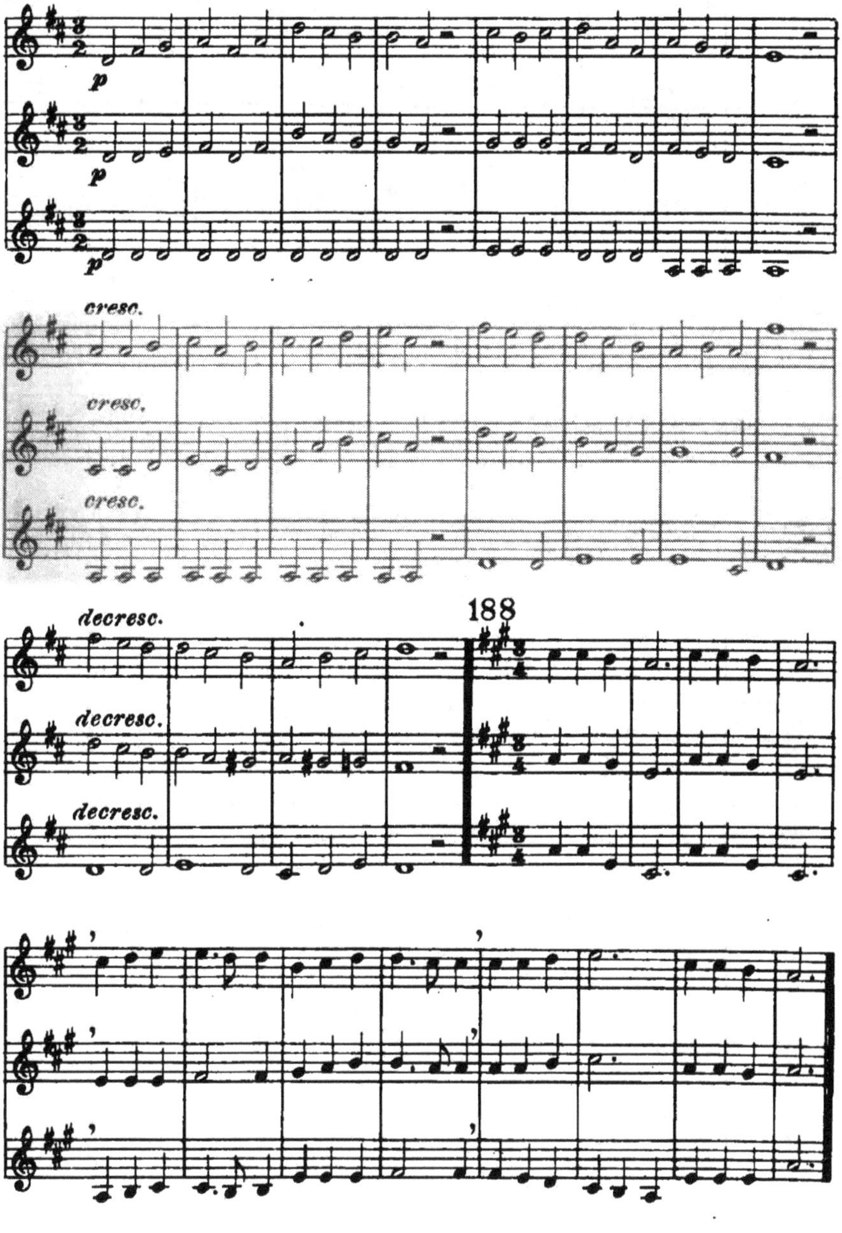
p
p
p
cresc.
cresc.
cresc.
decresc.
decresc.
decresc.
188

42   SOLFAS.

194

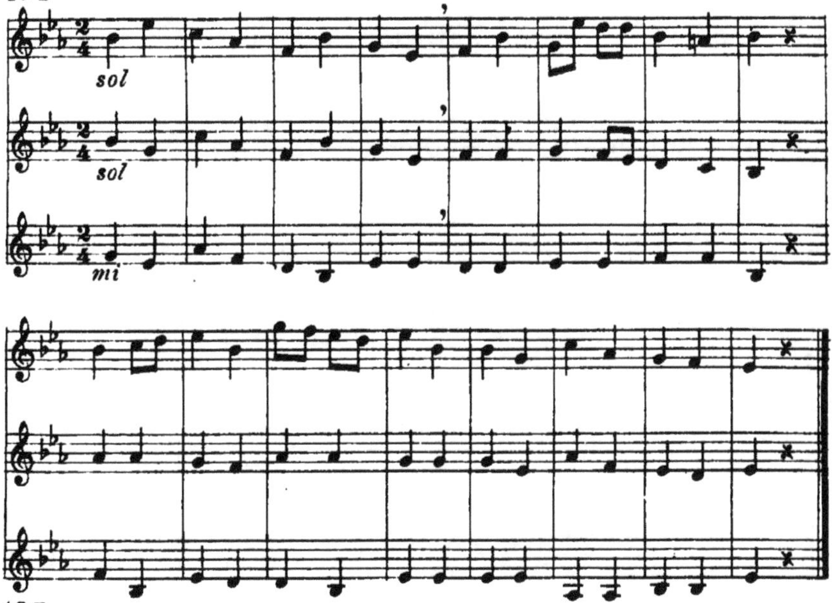
sol
sol
mi

195

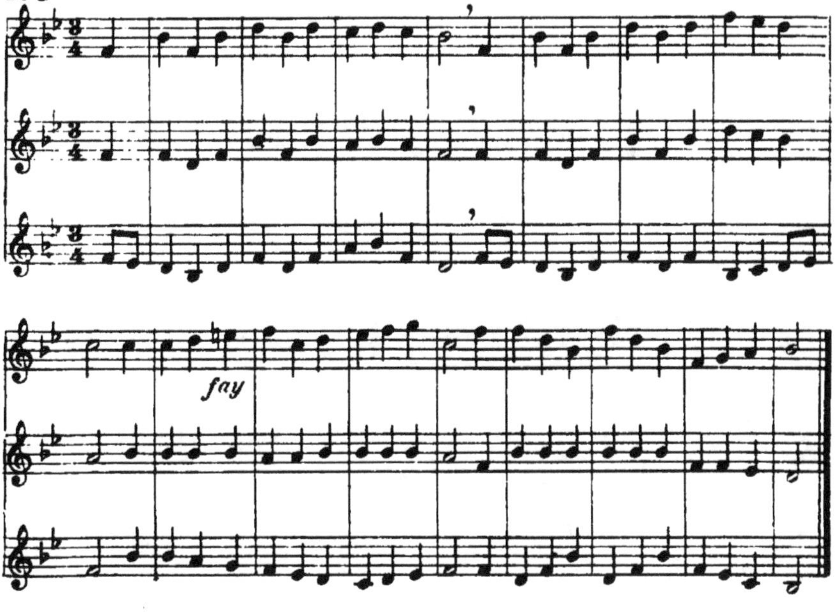
fay

196

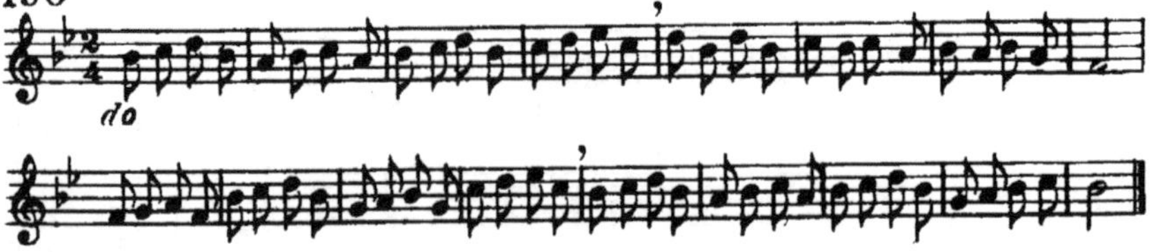
do

197

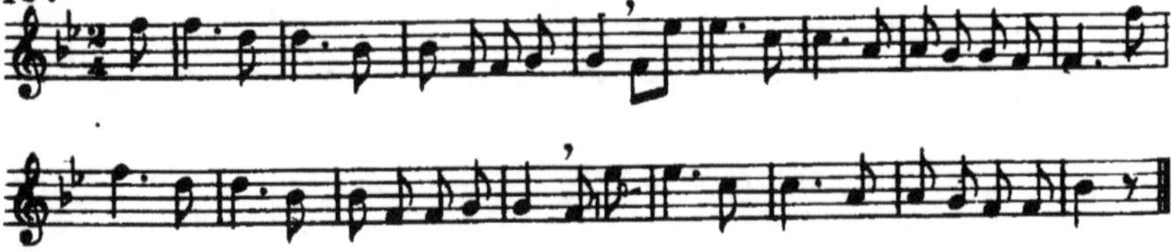

198

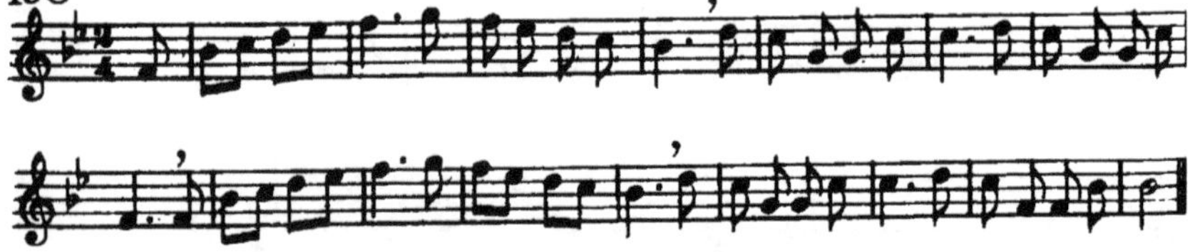

199

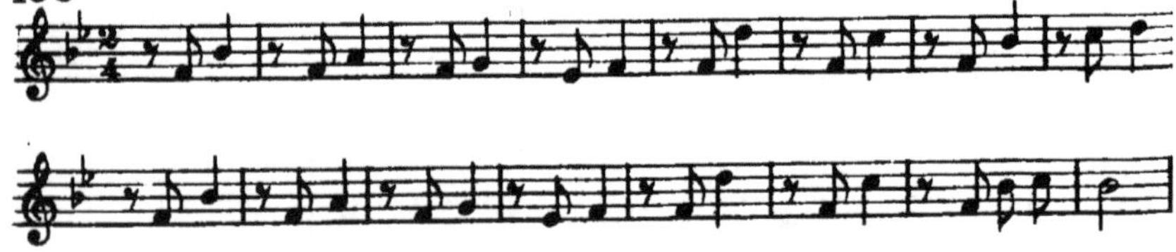

200

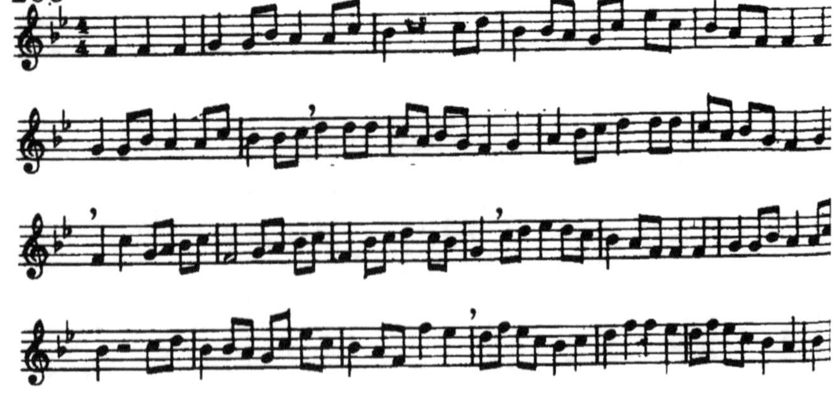

SOLFAS FOR THREE VOICES.

201 With Spirit. M.M. ♩= 120

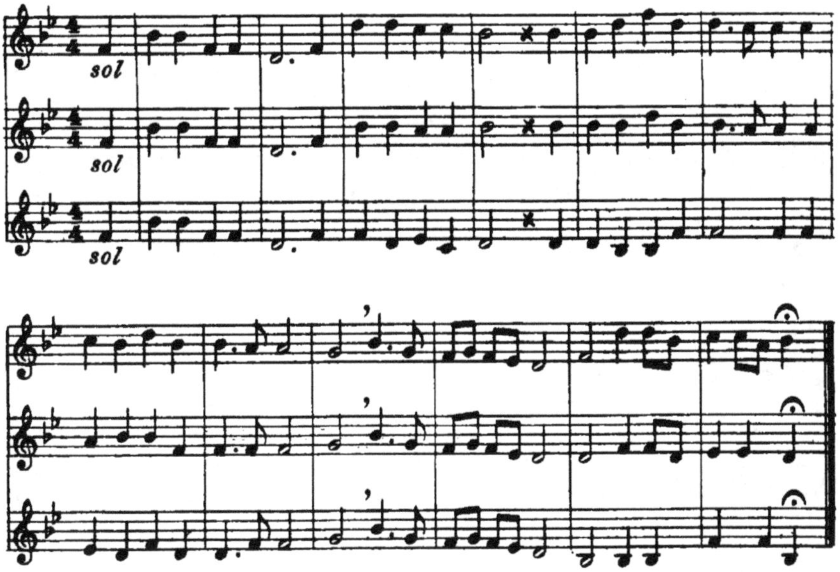
sol
sol
sol

202 M.M. ♩= 110

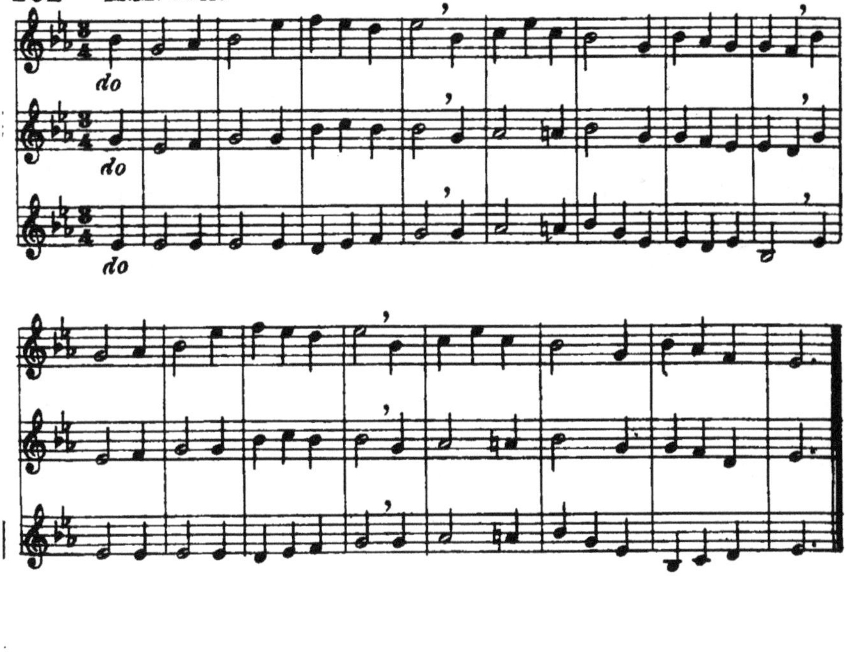
do
do
do

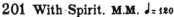

SOLFAS.

203

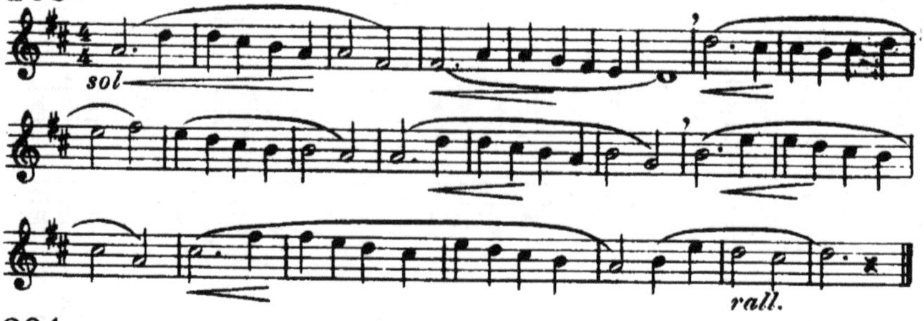
sol
rall.

204

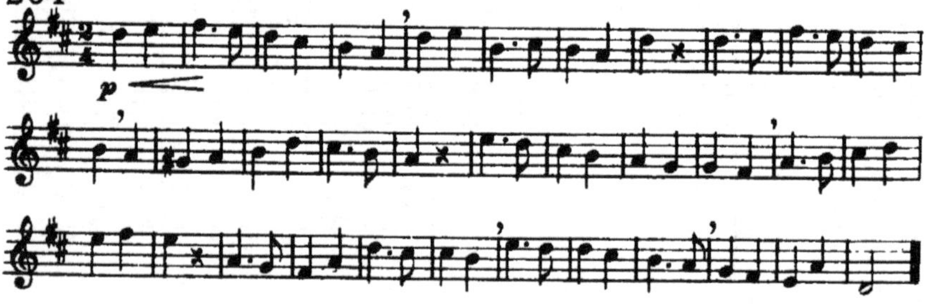
p

205

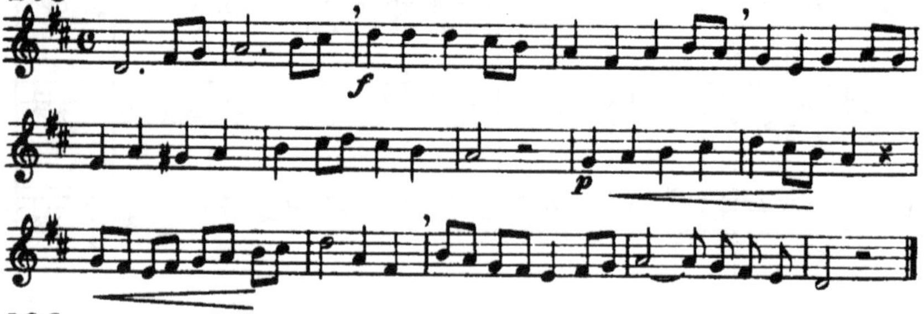
f
p

206

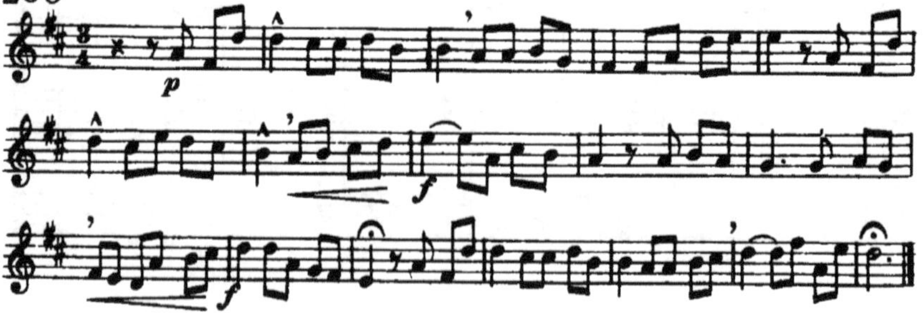
p
f
f

SOLFAS FOR THREE VOICES.

207 M.M. ♩= 104

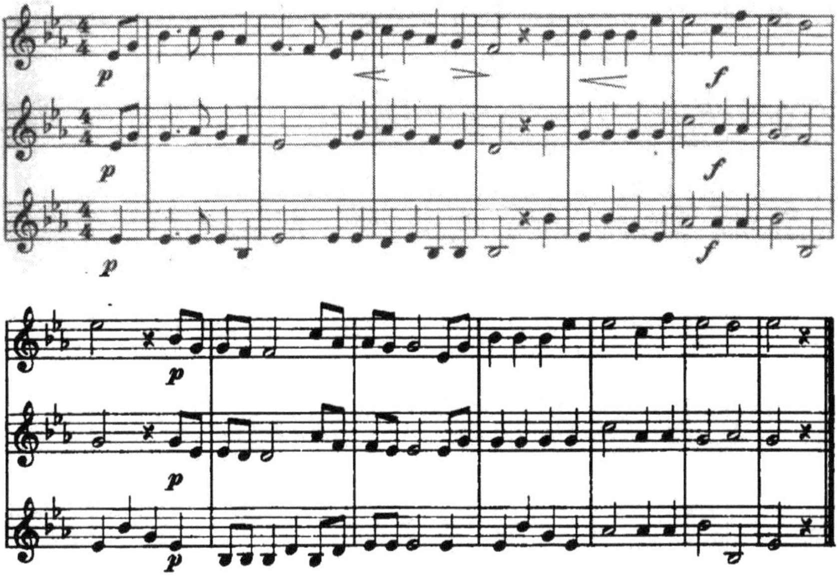
p
f

208

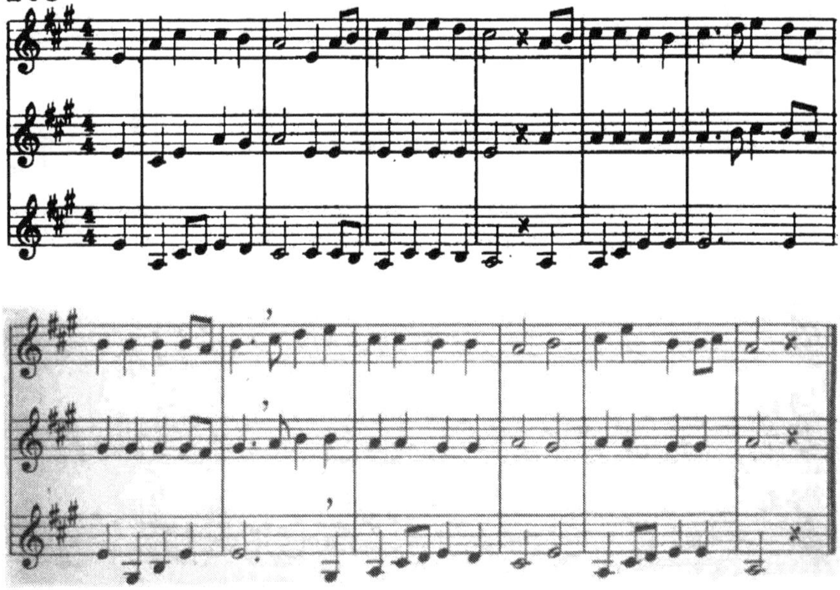

209

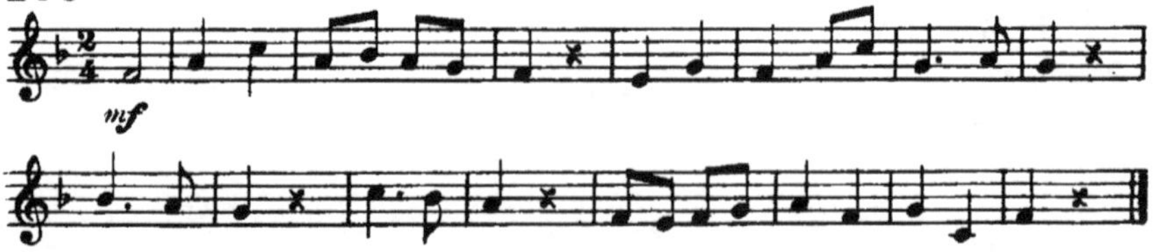
mf

210

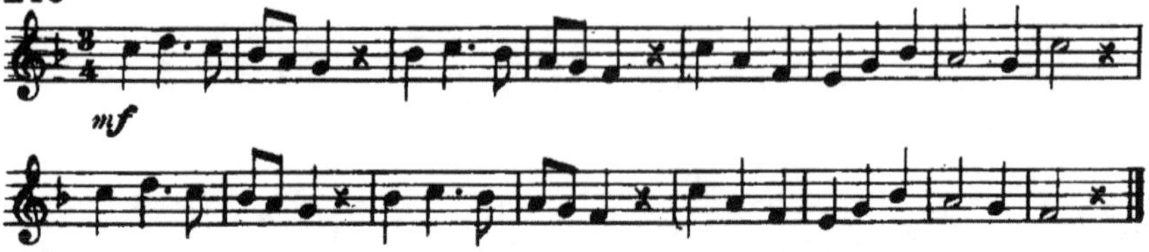
mf

211

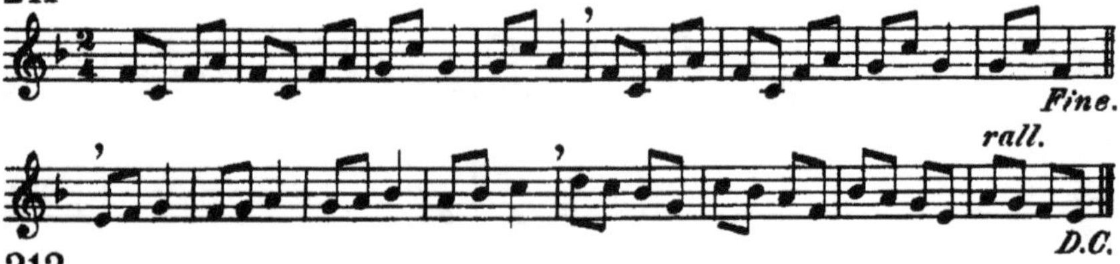
Fine.
rall.
D.C.

212

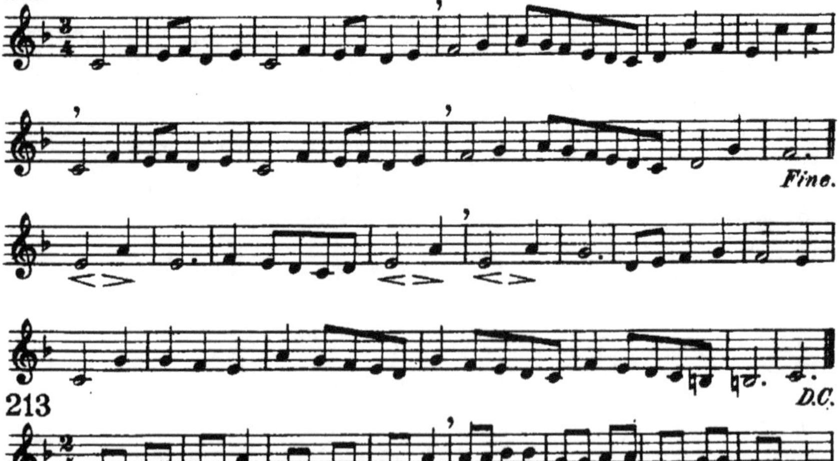
Fine.
D.C.

213

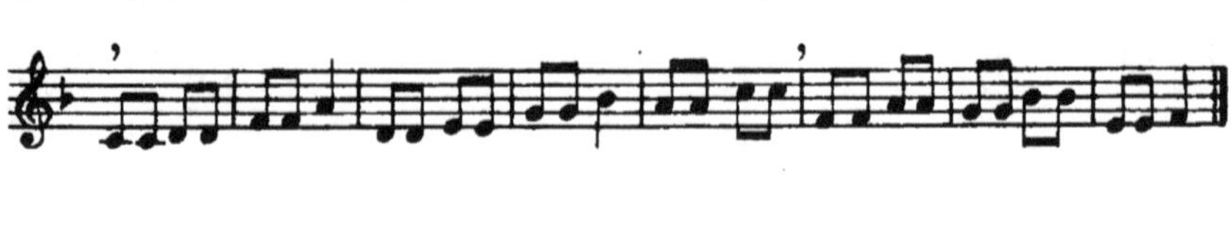

SOLFAS FOR THREE VOICES.

214

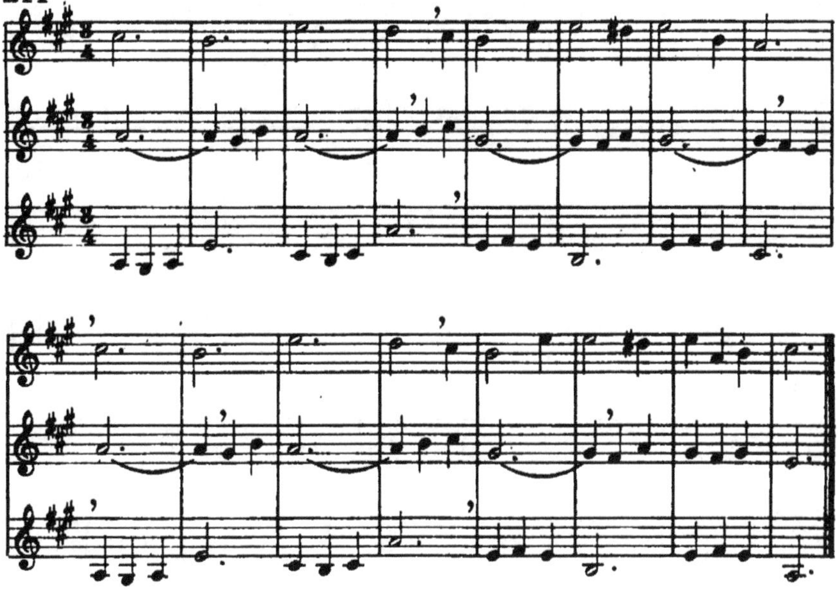

215 M.M. ♩= 96

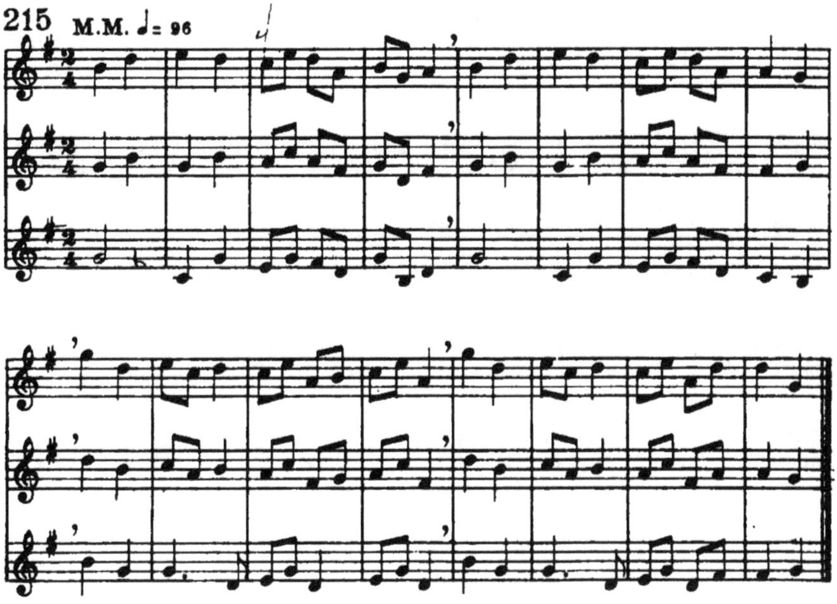

216

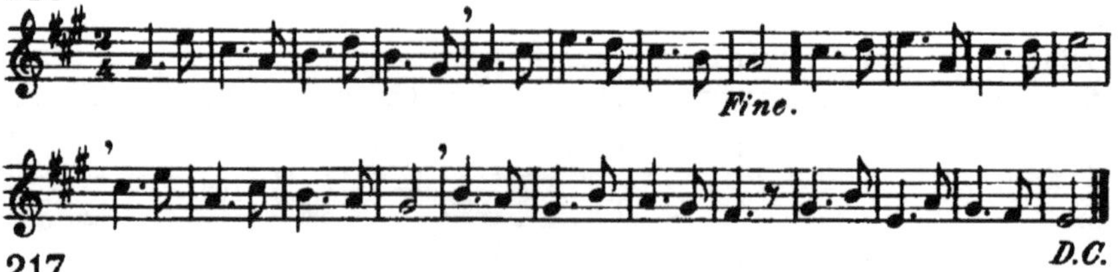
Fine.
D.C.

217

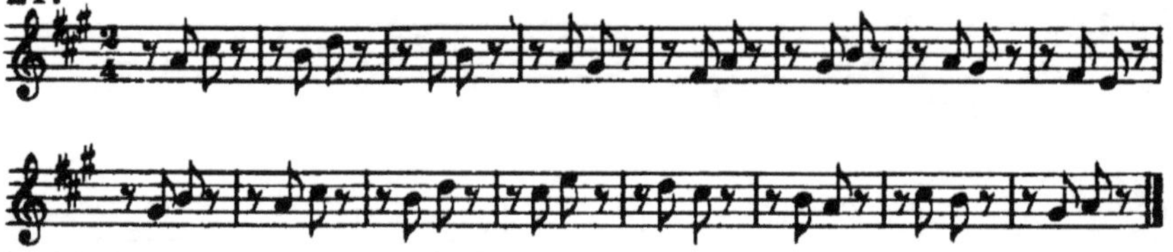

218

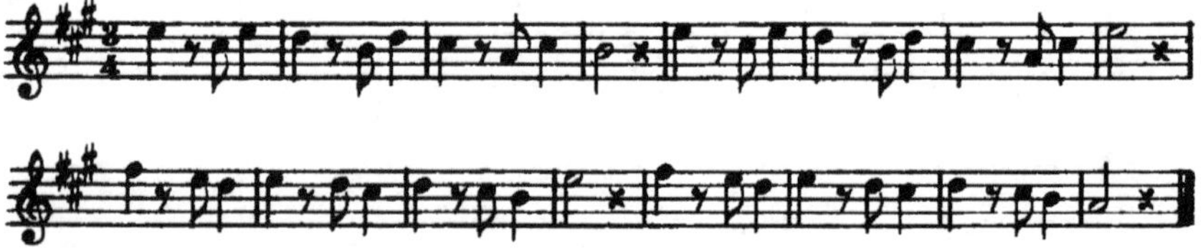

219

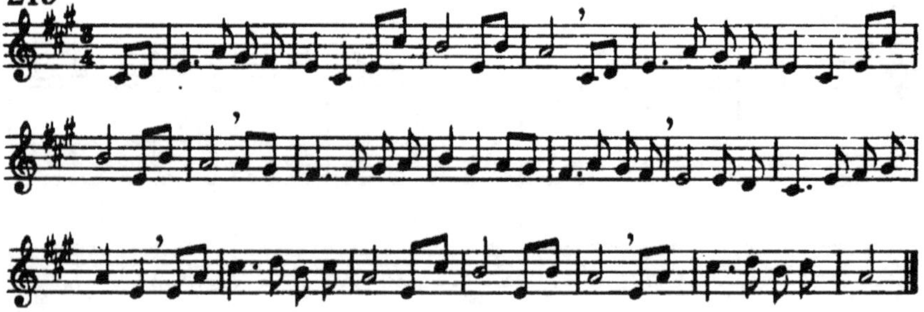

220

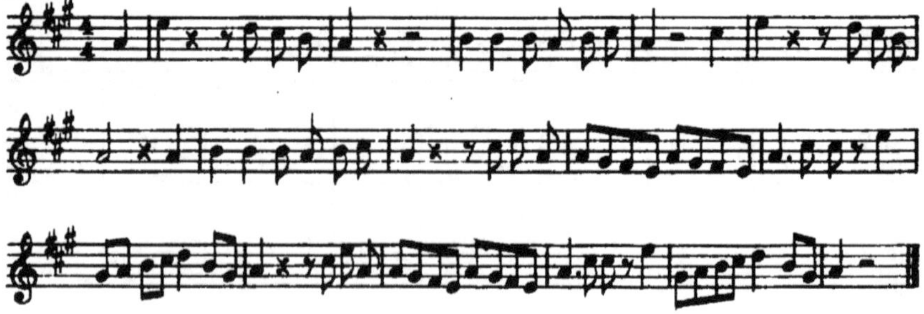

221 Leggiero. M.M. ♩= 112

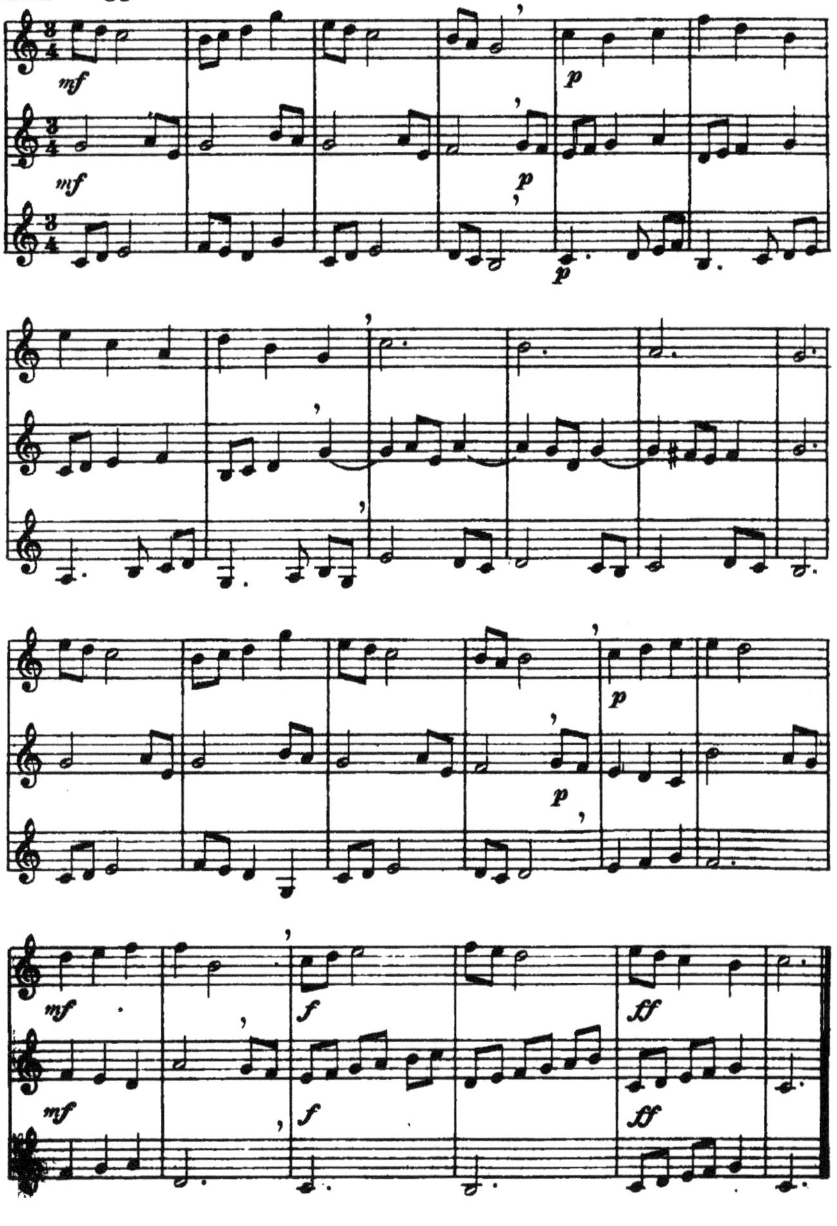

SOLFAS FOR THREE VOICES.

222 Allegretto.

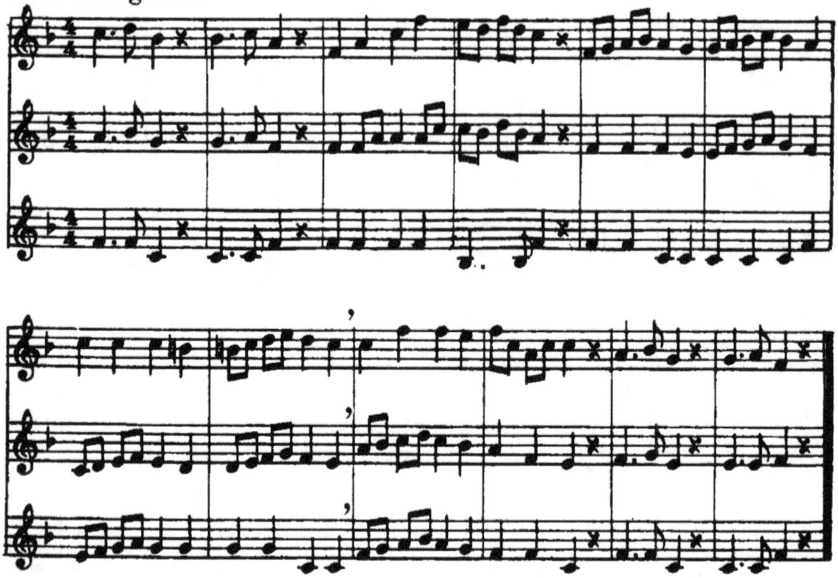

222a

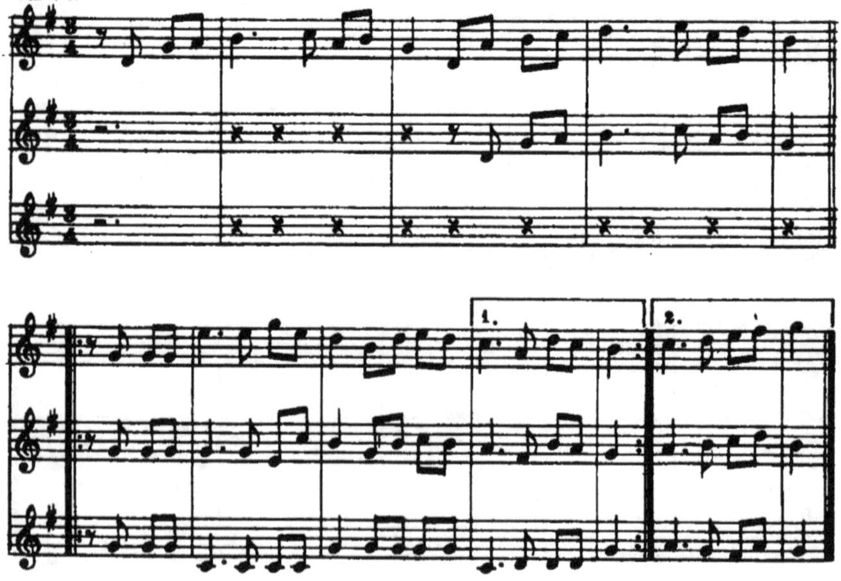
1.
2.

SOLFAS FOR TWO VOICES.

223

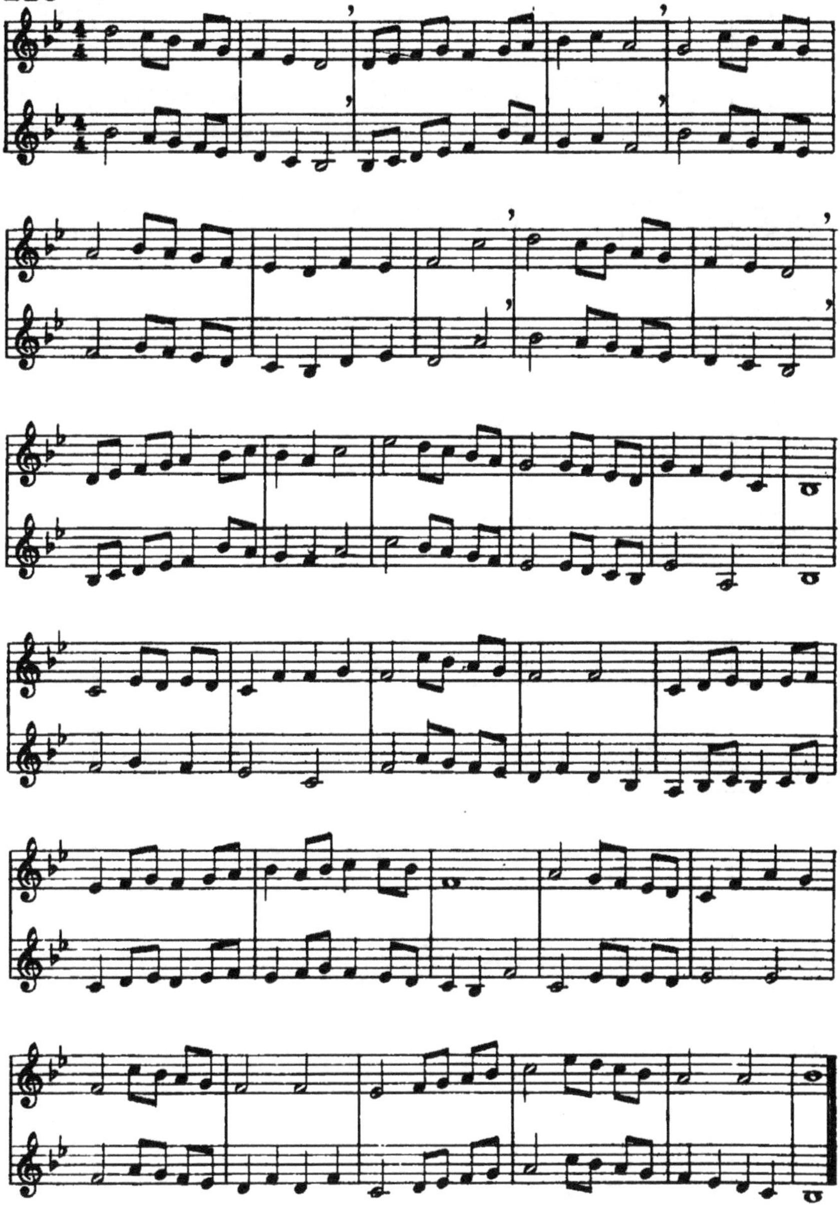

Exercises Nos. 224 to 229 inclusive to be *named only* by syllables - not to be sung.

224

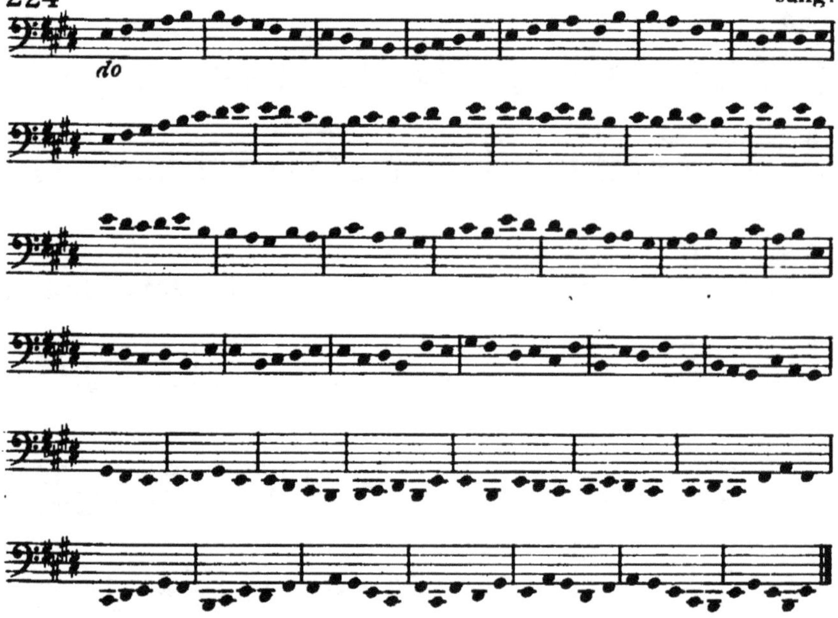
do

225

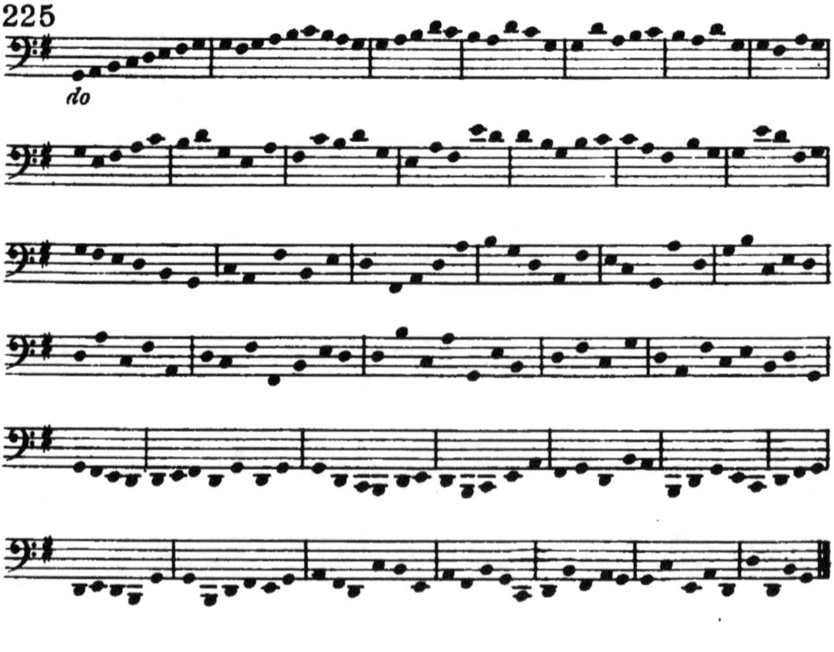
do

226

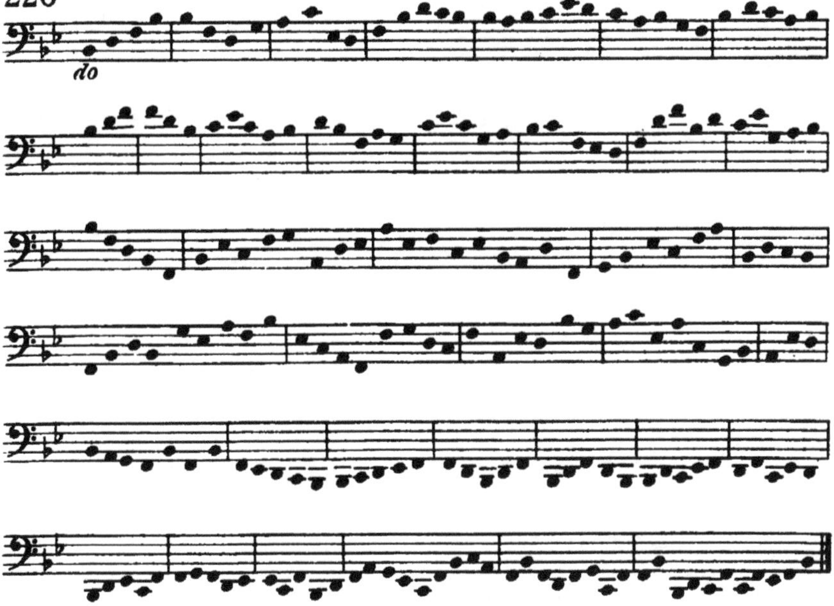
do

227

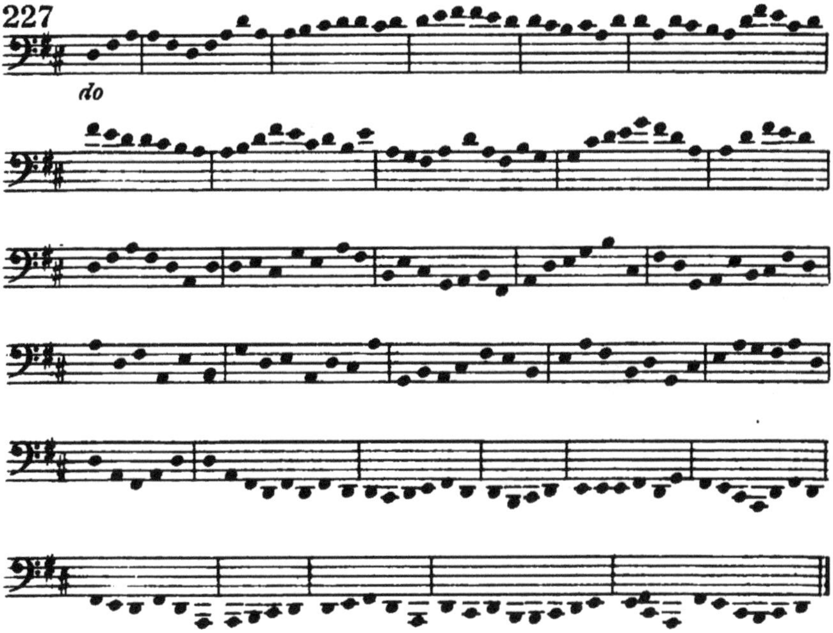
do

228

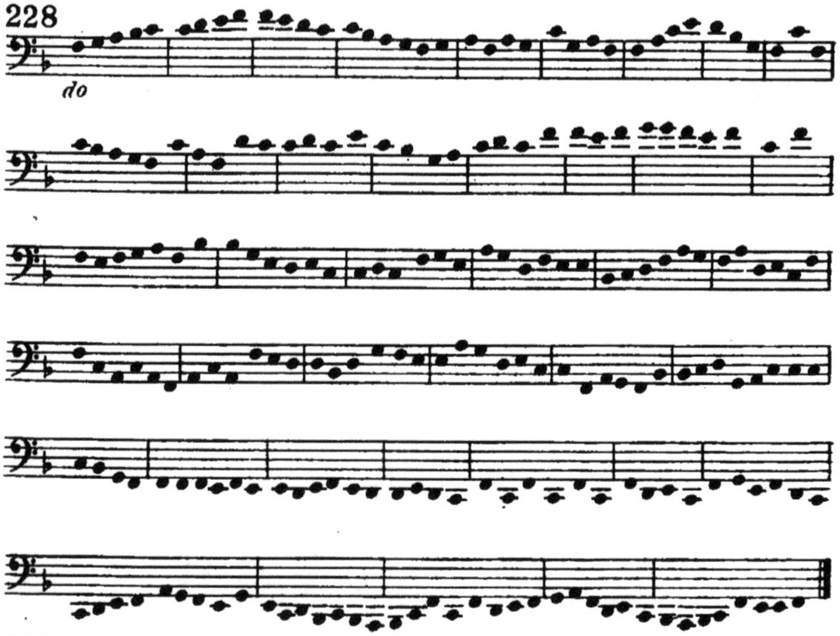
do

229

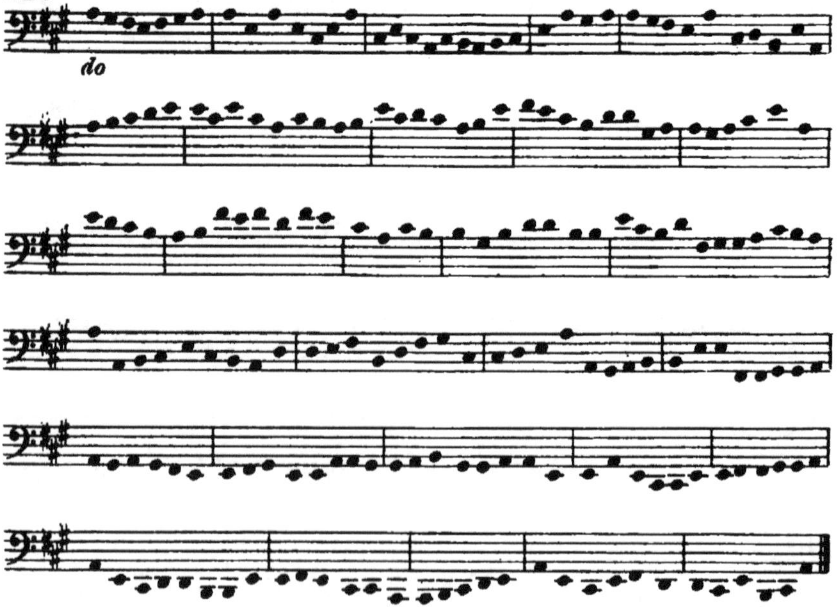
do

INTONATION EXERCISES.

230

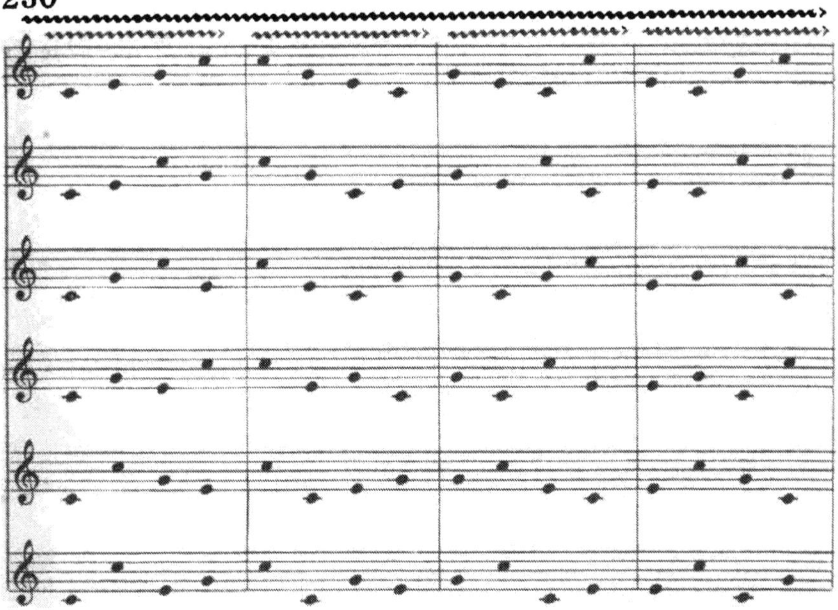

231

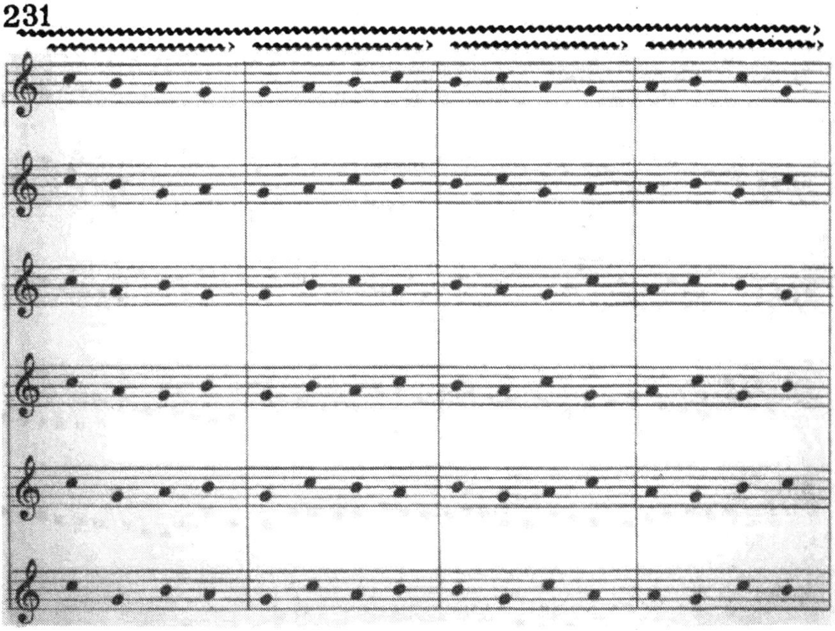

232

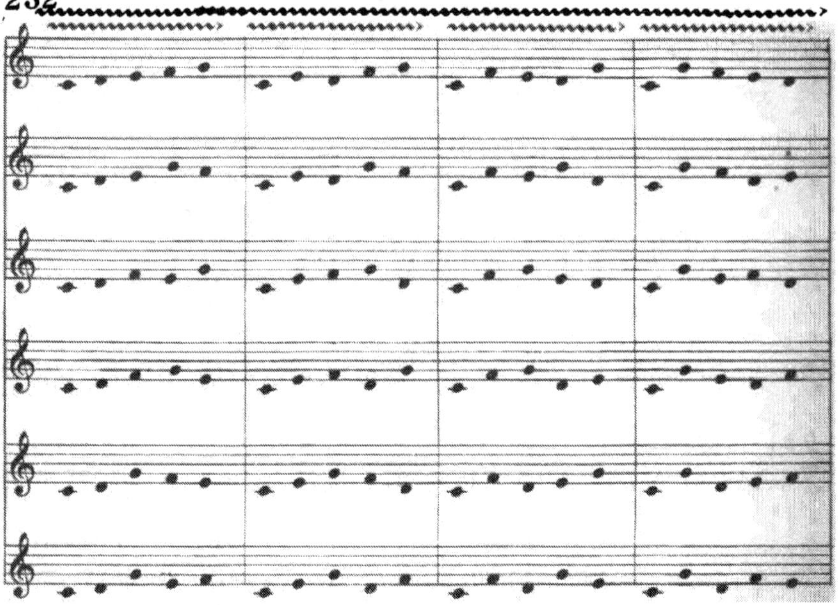

233

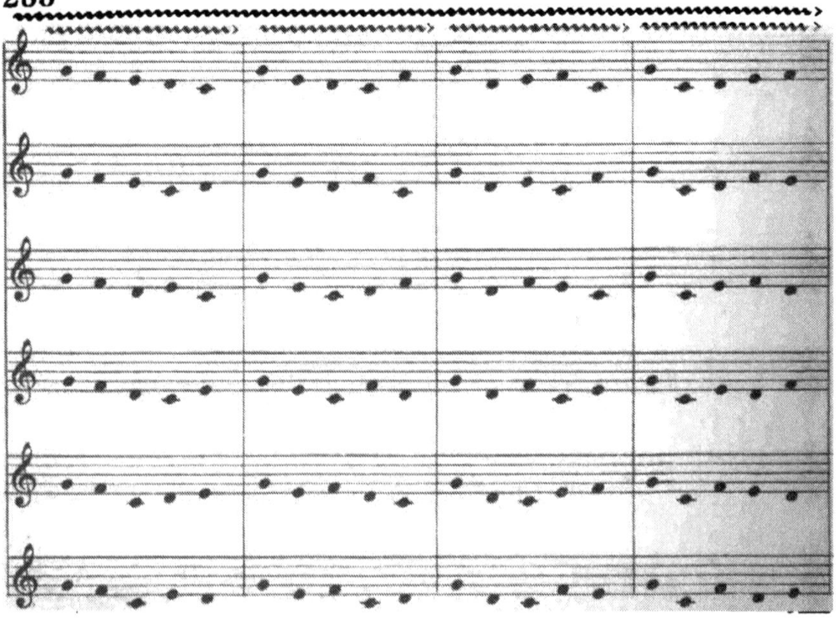

234

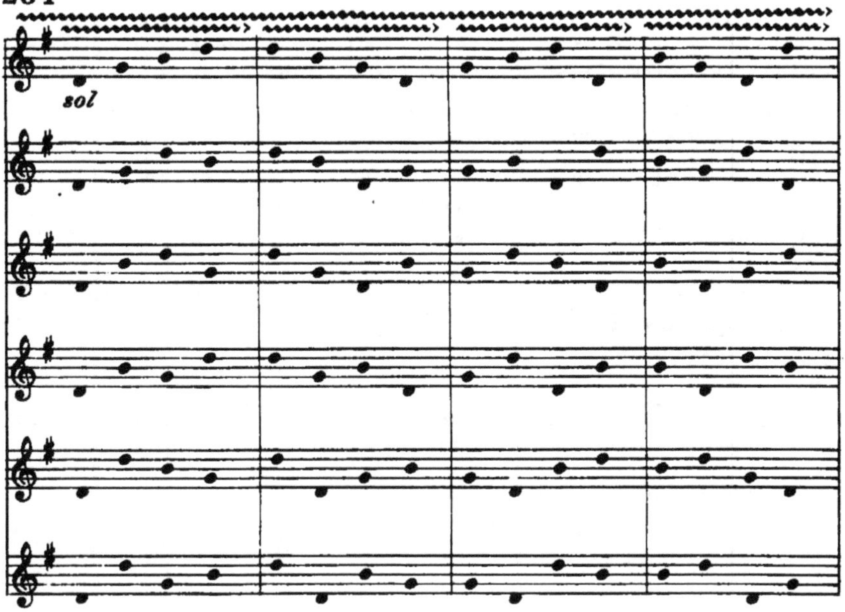
sol

235

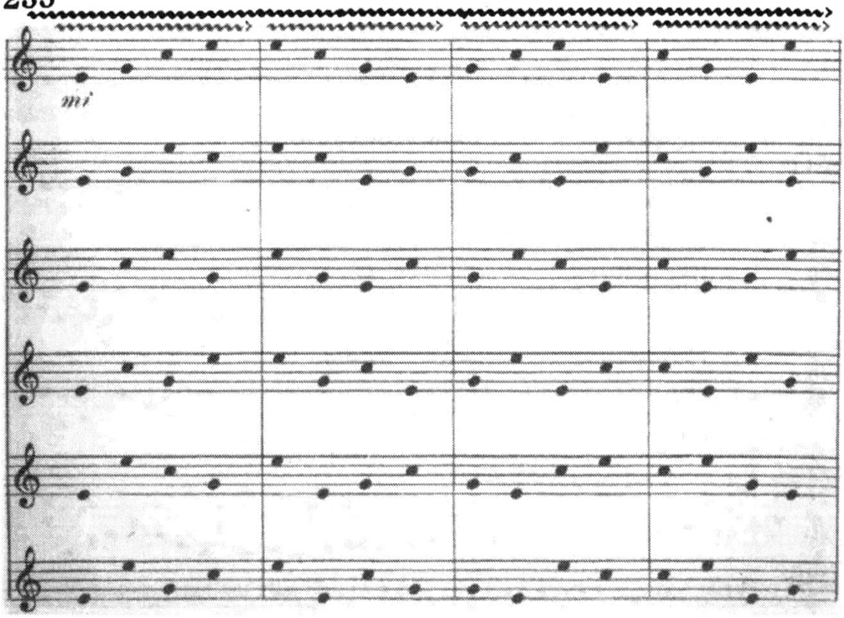
mi

STUDY OF CHROMATIC SCALE BY SHARPS.

Pupils sing several times DO-SI-DO then exactly on the same pitch the different new syllables under it carefully listening to themselves and watching that they correctly reproduce the pattern-tune DO-SI-DO.

Each line should be *thoroughly* mastered before passing to the next. Teacher gives the sound of SOL for DO.

236

Pattern-tune.	DO-SI-DO	DO-SI-DO	DO-SI-DO	DO-SI-DO	DO-SI-DO
New syllables.	SOL-FAY-SOL	RE-DAY-RÉ	LA-JAY-LA	MI-RAY-MI	SI-LAY-SI
Figure notation.	5 4 5	2 1 2	6 5 6	3 2 3	7 6 7

237

DAY
RAY
FAY
JAY
LAY

238

DAY
RAY
FAY
JAY
LAY

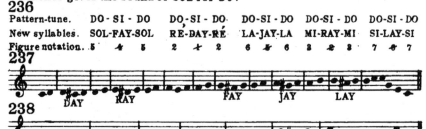

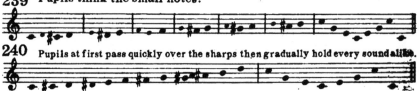

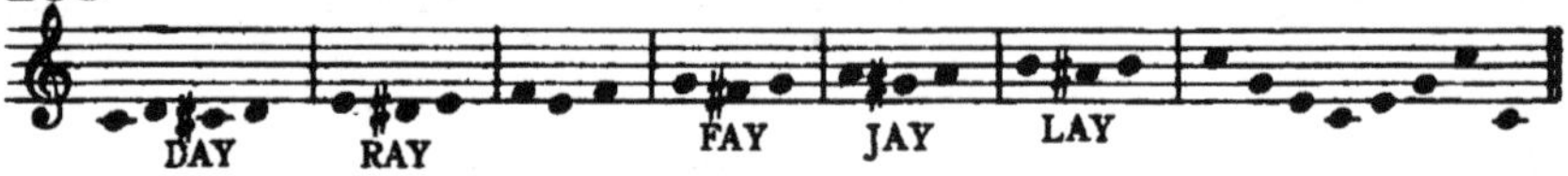

239 Pupils think the small notes.

240 Pupils at first pass quickly over the sharps then gradually hold every sound alike.

STUDY OF CHROMATIC SCALE BY FLATS.

Pupils sing several times MI FA MI and on the same pitch the new syllables under it; the termination IR to be pronounced as in SIR.

241

Pattern tune.	MI-FA-MI	MI-FA-MI	MI-FA-MI	MI-FA-MI	MI-FA-MI
New syallables.	LA-SIR-LA	RÉ-MIR-RÉ	SOL-LIR-SOL	DO-RIR-DO	FA-JIR-FA
Figure notation.	6 7 6	2 3 2	5 6 5	1 2 1	4 5 4

242

SIR
LIR
JIR
MIR
RIR

243

SIR
LIR
JIR
MIR
RIR

244 Pupils think the small notes.

245 Pupils at first pass quickly over the flats then gradually hold every sound alike.

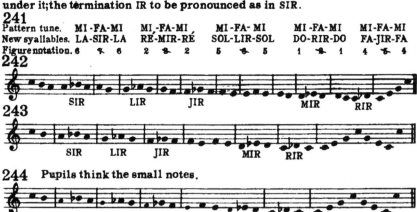

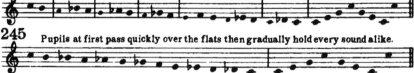

FOUR PART EXERCISES FOR MIXED VOICES.

246

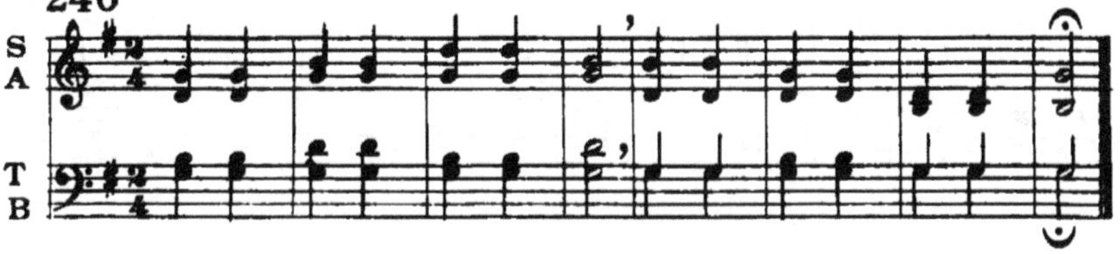
S
A
T
B

247

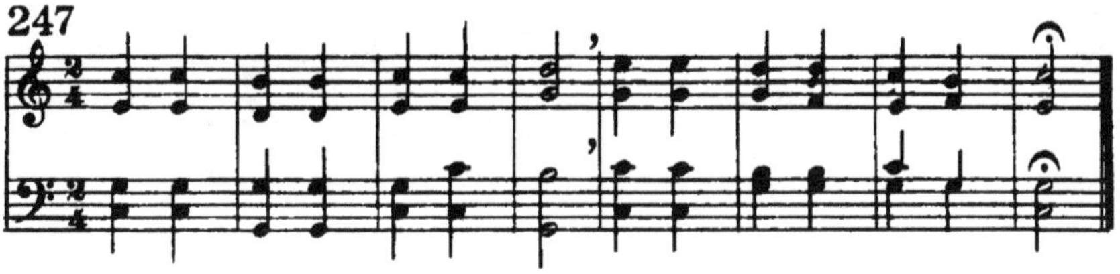

248

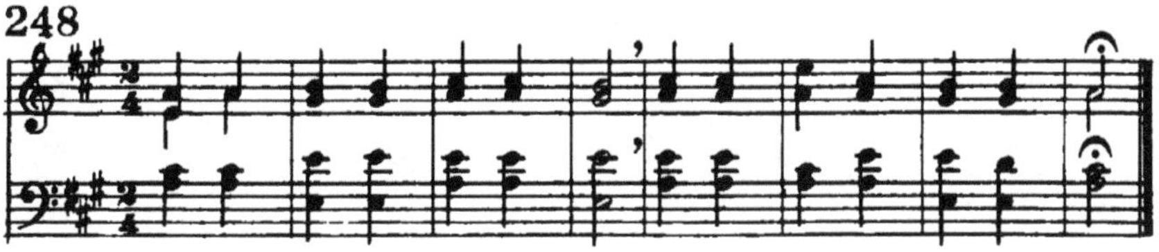

249 Chants - After having sung to LA repeat to GLORIA.

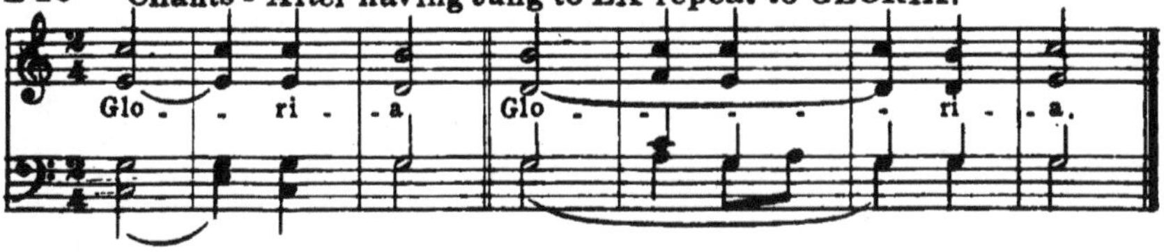
Glo - - ri - - a
Glo - - - - - ri - - a.

250

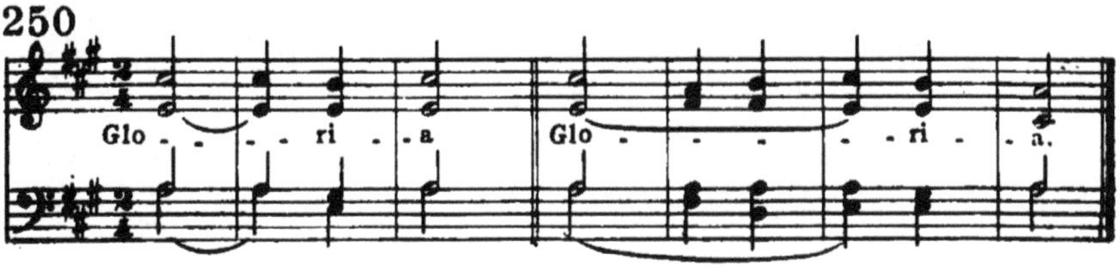
Glo - - - - ri - - a
Glo - - - - - ri - - a.

251

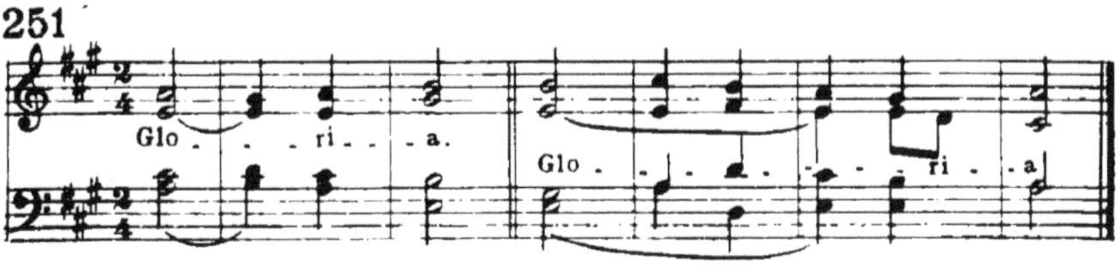
Glo - - - ri - - - a.
Glo - - - - - - - ri - - a

252

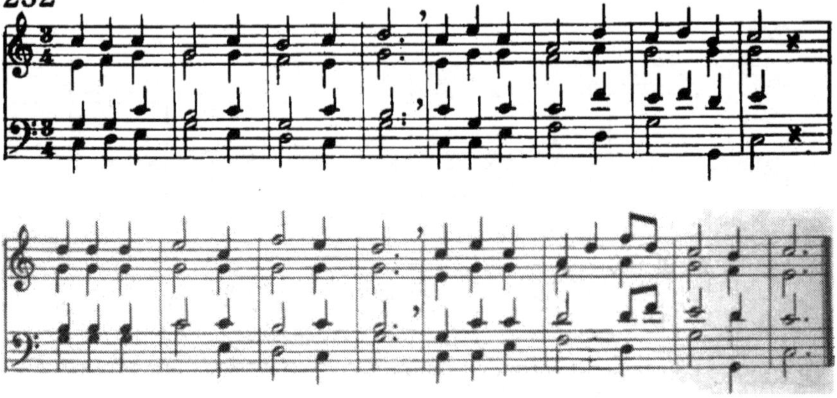

253

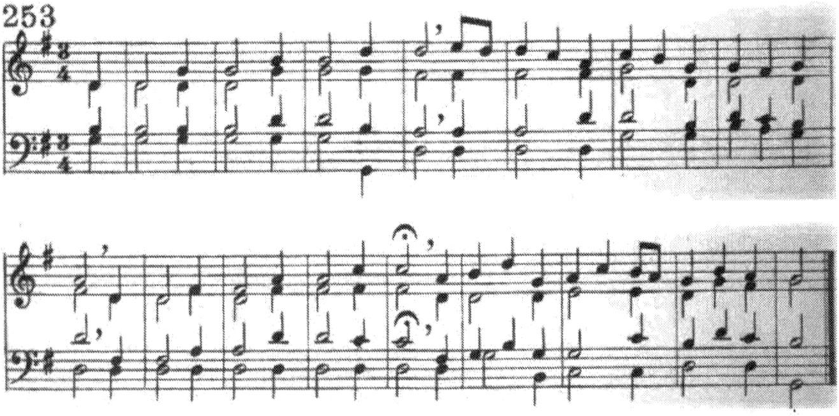

254

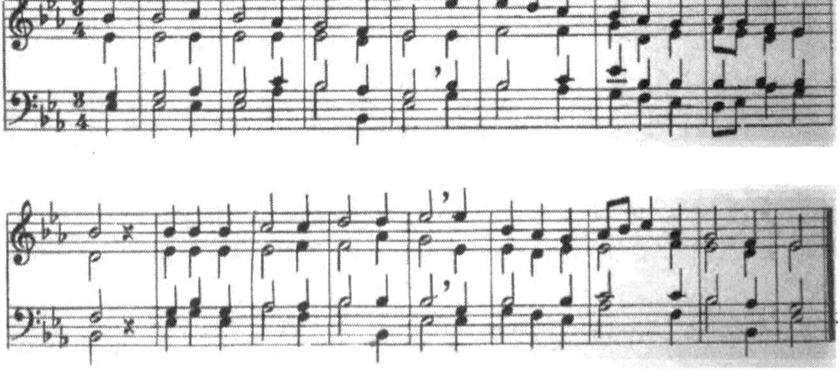

255

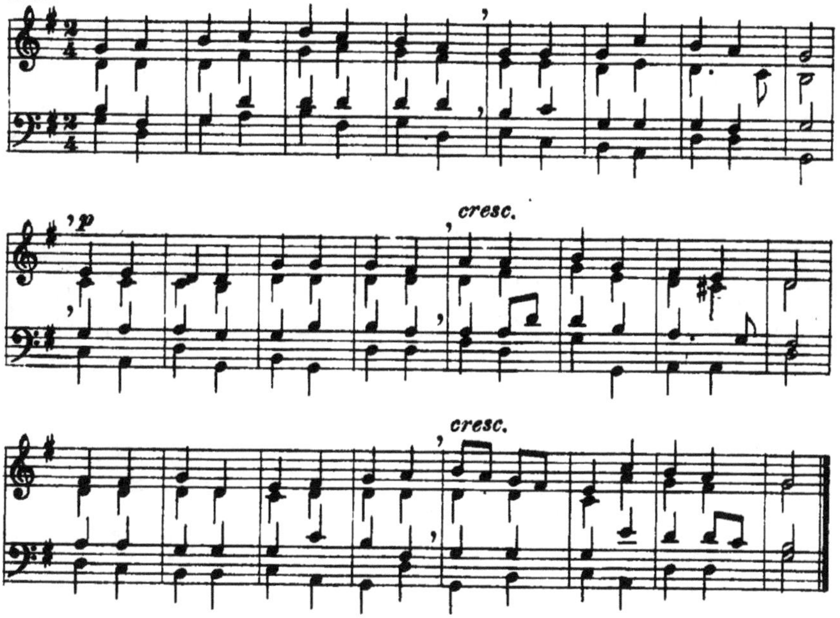
p
cresc.
cresc.

256

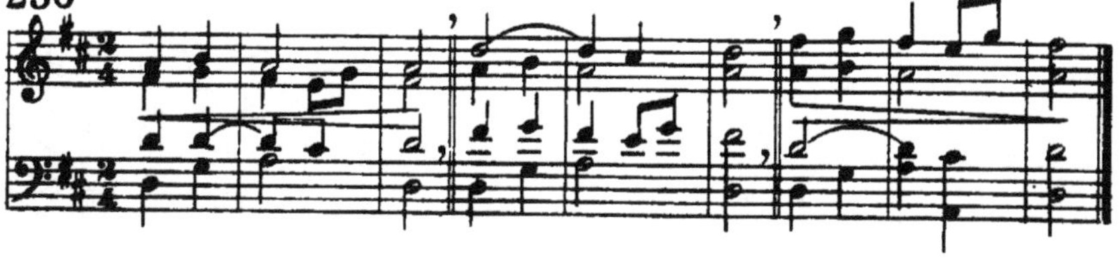

257

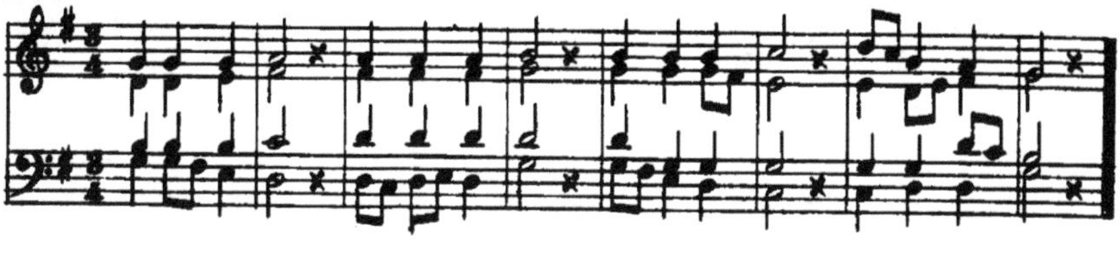

258 **Exercise on suspended discords.**

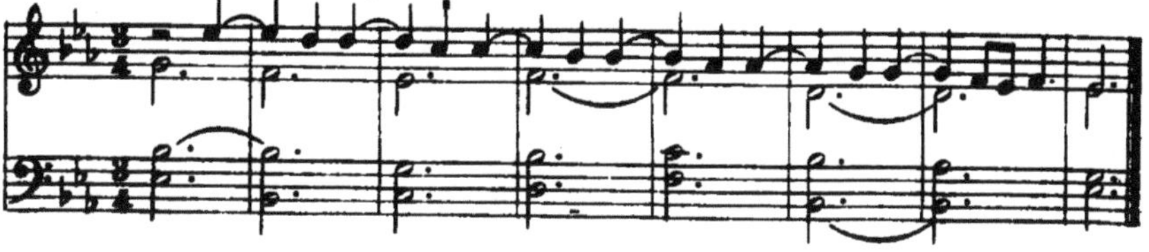

259

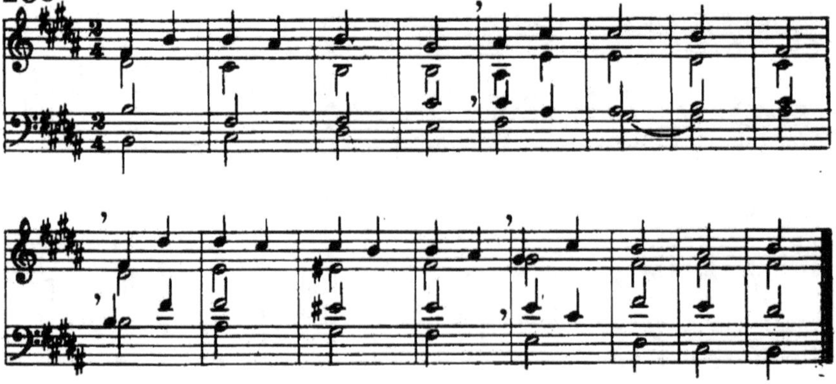

260

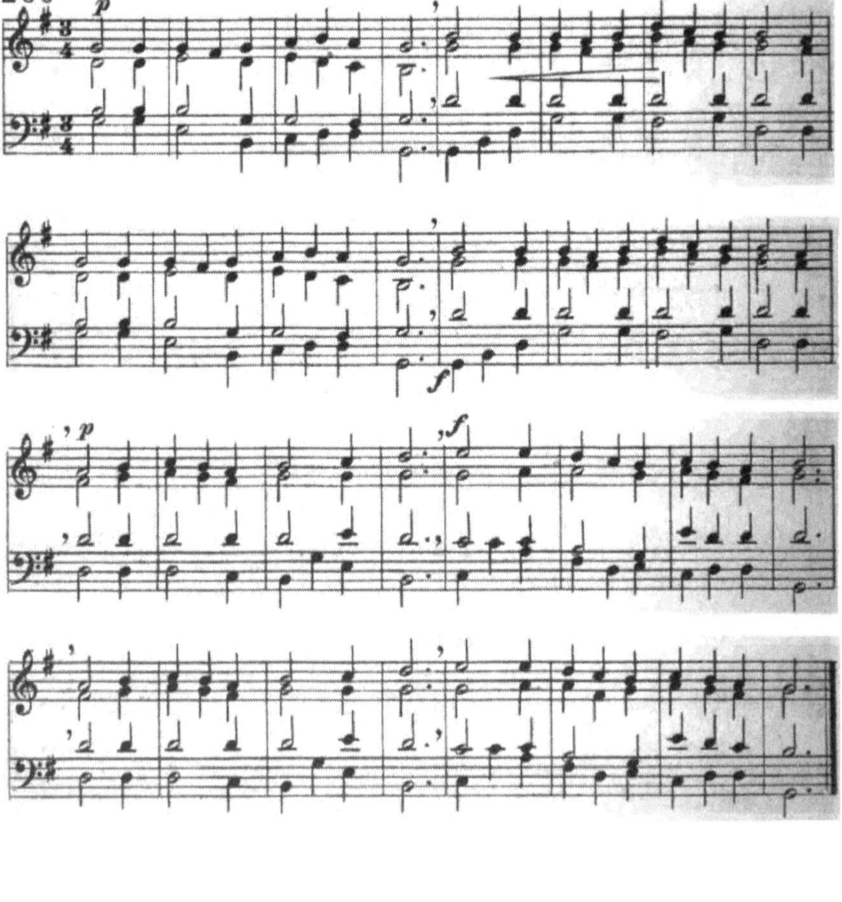
p
f
p
f

In singing by transposition when a natural ♮ cancels a flat ♭ of the signature Pupils sing a sharp. When a natural ♮ cancels a sharp ♯ of the signature pupils sing a flat.

261

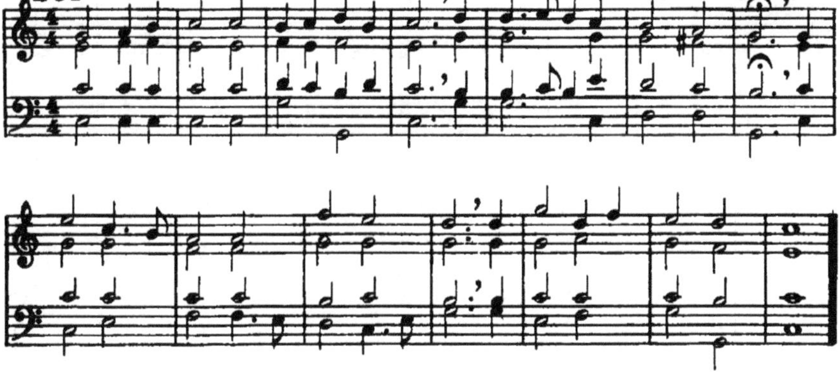

262

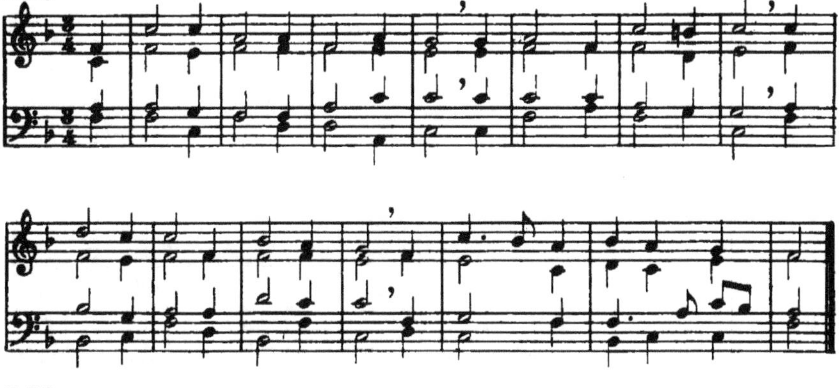

263

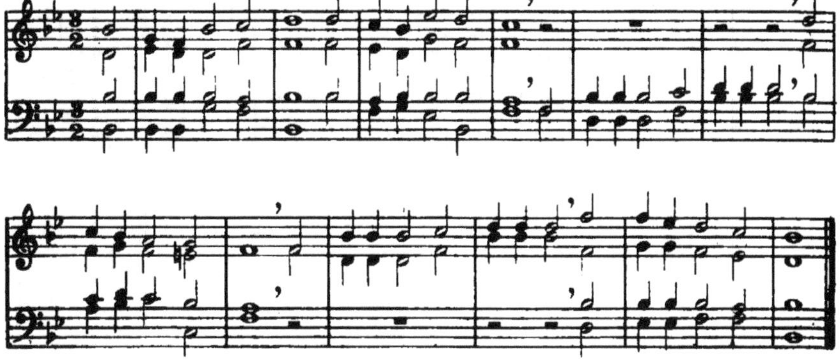

Teacher will prepare for the sharp as it is rather difficult to intone without the helping note.

264

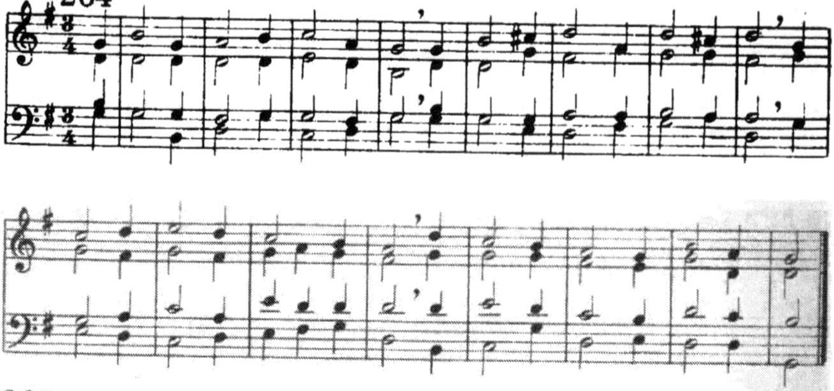

265

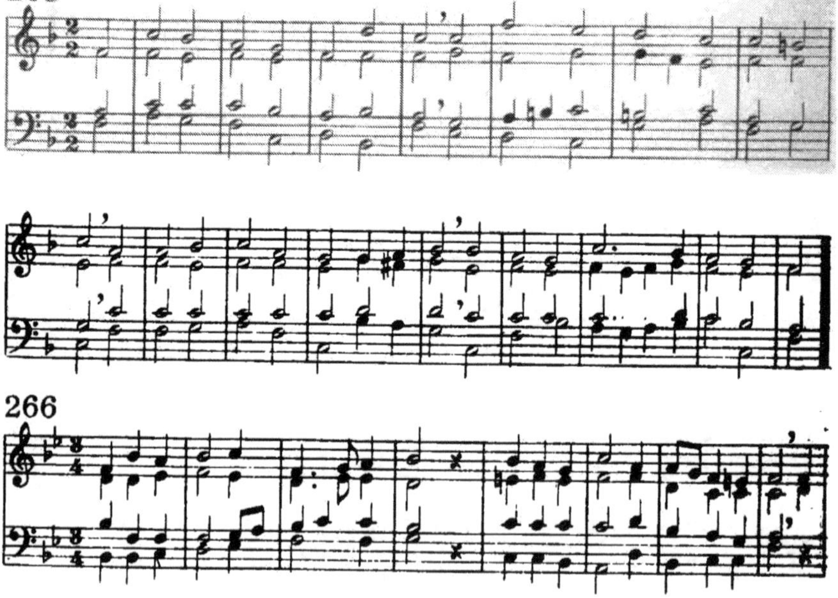

266

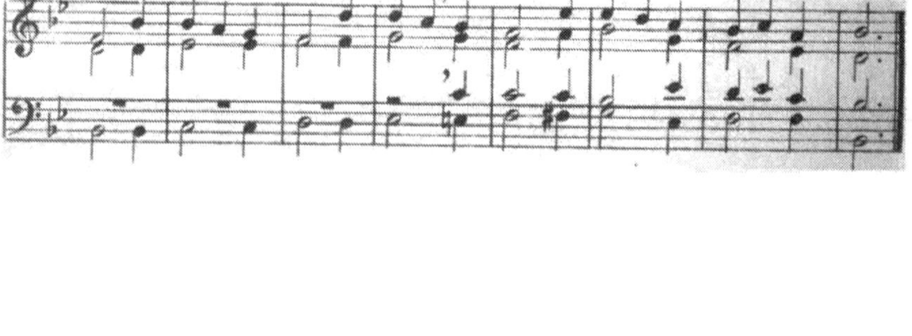

267

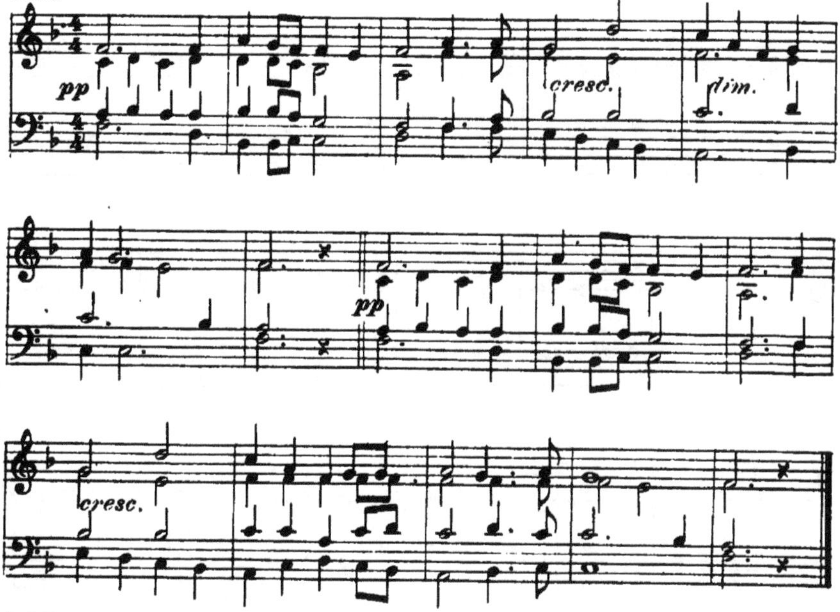
pp
cresc.
dim.
pp
cresc.

268

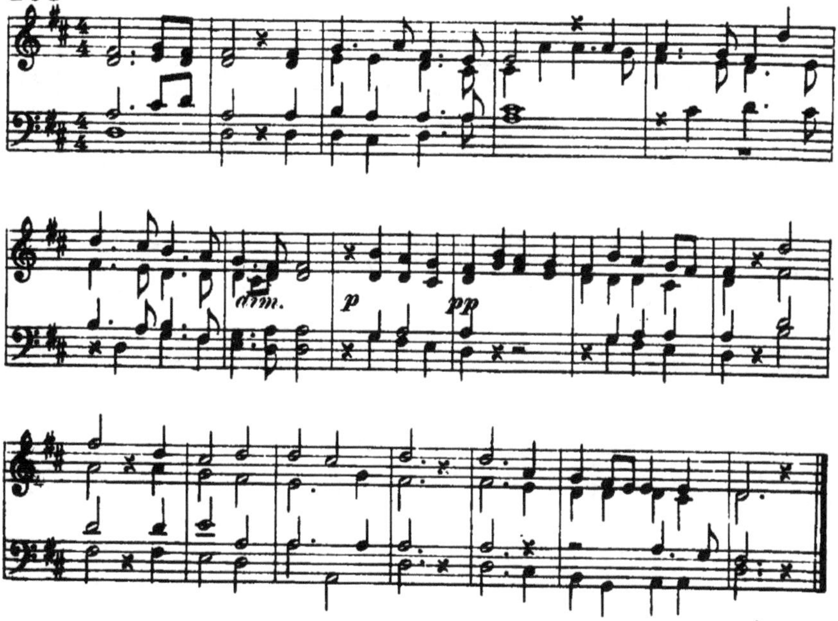
dim.
p
pp

269

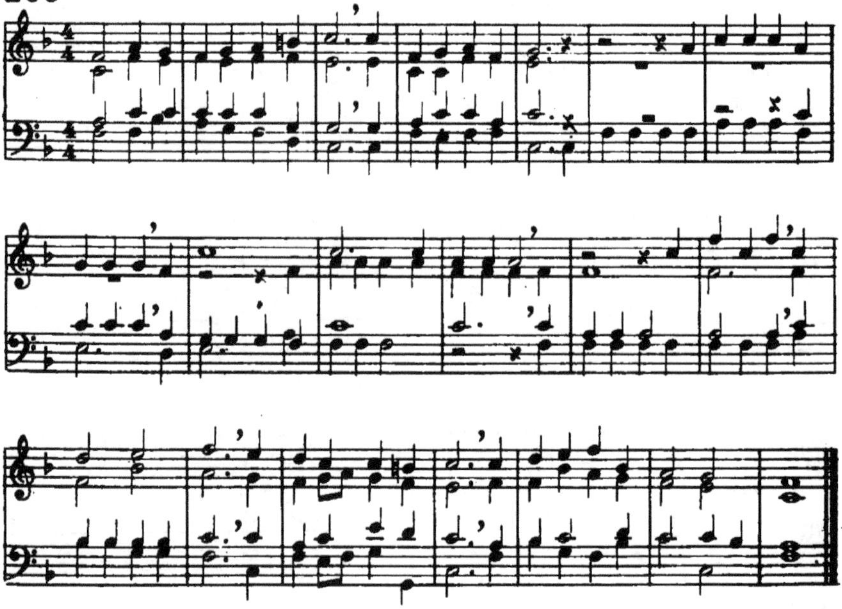

270

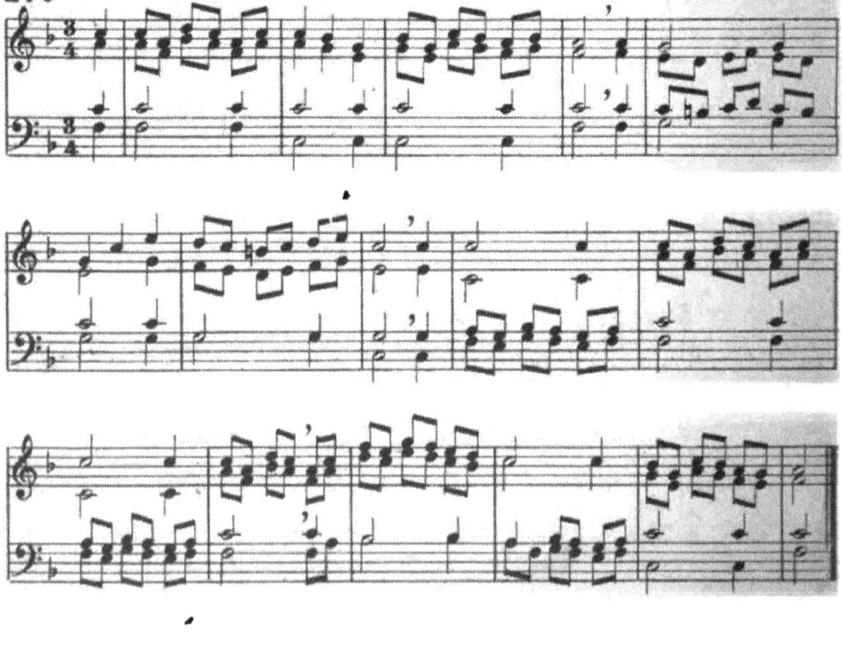

William A Lincoln
    383 Decatur Str.
        Brooklyn

New Reid Ave

4 -